Bakhtinian Perspectives on Language, Literacy, and Learning

The book represents a multidisciplinary collaboration that highlights the significance of Mikhail Bakhtin's theories to modern scholarship in the field of language and literacy. The chapters examine such important questions as: What resources do students bring from their home/community environments that help them become literate in school? What knowledge do teachers need in order to meet the literacy needs of varied students? How can teacher educators and professional development programs better understand teachers' needs and help them to become better prepared to teach diverse literacy learners? What challenges lie ahead for literacy learners in the coming century? Chapters are contributed by scholars who write from varied disciplinary perspectives. In addition, other scholarly voices enter into a Bakhtinian dialogue with these scholars about their ideas. These "other voices" help our readers push the boundaries of current thinking on Bakhtinian theory and make this book a model of heteroglossia and dialogic intertexuality.

Arnetha F. Ball is Associate Professor of Education at Stanford University. Her research interests focus on literacy studies, writing research, and the preparation of teachers to work with culturally and linguistically diverse populations in the United States and South Africa. She has served on many boards and committees in her field and has published widely, with numerous book chapters and articles in journals that include *Linguistics and Education, Applied Behavioral Science Review, Language Variation and Change,* and *Written Communication.* Dr. Ball's recent publications include *Black Linguistics* with Makoni, Smitherman, and Spears and two forthcoming books: *Carriers of the Torch: Addressing the Global Challenge of Preparing Teachers for Diversity* and *Literacies Unleashed* with Ted Lardner.

Sarah Warshauer Freedman is Professor of Education at the University of California, Berkeley, and was Director of the National Center for the Study of Writing and Literacy from 1985 to 1996. Her previous books include *Inside City Schools, Exchanging Writing, Exchanging Cultures: Lessons in School Reform from the United States and Great Britain,* and *Response to Student Writing,* and she edited *The Acquisition of Written Language.* Her research interests focus on literacy learning as well as the role of education in promoting peace, democracy, and human rights.

Learning in Doing

Social, Cognitive, and Computational Perspectives

Series Editor Emeritus
John Seely Brown, Xerox Palo Alto Research Center

General Editors
Roy Pea, Professor of Education and the Learning Sciences and Director,
   Stanford Center for Innovations in Learning, Stanford University
Christian Heath, The Management Centre, King's College, London
Lucy A. Suchman, Centre for Science Studies and Department of Sociology,
   Lancaster University, UK

Plans and Situated Actions: The Problem of Human–Machine Communication
Lucy A. Suchman

The Construction Zone: Working for Cognitive Change in Schools
Denis Newman, Peg Griffin, and Michael Cole

Situated Learning: Legitimate Peripheral Participation
Jean Lave and Etienne Wenger

Street Mathematics and School Mathematics
Terezinha Nunes, David William Carraher, and Analucia Dias Schliemann

Understanding Practice: Perspectives on Activity and Context
Seth Chaiklin and Jean Lave

Distributed Cognitions: Psychological and Educational Considerations
Gavriel Salomon

The Computer As Medium
Peter Bogh Andersen, Berit Holmqvist, and Jens F. Jensen

Sociocultural Studies of Mind
James V. Wertsch, Pablo Del Rio, and Amelia Alvarez

Sociocultural Psychology: Theory and Practice of Doing and Knowing
Laura M. W. Martin, Katherine Nelson, and Ethel Tobach

Mind and Social Practice: Selected Writings of Sylvia Scribner
Ethel Tobach, Rachel Joffee Falmagne, Mary Brown Parleee, Laura M. W.
   Martin, and Aggie Scribner Kapelman

Continues on page 350

To our parents, Mildred and James Mathews
and Miriam and Samuel Warshauer,
who have supported and encouraged us over the years.

Bakhtinian Perspectives on Language, Literacy, and Learning

Edited by

ARNETHA F. BALL
Stanford University

SARAH WARSHAUER FREEDMAN
University of California, Berkeley

CAMBRIDGE
UNIVERSITY PRESS

PUBLISHED BY THE PRESS SYNDICATE OF THE UNIVERSITY OF CAMBRIDGE
The Pitt Building, Trumpington Street, Cambridge, United Kingdom

CAMBRIDGE UNIVERSITY PRESS
The Edinburgh Building, Cambridge CB2 2RU, UK
40 West 20th Street, New York, NY 10011-4211, USA
477 Williamstown Road, Port Melbourne, VIC 3207, Australia
Ruiz de Alarcón 13, 28014 Madrid, Spain
Dock House, The Waterfront, Cape Town 8001, South Africa

http://www.cambridge.org

First published 2004

Printed in the United States of America

Typeface ITC New Baskerville 10/12 pt.   *System* LATEX 2$_\varepsilon$ [TB]

A catalog record for this book is available from the British Library.

Library of Congress Cataloging in Publication Data
Bakhtinian perspectives on language, literacy, and learning / edited by Arnetha F. Ball,
   Sarah Warshauer Freedman.
         p.   cm. – (Learning in doing)
   Includes bibliographical references and index.
   ISBN 0-521-83105-9 – ISBN 0-521-53788-6 (pbk.)
      1. Literacy – Social aspects.   2. Language and education.   3. Critical pedagogy.
   4. Bakhtin, M. M. (Mikhail Mikhaælovich), 1895–1975.   I. Ball, Arnetha F., 1950–
   II. Freedman, Sarah Warshauer.   III. Series.
   LC149.B25   2004
   302.2′244 – dc22   2003065262

ISBN 0 521 83105 9 hardback
ISBN 0 521 53788 6 paperback

Contents

Contributors

Arnetha F. Ball
Stanford University

Charles Bazerman
University of California, Santa Barbara

Allison Weisz Brettschneider
The Education Alliance at Brown University

Verda Delp
University of California, Berkeley

Mark Dressman
University of Illinois at Urbana–Champaign

Sarah Warshauer Freedman
University of California, Berkeley

James Paul Gee
University of Wisconsin-Madison

Cynthia L. Greenleaf
Strategic Literacy Initiative/WestEd

Judy Kalman
DIE-Centro de Investigación y Estudios Avanzados

Mira-Lisa Katz
Sonoma State University

Christian P. Knoeller
Purdue University

Eileen Landay
Brown University

Carol D. Lee
Northwestern University

Jabari Mahiri
University of California, Berkeley

Alice A. Miano
University of California, Berkeley

Gary Saul Morson
Northwestern University

Melanie Sperling
University of California, Riverside

Guadalupe Valdés
Stanford University

Acknowledgments

We would like to thank James E. Williams for his reviews and insightful comments during the early development of this project. Many of the ideas discussed in this volume first had their airing at the 2000 National Council of Teachers of English, Assembly for Research Mid-Winter Conference, *New Literacies for New Times: Bakhtinian Perspectives on Language, Literacy, and Culture for the 21st Century*. We are grateful to all members of the group for their intellectual contributions and we would like to thank all the students who volunteered during that conference and those who subsequently participated in the course that we jointly taught on Bakhtinian Perspectives. We also want to express our gratitude to family, friends, and colleagues, especially Alexei Yurchak and Gary Saul Morson, who provided critical advice and support just when it was needed. And finally, we are grateful to Roy Pea and Phil Laughlin for their continuing support and encouragement throughout this project.

PART I

IDEOLOGIES IN DIALOGUE

Theoretical Considerations

1

Ideological Becoming

Bakhtinian Concepts to Guide the Study of Language, Literacy, and Learning

Sarah Warshauer Freedman
Arnetha F. Ball

In his recent exhibit, "Migrations," photographer Sebastiao Salgado (2000) looks through his camera's eye to tell what he calls "a story of our times," a story of massive and global movements of people. Most often these people are migrating because they seek refuge from rural poverty, or because they are refugees or displaced persons whose movements are caused by war or other political, ethnic, or religious conflict. Salgado presents haunting images of outstretched hands reaching for a new life that is just out of grasp, hungry children in parched landscapes that yield no food, masses on the move with nowhere to go. These images come from Asia, Africa, Europe, and the Americas. These are not the typical media images of globalization, which associate modernity with progress and prosperity, new technologies, and high-speed travel. We acknowledge the typical modern images, but we also think it critical not to forget Salgado's more disturbing images, which are also images of our times.

Salgado could just as easily have fixed his lens on disturbing scenes in the United States: the hungry and homeless who migrate from shelter to street in search of spare change or a bite to eat, undernourished school children moving from home to school on unsafe streets, gangs of teenagers crossing neighborhood boundaries to mark territory and engage in seemingly senseless battles. In everyday life, these scenes occur in the context of great wealth and plenty that often exists right around the corner.

It is across these twenty-first-century divides – between the haves and the have nots, between those with place and those who are displaced, between those with access to high-speed travel and technology and those who have little access, and for those at all points along these continua – that we must find ways to communicate that establish bonds rather than create barriers.

Much prior research on language, literacy, and learning has examined the nature of the divides that separate us and the clashes that occur when disparate people come together, often in our schools but in other social institutions as well (e.g., Ball, 1992, 1998; Ball & Lardner, 1997; Cazden, John, & Hymes, 1972; Freedman & Sperling, 1985; Freedman & Katz, 1987; Michaels, 1981). We use this chapter to argue for a new direction for research, one that focuses more directly on how people can and do communicate across these divides and the role such communication plays in teaching and learning. The earlier research on clashing cultures provides an important foundation for this new research agenda, for we need to know what goes wrong in order to understand what does and can go right. We argue for this new focus because more different kinds of people *are* coming together – in classrooms, in workplaces, over the Internet, in cities all around the globe. New communication technologies, easier access to faster modes of travel, as well as the global migrations Salgado depicts, argue for a global picture of increasingly diverse populations existing side by side and interacting together. Diverse people will struggle to understand one another. We therefore will need to understand the nature of that struggle. We will have before us opportunities to watch what goes wrong just as we have done, but we also will have opportunities to watch and learn from effective communication as it occurs.

DEFINING IDEOLOGICAL BECOMING

We are specifically interested in understanding how effective communication leads to the development of language, literacy, and learning in these new contexts. In seeking this understanding, we have found the theories of Mikhail Bakhtin and his whole school, including Medvedev and Voloshinov, extraordinarily helpful, especially their concept of "ideological becoming."

Before discussing why we find this concept so helpful, we define ideology in order to clarify what Bakhtin and his followers mean by the term. According to the *American Heritage Dictionary* (2000), ideology means:

1. The body of ideas reflecting the social needs and aspirations of an individual, group, class, or culture
2. A set of doctrines or beliefs that forms the basis of a political, economic, or other system

The second, more political meaning is often ascribed to Bakhtin. However, the Russian word *ideologiya* does not carry strong political connotations. Morris (1994), who writes about British English, sees Bakhtin's meaning as most consistent with the first definition:

The Russian '*ideologiya*' is less politically coloured than the English word 'ideology'. In other words, it is not necessarily a consciously held political belief system; rather it can refer in a more general sense to the way in which members of a given social group view the world. It is in this broader sense that Bakhtin uses the term. For

Bakhtin, any utterance is shot through with '*ideologiya*', any speaker is automatically an '*ideolog*'. (p. 249)

Emerson (1981) makes a similar but somewhat expanded point, writing from a U.S. vantage:

Its English cognate "ideology" is in some respects unfortunate, for our word suggests something inflexible and propagandistic, something politically unfree. For Bakhtin and his colleagues, it means simply an "idea system" determined socially, something that *means*. (p. 23)

In Bakhtinian writings, *ideological becoming* refers to how we develop our way of viewing the world, our system of ideas, what Bakhtin calls an ideological self. Although the Bakhtinian school's concept of ideological becoming does not necessarily have a political edge, it does not exclude the development of a political idea system as part of ideological development. In the case of language and literacy learning, especially as we consider diverse populations talking and learning together, we believe that politics are an inevitable consideration. Language use and literate abilities provide ways for people to establish a social place and ways for others to judge them (see Trudgill, 1995). The choices learners make about what types of language to acquire and use are political just as the decisions teachers make about what types of language to promote and accept in the classroom are political. Students make conscious and unconscious decisions about how much to identify with and acquire school language and school ways; they come to school with ways of talking that mark them as members of a particular socioeconomic class, and they decide whether to move away from those ways; they decide what to read and write and whether they care most about pleasing the teacher or their peers or both or neither. Broadly speaking, these are all political decisions. Likewise, teachers decide how to respond to diverse language patterns in their classrooms; how much controversy to introduce into the classroom; how to group or not group students for learning; how to respond to individuals and the group; whether to teach critically, in ways that push students to examine the established social order. Again, these are all political decisions, some more explicitly and consciously so than others.

It is also important to note that the concept of ideological becoming does not refer to the development of isolated concepts or ideas. Bakhtin and his followers are interested in the development of the whole person and his or her complex of ideas and concepts, including political ideas, but not to the exclusion of other parts of the idea system. Bakhtin is concerned with more than individual growth because he places the individual firmly within a social context and shows that the individual influences the social world, just as the social world influences the individual.

HOW IDEOLOGICAL BECOMING RELATES TO LANGUAGE, LITERACY, AND LEARNING

To understand the importance of ideological becoming for language, literacy, and learning in contexts where diverse people come together, we first note that according to Bakhtin/Medvedev (1978), ideological becoming happens within what he calls "the ideological environment" (p. 14).[1] According to Bakhtin/Medvedev, "Human consciousness does not come into contact with existence directly, but through the medium of the surrounding ideological world" (p. 14). In effect, the ideological environment – be it the classroom, the workplace, the family, or some other community gathering place – mediates a person's ideological becoming and offers opportunities that allow the development of this essential part of our being. In ideological environments characterized by a diversity of voices, we would expect not only new communication challenges, but also exciting opportunities and possibilities for expanding our understanding of the world.

Bakhtin (1981) notes that the coming together of the voices of the different individuals within these environments is essential to a person's growth: "Another's discourse performs here [in ideological becoming] no longer as information, directions, rules, models and so forth – but strives to determine the very basis of our ideological interrelations with the world, the very basis of our behavior" (p. 342). All learning is at its core social. According to Bakhtin, the social interactions that are most effective in promoting learning are those that are filled with tension and conflict. Individuals struggle with these tensions as they develop their own ideologies. Bakhtin argues that the struggles are needed for people to come to new understandings: "The importance of struggling with another's discourse, its influence in the history of an individual's coming to ideological consciousness, is enormous" (p. 348). Although miscommunication of the type that has been so carefully studied inevitably occurs along the way, Bakhtin's theory implies that it is essential to look beyond the moment of miscommunication to the longer-term, ongoing dialogic process if we want to understand the struggles that lead to learning. According to Bakhtin "our ideological development is . . . an intense struggle within us for hegemony among various available verbal and ideological points of view, approaches, directions and values" (p. 346). We go through a "process of selectively assimilating the words of others" (p. 341). The role of the other is critical to our development; in essence, the more choice we have of words to assimilate, the more opportunity we have to learn. In a Bakhtinian sense, with whom, in what ways, and in what contexts we interact will determine what we stand to learn.

---

[1] The question of authorship is disputed, although according to Morson (personal communication, 2002), it is now widely believed that this text was written by Medvedev. When we refer to it in the text, however, we use Bakhtin/Medvedev because this is the authorship ascribed on the text from which we are quoting.

Bakhtin (1981) argues that when diverse voices interact, we struggle to assimilate two distinct categories of discourse: (1) authoritative discourse, and (2) internally persuasive discourse. Because of their different properties, we struggle with them in different ways. Bakhtin defines authoritative discourse:

The authoritative word is ... so to speak, the word of the fathers. Its authority was already *acknowledged* in the past. It is a *prior* discourse. It is therefore not a question of choosing it among other possible discourses that are its equal. It is given [it sounds] in lofty spheres, not those of familiar contact... for example, the authority of religious dogma, or of acknowledged scientific truth or of a currently fashionable book. (pp. 342–3)

The nature of our struggles with an authoritative discourse depends on our relationship with it. Bakhtin (1981) explains that literary characters often struggle against "various kinds and degrees of authority," against the "official line" (p. 345); such is also the case in everyday life, which art imitates. These struggles occur in what Bakhtin calls a "contact zone," that "zone of contact" where we "struggle against various kinds and degrees of authority" (p. 345).[2] This is not to say that all people struggle against all authority or all authoritative discourses, but rather that there are times in our lives when what we think as an individual is not the same as some aspect of the official doctrine of our larger world. It is at those moments of struggle that we develop our own ideologies. Bakhtin explains that the struggle occurs because

[t]he authoritative word demands that we acknowledge it, that we make it our own; it binds us, quite independent of any power it might have to persuade us internally; we encounter it with its authority already fused to it. (p. 342)

---

[2] Mary Louise Pratt (1991/1999, 1992) has been widely quoted for her use of the term "contact zone"; she does not derive her use from Bakhtin, but rather from linguists who talk about what occurs when different languages come into contact with one another. Contact languages refer to "improvised languages that develop among speakers of different native languages who need to communicate with each other consistently, usually in the context of trade. Such languages begin as pidgins, and are called creoles when they come to have native speakers of their own. Like the societies of the contact zone, such languages are commonly regarded as chaotic, barbarous, lacking in structure" (Pratt, 1992, p. 6). She uses the term more specifically than Bakhtin does "to invoke the spatial and temporal copresence of subjects previously separated by geographical and historical disjunctures, and whose trajectories now intersect" (p. 7). Like Bakhtin, she is interested in "social spaces where cultures meet, clash, and grapple with each other," but she is concerned with "contexts of highly asymmetrical relations of power, such as colonialism, slavery, or their aftermaths as they are lived out in many parts of the world today" (Pratt, 1991/1999, p. 584). She goes on to apply the term to modern contexts where contested cultures come together and uses it to provide a contrast to the common term "community" derived from "speech community," which is often conceptualized as a homogeneous and coherent group of speakers.

Morson (this volume) explains that the authoritative word is not the same as the authoritarian word. The authoritative word may or may not be authoritarian. Although some people take authoritarian words as authoritative, Wertsch (2002) shows that some may resist. He gives the example of people living under an oppressive government who in their private discourses oppose the authoritarian words of the government, even though in public they act as though they accept these words as authoritative. The point is that it is important to determine whether what one voices as authoritative really functions authoritatively for an individual.

As we develop our idea systems or ideologies, besides struggling with the official authoritative discourses in our world, we also come into contact with and struggle with the everyday discourse of the common people we encounter. This everyday discourse is what Bakhtin calls internally persuasive discourse. Internally persuasive discourse has an almost opposite set of properties to those of authoritative discourse. According to Bakhtin (1981), internally persuasive discourse is "denied all privilege, backed by no authority at all, and is frequently not even acknowledged in society" (p. 342). It is what each person thinks for him- or herself, what ultimately is persuasive to the individual. As we form our own ideas, we come into contact with the discourses of others and those discourses enter our consciousness much as authoritative discourse does. The discourse of others also influences the ways we think and contributes to forming what ultimately is internally persuasive for us. However, unlike its authoritative cousin, internally persuasive discourse is subject to change and is constantly interacting with our ever-evolving ideologies. Indeed, "a variety of alien discourses enter into the struggle for influence within an individual's consciousness (just as they struggle with one another in the surrounding social reality)" (p. 348).[3]

If we take the case of U.S. schools today, we can see the importance of considering learning and development in terms of ideological becoming. U.S. schools are changing demographically. Classrooms are more varied than ever before, with students coming together across what used to be considered uncrossable linguistic and cultural divides. These diverse populations bring a range of internally persuasive discourses, which will impact the process of ideological development and ideological becoming of all students inside our classrooms. They ensure plentiful tensions among a range of authoritative discourses to which different students will orient and among a wide range of internally persuasive discourses as well. They also ensure tensions between the authoritative discourses and the internally persuasive discourses. This rich and complex "contact zone" inside the classroom yields plentiful opportunity for students to decide what will be internally persuasive

---

[3] Landay (this volume) offers extended examples of the interplay of authoritative and internally persuasive discourse in the classroom. Morson (this volume) discusses the differences between the authoritative and the authoritarian, as well as offers further examples of the interplay of authoritative and internally persuasive discourses.

for them, and consequently, for them to develop their ideologies. This diversity, which includes the diversity within the world that surrounds the classroom, presents both challenges and opportunities as teachers seek to guide their students on this developmental journey.

SETTING A RESEARCH AGENDA

As we forge a research agenda for language, literacy, and learning for the twenty-first century, we need to consider the multiplicity of voices in our classrooms. Furthermore, we must think globally, and we must think about language, literacy, and learning in schools and in nonschool settings. In these contexts, we need to consider how the multiplicity of voices shapes the ideologies that the next generation will develop and that will guide us all in the coming century. These voices demand that we set a research agenda that includes the complexities of our world's societies, its schools, and its other settings where ideological becoming is nurtured.

We propose that if we take seriously the Bakhtinian notion of ideological becoming, there are at least three important implications for the future of research and practice:

1. Researchers and practitioners must take diversity seriously and see how it can be a resource.
2. Researchers and practitioners must seek to understand the mechanisms of growth and change, which is always occurring.
3. Researchers and practitioners must seek to understand peoples' struggles to creatively manage those tensions and conflicts that are critical to learning.

Next, we will explain what we think it means to take these Bakhtinian concepts seriously, using our own cross-national work in the areas of language and literacy learning and teacher education.

OUR RESEARCH IN CROSS-NATIONAL CONTEXTS

Ball presents her research in South Africa, and Freedman presents her research in Bosnia-Herzegovina and Rwanda (Freedman, Corkalo et al., in press; Freedman, Kambanda et al., in press). These cross-national studies have proven especially useful in helping us broaden our assumptions about diversity, growth and change, and the nature of the Bakhtinian struggles and tensions that are characteristic of our new times.

Ball's study (2000a, 2000b) focuses attention on the first implication for research, what it means to take diversity seriously and see how it can become a resource. Ball's study is based on a teacher education course implemented over a 3-year period in the United States and South Africa in an effort to help teachers become better prepared to teach culturally and linguistically diverse students. Using data collected from more than 100 U.S. and South African preservice and in-service teachers, this research investigates the evolving perspectives of teachers as they prepare to face challenging situations in diverse schools. The data include the classroom discussions, narrative essays, journals, and autobiographies of the teachers' literacy experiences. This study shares the developing voices of these U.S. and South African teachers over time as they engage with issues of literacy and diversity in the course.

Freedman and her colleagues are studying the role of the schools in social reconstruction in two parts of the world that experienced war and genocide in the early 1990s: Rwanda and the former Yugoslav country of Bosnia-Herzegovina.[4] The study includes interviews and focus groups with educational officials as well as with local stakeholders (teachers, parents, and secondary students). The goal is to introduce local voices into the national and international debates about the roles schools are playing and might play in shaping the countries' futures. Freedman describes the official debates about the schools and then provides excerpts from interviews with local stakeholders. Freedman's work focuses attention on the second and third research implications, what is involved in understanding the mechanisms of growth and change, and what is involved in understanding struggles to creatively manage the tensions and conflicts that underlie learning.

Ball's Project: Taking Diversity Seriously While Seeking to Understand the Mechanisms of Change

Current reform movements in the United States and abroad are challenging teacher education programs to prepare teachers who are able and interested in teaching in the schools of the twenty-first century. U.S. demographers predict that by 2020, 46 percent of the U.S. school population will be students of color, whereas in South Africa students of color comprise well over 50 percent of the school population. Reports on educational achievement in both countries confirm that a large number of these students attend schools in poor, underresourced areas and that many of them are failing to achieve at their full potential. Many of these students move from home to school on unsafe streets. They represent society's have nots, who are often displaced, and who lack access to high-speed travel and technology. Twenty-first-century classrooms in the United States and South Africa are becoming more varied

---

4   Data were collected in three towns in different areas of Rwanda where the wars and genocide were experienced differently – Kibuye and Rubengera in Kibuye province, Save in Butare province, and Byumba in Byumba province. See related studies with complementary data collected in these same cities and in other parts of Rwanda in Stover and Weinstein, in press.

   In the Balkans, data were collected in one town in BiH, Mostar. Additional data were collected in Vukovar in Croatia, but because they were collected later, they are not included in this chapter. Related studies with complementary data collected in these same cities, as well as in other parts of BiH and Croatia, can be found in Stover and Weinstein, in press.

than ever before. With students and teachers coming together across linguistic and cultural divides, it is more imperative than ever that teacher education programs prepare teachers to work effectively with diverse student populations. Clearly, an important goal of teacher preparation programs globally must be to prepare teachers to work effectively with students from culturally and linguistically diverse backgrounds.

Ball's interest in investigating the changing perspectives of U.S. and South African teachers emerged because these two countries share striking similarities in their need to prepare teachers to work with diverse student populations and in their histories concerning the education of marginalized people of color. These two countries have historically shared many of the same language policies toward linguistically diverse students and the mechanisms they use to implement those inequitable policies. South Africa and the United States in past years promoted apartheid and segregation, which resulted in separate and unequal systems of education that deliberately miseducated Blacks in an attempt to lower their aspirations and prepare them for a subordinate role in society. Both countries share a history of racial disparities in the quality of schools, in educational access, and in the preparation of teachers to work with culturally and linguistically diverse students.

The cross-national study that is reported on here is based on a teacher education course that was implemented over a 3-year period with teachers from these two countries as they prepared to face challenging situations in diverse schools. This course drew on the works of Vygotsky (1978), Leont'ev (1981), and Luria (1981) to build a sociocultural theoretical frame that would help to explain how teachers develop commitment to issues of diversity, as well as how their commitments are revealed in their oral and written discourses, as they consider possibilities of teaching culturally and linguistically diverse students. It was hypothesized that, as teachers were exposed to strategically designed readings and activities within a teacher education program, their perspectives on literacy and commitments to teaching diverse student populations would be affected in positive ways. Using data collected from more than 100 U.S. and South African preservice and in-service teachers, this research investigated how teachers' developing perspectives and commitments can be facilitated by exposure to the internally persuasive discourses of diverse writers about literacy and through engagement with particular classroom activities. The research reveals how the teachers' developing perspectives and commitments are revealed in their changing patterns of discourse (Ball, 2000a, 2000b). The research involved discourse and text analyses of narrative essays, literacy autobiographies, journals, interviews, small-group discussions, and videotapes of teaching collected from the teachers enrolled in the course. These data illustrate the teachers' changing ideologies concerning theoretical principles and teaching practices. In a Bakhtinian sense, this research investigates the notion of ideological becoming. Ball conceptualized the teacher education program as a learning environment and social setting – a contact zone – where ideological becoming would be nurtured. She realized that the teachers came to the course with a body of assumptions and beliefs that had been shaped by the authoritative discourses that they had encountered prior to this course. Knowing that each teacher began the course with a body of assumptions and beliefs, which constitute their internal ideologies, she exposed the teachers to a range of theoretical readings representing the internally persuasive discourses of others, which she hoped would be added to the multiplicity of voices that would shape and guide the developing ideologies of our next generation of teachers. She also exposed the teachers to readings about pedagogy and best practices that would enlighten them about working with diverse student populations and cause them to give serious consideration to ways that diversity could be viewed as a resource in their classrooms.

The teachers in this study brought a range of internally persuasive discourses to the course, which had been influenced by the authoritative discourse that shapes traditional approaches to teaching mainstream students. The internally persuasive discourses that each teacher brought to the course impacted their ideological becoming as they engaged with new ideas within our teacher education classroom. As most teachers enter teacher education programs, they bring with them very limited perspectives on what literacy is, what it means for a person to be literate, and ways that they can strategically use the diverse language and literacy practices that students bring to the classroom as a resource. Linked to these limited views is the fact that many of these teachers have also given little thought to teaching students who are different from themselves or who have had different literacy histories from their own. The teachers in this study were exposed to diverse readings that were carefully selected to broaden and challenge their previously held ideologies concerning the use of literacies in classroom practice. In essence, exposure to these theoretical readings and practical strategies, coupled with reflective writing, student case studies, and authentic teaching experiences, were designed to serve as a catalyst to motivate tensions between authoritative discourses and a wide range of internally persuasive discourses that were present in our class. This rich and complex "contact zone" inside the teacher education classroom yielded plenty of opportunities for students to decide what would become internally persuasive for them; in other words, it yielded plenty of opportunities for teachers to further develop their ideologies.

As we have noted earlier, it is what each person thinks for him- or herself, what ultimately is persuasive to the individual, that determines the development of their ideologies. As teachers form our own ideas, they come into contact with the internally persuasive discourses of others, and those discourses enter their consciousness much as authoritative discourse does. It was hoped that the discourses of the carefully selected theories of others would influence the ways these teachers came to think about diversity, and contribute to forming what ultimately was internally persuasive for them. According to Bakhtin, the internally persuasive discourse of these teachers would be open and subject to change and would constantly interact with other ideas in ever-evolving ways. In the account that follows, excerpts collected from one of the teachers are presented in order to trace her changing discourses over time and to show evidence of her developing ideologies and plans for future practice. These brief excerpts are taken from the students' personal narratives, reflections on the course readings, and the teacher's discussions of how her participation in the course as a strategically designed activity system influenced her ideological becoming (see Ball, 2000a, 2000b, for a more detailed description of the complex mechanisms of change that influenced this student and her fellow classmates).

One South African teacher, Dorene, was a female in her late twenties who came from a lower-class, Black South African background. Dorene attended a teacher education program that was offered at a major university located in the Western Cape Province of South Africa. Although the university offered a traditional teacher education program, Dorene and her classmates were enrolled in a course for practicing teachers who were seeking certification in a Further Diploma in Education program. This teacher education program was designed to prepare teachers to teach in the newly emerging multilingual and multicultural schools. When she enrolled in the course, Dorene had been teaching for 3 years and living in an area of the city designated for "Blacks" during apartheid. Like all participants in the course, Dorene wrote an autobiography of her early literacy experiences in order to bring to a metacognitive level of awareness those experiences that helped to influence the development of her ideologies concerning literacy and what it means to be a teacher. In her autobiography, Dorene revealed that she grew up in a township and recalled starting school at a rather late age:

I was then nine years old. Neither of my parents attended school, they are illiterate. But, what I vaguely remember is that my mother used to show me pictures and tell me what was going on, i.e., a woman is carrying a basket, she is coming from town, etc. What I liked best was when she told me stories, some I still remember even today. When I was about seven years old I was hospitalized and I remember the nurses used to read us stories from books in Afrikaans and English. I was in the hospital for six months and I loved to listen to what was read and also joined the other children in a class where on certain days a lady use to come and teach us to read, write and count. We also attended Sunday school and reading was done all the time there. I learned to read and write on a slate. When I could master reading in standard 3, I used to read for my mother from the schoolbook and she would sit down and listen to me. If she didn't, I used to cry.

My reflections on my experiences are both positive and negative. Positive in the way that I developed a love for reading and school work and a love for teaching pupils the happiness and fulfillment a person gets from reading. But there were also negatives. I often thought of dropping out of school because my father did not see the importance of me going to school, not allowing me to read my books at home. The only time I could look into my books was late at night . . . I passed my school years having to study only at school . . . or else I had to wait until he was asleep. Sometimes I was beaten at school and sometimes I was beaten at home for separate reasons. I was the only one who survived . . . my brother and sister dropped out of school at an early age and I blame my father for that. Having someone to encourage you in what you do helps and motivates you to go further. I thank my mother and my teachers for encouraging me. I always think of my teacher who used to say "one who strives never loses," and that is how I endured my school years. . . .

This autobiographical activity served as a readiness exercise that prepared Dorene and her fellow classmates to consider new and different perspectives, attitudes, and visions for language and literacy learning, inclusion, and teaching practices in the classroom.

Following their experiences of sharing and reflecting on their personal literacy histories, the teachers in the course were exposed to assigned readings that were carefully selected to broaden their previously held ideologies on literacy and classroom practice. They were exposed to the internally persuasive discourses of others through writings by McElroy-Johnson (1993) on giving voice to the voiceless, Giroux (1988) on teachers as transformative intellectuals, Freire (1994) on the pedagogy of the oppressed, Gee (1989) on discourse as identity, and Delpit (1992, 2000) on the acquisition of literate discourse and on teaching other peoples' children. In essence, exposure to these theoretical readings and to practical strategies, coupled with reflective writing and authentic teaching experiences, served as a catalyst that motivated the teachers to consider new possibilities for their teaching practices. As the teachers' metacognitive levels increased concerning their own literacy experiences, many began to look outward and to question and challenge some of their long-held perspectives that they may not have been consciously aware of earlier.

After reading Giroux's (1988) thoughts on teachers as transformative intellectuals and teachers as critical thinkers, Dorene wrote in her reflective journal her critique of the educational system as she now saw it:

There are problems in our system in that firstly our teacher training was not of equal quality and level as that of our white compatriots and because of that our teaching ways are poor because there is rote learning in our schools that does not give the time or opportunity for critical and logical thinking. I see a need for in-service training for teachers, so that teaching can be more conducive to student success and more creative so we can develop the pupils' skills in literacy in an adequate manner.

After reading excerpts from Vygotsky (1981) on the process of internalization and from Au (1993) on expanding definitions of literacy, Dorene wrote the following in her reflective journal:

The theory that relates to my action research project is the one by Vygotsky that says we should internalize the activities that happen with our learners and assist them in learning more than I was as a teacher. We should not be doing the thinking for the student, but rather, we should be acknowledging the child's knowledge and make him/her more accessible to learning and not stay egocentric. I as a teacher should think, "am I transferring knowledge or am I helping to develop the child holistically in all aspects of life. I should reflect on these things myself, as I want prosperity in my students. . . . In addition, the five strategies from Au (1993) are very important in that a child is not encouraged to be a convergent thinker, but he/she is encouraged to use resources and embark on projects that have different topics.

As the course readings became internally persuasive for Dorene, she indicates their persuasive force as she voices what she wants for the students in her classroom:

Culturally, the learner has to identify with themselves, knowing their own language and then acquiring the ability to communicate in the other languages that are around them, thereby understanding the society they live in. . . . The linguistic growth of students is increased when parents also see themselves as co-educators. There must develop this relationship. Schools should help to establish these collaborative relationships. Parents should be encouraged to participate in promoting their children's progress in the education of their pupils. This can be done if parents listen to their children reading books sent from home. . . . I can truly say that I am what I am today because of my mother and I thank the Lord for having her and myself for obeying authority even under excruciating circumstances. I now realize that these experiences helped to make me the grown up that I am: one who loves children and wants to help them in their learning. . . . I am interested in helping small children to acquire knowledge and through it they can learn to be better persons who can work for themselves and their community, to build the children's confidence so they will not be afraid to talk even if they don't know the other languages.

After many classroom hours spent in discussions, reading about various theoretical perspectives, working with diverse students, and implementing practical strategies within their classrooms, bridges were formed between the texts they read, the teachers' internally persuasive discourses, and the internally persuasive discourses of others – the diverse perspectives and the new voices that were being represented in the course. Dorene's final reflection on her expanding definition of literacy reveals her emerging thoughts about literacy and teaching in diverse classrooms. Dorene's definition of literacy evolved from one that included the ability to "read, write, and speak on social context and academic context," to one that "also takes into consideration the cultural background of the students." For Dorene, the concept of literacy was greatly influenced by her reading of Au (1993). She shared this thought in her journal:

As I have read Kathryn Au's views on the definition of literacy, I fully agreed that literacy is not just the ability to read and write but also having insight to extract meaning from a text, read with comprehension and be able to recall information.

To communicate in a logical and critical way, we must be finding out about common-alities among different cultures and understanding one another, developing skills in implementing the acquired knowledge both academically and socially.

From her reading of McElroy-Johnson (1993), she also included "the ability to voice out your thoughts orally" and, as she noted earlier, "having the confidence so they will not be afraid to talk even if they don't know the other languages." These statements illustrate that, for Dorene, the course activities greatly helped her to gain the strength needed to voice her feelings and to be an active agent of change for students of color in a system that desperately needs restructuring.

Dorene clearly represents a student engaged in ideological becoming as she indicates her teaching plans that have emerged as a result of the course along with the multiplicity of voices that she will need as she goes out into the system to impact change. She says, "I want as a teacher to help my pupils to achieve their goals, i.e., reading writing and speaking. I want them to be proficient in reading all the languages we teach at school." Further evidence of Dorene's ideological becoming was heard in her emerging internally persuasive voice as she says,

Now I can allow a buzz to take place in my classroom that makes the pupils feel free. I converse with them so that they may see I have an interest in their lives. As from when I started learning about the action research project, I let my pupils do activities like interviewing prominent figures in their community like policemen and nurses. This way, my pupils develop confidence in speaking with professional people besides at school. I have come to the realization that in order for the teacher to be effective in the class, she needs dedication and love for what he/she does. The teacher should be supportive to the children and not have a teacher-centered class. Guiding children and being a role model helps very much when allowing the children to make their own choices. But we must make a rule that each person is responsible for his/her choice of action. Effectiveness goes with planning. Without planning properly, what are you going to do with results that end in failure? That is why it is important to assess yourself and know your goals. And finally, the tone of your voice also plays a very important part. If you speak soft or if you scream, your pupils will imitate you.

The implementation of these changes and emerging plans were con-firmed by Ball's observation of the changes in Dorene's teaching practices over time – during her 1997 visit to South Africa and again during her 2000 visit (see Ball, in press). As we came to the close of the course, Dorene penned the following letter:

Dear Dr. Ball:

Time flew by so quickly that I was taken aback with I heard that your time in South Africa is over. I will miss you. To tell the truth you came when I was fumbling – having hard times when I said I was quitting from the course. But you came with your fire – with Vygotsky and Au flying – and you boosted my spirits. I am thankful for the help you have been, for the insights you have given. Now I know I have to be aware of every detail I venture into. In my schoolwork, I must have a far researching mind – to develop myself and ensure the progress of my pupils. I know now that for my pupils to be bilingual, I have to encourage them positively, not teaching them for the purpose of academic achievement only. But to let them adapt to all situations. Your handouts have been a great help and will keep on helping me. Whenever I am uncertain of something and need guidance, I will take a look at my handouts. The handout on classroom-based assessment by Fred Genesee has been a great help, together with the one on how to teach a second language to first language speakers. They have been very important and will continue to be. Instructing pupils is always a challenge, but the end results of our acquired skills will be for the betterment of our students. I wish you, doctor, a safe and peaceful journey home. Please come back again soon and keep us on our toes.

Thank you again very much.

Dorene

When many of the teachers first entered Ball's course, like Dorene, they freely admitted that they had not given a great deal of conscious consideration to the notion of working as advocates for social change concerning the learning environments available for critically thinking students from poor and marginalized backgrounds. During the course, teachers were confronted with the challenge of considering these issues through interpersonal and socially mediated forums, including readings representing the discourses of others, individual and shared reflections on a range of related issues, written engagement with carefully designed prompts on these topics, and challenging classroom discussions that cause them to consider issues of diversity in different ways. Exposure to theoretical readings and practical activities took place during the course as a catalyst for engaging teachers in oral and written conversations that Ball hoped would have a positive impact on their thoughts and developing ideologies on issues of equity and educational reform.

At the time of this research, South Africa was emerging from the systematic implementation of apartheid and a history of social, economic, and educational inequalities in the education of marginalized populations. When I conducted my research in 1997 and 2000, South Africa was seeking ways to more effectively educate large numbers of poor, marginalized, and underachieving students. Many of these students were from culturally and linguistically diverse backgrounds, and they were educationally different from the students for whom the majority of instructional materials and school expectations had been tailored. At the time of my visits, it was clear that South Africa perceived the state of its educational program for underserved populations to be in crisis. With an end to official forms of social and economic segregation and degradation, as well as an apparent need for massive reconstruction of their educational system, South Africa welcomed innovations and collaborations that would support them in achieving their goals toward educational reform.

Dorene and many other students who participated in this course experienced challenges to their existing internally persuasive discourses that motivated them to struggle with the official authoritative discourses that they had previously encountered. They also came into contact with, and struggled with, the everyday discourses of their classmates and the common people they encountered. The changes that took place as a result of these encounters are what Bakhtin and his followers call ideological becoming.

Freedman and Her Colleagues' Project: Understanding Struggles To Resolve Tensions and Conflicts

Freedman turns to the second and third implications for future research, those aspects of ideological becoming that focus on the mechanisms of growth, and how learners struggle with the tensions and conflicts that lead to learning. Whereas the Bakhtinian school discusses the positive role these struggles play in learning, tension and conflict take on a special intensity in the countries where Freedman and her colleagues' research is situated: Rwanda and Bosnia-Herzegovina (BiH). These countries are in the throes of recovering from the mass atrocity of recent war and genocides. Many of their citizens have suffered serious trauma, and many are undergoing major shifts in identity. They are struggling to survive their psychic and physical wounds, and they are struggling with how to understand their nationality and nationhood. They further are struggling with what democracy means for them personally and for their countries. The citizens of BiH also live under the supervision of the international community because the UN Office of the High Representative (OHR) enforces the implementation of the Dayton Peace Accords. Many feel that the OHR sits unrelentingly in judgment of their actions. In both Rwanda and BiH, the schools carry the responsibility of inculcating ideologies in the next generation that will do nothing less than support reconciliation and a lasting peace. The stakes for the ideological becoming of the young are high and the teaching tasks complex.

In Rwanda during 4 months in the spring of 1994, the Hutu government organized and oversaw the slaughter, by conservative accounts, of at least a half million people (Des Forges, 1999) and, by some estimates, of as many as 800,000 people (Sibomana, 1999). The current Tutsi-dominated government espouses a philosophy of national unity and reconciliation, although it was involved in massacres of up to 300,000 people in Rwanda and Congo (Prunier, 1995; Sibomana, 1999). As Sibomana (1999) assesses the situation, "Official declarations are one thing; reality is another" (p. 139). The current Rwandan government has strongly discouraged all official identification by ethnicity, and many believe it is illegal to identify as belonging to a particular ethnic group. The government also discourages even unofficial displays of ethnic identity. There is little space for disagreement or debate, and people fear retribution for any disagreement with any government policy (Longman & Rutagengwa, in press). This climate of repression creates ongoing tensions, which have few outlets for resolution.[5]

During the breakup of Yugoslavia between 1991 and 1995, approximately 200,000 people including 22,000 children were murdered (Maass, 1996). Whereas fear and suppression underlie the many silences found in Rwanda, unresolved anger underlies the frequent and explicit disagreements in BiH. Nationalist tensions surface on the streets, in the homes and schools, and in the churches. Particularly in Serbian and Croatian areas of BiH, many politicians and their followers still seem to be fighting the war. Besides the verbal battles, violent cross-national outbreaks continue to occur periodically, with the UN troops stationed in the country for purposes of keeping the peace. Although those who have watched the region closely since the early 1990s see some improvements, especially in the elected leadership, different national groups remain reluctant to take any responsibility for their role in the atrocities associated with the recent wars, and tensions are far from resolved (The Human Rights Center/UC Berkeley et al., 1999).[6]

These international contexts force a careful consideration of how individual and social development interact with political life and of how struggle and conflict can sometimes lead to the hardening of ideas. Of particular interest in these contexts is how the official authoritative discourses in the two countries interact with the internally persuasive discourses of everyday people. The ways the discourses interact complicate Bakhtinian ideas about the role of tension and struggle in ideological becoming and suggest a relationship between ideological becoming, the mechanisms behind the management of conflict, and those processes that ultimately could lead to reconciliation (see Stover, 1998, for a discussion of the processes underlying reconciliation).

Freedman, Corkalo et al., and Freedman, Kambanda et al. (in press) in their research on the schools compare the internally persuasive discourse of local stakeholders – teachers, parents, and students – with the official authoritative discourse of policy makers and education officials. In this chapter, Freedman explores how these discourses come together ultimately to determine students' opportunities to learn. In both countries, the schools play a critical role in all official plans for rebuilding the societies. In both countries, people seem to place their greatest hopes on the next generation, which has not directly experienced the traumatic events of the recent past and whose attitudes are not yet hardened.

---

[5] For detail on the political situation that led to the Rwandan genocide, for reports of the genocide, and an analysis of the current political situation, see Des Forges (1999), Prunier (1995), and Sibomana (1999).

[6] For detail on the political situation that led to the mass atrocities in the Balkans, and for a full report of them and an analysis of the current political situation, see Glenny (2000), Maass (1996), and Silber and Little (1997).

There is a sense in both BiH and Rwanda that education gone wrong contributed in powerful ways to the violence. Not only was hatred taught explicitly through the curriculum, but also in Rwanda educational opportunities were systematically denied to the Tutsis by the Hutu who held power, just as the Tutsi earlier had denied opportunities to the Hutu when the Tutsi held power. In both cultures there was the expectation that educated people should be civilized, cultured, and refined, and therefore would not commit crimes against humanity or genocide. When they did, there was the widespread belief that the educational system, on a very fundamental level, was not doing a good job. One high-ranking Rwandan education official puts forth these widely held views:

An education that leads to genocide is a terrible education as far as we're concerned . . . if someone who has a degree, the diploma, or the PhDs could go out of their way and could either kill or allow others to kill or plan to kill, that gave the feeling that that education was wrong. . . . What kind of education have I got if I have no feelings at all?

Just as the educational system was believed to have contributed to the genocide, today people believe that education, done well, could play an equally powerful role in preventing future violence. The stakes for the schools in both countries are extraordinarily high. Many players, from national and local government officials to official representatives of the international community who enforce the Dayton Peace Accords in BiH, attempt to keep tight control over what happens inside the schools. Local citizens, including teachers, parents, and students, who are most affected by school policies, seldom have any forum for voicing their opinions to official decision makers. Those who work in the schools enact the official decisions or find their ways around them; even if they do not exert official power, like families and other parts of the community, they exert unofficial power. To use Bakhtin's terms, how local citizens' internally persuasive discourses interact and how those discourses interact with the official discourses within the country determine what actually happens in the schools. Local citizens ultimately exert a great deal of influence over the ideological becoming of the next generation, regardless of how much influence they have over school policies.

Freedman analyzes the views of teachers, parents, and students about one tension-filled topic, the language of instruction. Both countries grapple with issues related to national languages and the languages of instruction. In both countries, local citizens hold strong opinions about this issue. In both countries, these opinions relate to the state of intergroup relations and readiness for reconciliation.

In Rwanda during the summer of 2001, Freedman, Longman, and Samuelson interviewed twenty-two educational leaders, including officials from government ministries, church groups, and nongovernmental organizations working on educational issues. In the fall of 2001, Freedman's team from the National University of Rwanda interviewed eighty-four Rwandan students, parents, and educators. Approximately half were Tutsi and half Hutu (see Freedman, Kambanda et al., in press). In BiH during the summer of 2000, Freedman and Leebaw interviewed thirty-three educational leaders in Sarajevo, Mostar, and Banja Luka. In the fall of 2001, Freedman's team from the Human Rights Centers in Sarajevo and Mostar interviewed forty stakeholders in Mostar, including students, parents, and educators. Approximately half were Bosnian Moslems and half were Bosnian Croats (see Freedman, Coralka et al., in press).

Rwanda

In Rwanda, the situation for communication in the schools is complicated by the fact that there are three languages of instruction – the local home language of Kinyarwanda, which Rwandans learn as their native language, and the academic languages of French and English, which are learned in school and are by policy the languages of instruction from the fourth year onward. French became the language of the academy and the government when the Belgians colonized Rwanda in 1919. English was introduced after the genocide by returnees from Uganda and other English-speaking countries of the Diaspora. Many current government leaders, including the president, grew up speaking English. Although relatively few Rwandans are returnees who speak English as their native language, those who do have a great deal of power.[7] Not surprisingly, they legislated English as a third official language for the country and as a language of instruction. This multilingual policy creates practical difficulties for the schools.

The same Rwandan education official who blamed the schools for the genocide explained the link he sees between reconciliation and language policies:

A person of my age might find it hard to forgive if the whole of your family say is wiped out and you yourself remain, but my child should grow up in a different environment.

---

[7] Many Tutsis were driven out of Rwanda in the early 1960s. At this time, the Hutu who are the majority group in Rwanda had gained control of the government, and the Belgian colonialists, who had always protected the minority Tutsi population, left Rwanda and returned the country to the Rwandan people. The Tutsi who fled Rwanda in the early 1960s formed a diaspora mostly in neighboring countries, and many of them organized and mounted a series of attacks to try to regain power. During these years, the Hutu government in Rwanda claimed that local Tutsi were aiding the Tutsi attackers from the exterior. The Hutu government carried out a series of massacres of local Tutsi to stop their supposed support of the invading Tutsi. Part of the propaganda that led to the genocide of 1994 involved invoking Hutu fear of these Tutsi rebels from the exterior, who the Hutu claimed were still being supported by local Tutsi. Currently, these Tutsi from the exterior are in control of the government. They returned to Rwanda in 1994, stopped the genocide, and took power at that time.

And even if they are not able to forget, they should at least have a new attitude, a new environment of peace, of reconciliation, of tolerance, of living together. It should be different from the current generation. Today some wounds are still in effect. But twenty years, ten years down the road, we think that that generation will be much better at forgiving [pause] That explains [why] we also have bilingualism as a national policy because we want to use communication, you know, English, French, you know, as part of the [reconciliation] courses. Because Rwandan society, among other things, has been divided along Anglophone-Francophone lines. And what we are saying is that, how does it help you if you consider yourself Anglophone or Francophone, as a Rwandese? As a Rwandese, we have specific problems for Rwanda, and we are also together as Rwandese, never mind if your educational background was Burundi, or Congo, or Uganda, or America for that matter.

This official uses the third person and first person plural "we" as the subject of his sentences above, marking his discourse as authoritative and official; he never uses the first person to indicate that he is expressing his own opinion. When officials we interviewed wanted to express their personal opinions, they always marked a shift from speaking in their official capacity to speaking in a personal capacity with a shift to the first person pronoun, "I." Note also how after only a brief pause, this official shifts from the topic of the population's ability to forgive and reconcile after the genocide, to the topic of language policy and communication as central to the reconciliation process. As he indicates, the Rwandan returnees who are in power speak either French (if they are from Congo, Burundi, or some other Francophone country) or English (if they are from Uganda, Kenya, Tanzania, or some other Anglophone country). Some returnees, but not all, also speak Kinyarwanda. He expresses a basic understanding that communication is essential to reconciliation, but his focus is on returnees, in his circle of government officials, who do not have the common language of Kinyarwanda. Some of these returnees are from Francophone countries ("Burundi, or Congo") and some are from Anglophone countries ("Uganda or America for that matter"). He is not talking about communication among people who were born in Rwanda and speak Kinyarwanda and those who were raised speaking Kinyarwanda when they were living abroad.

The local citizens – be they Hutu or Tutsi or teachers, parents, or students – expressed general enthusiasm for the current multilingual policy of the government. The citizens claimed that knowledge of multiple languages would be useful for travel abroad, the nation's ability to have contact with the outside world, access to a wider range of books, interactions with neighboring countries that have both French and English as their languages, opening minds to other cultures. They particularly favored the introduction of English because of its status as a global language and its usefulness as Rwandans interact with the world beyond their country's borders. Given the current leadership, they also understood the necessity of adding English to stimulate better and wider communication within the country, to promote national unity, and to further future national development. The government-inspired official discourses favoring English as a third official language coincided with what in the ideal and in the abstract was internally persuasive to the local citizens.

In spite of this apparent widespread enthusiasm for English, language practices in the schools seemed slow to change. The internally persuasive discourse of the interviewees indicated definite ambivalence about introducing English as a language of instruction. Although the schools are supposed to shift the language of instruction to French and English in the fourth year, in practice many elementary schools teach only in Kinyarwanda. In some cases, they do not have staff proficient enough in either French or English to teach in those languages. When students have difficulty understanding French, some reported that teachers resorted to Kinyarwanda in order to communicate, even in the secondary schools. One Tutsi student whose family returned to Rwanda after the wars and genocide observed: "Teachers are obliged to appeal to Kinyarwanda when students themselves complain that they don't understand." A university official recognized, "We have Kinyarwanda as a common language. That has helped a lot as far as communication is concerned." The "contact zone" inside Rwandan secondary schools includes a far-ranging political space, with influences from Congo, Burundi, and Uganda intermixing with influences from Rwanda itself and Belgium, as well as other countries that housed the Rwandan Diaspora.

French, not English, remains the preferred language of instruction for the upper grades. English is most commonly taught as a foreign language. The exception was a school with a substantial population of Anglophone students, which offered courses to these students in English and courses to the Francophone students in French. The effect was that in this school students were segregated according to language.

Some Hutu in particular resented the idea that they might be instructed in English, which is a language they did not know well. As one student explained,

I started to learn in French from primary form up to now, and if I were to be taught in English now, it would be too difficult for me to understand what they are teaching me. So, lessons should continue being given in French because it is the language we understand, and it does not give us hard time like English would do if it is introduced as a teaching language now.

A Tutsi teacher agreed on the grounds that students have to juggle too many languages:

I think it is good to study in French because students are Rwandans. But if we used other languages, it would confuse students.... It is good because we also teach English as a course... but using many languages in teaching is difficult, because even Kinyarwanda is difficult [because some do not speak it either and it is not the language commonly used for academic talk].

A teacher interviewed by the project team blamed the lack of use of French in the lower grades for the difficulties he found some students to have when they reached secondary school. He gave the example of "one student who failed to adapt to French as a language of instruction." He claimed this student's difficulties "could be solved if pupils in upper primary could be taught in French to prepare them for secondary education." Another teacher stated that his "students are more familiar with Kinyarwanda than other languages" and for this reason have difficulty in secondary school. One teacher who did not speak Kinyarwanda was particularly aware of its importance for helping pupils understand their lessons at the secondary level:

As I didn't study Kinyarwanda, I have difficulties communicating with my students. For other teachers, when they meet such problems, they try to translate the message in Kinyarwanda. This is an obstacle. I try to adapt my French and English to the level of students.

Some educators also pointed out the impracticality of introducing a new language of instruction. Schools in Rwanda have difficulty paying teachers, have poor facilities, and have few books or other school supplies. Furthermore, many teachers lack sufficient training. Introducing a new language of instruction was recognized to be costly in both personnel and materials:

If students are to learn in both languages, first of all, teachers must master those languages. I am silent about the lack of textbooks of both languages. So, I think using both languages now doubles the problems.

Another Hutu school administrator explained:

If they [policy-makers] want utilisation of these languages at the same rate, it requires much money. First of all, having the syllabus designed in those languages in which they want to teach, you must have qualified teachers who are able to teach in these languages. In my opinion, this is a too ambitious of an objective.

These comments make the following remarks of a government official seem naive:

Owing to the shortage of manpower, womanpower in our schools, if I move into a classroom, and I speak English, which is what I do, those who speak French will follow my lesson. Someone is doing, who speaks French only, will march into the classroom and kids who come from so-called Anglophone background could follow the lesson. It is happening, yeah.

Although this official understands the problems in resources and that bilingualism is not always a reality, he nevertheless constructed for himself and the interviewer an ideal picture of language use in the schools.

For Rwandan schools to be seen as social institutions that deal with the tensions that plague the society writ large, they must address the issue of languages of instruction. Bakhtin and his followers show that students must interact with multiple voices, which express multiple points of view, in or-der to learn and grow. They need a common language through which to interact, and they must be able to hear clearly what others say and mean. They also must have teachers who understand and can mediate among the different voices that enter the dialogue. It may be impractical at this time to introduce English as a new language of instruction in Rwanda; in prac-tice, many schools seem to have made the decision not to introduce English as anything more than another foreign language. It may also be the case that Kinyarwanda should be used for certain kinds of conversations; in prac-tice, many schools seem to have made the decision to use Kinyarwanda as needed. It is also the case that people in a society need to feel safe enough to express their points of view. It will also be critical to have open debates about language in order to come to realistic and sensitive decisions. The same debates will also be necessary in other arenas, particularly as people develop internally persuasive discourses to explain the recent past and make decisions about the future.

Bosnia-Herzegovina

In BiH, the tensions and struggles around the languages of instruction in the schools are just as complex as they are in Rwanda. These tensions further complicate the Bakhtinian notion of how struggles lead to learning. Before the Balkan wars of the 1990s, Bosniaks (Bosnian Moslems), Bosnian Croats, and Bosnian Serbs all spoke Serbo-Croatian. Now the Bosnian Croats call their language Croatian, the Bosnian Serbs call their language Serbian, and the Bosniaks call their language Bosnian. The three languages are mutu-ally comprehensible and have essentially the same syntactic structures; the differences are mostly at the word level. Michael Ignatieff (1998) explains that the different groups in the former Yugoslavia tend to magnify minor differences, such as those within the languages, to achieve separatist polit-ical ends. He calls this phenomenon the narcissism of minor differences. Linguist Peter Trudgill (1995) agrees, characterizing the motivations behind magnifying these small linguistic differences as purely political, "[T]he new governments of the former Yugoslavia are attempting to stress their separate nationhoods and ethnicities by focusing on lexical differences" (p. 45).

Unlike in Rwanda, in BiH multiple official discourses are espoused by varied governments in the region, including the federal governments of the newly formed countries, varied local governments within the countries, and the international community that oversees the enforcement of the Dayton Accords. What proved internally persuasive for the local stakeholders in the interview study varied in relatively systematic ways, depending on the speaker's national group affiliation. This affiliation led the interviewees to align with different official national discourses. The project collected data in Mostar because of ongoing tensions between the Bosniaks who live on the East side of the city and the Bosnian Croats who live on the West side.

Although there has been improvement, people generally do not cross the bridges that join one side of the city to the other, either literally or figuratively; however, it is more common for Bosniaks to cross to the West side than for Croats to cross to the East (Ignatieff, 2002). The schools are segregated, and the opportunities for cross-national dialogue are pitifully few for most people. Although the Dayton Peace Accords support school integration, local officials have found ways of interpreting Dayton so schools can remain separate. Currently, in the town of Stolac, schools are integrated by having students of different nationalities go to school in the same building but not in the same classes. In some schools, students are on shifts so students from different national groups do not have to be in these so-called integrated schools at the same time. This notion of shared facilities, but different curriculum and classes, is now called the Stolac model. Such an interpretation of what is meant by school integration remains a point of tension between local officials and the UN's OHR, which enforces Dayton. As one OHR representative explained:

Literally what you are talking about [with school segregation] is the fight for territory, but there is also a fight for language, identity, culture, history, heritage, and all of that. It started, again, early '99 . . . the language, and heritage, and culture of education card has been played a lot.

In BiH the issue of language of instruction is intimately tied to issues of school integration. Because the different nationalities claim to have different languages, they claim that their children have a right to be educated in their national language. The issue has been twisted into an issue of minority language rights, which is part of a larger argument for the preservation of minority cultures. The Bosniaks are quite impatient with these arguments. In interview after interview, teachers, students, and parents asserted that in reality, the language is all the same:

Officially there are unfortunately, three languages, but the thing is that we do not have interpreters. There is Bosnian, Serbian, and Croatian. This is a one language . . . damned nationalism is so strong and opposing, politics opposing although it is completely the same language. . . . No one needs an interpreter, but it is as it is. (history teacher)

Basically, we all speak the same language. Well in the books, this making of new books, Bosnian, Croatian or Serbian. Well that is all one language. (parent)

Bosnian, Croatian, Serbian. It is the same language. Maybe it has some differences in some words, but everybody understands each other. (student)

The Bosnian Croats, in contrast, argued for their language rights, and rarely mentioned the similarities across the languages. Their internally persuasive discourses sound quite different from those of their Bosniak neighbors. They espoused the same rights for other national groups, and claimed every group had the right to keep its language and school curriculum separate.

I think there should be national schools. So the lectures would be held in Croatian for Croat people, Serbian for Serbs, and Bosniak for Bosniaks . . . every ethnic group has to have rights. By some rules of democracy they have right to live, work, and use their own language. (Bosnian Croat student)

This same student admits similarities in the languages, but immediately moves on to stress the special differences that justify their separateness:

Of course all three languages don't have too many differences, but each has certain special things, and every person likes it because of something beloved in it.

Most interesting is this student's claim that she has discussed her views with students of other nationalities and that they agree with her. "I talked about it with friends of different nationality, and they also agree." Her claim about what others think conflicts with what the Bosniaks say in their interviews.

This student also voices strong views about what she feels is needed for reconciliation. She resents the foreign intervention that brokered the peace. She knows that ultimately Bosnians with different national affiliations will have to communicate with one another and find ways to cooperate, but she still holds on to her philosophy of separateness and incorrectly ascribes her philosophy to all local sides:

We have to build this country by a model and structure that is not imposed by some violent or even foreigner suggestions. I think that people of Bosnia know what's best for them. . . . Cooperation is needed in B-H, and with other countries, but it should be somehow dominant what people from here want, and for sure everyone wants their language. That is definitive.

A Bosniak parent offers a contrasting way of thinking about a mixed society. He imagines ways to preserve what he understands to be the linguistic desires of the "others," but in a context of integrated schools and classrooms:

It [classrooms] would be mixed. It would be logical to me that everyone speaks in their own language. If the professor is Croat, let him speak in Croatian. If he is a Serb, let him speak in Serb language, and the children should speak in their own languages. If by chance someone doesn't understand, he should ask what does it mean, and not to correct.

Another Bosniak teacher stresses the importance of teaching language tolerance:

If I am explaining, I had a custom to say, well, tacka and tocka [Bosnian and Croatian word for full stop, op.trans], and then said to children that both words are correct. It is nice to know both words, you know. This is a way that I am acting today. . . . Children register all of that.

When educators, students, and parents demonstrate such different and conflicting ideologies depending on their national group and when students do not have opportunities to meet in school to grapple with these differences, it creates obstacles for schools' attempts to support the kind of ideological development that could lead to mutual understanding.

CONCLUSION

In both BiH and Rwanda, Bakhtinian theories about the academic and verbal struggles that lead to learning take on an added intensity. These are parts of the world where ordinary people had little opportunity for honest verbal struggle. The situations that led to the wars and genocides of the 1990s remain in place in too many ways for comfort. The issue of the language of instruction in the schools demonstrates how difficult it is for people to communicate honestly and work through their ongoing difficulties. As Bakhtin emphasizes, internally persuasive discourses need opportunities for testing against opposing points of view. In Rwanda, the issues are suppressed and the language of the schools often serves to depress rather than support communication. In BiH, the issues are raw and on the surface, and the tensions are so great that communication is difficult. Furthermore, many schools remain segregated. In both contexts, political leaders continue to manipulate societal structures and attitudes, making it difficult for the youth to move in different directions than their parents did. In these countries, the concept of ideological becoming offers a framework for mediation, a way to consider the kinds of dialogues that could lead to change. However, the "contact zones" reference very real and very recent violent physical conflicts, making ideological becoming all the more important and all the more complex.

In both countries, discourses work on several levels; therefore, dialogues must occur within and across these levels – from the official and authoritative words of the international community and national leaders, to the words of everyday people. Freedman and her colleagues found that everyday people are full of good will, especially given what they have experienced in the past decade and given the political contexts in which they live. The national and international leaders with their varied authoritative discourses could learn a great deal from the internally persuasive discourses of the citizens of Rwanda and BiH. The schools could also be more effective if they were to teach young people to question the authoritative discourses that seek to manipulate them and that even manipulate the schools they attend. Manipulative leaders in both countries played a major role in creating the conditions that led to the wars and genocides. In the aftermath, it is critically important for all sides to find ways to learn from the recent past so mass atrocity does not occur again. In the conclusion to her book, which documents the Rwandan genocide, Allison Des Forges (1999) presents a Bakhtinian image of resonating voices of protest as what will be necessary to prevent future genocides:

We must find ways to increase the numbers and effectiveness of resisters against such crimes, whether within or outside the society at risk. We must understand how local and international protest can resonate back and forth to create the swell of outrage that will prevent or halt future genocides. (p. 771)

A WORD ABOUT METHODOLOGY

Bakhtinian theories support empirical research. They emphasize the fact that ideology is not a hidden inner process but rather is external, visible, and amenable to empirical study. Bakhtin/Medvedev (1978) argues, "We are most inclined to imagine ideological creation as some inner process of understanding, comprehension, and perception, and do not notice that it in fact unfolds externally, for the eye, the ear, the hand" (p. 8). Ideology is "not in the soul, in the inner world, ... but in the world, in sound, in gesture, in the combination of masses, lines, colors, living bodies" (p. 8). The implication for research is that ideological becoming "is completely accessible to a unified and essentially objective method of cognition and study" (p. 8). Bakhtin/Medvedev continues to explain: "Every ideological product (ideologeme) is a part of the material social reality surrounding man, an aspect of the materialized ideological horizon. Whatever a word might mean, it is first of all materially present, as a thing uttered, written, printed, whispered, or thought. That is, it is always an objectively present part of man's social environment" (p. 8). This social environment includes the cognitive and affective worlds of the people in the society and the actions that surround them.

Bakhtinian theories support the study of social processes, not isolated individuals. Ideology is part of a social process, and can only be understood by analyzing its social and interactive essence. Bakhtin/Medvedev explain the completely social nature of the process of ideological development:

> that the individual, isolated person does not create ideologies, that ideological creation and its comprehension only take place in the process of social intercourse. Each individual act in the creation of ideology is an inseparable part of social intercourse, one of its dependent components, and therefore cannot be studied apart from the whole social process that gives it its meaning". (p. 126, in Morris from *The formal method in literary scholarship*, 1928)

If one understands the developmental process in this way, one realizes that, "It [ideology] is not within us, but between us" (Bakhtin/Medvedev, 1978, p. 8).

THE DEVELOPMENT OF THIS BOOK

We ourselves have gone through a process of ideological becoming in the development of this book. As scholars in the academy, we began with the authoritative voices that so often dictate our perceptions and interpretations. To these, we have added the internally persuasive discourses in our worlds. These include the images of artists like Salgado, as well as the images we see and the voices we hear in our daily lives – each others' discourses, our students', our colleagues', our friends' and families', our research experiences. These images and discourses push us to move beyond the comfortable topics we so often embrace to consider some of the more difficult challenges facing education – challenges such as making space in the academic agenda of schooling for the nonauthoritative voices of disenfranchised students (Landay, Lee, and Knoeller) and equipping teachers to think critically about their enactment of this agenda (Sperling and Greenleaf & Katz). To deal with these realities, for both teachers and students, we need what Dressman refers to as "a new map"; we need to reflect on the scholarly journeys we take, in the way that Bazerman does; we need to open our scholarly inquiry to new voices in the way that Valdés does. Only by being equipped with new ways of seeing and interpreting the discourses around us can we reenvision our future and face such challenges as those posed by new technologies (Mahiri), by adults who strive to reshape their opportunities (Kalman), and by the next generation of what Gee calls "shape shifters," who are in the process of reinventing the world.

While we were working on this book, we also incorporated the voices of a group of graduate students at Stanford and Berkeley, where we cotaught a course using many of the chapters from this book. Just as we struggled with our own ideological becoming, so did these students. They engaged in dialogue with a number of the chapter authors and wrote a series of "voices in dialogue," which are published at the ends of the sections to come. At many points they found themselves facing tensions between the authoritative words of the academy and their classmates' understandings of the material they were reading and interacting with.

It has now been over 25 years since Bakhtin's writings began to impact Western thought. His perspectives remain as current today as when they were first published. He teaches us that we in education have to be clear about who we are and what we think, about not just what a single individual thinks but about systems of thought and how they interact together. We have to recognize that our thought systems are always in a state of flux and growth. And we have to understand that we are responsible for an aspect of teaching that we don't always consider – nurturing and guiding ideological becoming.

References

American Heritage dictionary of the English language, fourth edition. (2000). Houghton Mifflin Company.

Au, K. (1993). An expanded definition of literacy. In *Literacy instruction in multicultural settings* (pp. 20–34). New York: Harcourt Brace College Publishers.

Bakhtin, M. M. (1981). Discourse in the novel. In M. Holquist (Ed.), *The dialogic imagination: Four essays by M. M. Bakhtin.* (Trans. Caryl Emerson and Michael Holquist). Austin: University of Texas Press.

Bakhtin, M. M./Medvedev, P. N. (1978). *The formal method in literary scholarship: A critical introduction to sociological poetics.* (Trans. Albert J. Wehrle). Cambridge, MA: Harvard University Press.

Ball, A. F. (1992). Cultural preference and the expository writing of African-American adolescents. *Written Communication, 9*(4), 501–32.

Ball, A. F. (2000a). Preservice teachers' perspectives on literacy and its use in urban schools: A Vygotskian perspective on internal activity and teacher change. In C. Lee & P. Smagorinsky (Eds.), *Worlds of meaning: Vygotskian perspectives on literacy research* (pp. 314–59). Cambridge, UK: Cambridge University Press.

Ball, A. F. (2000b). Preparing teachers for diversity: Lessons learned from the U.S. and South Africa. *Teaching and Teacher Education, 16,* 491–509.

Ball, A. F. (in press). *Carriers of the torch: Addressing the global challenge of preparing teachers for diversity.* New York: Teachers College Press.

Ball, A. F., & Lardner, T. (1997). Dispositions toward literacy: Constructs of teacher knowledge and the Ann Arbor Black English case. *College Composition and Communication, 48* (4), 469–85.

Cazden, C., John, R., & Hymes, D. (Eds.), (1972). *Functions of language in the classroom.* New York: Teachers College Press.

Delpit, L. (1992). Acquisition of literate discourse: Bowing before the master? *Theory Into Practice, 31*(4), 296–302.

Delpit, L. (2000). The silenced dialogue: Power and pedagogy in the education of other peoples' children. *Harvard Educational Review, 58* (3), 280–98.

Des Forges, A. (1999). *Leave None to Tell the Story: Genocide in Rwanda.* New York and Paris: Human Rights Watch and International Federation of Human Rights.

Emerson, C. (1981). The outer world and inner speech: Bakhtin, Vygotsky, and the internalization of language. In G. S. Morson (Ed.), *Bakhtin: Essays and dialogues on his work.* Chicago: The University of Chicago Press.

Freedman, S., Corkalo, D., Levy, N., Abazovic, D., Leebaw, B., Ajdukovic, D., Djipa, D., & Weinstein, H. (in press). Public education and social reconstruction in Bosnia-Herzegovina and Croatia. In E. Stover & H. Weinstein (Eds.), *My neighbor, My enemy: Justice and community in the aftermath of mass atrocity.* Cambridge, UK: Cambridge University Press.

Freedman, S., Kambanda, D., Mukashima, I., Mukama, E., Mugisha, I., Mutabaruka, J., Samuelson, B., & Weinstein, H. (in press). Confronting the past in Rwandan schools. In E. Stover & H. Weinstein (Eds.), *My neighbor, My enemy: Justice and community in the aftermath of mass atrocity.* Cambridge, UK: Cambridge University Press.

Freedman, S., & Katz, A. (1987). Pedagogical interaction during the composing process: The writing conference. In A. Matsuhashi (Ed.), *Writing in real time: Modelling production processes* (pp. 58–80). Norwood, NJ: Ablex.

Freedman, S., & Sperling, M. (1985). Teacher student interaction in the writing conference: Response and teaching. In S. Freedman (Ed.), *The acquisition of written language: Response and revision* (pp. 106–30). Norwood, NJ: Ablex.

Freire, P. (1994). *Pedagogy of the oppressed.* New York: The Continuum Publishing Company.

Gee, J. P. (1989). What is literacy? *Journal of Education, 171*, 18–25.

Giroux, H. A. (1988). *Teaching as intellectual: Toward a critical pedagogy of learning.* New York: Bergin and Garvey.

Glenny, M. (2000). *The Balkans: Nationalism, war, and the Great Powers, 1804–1999.* New York: Viking.

The Human Rights Center/UC Berkeley, the International Human Rights Law Clinic/Boalt Hall, UC Berkeley, and the Human Rights Centre/University of Sarajevo. (1999). Justice, accountability, and social reconstruction: An interview study of Bosnian judges and prosecutors. *Berkeley Journal of International Law, 18*(1), 102–64.

Ignatieff, M. (1998). *The warrior's honor: Ethnic war and the modern conscience.* New York: Henry Holt and Company.

Ignatieff, M. (2002, October 27). When a bridge is not a bridge. *The New York Times Magazine,* p. 56.

Leont'ev, A. N. (1981). The problem of activity in psychology. In J. Wertsch (Ed.), *The concept of activity in Soviet psychology* (pp. 37–71) (actually from Voprosy filosofi, 1972, no. 9, pp. 95–108). Armonk, NY: Sharpe.

Longman, T., & Rutagengwa, T. (in press). Memory, identity, and community in Rwanda. In E. Stover & H. Weinstein (Eds.), *My neighbor, My enemy: Justice and community in the aftermath of mass atrocity.* Cambridge, UK: Cambridge University Press.

Luria, A. R. (1981). *Language and cognition* (Trans. and Ed. J. V. Wertsch) New York: Wiley Intersciences.

Maass, P. (1996). *Love thy neighbor: A story of war.* New York: Alfred A. Knopf.

McElroy-Johnson, B. (1993). Teaching and practice: Giving voice to the voiceless. *Harvard Educational Review, 63*(1), 85–104.

Michaels, S. (1981). "Sharing time"; Children narrative styles and differential access to literacy. *Language in Society, 10*, 423–42.

Morris, P. (Ed.). (1994). *The Bakhtin reader: Selected writings of Bakhtin, Medvedev, Voloshinov.* London: Arnold.

Pratt, M. L. (1991/1999). Arts of the contact zone. In D. Bartholomae & A. Petrosky (Eds.), *Ways of reading: An anthology for writers* (5th ed., pp. 582–96). Boston: Bedford/St. Martin's. (Originally published 1991, *Profession 91.* New York: MLA, 33–40.)

Pratt, M. L. (1992). *Imperial eyes: Travel writing and transculturation.* London: Routeledge.

Prunier, G. (1995). *The Rwanda crisis: History of a genocide.* New York: Columbia University Press.

Salgado, S. (2000). *Migrations.* Paris: AMAZONAS Images.

Sibomana, A. (1999). *Hope for Rwanda: Conversations with Laure Guilbert and Hervé Deguine.* London: Pluto Press.

Silber, L., & Little, A. (1997). *Yugoslavia: Death of a nation.* New York: Penguin Books.

Stover, E., & Weinstein, H. (in press). My neighbor, My enemy: Justic and community in the aftermath of mass atrocity. Cambridge, UK: Cambridge University Press.

Trudgill, P. (1995). *Sociolinguistics: An introduction to language and society.* Harmondsworth, Middlesex, UK: Penguin Books.

Vygotsky, L. S. (1978). *Mind in society: The development of higher psychological processes.* M. Cole, V. John-Steiner, S. Scribner, & E. Souberman (Eds.). Cambridge, MA: Harvard University Press.

Vygotsky, L. S. (1981). The genesis of higher mental functions. In J. Wertsch (Ed.), *The concept of activity in Soviet Psychology,* pp. 144–188 (from Razvitie Vysshikh psikhicheskikh funktsii [The development of higher mental functions]. Moskow, 1960, pp. 182–223). Armonk, NY: Sharpe.

Wertsch, J. (2002). *Voices of collective remembering.* Cambridge, UK: Cambridge University Press.

2

Dewey and Bakhtin in Dialogue

From Rosenblatt to a Pedagogy of Literature as Social, Aesthetic Practice

Mark Dressman

For more than 50 years, academic conversations in colleges of education across the United States have mapped out the possibilities for a pedagogy of literature within a two-dimensional world. Along the horizontal or instructional axis, the roles of teacher and student have been conceived along a continuum, with teachers described at one end as master readers and students as apprenticed supplicants and at the other with teachers described as facilitative guides and students as autonomous meaning makers. Along the vertical or curricular axis, the purposes and focus of reading have been depicted as extending from the purely pragmatic, quasiobjective analysis of texts as biographical-historical documents, to the subtle and subjectively nuanced, highly personalized aesthetic appreciation of texts as works of art. Despite recent attempts to redraw this map (e.g., see Appleman, 2000; Faust, 2000; Langer, 1990; McCormick, 1994; Rabinowitz & Smith, 1998; Scholes, 1985), the view it permits of literary experience and the assumptions this map encodes about readers, authors, texts, and teachers remain unchallenged by the vast majority of English educators in research, teacher education, and practice today.

Like all maps, however, over time and experience, this one has begun to fray along the edges and in its creases, while its relation to the world that its users hope it mirrors and produces through the direction it provides has become increasingly more open to question. Consider the wear such a map receives in urban classrooms when students are gathered into literature circles to discuss their response to young adult novels beyond the reading ability of half the class, or when, outside the occasional advanced placement class, high school teachers struggle to make the body of ancient and arcane texts that comprise the English canon even minimally comprehensible to 16-year-olds. Or consider how little direction such a map provides when, in multicultural classrooms, students of color encounter images in that canon of themselves as subhuman others, or when the "workshop" approach leads students' tastes to run away from literature and culture and aesthetic experience and into the world of Sweet Valley High and other equally "trashy" pulp-fiction series (Christian-Smith, 1990). As a teacher in circumstances like these, one can quickly become torn between the simulated world of best practice traced by our present map and the pressing realities of one's own classroom terrain.

The fundamental assertion of this essay, then, is that we – teacher educators, researchers, and most of all classroom teachers – need a new map, one that does not set the functional against the aesthetic, or the personal against the social, and that is not as quick to distinguish what is literature from what is "trash." We need one whose edges connect to the curricular maps of other disciplines and ways of knowing, and one, as Alan Purves (Saks, 1995) once noted about the old one, that does not mask prescription as description in its efforts to "facilitate" teachers' work. Then we might imagine a pedagogy of literature in which teachers would be encouraged to provide authoritative but not authoritarian support for struggling readers, and in which readers would become critical appraisers of authorial intentionality and critical users of historical and biographical background information. Such a map would chart a pedagogy in which students could find the means to "talk back" to oppressive images and their canonizers, and in which the aesthetic wonder of reading complexly crafted texts would come from an experience of them as living traces of conversations among people who came before us, progenitors whose struggles and whose language thread throughout the words and deeds of all of us today.

In pursuit of that goal, in this chapter I consider the ways in which the aesthetics and educational philosophy of John Dewey and the linguistic and literary insights of Mikhail Bakhtin could serve as critical landmarks for a new map of literature education. My turn to Dewey, whose work, ironically, is routinely cited as the principal influence and source of inspiration for the old map (e.g., see Faust, 2000; Rosenblatt, 1938, 1968, 1976, 1978/1994, 1983, 1995), is prompted by two recent analyses that Joan Webster and I conducted in collaboration. The first study examined shifts in the pedagogical stance of literature educator and theorist Louise Rosenblatt (1938, 1995) between the first and fifth editions of *Literature as Exploration*, (Dressman & Webster, 2001a), whereas the other investigated the influence of Rosenblatt's work in English education research and practice (Dressman & Webster, 2001b). Findings from the first study led us to question the extent of Dewey's influence on Rosenblatt's work in two critical areas, Rosenblatt's adoption of Dewey's theory of *transactional experience*, and her understanding of Dewey's interest in the role of aesthetic experience in promoting democratic values. The second study provided evidence of Rosenblatt's extraordinary influence on the ways that researchers and practitioners in the field of English education have, in turn, adopted her interpretation of Dewey's ideas in these two areas. My turn to Bakhtin is guided by a concern for the lack of detailed discussion in Dewey's work on aesthetics about the ways that literary texts,

and in particular literary language, function as discursive touchstones or
focal points within societies.

As a way of clarifying the significance of the differences between Dewey's
views and Rosenblatt's use of them in her work on literature education, the
first part of this chapter contrasts their explanations of aesthetic and transactional experience in some detail. It also considers what a fully Deweyan
view of literary experience, if diagrammed, might look like compared with
the view provided by a diagram of the Rosenblattian view. The chapter then
turns to the explication of a diagram illustrating how I believe Bakhtin
conceived of literary reading, and compares its similarities and differences
to the Deweyan diagram. The final section provides an argument for the
strengths of a pedagogy of literature that draws on what I perceive to be the
complementary relationship between the two philosophers' work. It also
considers the practical implications of such an approach on the teaching of
literature in U.S. secondary schools, and illustrates these implications with
a discussion of how such an approach could illuminate the teaching of a
controversial text such as *The Adventures of Huckleberry Finn*.

DEWEY AND ROSENBLATT

Figure 2.1 presents an analysis of Rosenblatt's work in diagram format, taken
from the analysis of the first study and from Joan Webster's and my analysis
in the second study of how others read her work. Because of Rosenblatt's
argument that the meaning of a text is something neither in the text nor in
the reader, and that it is something made from the visual symbols on a page
of text as a reader's own past and present condition perceives and orders
them, the "poem" in this diagram is represented as an irregularly shaped
(and, although not represented here, an ever-developing) figure placed, as
Rosenblatt has described it, "between" the reader and the text. At points in
her explication, Rosenblatt has argued – in congruence with Dewey – that it
is not only the reader's "mind" but her whole being that makes sense of the
text; yet the processes and influential factors in Rosenblatt's description of
this transaction – in unacknowledged contradiction to Dewey's – are almost
exclusively mental ones. For this reason, it is the reader's *cognition* that is
represented in Fig. 2.1, in a vertically layered sequence that is not explicitly
described by Rosenblatt, but that is certainly implied by the primary emphasis she places on readers' conscious apprehension of what they are feeling
and thinking as they read. This is also implied by the secondary emphasis –
indeed, her strident criticism of psychoanalytical approaches that depend
on the reader's *unconscious* apprehensions – she places on thoughts and feelings that are remote or hidden from the immediate context of the reading
event. The two sets of two-way arrows indicate some exchange between the
different layers of the reader's cognition.

Rosenblatt has had little to say about exactly how the internal structure
or language of a text "channels" readers' experiences. For that reason, the

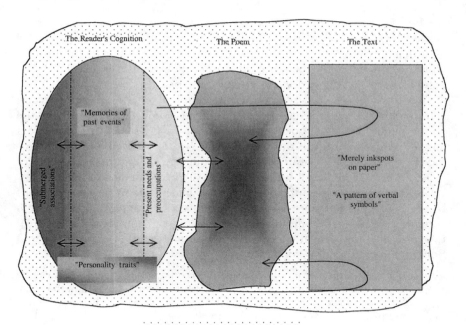

FIGURE 2.1. A Rosenblattian view of the aesthetic reading event.

From *Literature as Exploration* (Rosenblatt, 1995):
A novel or poem or play remains merely inkspots on paper until a reader transforms them into a set of meaningful symbols. The literary work exists in the live circuit set up between reader and text: the reader infuses intellectual and emotional meanings into the pattern of verbal symbols, and those symbols channel his thoughts and feelings. Out of this complex process emerges a more or less organized imaginative experience. (p. 24)

Language is socially evolved, but it is always constituted by individuals, with their particular histories. (p. 25)

The special meanings and, more particularly, the submerged associations that these words and images have for the individual reader will largely determine what the work communicates to *him*. The reader brings to the work personality traits, memories of past events, present needs and preoccupations, a particular mood of the moment, and a particular physical condition. (p. 30)

... [T]he two-way, reciprocal relation explains why meaning is not 'in' the text or 'in' the reader. Both reader and text are essential to the transaction process of meaning making. (p. 27)

From *The Reader, the Text, the Poem* (Rosenblatt, 1978/1994):
Memory functions in an important way in this selecting, synthesizing, organizing process. I refer here not simply to the overall role of the linguistic- and life-memories the reader brings to the text, but to the way in which during the reading the reader keeps alive what he has already elicited from the text. At any point, he brings a state of mind, a penumbra of "memories" of what has preceded, ready to be activated by what follows, and providing the context from which further meaning will be derived. (p. 57)

figure representing the text is left plain, with two of her better-known phrases included in it to indicate Rosenblatt's regard for the text as a source of material. Rosenblatt has described the reading process as one in which the reader uses the signs on a page of text as material to construct its meaning, and so this process is represented in Fig. 2.1 by the curved arrows, which reach from the most conscious region of the reader's cognition into the text and then into the poem. Because of the need to continually sample and adjust meaning as the reader proceeds through a text, a pair of two-way arrows run from the poem to the most conscious areas of the reader's cognition. Finally, because there is some indication in Rosenblatt's work that she believes the context in which texts are read has an impact on readers' aesthetic experiences of them, that context is represented as a patterned area that surrounds the reading event, but one that is bordered and that allows for no direct interpenetration either with external historical or social conditions or with the reader, the text, or the poem.

As Fig. 2.1 also shows, even though Rosenblatt's model of literary trans-action allows for some exchange of signification between the text and the reader and between the poem and the reader, each also remains a discreet and autonomous entity. If this is an accurate representation of Rosenblatt's model, then it raises serious questions about how Deweyan her concept of transaction may be. In distinguishing between interactive and transactive views, for example, Rosenblatt (1978/1994) used the example of billiard balls colliding to illustrate how an interactive view "implies separate, self-contained, and already defined entities acting on one another" (p. 17). Interestingly, however, in their explanation of the difference, Dewey and Bentley (1949) used the same example, but extended it:

> If we confine ourselves to the problem of the balls on the billiard table, they can be profitably presented and studied interactionally. But a cultural account of the game in its full spread of social growth and human adaptations is already transactional. And if one player loses money to another we cannot even find words in which to organize the fully interactional account by assembling together primarily separate items. Borrower can not borrow without lender to lend, nor lender lend without borrower to borrow, the loan being a transaction that is identifiable only in the wider transaction of the full legal-commercial system in which it is present as an occurrence. (p. 133)

From their example, one may wonder if reading events are not the type of events that require an account in their "full spread of social growth and human adaptations." Yet Rosenblatt's limiting phrasing of "an individual reader and a text" producing their own environment is more similar to an interactional account of billiards than a transactional one. The most important point here, however, is that for Dewey and Bentley, transactions cannot be viewed either as the collision of two bodies, *or as the dance of two bodies in isolation.* They must be viewed, if they are to be accounted for transactionally at all, within their immediate social and full cultural context, and in transaction with that context.

In contrast to Fig. 2.1, Fig 2.2, which represents my interpretation of a Deweyan view of reading as a transactional experience based largely on *Art as Experience* (Dewey, 1934) and *Knowing and the Known* (Dewey & Bentley, 1949), shows how permeable the boundaries of reader, reading, text, and the immediate and enduring contexts of human social experience were as Dewey described them. Figure 2.2 shows that for Dewey, a reader's ex-perience of a text, and, in particular, an *aesthetic* experience of that text, depended on a balanced integration of three aspects of the reader's prior experience–practice, intellect, and emotion – and their prior experience of

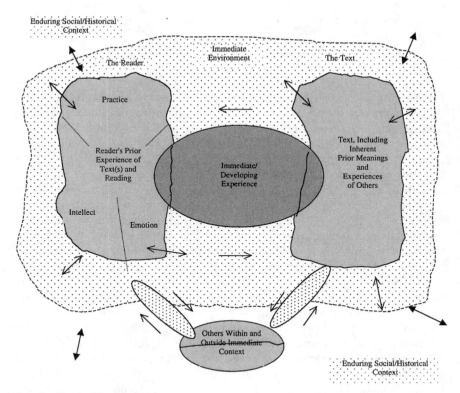

From *Art as Experience* (Rosenblatt, 1934):

Thinking goes on in trains of ideas, but the ideas form a train only because they are much more than what an analytic psychology calls ideas. They are phases, emotionally and practically distinguished, of a developing quality.... (p. 37)

In an experience, things and events belonging to the world, physical and social, are transformed through the human context they enter, while the live creature is changed and developed through its intercourse with things previously external to it. (p. 246)

... [A]n influential manner of thinking has ... treated mind as an independent entity *which* attends, purposes, cares, notices, and remembers. This change of ways of responding to the environment into an entity from which actions proceed is unfortunate, because it removes mind from necessary connection with the objects and events, past, present, and future, of the environment with which responsive activities are inherently connected. (pp. 263–4)

Any psychology that isolates the human being from the environment also shuts him off, safe for external contacts, from his fellows. (p. 270)

From *Knowing and the Known* (Dewey & Bentley, 1949):

In ordinary everyday behavior, in what sense can we examine a talking unless we bring a hearing along with it into account? Or a writing without a reading? Or a buying without a selling? Or a supply without a demand? ... We can, of course, detach any portion of a transaction that we wish, and secure provisional descriptions and partial reports. But all this must be subject to the wider observation of the full process. (p. 134)

FIGURE 2.2. A Deweyan view of readings as experience.

reading as these were influenced by the reader's immediate environment and experience of the text as one read. Moreover, one's immediate and developing experience of a text would never be described as something occurring outside the reader or the text; rather, it would involve a transaction that was transformative not only for the reader, *but also for the text* when meanings were shared with others inside and outside the immediate context of the event. Such an experience would also be transformative for the immediate environment and for the enduring social and historical environment or context to which the event of reading contributed, however minimally.

Dewey's concern for understanding events in their full transactional context extended to his view of aesthetic experience as critical to the daily functioning and development of democratic societies. Although Dewey did make a distinction between the instrumental and the enjoyable uses of events and objects, he never argued that one sort of use precluded the other. Indeed, his instructional goal, at least in *Art as Experience* (Dewey, 1934), seemed to be to argue that much of what is wrong with modern life springs from the separation of the two. For example, he was very critical of museums as institutions, arguing they not only isolated and elevated artistic objects from everyday life, but that they also signaled a division in modern life between the aesthetic and the everyday that was injurious to the well-being of individuals and society. Instead, for Dewey, aesthetic experiences, even of those events and objects that are specifically "works of art," such as plays, paints, or novels, are always part of situations that have both enjoyment and some instrumental goal as their purpose. Multiple experiences of an object or event in multiple situations, knowledge of how that object or event was used and perceived throughout history, and the experiences of multiple users of that object, both instrumentally and enjoyably, all produce extrinsic meanings, that, through reflection, become an intrinsic part of what is perceived in an experience of the event or object (Jackson, 1998). Thus, for Dewey (1934), "The enemies of the esthetic are neither the practical nor the intellectual. They are the humdrum; slackness of loose ends; submission to convention in practice and intellectual procedure" (p. 40).

It is in this context that the several differences between Rosenblatt's and Dewey's aesthetic theories are made clear. For example, what would Dewey have made of Rosenblatt's elevation of "the literary work of art" above "trash" (Rosenblatt, 1995, pp. 200–1) and works of "mediocrity" (Rosenblatt, 1978/1994, p. 159) as preferred objects for aesthetic experiences? In contrast, Dewey (1934) noted that "the arts which today have the most vitality for the average person are things he does not take to be arts: for instance, the movie, jazzed music, the comic strip, and, too frequently, newspaper accounts of love-nests, murders, and exploits of bandits" (pp. 5–6). More significantly, I believe that Dewey would have taken the distinction Rosenblatt (1968) made from the second edition of *Literature as Exploration* onward between aesthetic and efferent stances toward texts to be yet another socially injurious attempt to naturalize the separation of the aesthetic from the means of production – the instrumental labor – that characterizes much of modern life's experiences. That Rosenblatt described this distinction as occurring on a "continuum" would not reassure him, I believe, for the image of a continuum, while allowing for some "mixture" of its two ends, also reinforces the fundamental distinctiveness of the two concepts. It does not capture, as Dewey explained, the transactional process by which a sense of instrumental uses and extrinsic meanings first adhere, and then through reflection, inhere in an object or event and its meaning; nor does it imply how, in a better world, aesthetic pleasure would be an intrinsic aspect of the most instrumental of daily activities.

Finally, note how different Dewey's argument for the social and cultural function of the arts and of aesthetic experience, particularly of literature, is from Rosenblatt's. Paradoxically for Rosenblatt, the social and cultural effects of literature accrued from an almost entirely personal and private experience of a text. For example, in her later work Rosenblatt (1978/1994) explained that "Literary texts provide us with a widely broadened 'other' through which to define ourselves and our world. Reflection on our meshing with the text can foster the process of self-definition in a variety of ways" (p. 145). In another work, she continued in the same vein: "In a world of such vast technological change, of such a desperate sense of international tensions, the individual needs to build for himself a mental and emotional base from which to meet the fluctuating currents about him" (Rosenblatt, 1995, p. 162). The view of society suggested by these and other passages is of a world of highly autonomous beings, each seeking her or his own "personal" connection to that world on her or his own terms.

The contrast with Dewey's view of society and of the role of literature and other works of art could not be more stark. For Dewey, the personalization of aesthetic experience contributed to art's cultural trivialization. Instead, he argued that

Esthetic experience is a manifestation, a record and celebration of the life of a civilization, a means of promoting its development, and is also the ultimate judgment upon the quality of a civilization. For while it is produced and is enjoyed by individuals, those individuals are what they are in the content of their experience because of the cultures in which they participate.

... Art is the great force in effecting [cultural] consolidation. The individuals who have minds pass away one by one. The works in which meanings have received objective expression endure. They become part of the environment, and interaction [i.e., transaction] with this phase of the environment is the axis of the continuity in the life of civilization. (Dewey, 1934, p. 326)

The image here is of a culture transcending individual experience, and of art as a civilization's embodiment and enduring transmitter of a culture's values, forms, and content. Thus, for Dewey, the individual experiences of people are not what matter, either in an individual's, or in a civilization's, cultural development.

What mattered for Dewey was the *collective* aesthetic experience of a society– that is, the meanings, both extrinsic and intrinsic, that are communally disputed and shared within a culture – in its transactions with events and with objects of art. As an example, Dewey (1934) noted, "The Magna

Carta is held up as the great political stabilizer of Anglo-Saxon civilization. Even so, it has operated in the meaning given it in imagination rather than by its literal contents" (p. 326). More contemporary examples of such collective aesthetic experience in the United States might include the current controversy over the implications of naming *The Adventures of Huckleberry Finn* "the great American novel" (Arac, 1997; Corporation for Public Broadcasting, 2000), or the ways that television sitcoms like "All in the Family" and the weekly melodrama "ER" have simultaneously challenged the conventions of those genres and the conventions of public discourse about bigotry, patriarchy, and health care reform. In other words, it isn't so much individual readings of texts, but collective conversations about a text or texts that bear cultural and historical consequences.

TURNING TO BAKHTIN

This analysis raises important questions about the implications of a pedagogy of literature that focuses educators' attention on the encounters of individualized readers with decontextualized texts, and that divides the functional, or "efferent" uses of texts from their artistic and personal, or "aesthetic," appreciation. Consider, for example, a situation I encountered in a preservice methods course, when I presented the poem, "Elena" (Mora, 1994), in which an immigrant mother mourns that when her children laugh and joke in English, she cannot join in because she speaks only Spanish. When I asked how they would teach this poem, my students suggested having their future students "write about a time when they felt left out." When I pointed to the cultural and political implications of the poem and asked how they would address these (pointing out also that they were likely to have students whose mothers did not speak English either), the students balked. One confessed that if that were the case, she wouldn't teach the poem, because, as an English teacher, it "wasn't (her) job to get politically involved." Or consider the opposite case of a teacher I know whose passion for social justice leads him to focus exclusively on issues of race, class, and gender in his teaching of literary texts in his classroom, and to regard the pleasure students might take from a text and issues of form, style, and genre as educationally misdirected. Finally, consider the national controversy over the standing of Mark Twain's work in the literary canon of the United States (Arac, 1997; Quirk, 1995) and the teaching of *The Adventures of Huckleberry Finn* in secondary schools (Corporation for Public Broadcasting, 2000). A map of literature pedagogy directed by an ethos of individualism and in the separation of pleasure from purpose, I argue, would not suggest an adequate response to the preservice teacher who can't bring herself to "get political" when that is called for, or to the practicing teacher who can't see past his own convictions, or to the critics and educators who struggle to reconcile an icon's literary and cultural influence with the consequences of that influence for the nation's literary and social present and future. Yet this approach remains the one most often recommended by mainstream experts for literature education in secondary schools and teacher education programs.

These findings have led me to consider how a theory of language and literacy grounded firmly in Deweyan concepts of transactional experience and aesthetics might better inform research and the development of curricular practices about the ways that readers and texts might come together in the classroom in furthering the goals of a pluralistic, democratic society. Yet I must also concede that this task is significantly limited by the absence in Dewey's work (or at least, in my reading of Dewey thus far) of a comprehensive description of how either language or the reading of texts figures into transactional and aesthetic experiences. It is for this reason that I turned to the work of Mikhail Bakhtin, whose historicized, materialist views of language, literature, and of the process of dialogue, at least as I currently understand them, share some points of congruence with Dewey's work.

This section of the chapter, then, examines the congruence between Dewey's work and Bakhtin's, in order to see what each might offer to a theory of language and literacy and a practice of literacy education at the beginning of the new century. At the same time, however, I want to emphasize that I am also aware of – and wary of – the temptation to overlook points of *incongruence* between the two that ought not to be overlooked, to find points of similarity that are not quite congruent, and to do serious damage to the work of each in my enthusiasm to forge something new from their union. That is not my goal. Rather, I seek a preliminary examination of points of congruence, and to engage in a very tentative conversation about what the two, when considered in tandem, might contribute to researchers' and practitioners' developing theories of language and literacy.

Figure 2.3 provides a diagram of my developing understanding of Bakhtinian dialogism. In this diagram, the use of language across space and time as the permeating condition of a reader's present experience of a text is the irregularly shaped pattern of dots that pervade the diagram. The four sources of influence over the meaning a reader makes of a text at a moment in time – the reader as "author of self," other texts, others' uses of language and readings of texts, and the text itself as utterance or construction of utterances by an author in another time/space – are represented as circles and ovals with permeable boundaries. Dialogic exchange among these four influences is represented by flat, elliptical ovals that "flow" between the influences. The sets of arrows represent the give-and-take of linguistic intercourse, or dialogue, which is the "engine," or source, of movement in Bakhtin's work. In the center of the diagram is the reading of a particular text in time and space, formed through a dialogue between reader and text – a dialogue that leaves its imprint on both the reader and the text, and that dialogically contributes to others' readings and uses of language and the construction of other texts and utterances across time/space.

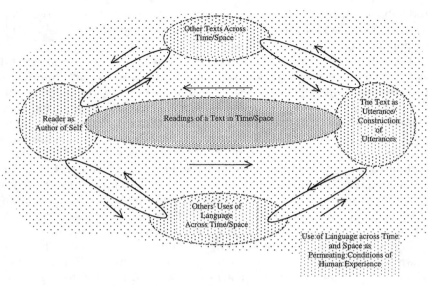

From *The Dialogic Imagination* (Bakhtin, 1981):
The novel can be defined as a diversity of social speech types (sometimes even diversity of languages) and a diversity of individual voices, artistically organized. The internal stratification of any single national language into social dialects, characteristic group behavior, professional jargons, generic languages, languages of generations and age groups, tendentious languages, languages of authorities, of various circles and of passing fashions, languages that serve the specific sociopolitical purposes of the day, even of the hour ... this internal stratification present in every language at any given moment of its historical existence is the indispensable prerequisite for the novel as a genre. ... These distinctive links and interrelationships between utterances and languages, this movement of the theme through different languages and speech types, its dispersion into the rivulets and droplets of social heteroglossia, its dialogization – this is the basic distinguishing feature of the stylistics of the novel. (pp. 262–3).

[L]iterary language itself is only one of these heteroglot languages. ... Every concrete utterance of a speaking subject serves as a point where centrifugal as well as centripetal forces are brought to bear. ... And this active participation of every utterance in living heteroglossia determines the linguistic profile and style of the utterance to no less a degree than its inclusion in any normative-centralizing system of a unitary language. ... The authentic environment of an utterance, the environment in which it lives and takes shape, is dialogized heteroglossia, anonymous and social as language, but simultaneously concrete, filled with specific content and accented as an individual utterance. (p. 272)

From *Art and Answerabilty* (Bakhtin, 1990):
An aesthetic event can take place only when there are two participants present; it presupposes two noncoinciding consciousnesses. When the hero and the author coincide or when they find themselves standing either next to one another or in the face of a value they share or against one another as antagonists, the aesthetic event ends and an *ethical* event begins. ... (p. 22)

From *Dialogism: Bakhtin and His World* (Holquist, 1990):
... the Bakhtinian just-so story of subjectivity is the tale of how I get my self from the other: it is only the other's categories that will let me be an object my own perception. I see my self as I conceive others might see it. In order to forge a self, I just do so from *outside*. In other words, *I author myself.* (p. 28)

FIGURE 2.3. A Bakhtinian view of reading as dialogue.

Finally, although not indicated in the diagram, in Bakhtin's view there are centrifugal and centripetal forces, (e.g., the historical "weight" of linguistic continuity and the semantic indeterminance of signs) in operation within each dialogic exchange that account for the balance between language's and humans' ironic capacity to adapt and yet remain the same simultaneously – to produce and reproduce – as material conditions shift. Thus, what keeps Bakhtin's view of reading from falling prey to a "mushy" mysticism grounded in slogans insisting that "everything is connected" and "we are all one" is the nature and historical materiality of language itself, and the very concrete traces of prior use that authors leave and that language produces in the texts of the past and present.

When Fig. 2.3 is compared and contrasted with the Deweyan representation of Fig. 2.2, two important similarities between the work of Dewey and Bakhtin can be observed. First, a comparison of the diagrams suggests a congruence between Dewey's description of *transactional experience* and the uses of the term *dialogue* in Bakhtin's work (Bakhtin, 1981). As Kenneth Hirschkop (1999) remarked, Bakhtin's use of *dialogue* is much broader than our contemporary notion of "conversation," and embraces any fully contextualized, living process of exchange between an author and his text, between readers and a text, and between the text and the society of which it and readers are a part. From this perspective, dialogue acts as a linguistic metaphor for the transactional medium in which experience takes place (Sarah McCarthey, personal communication). Similarly, Dewey argued that a full understanding of an event must involve observation not only of an interaction between two entities, but also of the circumstances, historical and present, that have brought them together and of the history and dynamic experience of previous encounters between other entities that they share and exchange in their encounter.

Second, both share a concern for aesthetics as dialogic/transactional processes that are socially, culturally, and historically transforming, rather than processes somehow removed from the material conditions of one's lifeworld. Both Dewey and Bakhtin viewed individuals as constructed by others, that is, as needing the presence of others to define their own experience of themselves and of events. This congruence becomes particularly evident when the views of Dewey and Bakhtin are compared with Rosenblatt's work. For Rosenblatt, and particularly in her later work, aesthetic experiences may have a transformative effect on one's lifeworld, but only as they affect the beliefs and attitudes of individual readers one at a time. Rosenblatt's focus on the conscious intentionality and agency of readers in making their own sense of texts as they read, in combination with repeated arguments in later editions of her work that to attend consciously to the historical and social implications of literary texts is to read them "efferently" as "mere social documents," would seem to be an active denial of the desirability of a close relationship between social and personal spheres of interest.

Finally, although the diagrams in Figs. 2.2 and 2.3 do not reveal this third point of congruence, both Dewey and Bakhtin share a focus on the everyday, in-use quality of human experience – a focus, incidentally, which stood in opposition to, and as a critique of, prevailing opinion in their time. Dewey argued that aesthetic experiences are a vital part of societal growth and renewal, and that it was through everyday aesthetic practices that this transformation was most likely to occur. Similarly, Bakhtin argued against the prevailing arguments of his time that a prose stylistics of the novel was not contradictory, and that a stylistics of the novel must involve an examination of the social origins of everyday speech – the type of speech of which novels were composed.

There are, of course, important points of incongruence between the work of Dewey and Bakhtin that must also be taken into account as one considers them in combination. Primary among these are the greater emphasis on historical circumstance that Bakhtin saw operating in present events, and, as a comparison of Figs. 2.2 and 2.3 suggests, the greater permeability of reader and text, not only by each other, but also by others in their immediate and past environments. This is largely due to differences in the type and variety of motive forces each ascribes to readers, texts, and other entities. In Dewey's work, agency seems to be an ontological characteristic of all beings, and it is exercised in a variety of processes that are both linguistic and physical, that is, in the course of human and nonhuman entities' resistance or conformity to others, they transform and are transformed by them, sometimes in minute and other times in grosser, more perceptible, ways. For Bakhtin, all exchange among entities, or at least all human perception of exchange, is mediated by language through a process that is at times broadly metaphorized, and at other times more conventionally characterized in linguistic terms, as *dialogue*. Thus, what seems to be lacking in Dewey for theorists of literature education is a detailed explanation of how the material of texts, language, works. Yet what may be an objectionable overemphasis on language and linguistic metaphors in Bakhtin's work for literacy educators – such as a lack of concern for the physical environment or immediate social environment of the classroom and its relationship to broader, more enduring conditions– may, with some imagination, be seen as a complement to Dewey's view of transactional experience. It is to the practical implications of a theory of literature education grounded in a Rosenblattian concern for what readers make of texts, but explicated by the pragmatic and dialogic focuses of Dewey and Bakhtin, that I turn in the conclusion to this chapter.

CONCLUSION: PRACTICAL IMPLICATIONS

My understanding of the potential significance of a dialogue/transaction between the ideas of Dewey and Bakhtin for language and literacy education in theory is presented in summary form in Table 2.1. Perhaps the most important contribution Bakhtin offers to a Deweyan perspective is a linguistic and textual trope by which a theoretically rigorous practice of language and literacy education can be imagined. Why, then, bother with Dewey at all? I would argue, from a Bakhtinian perspective, that what Dewey offers is a view of experience more in touch with Western sensibilities – that is, one that is fully contextual, but less centered in a history of imperial oppression as ponderous as the Russian context in which Bakhtin wrote, and that is therefore in closer dialogical relation to our own historical and pedagogical experience. This is not to say that Dewey's work can or should be

TABLE 2.1. *Deweyan and Bakhtinian Contributions to Literacy Education*

What Dewey Offers Beyond Rosenblatt	What Complements Bakhtin in Dewey	What Complements Dewey in Bakhtin
A revised definition of transaction that ascribes agency to the text and to the immediate and historical context of the reading event	A focus on pedagogy that is more inclusive than Bakhtin's preoccupation with the novel	A focus on language and a theory of language as mediator of historical, cultural, and social experience
A revised definition of aesthetics that does not separate functionality from emotional or personal appeal	A focus on the reader's response to artistic works	An explication of the historical weight of language and narrative on present events
A definition of personal response that is sociocultural and historical in origin	An explicit concern for social progress and the cultural function of aesthetic experience	An explication of the architectonics of the novel, and, by extension, of other forms of text
	A broader discussion of artistic works in general	A focus on the agency of texts and authorship within dialogic/ transactional experience
	An explicitly American, pragmatic expression of how art functions within our present sociohistorical context	

viewed as "Bakhtin-Lite," but rather that, from a U.S. historical perspective, an appropriation of Bakhtinian views of language and literacy read through the lens of Deweyan pragmatism and educational theory is likely to be more open to reception and application.

What does a theory of literature education grounded in a dialogue between Dewey and Bakhtin suggest in terms of classroom practice? One way to understand the significant differences between a pedagogy based solely in the work of Louise Rosenblatt and one that is grounded in a dialogue/transaction between the work of Dewey and Bakhtin is to imagine how a Rosenblattian approach would differ from one based on the work of Dewey and Bakhtin in the teaching of a currently controversial text, such as *The Adventures of Huckleberry Finn.*

To begin with, such an approach would significantly extend the context in which "literary transactions" are conceived beyond the autonomous subjectivity of "an individual reader" implied in Rosenblatt's later work, to view readers as *social* subjects, whose "personal" responses are the result of their unique history of experiences within the world as literate, social beings. Dewey's aesthetics also extend the social and cultural agency of texts themselves (see Jackson, 1998), beyond Rosenblatt's famous description of texts as "mere ink spots on a page" to objects whose history of use and appreciation has a profound effect on the meanings readers make or take from them. Thus, the transaction that readers experience when they become fully, aesthetically engaged with a text is most comprehensively and clearly understood as an event occurring not merely between the reader/subject and the text/object, but as the nexus of the complex social, economic, political, and historical conditions that have produced both agents in their coming together.

A recapturing of Dewey's work also demonstrates the folly of locating readers' stances along a single continuum ranging from "aesthetic" to "efferent," and instead urges researchers and theoreticians of literature education to find or remake the potential for aesthetic experiences of literary and other types of text within a broad range of literate activities – from the reading of novels individually or in small groups to the researching and writing of reports to the performance of poetry to the viewing of television and movies to the use of the Internet – rather than to draw a box around some reading practices and label them "aesthetic," and therefore somehow "better" than other, more instrumental, and so "lesser," ways of reading. In short, a pedagogy founded on Deweyan principles of aesthetic response would not sacrifice personal readings for the sake of "academic rigor," but would, instead, build upon and resituate personal response within a socially, culturally, and sometimes politically responsive framework. Finally, such a pedagogy would not separate "aesthetic" activities such as literary response from more "efferent" activities such reading to write reports and essays, but rather would invite teachers to find ways to remake the activity of reading for persuasive or expository writing into a form of activity that is also emotionally, intellectually, practically, and so *aesthetically*, engaging.

Practically speaking, this does not imply that an approach based on discussions centered around readers' personal responses should be abandoned, but rather that in the course of discussions, readers need to be invited to understand their personal responses as the result of their historical and cultural position in relation to the text. For readers of *Huckleberry Finn*, responses are likely to center around Twain's use of the n-word and the relationship between Huck and Jim, and in particular around whether Huck ever comes to see Jim – and by extension, all African Americans – as his moral and intellectual equal. In this case, rather than simply asking students to explain or clarify their views on these issues, from a Deweyan perspective it would also be important for a teacher to have students explore the origins of their opinions in their own cultural and historical backgrounds, to share these origins as a class, and to consider how they relate to the public and critical commentary that has surrounded the novel since its publication. This would necessarily involve some research or at least the introduction of texts such as book reviews and editorials published in the past and present that discuss the significance of *Huck Finn*, and a reporting of those discussions and class discussions in some text-based format. Finally, such an approach would require teacher and students to examine the craft and craftiness of author Mark Twain – that is, to consider how he crafted a set of narrative circumstances and a relationship between two characters that continues to speak to the issues of race and racism in the United States today.

A Deweyan pedagogy of *Huckleberry Finn*, then, would invite teachers and students to examine the why and how of their aesthetic response and relationship to the text as a cultural icon, with the hopeful outcome being a renewed and clarified understanding of the issues that continue to make the novel a vital part of the nation's political and cultural life. However, such an approach would not necessarily invite or provide a framework for a detailed investigation of the language and structure of the text itself. This is particularly unfortunate in the case of *Huckleberry Finn*, because one of its main claims to the status of "classic" is based in the argument that its use of "vernacular" language represents a significant break, not only from previous U.S. literary works, but also from the British and European tradition.

Bakhtin's dialogism, however, does offer such a framework, consisting of multiple levels, for investigating Twain's use of the vernacular in *Huckleberry Finn*. First and most simply, there is the actual dialogue of the book, which is marked by Twain's appropriation of the language and dialects of the mid-Mississippi Valley in the early and mid-nineteenth century, and of his appropriation also of performative "set" pieces, such as the lectures and theatricals of the Duke and Dauphin. Practically, as a way of raising students' awareness of these aspects of the novel, teachers may invite students to practice reading the dialogue aloud, to point out Twain's appropriation of the uses of language in his childhood, and then perhaps to invite students to write dialogue taken from their own backgrounds, and to appropriate performative "set" pieces that appear in their own lives, such as television commercials, the language of VJs on MTV, etc.

A second level of dialogue that would need to be considered is one that was alluded to above in the discussion of a Deweyan approach to the novel, and that is the dialogue between author and readers that Twain, as an author who was very interested in both art *and* commerce, continues to engage us. This is particularly the case with respect to Twain's use of the vernacular – which was regarded by some critics as crude and "low class" when the book was first published – and, more recently, his use of the n-word. In classroom settings, the important question to be raised in discussion and then researched is not what Twain's "real intentions" were in his use of language and his construction of the circumstances that surround Jim and Huck, but rather how he continues to engage his current audience in wondering what he "really" meant, how he "really" felt about the characters of Huck and Jim, if he was "really" a racist or not, and why, finally, we should care about these issues.

A third level of dialogic investigation, then, would be the continuing dialogue, past and present, about *Huckleberry Finn* and its status as a classic. It would be important for readers to understand that even if they'd never read the novel or seen any movie version of it before coming to the text, they still had some opinion of the novel's worth before they read it, not only because of its place on the course's and school's reading list, but also because of what they'd "picked up" about it, if only unconsciously, from others. This implies some discussion in class, then, of the novel's status over time, if only to indicate to students that its status remains a topic of dialogue in both public and academic spheres.

Finally, a fourth level of dialogic investigation would necessarily take the form of a self-reflexive investigation of the dialogue about the novel that takes place within the classroom over time. If students are keeping response journals as they transact with both the text and others in the class, at home, and with their teacher, we might hope for some noticeable development or adjustments in those responses to be taking place. One very valuable activity at some point would be for students to revisit their own responses to see if they could trace that development or adjustment, and if they could place the source or sources of the changes in perspective that they noted.

In conclusion, then, a practice of literature education grounded in a dialogue between the work of Dewey and Bakhtin would emphasize how indivisible the sociocultural, historical, political, and instrumental functions of a text are from its aesthetic experience. To be sure, literary texts are never fully appreciated as "mere social documents." However, to abjure the historical, social, and political history of artistic works produces a reading of them that is not more aesthetic, but merely more naive – in some ways more esoteric and further removed from the educational, cultural, and democratic effects that Rosenblatt, Dewey, and Bakhtin claimed are the most critical products of aesthetic experience.

This does not suggest a call for the reading of texts as "mere social and historical documents," as proponents of a Rosenblattian view of reader response might suggest. Rather, it suggests that a vital aspect of readers' responses to literature involves a developing awareness of *all the sources of those responses*, as well as the multiple sources of language within a text that prompt such responses. In other words, it calls for a shift in focus from individual readers' "personal" responses to a focus on the dialogic interplay – the *transaction* – between the initial meanings readers take or make from texts, and the full range of historical, cultural, and ideological meanings a text's genre, style, and content might support. Such an approach would ask readers to reflect on the origins of their own readings of a literary text; it would invite a pluralistic approach to understanding how some texts are written to appeal to a specific group of readers; and it would invite the critical appraisal of popular texts. Finally, it would require teachers both to support their students' readings and to provide alternative cultural and historical readings not generated within a classroom, and then ask students to respond to these from their own perspectives.

References

Appleman, D. (2000). *Critical encounters in high school English: Teaching literary theory to adolescents.* New York: Teachers College Press.

Arac, J. (1997). *Huckleberry Finn as idol and target: The functions of criticism in our time.* Madison: University of Wisconsin Press.

Bakhtin, M. M. (1981). *The dialogic imagination: Four essays by M. M. Bakhtin.* (Trans. C. Emerson & M. Holquist). (Ed. M. Holquist). Austin: University of Texas Press.

Bakhtin, M. M. (1990). *Art and answerability: Early philosophical essays by M. M. Bakhtin.* (Trans. V. Liapunov). Austin: University of Texas Press.

Christian-Smith, L. K. (1990). *Becoming a woman through romance.* New York: Routledge.

Corporation for Public Broadcasting. (2000). *Culture shock: Born to trouble: Adventures of Huck Finn.* ([online]: http://www.pbs.org/wgbh/cultureshock/beyond/huck.html).

Dewey, J. (1934). *Art as experience.* New York: Minton, Balch, & Co.

Dewey, J., & Bentley, A. F. (1949). *Knowing and the known.* Boston: Beacon Press.

Dressman, M., & Webster, J. P. (2001a). Retracing Rosenblatt: A textual archaeology. *Research in the Teaching of English, 36,* 110–45.

Dressman, M., & Webster, J. P. (2001b). Description, prescription, or cultural reproduction? Rosenblattian criticism in reader-response research and teaching. *National Reading Conference Yearbook, 50,* 164–77.

Faust, M. (2000). Reconstructing familiar metaphors: John Dewey and Louise Rosenblatt on literary art as experience. *Research in the Teaching of English, 35,* 9–34.

Hirschkop, K. (1999). *Mikhail Bakhtin: An aesthetic for democracy.* New York: Oxford University Press.

Holquist, M. (1990). *Dialogism: Bakhtin and his world.* London: Routledge.

Jackson, P. W. (1998). *John Dewey and the lessons of art.* New Haven, CT: Yale University Press.

Langer, J. A. (1990). The process of understanding: Reading for literary and informative purposes. *Research in the Teaching of English, 24,* 229–60.

Mackey, M. (1997). Good-enough reading: Momentum and accuracy in the reading of complex fiction. *Research in the Teaching of English, 31,* 428–58.

McCormick, K. (1994). *The culture of reading and the teaching of English.* Manchester, UK: Manchester University Press.

Mora, P. (1994). Elena. In D.C.D. Heyck (Ed.), *Barrios and borderlando: Culture of Latinos and Latinas in the United States* (p. 369). New York: Routledge.

Quirk, T. (1995). *Coming to grips with Huckleberry Finn: Essays on a book, a boy, and a man.* Columbia: University of Missouri Press.

Rabinowitz, P. J., & Smith, M. W. (1998). *Authorizing readers: Resistance and respect in the teaching of literature.* New York: Teachers College Press.

Rosenblatt, L. M. (1938). *Literature as exploration* (1st ed.). New York: D. Appleton-Century.

Rosenblatt, L. M. (1968). *Literature as exploration* (2nd ed.). New York: Noble & Noble.

Rosenblatt, L. M. (1976). *Literature as exploration* (3rd ed.). New York: Noble & Noble.

Rosenblatt, L. M. (1978/1994). *The reader, the text, the poem: The transactional theory of the literary work.* Carbondale: Southern Illinois University Press.

Rosenblatt, L. M. (1983). *Literature as exploration* (4th ed.). New York: Modern Language Association.

Rosenblatt, L. M. (1995). *Literature as exploration* (5th ed.). New York: Modern Language Association.

Saks, A. L. (Ed.). (1995). Viewpoints: A symposium on the usefulness of literacy research. *Research in the Teaching of English, 29,* 326–48.

Scholes, R. (1985). *Textual power: Literary theory and the teaching of English.* New Haven, CT: Yale University Press.

3

Intertextualities

Volosinov, Bakhtin, Literary Theory, and Literacy Studies

Charles Bazerman

Intertextuality forms one of the crucial grounds for writing studies and writing practice. Texts do not appear in isolation, but in relation to other texts. We write in response to prior writing, and as writers we use the resources provided by prior writers. When we read we use knowledge and experience from texts we have read before to make sense of the new text, and as readers we notice the texts the writer invokes directly and indirectly. Our reading and writing are in dialogue with each other as we write in direct and indirect response to what we have read before, and we read in relation to the ideas we have articulated in our own writing.

Understanding how we use intertextuality as writers and readers can improve our practice as individuals and as collectives. Our writing can be more sure-footed as we notice the intertextual ground we stand on. We can become more deft and precise in invoking texts that we want the reader to see as relevant context and in excluding those intertexts that might distract the readers from the vision we want to present. As readers we can note more exactly those intertexts the writer is invoking, and how and for what purposes. Further, we can also decide as readers if we want to bring other texts to bear to the issue that the writer has not seen as relevant.

As useful a concept as intertextuality is, we have difficulty making precise analytic use of it for rhetoric, composition, and literacy studies. That is because the term has been introduced through literary studies and has been defined and elaborated in ways that focus on issues of most interest to literary studies, rather than those issues most of interest to rhetoric, composition, and literacy studies. The literary genealogy for the term intertextuality has been reconstructed to start with Mikhail Bakhtin. This Bakhtin is assumed to have written V. N. Volosinov's *Marxism and the Philosophy of Language,* and thus that work is read in the light of Bakhtin's ideological concerns with monologic and dialogic forms of consciousness of the literary author as expressed in the author's literary work. The term intertextuality then developed within literary studies where the issue focused on the nature and status of the literary author. To gain a broader and more fundamental understanding of how texts rely on and relate to each other, we need to recover a definition and understanding of intertextuality that fits the needs of literacy practitioners, researchers, and educators, and then use that field-appropriate definition to refine practice, rather than to remain tied to definitions and understandings designed for the more limited domain of literary studies.[1]

I want to reframe literacy studies' concerns with intertextuality by two moves. First, I recover Volosinov from Bakhtin so as to point out his more fundamental and broader interests in the relations among utterances. Second, I remind us of the somewhat separate issues of intertextuality within writing studies – a story I tell from the perspective of my own developing interests. On the bases of these two moves, I then suggest how we might want to understand intertextuality.

The term intertextuality, or any Russian equivalent, appears nowhere in the works of either Bakhtin or Volosinov. The term was first coined by Julia Kristeva in a work of literary theory *Desire in Language: A Semiotic Approach to Literature and Art*, published in English translation in 1980. Drawing on a combined Bakhtin/Volosinov, she suggests that any text is a mosaic of quotations. She uses the concept of the textual mosaic to argue against the radical originality of any text and to locate common cultural experience in the sharing of text rather than any shared intersubjective state, for we always take up individual subject positions. Orientation to common utterances, she argues, creates the ongoing culture and evokes common objects of desire. Intertextuality, for Kristeva, is a mechanism whereby we write ourselves into the social text, and thereby the social text writes us.

The origins of the concept in Bakhtin and Volosinov – and I would distinguish between the two – have different motives and forces than used by Kristeva. In *Marxism and the Philosophy of Language* (first published in the Soviet Union in 1929; appearing in English translation in a limited edition in 1973 and more widely in 1986), Volosinov uses the relation among texts to argue against two idealized dichotomies Ferdinand de Saussure (1986; generally viewed as the founder of modern linguistics) makes in order to establish an autonomous linguistics. Saussure distinguishes between langue (an abstracted language system) and parole (particularized individual uses of that language). Then, Saussure designates langue and not parole as the proper object of linguistic study. Volosinov answers that language exists only in individual utterances located in particular moments and relations; one cannot properly understand language apart from its instances of use, embedded within many surrounding utterances. Saussure's second idealized distinction of diachrony (historical process) and synchrony (contemporary,

---

[1] Both Porter (1986) and Selzer (1993) also develop implications of intertextuality for composition and rhetoric, but they stay closer to literary critical understandings of intertextuality.

ahistorical form) is again to assert that language can and should be studied only in its idealized form in the present moment without respect to its history. Volosinov answers that every utterance draws on the history of language use, is responsive to prior utterances, and carries forward that history. In the interplay with past utterances, each new utterance takes on a stance to previous utterances. Volosinov, furthermore, begins a technical analysis of how texts position themselves to each other through linguistic systems of direct and indirect quotations.

Volosinov's work raises fundamental issues about the nature of all language and does not prejudge that any set of linguistically mediated relations is more valuable than any other. He points out that the relations exist and different linguistic forms and practices facilitate different sets of relations. As a linguist developing a philosophy of language,[2] he is primarily interested in the nature of language, which he sees as situated utterance. The relations among texts and other utterances are facilitated by certain linguistic mechanisms such as quotation. These mechanisms embed language in social interaction and social relations. Thus, Volosinov wants to explore the relations among texts technically in order to understand how language as utterance works in practice. Further, since he sees individual consciousness arising out of our particular experiences of language utterance, our consciousnesses are deeply dialogical (or as we would now say intertextual), just as our utterances are. Therefore, the mechanisms of textual relations are also part of the mechanisms of the formation of consciousness.

The dialogic formation of consciousness is a theme later pursued by Bakhtin (1981), in particular concerning the representation of novelists' consciousness within the form of the novel. However, because Volosinov's interests in consciousness concern the internal formation in socially situated nonliterary contexts,[3] they are much closer to issues raised by Lev Vygotsky's analysis of the internalization of the interpersonal words. In the words of Vygotsky's 1931 essay on the internalization of higher mental functions (in 1987):

An interpersonal process is transformed into an intrapersonal one. Every function in the child's cultural development appears twice: first on the social level, and later, on the individual level; first between people (interpsychological), and then inside the child (intrapsychological).

[2] Clark and Holquist (1984) report that, in 1927, Volosinov received a degree from the Philological faculty of Leningrad University and then enrolled as a graduate sudent in the Institute for the Comparative History of Literatures and Languages of the West and East. They report his dissertation topic seems to have been on reported speech, the main linguistic empirical matter in *Marxism and the Philosophy of Language.*

[3] See also Volosinov's (1926) essay, "Discourse in Life and Discourse in Art" (translated in *Freudianism,* Volosinov, 1987), in which he argues that even literature must be seen as socially situated utterance.

Volosinov in his (1927) book *Freudianism,* (translated in 1987) already was concerned with the issue of inner speech. In this context, he cites Vygotsky's 1925 paper on consciousness as a core problem of psychology (in 1987). In this paper, Vygotsky begins his investigation into the way language mediates consciousness and transforms reflexes, thus making available for consciousness and thought a form of cultural transmission of the historical experience of humankind. That is, by learning the culturally and historically formed language spoken by those around us our consciousness is formed; furthermore, our neural reflexes and consequent behavior are transformed. In this way our consciousness and behavior are formed in relation to the utterances that surround us and to which we respond in interaction. In modern terms, Vygotsky was showing us how our thoughts and actions could themselves be understood as deeply intertextual, regardless of how private and personal they seemed, or how much they lacked overt reference to the utterances of others. Over the next several years, Vygotsky was to investigate the role of signs in mediating action, directing attention, and the development of the infant into a mature social being. He also studied the processes by which signs and utterances came to regulate behavior and become internalized into the mind. These ideas, however, were only sketchily gestured at in the 1925 paper. Although Volosinov's 1927 citation provides direct evidence of Volosinov's awareness of Vygotsky, it is also reasonable to assume that Vygotsky was aware of Volosinov – given Vygotsky's extensive reading, the limited world of Soviet science at the time, and the consonance of their interests in developing Marxist historical theories of the formation of language, the mind, and consciousness.

Vygotsky's ultimate formulation of an internal plane of consciousness resulting from the internalization of language experience would provide a more robust model of socially formed individual consciousness and agency than Volosinov's formulation of inner speech and consciousness. Vygotsky, as a psychologist with developmental interests, was looking at how the outside (the interpersonal) got inside (the intrapersonal) in order to shape individual thought and action. He thus elaborated mechanisms by which internalized thought operated within the functional system of the self. The internal plane of consciousness, formed when language experience integrates with nonlinguistic experience, incorporates one's earliest social and linguistic relations and reformulates one's prelinguistic and nonsocial experience and perception. If Vygotsky shows more fully how society gets into the self, Volosinov as a socially oriented linguist points outward into how the self gets into society. Volosinov's formulation of inner speech arising out of socially embedded utterance reaches further outward in planting individual consciousness within a dynamic and complex social field. He points to the linguistic mechanisms by which we become intertwined with others in social dialogue and by which we necessarily become reliant on others' words in talking with and interacting among people. Because his work as a linguistic theorist and researcher did not extend much beyond his 1929 book (Volosinov, 1986), he never developed further his investigation of the sociolinguistic mechanisms of the embedding of the self in social relations and utterances. His work, nonetheless, has set important terms for contemporary sociolinguistics and anthropological linguistics. The strong complementarity between Vygotsky's inward mechanisms of the socially formed language-saturated consciousness and Volosinov's outward mechanisms of consciousness-forming sociolinguistic utterances provide a meeting point between psychology and social studies of language and interaction.

Bakhtin, rather than pursuing fundamental issues of the self formed in society, uses the relations of utterances to pursue narrower questions of literary value in the way that novels represent the utterances of the characters and narrators. In *Problems of Dostoevsky's Poetics* (Bakhtin, 1984a), a reworking of a 1929 book on Dostoevsky, and *The Dialogic Imagination* (Bakhtin, 1981), representing work in the 1930s and 1940s, he associates the form of the novel with a form of consciousness. He praises that form of novel that recognizes the variety of utterances incorporated and thus adopts a stance of multivocality, dialogism, or polyphony rather than authoritative univocality, monologism, or monophony, which obscures the complexity of human language, consciousness, and relation. Bakhtin's interest is in valuing appreciation of the existence of others, in the neo-Kantian tradition familiar to us in such moral thinkers as Martin Buber and Carl Rogers.[4] Bakhtin's moral stance starts with a morally accountable, autonomous self that must take responsibility for individual actions, as he articulates in his early works published in *Art and Answerability* (Bakhtin, 1990) and *Toward a Philosophy of the Act* (Bakhtin, 1993). Such an individual moral self implies a very different form of consciousness than that presented in the Volosinov and Vygotskian accounts of internalization of socially embedded speech. For Bakhtin, dialogism is a moral imperative rather than a fact of social development.

Bakhtin, in works such as *The Dialogic Imagination* (1981) and *Rabelais and His World* (1984b), is also interested in the stance or attitude or evaluation one utterance makes toward others, such as through double-voicing or carnivalesque. This often parodic or otherwise critical heteroglossia he considers typically in contexts critical of authority, power, and dominant classes. His treatment of double-voicing opens up the issue of the complex attitudes we have toward each other as we recognize and revaluate the character of each other's voice. Such complexity of evaluative attitude can serve to exclude or demote appreciation of the other, and is a frequent method for keeping at a distance those who are different from us, as we might parody a foreign accent

---

[4] For an excellent discussion of Bakhtin's neo-Kantian origins, see Dentith's (1995) introduction to the collection *Bakhtinian Thought*.

or nondominant dialect or we might mockingly repeat words we dismiss as absurd. Bakhtin, however, attempts to maintain a democratic, neo-Kantian appreciation of the other by limiting the targets of what we would now call attitude. The examples of carnivalesque or linguistic mockery that he examines typically aim to deflate oppressively powerful ruling forces rather than to stigmatize the powerless.

Bakhtin provides conceptual tools for understanding how authors engage or repress complexity of perspectives and represent evaluation and attitude toward the perspectives of the characters they represent. He uses those tools analyze in detail how the interplay of voices and perspectives is managed in different texts with particular ideological implications. In a number of works, he presents histories of different forms of consciousness associated with differing literary forms and the political struggles embodied in the replacement of one literary form by another. Later literary critics such as Kristeva, Barthes, and Riffaterre put aside analysis of the authorial handling of multiple voices and the historically shifting forms of fiction and literary consciousness. Rather they engaged broad, ahistorical questions of the status of the author, originality, and interpretation. As discussed earlier, Kristeva coined the term intertextuality to dissolve the autonomous integrity of both author and reader into the ocean of shared cultural experiences of common texts. Barthes (1977) took the implications of intertextuality a step beyond Kristeva's dissolution of authorship to a destabilization of the text itself because the text rests on the evocation of so many other texts. Riffatere (1984) sought to establish a basis for textual meaning and interpretation within the linguistic ambience, or intertexts, within which it is read. Among the literary critics, only most recently has Genette returned to a concrete analysis of how intertextuality works within specific texts. In several publications he has mapped out orderly sets of possible relations among texts, what he calls transtextuality: intertextuality (explicit quotation or allusion), paratextuality (the relation to directly surrounding texts, such as prefaces, interviews, publicity, and reviews); metatextuality (a commentary relation); hypertextuality (the play of one text off of familiarity with another); and architextuality (the generic expectations in relation to other similar texts) (Genette, 1992, 1997a, 1997b). Yet even this elaboration is only for the purpose of explicating literary meaning and effect. Transtextuality is a method by which texts make their meaning in a world of surrounding texts.[5]

The stakes of rhetoric, composition, and literacy studies in the relations among texts, self, society, and social action, however, are much broader than the concerns that have defined and elaborated the term intertextuality within literary studies. Our concerns harken back to the groundwork laid

---

[5] See Allen (2000) for a good overview of the various literary perspectives on intertextuality.

by Volosinov and Vygotsky, long before the term intertextuality was used. I am acutely aware of this because my own interests in the relations of text grew out of practical issues in composition before I had engaged with the work of any of the authors discussed in this paper. I then elaborated my interests through intense reading of Vygotsky starting in the mid-1970s and continuing as works became available in English, and then at the end of the decade by an interested, but less intense reading of Volosinov's *Marxism and the Philosophy of Language*. Only after my project based on the issues concerning the teaching of writing was fairly well formulated did the work of Bakhtin and Kristeva's term intertext start to wash across the American academic scene to provide the means by which teachers of writing and literacy researchers generally came to address issues of the relations among texts. I was pleased that the popularity of Bakhtin's and Kristeva's terms drew attention to how one used reading in the course of writing and how familiarity with texts developed one's consciousness and thought. I saw these terms providing useful tools for reorienting teaching of writing and literacy studies away from the isolated, individual writer toward the writer placed within a complex social, textual field.

However, I became increasingly uncomfortable with the focus and limitations those popular terms put on those issues of reading and writing. While I continued my own work following the issues as I saw them, I observed those terms were limiting the ability of the larger part of rhetoric, composition, and literacy studies to address the precise mechanisms by which writers were formed within a world of texts and the ways in which they deployed those texts to create social action. To reopen the question of how we can best examine the development of writers' consciousness, perception, and social relations within the world of texts which they engage with, I present how I see these issues by showing the path by which I came to see them as I do.

My work in academic writing, begun in the early 1970s before Bakhtin or intertextuality were known in the United States. I soon saw a critical aspect of academic writing to be writing about reading, which took me down a pathway of literacy development within schools, disciplines, professions, and other structured fields of communication. Rather than being concerned with the status of the author and the modes of consciousness expressed in fiction – as the literary definition of intertextuality might have directed me – I was drawn to considering the kind of skills and tasks necessary for people to develop into competent literate participants within the textually dense worlds of modernity. Enhanced agency as readers comes with noting how texts create social dramas of reference and sit in relation to the resources of prior and ambient texts. Enhanced agency as writers grows with our ability to place our utterances in relation to other texts, draw on their resources, represent those texts from our perspective, and assemble new social dramas of textual utterances within which we act through our words. How we use other texts frames social organization, relation, and action within the world of textual interchange.

The problem was first posed to me in the form of the standard but ill-defined assignment of the library research or term paper. In such assignments, students are expected to investigate and discuss some issue relevant to the course subject matter. Nobody at that time quite knew what this assignment entailed, and the only teaching materials available were little more than lists of references and resources along with footnote-style prescriptions. Teachers regularly complained, long before word processing and Internet research, of cut-and-paste jobs that strung together quotations, paraphrases, or verbatim plagiarism. Successful students, however, knew that there was a lot more to writing good research papers than locating some sources and following correct bibliographic form. There was a journey of learning, of problem formation and reformulation, of careful and thoughtful reading, of being able to interpret and restate what sources had to say, of evaluation and comment, of synthesis, of fresh argument. Such skills allowed a small group of students characterized as "academically talented" to climb up the slippery slopes of elite institutions and enjoy the pleasures of leisured academic life. As a writing teacher, I took as one of my fundamental problems to demystify what it took to climb this mountain.

I soon saw the problem of how to write the research paper as part of a bigger question of how to write well about nonliterary, knowledge-focused reading. My response to this question was a pedagogy that anatomized and practiced the various skills involved in writing about what you read – skills involving accurate portrayal of source materials as well as response, evaluation, commentary, analysis, synthesis, and incorporation into new ideas and projects. In addition, the pedagogy focused on students' reflective ability to analyze the systematic flow of genred texts that formed the context and resource for each piece of academic writing.[6] At this time, influenced by my reading of Vygotsky, I also became aware that active engagement with texts and developing articulate responses and thoughts in relation to those texts were significant parts of the development of students' educated and informed consciousnesses.

My interests in these issues developed just as the Writing Across the Curriculum (WAC) movement was being born. My work on academic reading and writing suggested to me that the expressivist and writing-to-learn theories behind early WAC in England and the United States did not give us a precise enough picture of the literacy demands of disciplinary coursework or of the experiences by which students' thought grew within academic contexts.

---

[6] This pedagogy took the shape of several textbooks, *The Informed Writer* (Bazerman, 1981, 1985, 1989, 1992, 1995), *The Informed Reader* (Bazerman, 1989), and *Involved: Writing for College, Writing for Your Self* (Bazerman, 1997).

As I surveyed the writing students were doing in university courses, it became clear that much academic writing was in response to particular texts, and that stances students were asked to adopt toward texts were organized along disciplinary lines. Texts provided a structure of role relationships that corresponded to disciplinary identities and that provided pathways for development of disciplinary forms of thought. Disciplinary differences seemed to be deeply rhetorical, psychological, sociological, and intertextual (as I was coming to understand the term as referring to the concrete relations among texts and utterances). The textual form appropriate to each kind of assignment emerged out of the argumentative relations authors took with each other's texts within the emerging social activity system of their fields. My comparative study of texts in literary studies, sociology, and biology considered the ways texts used the prior texts of the field, how they positioned themselves with respect to those prior texts, and how they anticipated being taken up as contributions to a literature (Bazerman, 1981). As my basic analytic heuristic, I expanded the traditional Aristotelean communication triangle of author-audience-subject matter by adding a fourth vertex – the literature – to create a communication pyramid. The text, in addition to establishing relations among author, audience, and subject creates relationships between the literature and those other three. The audience and author knowledge of the subject is built on prior texts; the audience knowledge and orientation is based on their reading; and the author's authority, resources, interests, and current stance grow out of an engagement with the literature. Thus intertextuality (as in Volosinov's relationship among utterances and Vygotsky's social language becoming the basis of consciousness and action) became built into my fundamental model of communication. I also began doing some historical work to see the features of scientific writing more distinctly through their emergence, and continuous repositioning against earlier texts. This was coincident with my settling on genre as a key concept, with genre being an historically emergent intertextual phenomenon.[7]

I have continuingly applied these ideas to my own writing, the writing of my students, and the writing I have examined in my research. As a result, I have come to appreciate how much reflective understanding of the intertextual landscape provides the writer with important strategic rhetorical tools. Developing a highly articulated picture of the ambient relevant texts can help the writer to define and even redefine the rhetorical situation, position the new text within larger organizations of textual utterances and activities, and bring deeper and richer resources to bear on the current task. Similarly, a highly developed view of the intertextual landscape helps a reader interpret, evaluate, and use a text more effectively. In short, intertextual awareness increases one's agency by planting literate activity in a richer context, increasing one's ability to move around within that context,

---

[7] These studies are represented in *Shaping Written Knowledge* (Bazerman, 1988).

and helping one deploy parts of it for one's own purposes.[8] We carry out our written speech acts on an unfolding landscape of unfolding intertexts, emergent structures of texts that condition the situation for future actions. Each text we write is a speech act, and the success of that text is in the consequences of what follows after, how the text creates a landmark of something done that needs to be taken into account in future utterances.[9]

To help students and other writers develop a fuller picture of the intertextual grounds and resources for their writing we can call their attention to a number of dimensions of intertextuality.[10] First is how explicitly and fully one text refers to and incorporates material from other texts. Are substantial amounts of material incorporated and taken at face value or is the other text only alluded to, or are other texts only there as an unspoken, assumed background?

Second is the form the reference takes, from direct extensive quotation with cited reference, through paraphrase, to unreferenced terms that echo recognizable discourses. Third is how far the text reaches out into distant texts. At one extreme is use of bits of text that appear earlier in the same text, echoing and building on it, in what we might call intratextual reference. Reference can reach a bit farther, but stay within closely related texts around a single case or issue – what we might call intrafile intertextuality. Intertextuality can stay within a specialty, disciplinary or professional domain, or may reach into different fields, different times, and different places. Fourth is how the intertextual material is transformed in its re-representation, and how the new author's stance or evaluation or synthesis places the intertextual

---

[8] I took an interest in how intertextual fields became historically organized and how individuals were able to build these systems for their own purposes. Such questions led me to examine the writings of Joseph Priestley, who it turns out was central in developing modern explicit citation practices (Bazerman, 1991). I took up the consequences of modern citation practice for the way the publication game is played now by examining a modern virtuosic tour de force of citation, Gould and Lewontin's (1979) "Spanderels of San Marcos" (Bazerman, 1993). During this period, several other people were working on parallel studies. Swales (1990) examined how research article introductions position new contributions to the literature, and Myers (1991) looked at how reviews of literature advance research agendas. Berkenkotter, Huckin, and Ackerman (1991), as well as Prior (1998), documented the way graduate students learn to navigate the literatures and other discussion of their fields to establish professional identity. Devitt (1991) examined the way intertextuality structures the work of the accountancy profession, and McCarthy (1991) researched the way a central text has organized the discourses of psychiatry.

[9] These themes of agency through creating presence in intertextual landscapes directed my book on the *Languages of Edison's Light* (Bazerman, 1999). The book examines how Edison took up positions in the major discourses – patent law, finance, corporations, technology and science, politics, journalism, consumer culture – as part of making incandescent light and power a reality. He had to complete many speech acts and create many social facts in multiple discursive worlds to give his emergent technologies presence, meaning, and value.

[10] I spell out tools for analyzing intertextuality in greater detail in the forthcoming *What Texts Do and How They Do It*, which I coedited with Paul Prior.

material in a new context, thereby modifying its meaning (see Linell, 1998). Fifth is how the intertextual material is used rhetorically in the new argument. These first five dimensions all concern how the intertext is deployed in the new text.

Three other dimensions call attention to the texts that lie behind the new text and that the writer can draw on or otherwise use to define the situation of the current text. First is the sequence of texts that have led up to and formed the current rhetorical situation. What memos, directives, and reports have created the necessity for a governmental agency to issue a new policy? What course syllabi and assignment sheets, assigned course readings, books cited in class lectures, and prior papers have led up to the paper that is to be handed in tomorrow? Second is the genre of any text or text to be written that grows out of a history of prior texts that set exemplars and expectations. Showing students models of prior texts that accomplish the tasks they are facing and helping them see how they can build on and modify that history of genre models can help provide guidelines as well as space for originality relevant to the specifics of the current task. Third is the entire range of relevant documents that can be brought to bear or used as a resource for a current document. The more broadly and precisely students and other writers envision the intertextual world they can draw on, the more powerful a set of flexible options they will have on hand. By bringing in new intertextual resources and contexts that they can show to be relevant, they can even redefine the fundamental rhetorical situation in major ways. A seemingly narrow issue of political expediency, for example, can be transformed into an issue of philosophical principle and moral integrity. Or a historical narrative can be transformed into a test of social theory. Or a muddle of conflicting interests can be sharpened into a small list of legally permissible choices.

Volosinov recognized that, as linguistic creatures, humans are inevitably caught up in the social drama of unfolding webs of utterances, to which we add only our next turn. It is worth serious attention how we place that next turn, how we draw on the history of utterances before us, and how we draw ourselves close to or distance ourselves from those utterances. On such questions rests what we are able to do.[11] Volosinov's understanding of language as historically situated utterance opens up many issues of the way writing is situated within, deploys, and re-represents the flow of prior texts, but it is up to composition and rhetoric to articulate the complex skills and knowledge by which we manage to articulate our position and contribution

[11] A concern for agency within intertextual worlds now leaves me wondering about what it means to live in an information age, and what intellectual and rhetorical skills students will need to succeed in such a world (see Bazerman, 2001). Information technologies are now reshaping all educational, social, and economic institutions, but the ideology of information misleadingly represents information as disembodied for human purposes and meaning-shaping contexts. It is urgent that we begin to understand how people gain agency in complex informational environments.

to that intertextual space. If we are to understand how we are acted upon, how we can react, and how we can act freshly in this complex literate world of ours, where major institutions and spheres of activity are saturated by texts, we need to move toward a richer and more participatory understanding of intertextuality. To do so, we need to develop analytical concepts and methods that extend beyond Volosinov's beginnings and head in directions quite different than the ways intertextuality has been taken up by the literary critical world. Composition and rhetoric's intertextuality is ultimately about agency within the complex, historically evolved, and continuingly mutating landscape of texts. Intertextuality for composition and rhetoric is about creating authority, agency, and powerful text, and not about their dissolution within everything that has been written before. We, after all, are concerned with helping students write themselves and their interests into the teeming world of language.

References

Allen, G. (2000). *Intertextuality*. London: Routledge.

Bakhtin, M. (1981). *The dialogic imagination*. Austin: University of Texas Press.

Bakhtin, M. (1984a). *Problems of Doestoevsky's poetics*. Minneapolis: University of Minnesota Press.

Bakhtin, M. (1984b). *Rabelais and his world*. Bloomington: Indiana University Press.

Bakhtin, M. (1990). *Art and answerability: Early philosophical essays*. Austin: University of Texas Press.

Bakhtin, M. (1993). *Toward a philosophy of the act*. Austin: University of Texas Press.

Barthes, R. (1977). *Image-music-text*. London: Fontana.

Bazerman, C. (1981). What written knowledge does: Three examples of academic discourse. *Philosophy of the Social Sciences 11*(3), 361–88.

Bazerman, C. (1981, 1985, 1989, 1992, 1995). *The informed writer*. Boston: Houghton Mifflin.

Bazerman, C. (1988). *Shaping written knowledge: The genre and activity of the experimental article in science*. Madison: University of Wisconsin Press.

Bazerman, C. (1989). *The informed reader*. Boston: Houghton Mifflin.

Bazerman, C. (1991). How natural philosophers can cooperate. In C. Bazerman & J. Paradis (Eds.), *Textual dynamics of the professions* (pp. 13–44). Madison: University of Wisconsin Press.

Bazerman, C. (1993). Intextextual self-fashioning: Gould and Lewontin's representations of the literature. In J. Selzer (Ed.), *Understanding scientific prose* (pp. 20–41). Madison: University of Wisconsin Press.

Bazerman, C. (1997). *Involved: Writing for college, writing for your self*. Boston: Houghton Mifflin.

Bazerman, C. (1999). *Languages of Edison's light*. Cambridge, MA: MIT Press.

Bazerman, C. (2001). Nuclear information: One rhetorical moment in the construction of the information age. *Written Communication, 18*(3), 259–95.

Bazerman, C., & Prior, P. (Eds.). (in press). *What texts do and how they do it*. Mahwah, NJ: Erlbaum.

Berkenkotter, C., Huckin, T., & Ackerman, J. (1991). Social context and socially constructed texts: The initiation of a graduate student into a writing research community. In C. Bazerman & J. Paradis (Eds.), *Textual dynamics of the professions* (pp. 191–215). Madison: University of Wisconsin Press.

Clark, K., & Holquist, M. (1984). *Mikhail Bakhtin*. Cambridge, MA: Harvard University Press.

Dentith, S. (1995). *Bakhtinian thought*. London: Routledge.

Devitt, A. (1991). Intertextuality in tax accounting: Generic, referential, and functional. In C. Bazerman & J. Paradis (Eds.), *Textual dynamics of the professions* (pp. 336–80). Madison: University of Wisconsin Press.

Genette, G. (1992). *The architext*. Berkeley: University of California Press.

Genette, G. (1997a). *Palimpsests*. Lincoln: University of Nebraska Press.

Genette, G. (1997b). *Paratexts*. Cambridge, UK: Cambridge University Press.

Gould, S. J., & Lewontin, R. C. (1979). The spandrels of San Marco and the Panglossian paradigm: A critique of the adaptationist program. *Proceedings of the Royal Society of London*, B 205, 581–98.

Kristeva, J. (1980). *Desire in language: A semiotic approach to literature and art*. New York: Columbia University Press.

Linell, P. (1998). Discourse across boundaries: On recontextualization and the blending of voices in professional discourse. *Text*, *18*(2), 143–57.

McCarthy, L. P. (1991). A psychiatrist using DSM-III: The influence of a charter document in psychiatry. In C. Bazerman & J. Paradis (Eds.), *Textual dynamics of the professions* (pp. 358–78). Madison: University of Wisconsin Press.

Myers, G. (1991). Stories and styles in two molecular biology articles. In C. Bazerman & J. Paradis (Eds.), *Textual dynamics of the professions* (pp. 45–75). Madison: University of Wisconsin Press.

Porter, J. (1986). Intertextuality and the discourse community. *Rhetoric Review*, 5, 34–47.

Prior, P. (1998). *Writing/disciplinarity*. Mahwah, NJ: Erlbaum.

Riffaterre, M. (1984). Intertextual representation. *Critical Inquiry*, *11*(1), 141–62.

Saussure, F. de (1986). *Course in general linguistics* (Trans. Roy Harris). LaSalle, IL: Open Court.

Selzer, J. (1993). Intertextuality and the writing process. In R. Spilka (Ed.), *Writing in the workplace* (pp. 171–80). Carbondale: Southern Illinois University Press.

Swales, J. (1990). *Genre analysis: English in academic and research settings*. Cambridge, UK: Cambridge University Press.

Volosinov, V. N. (1986). *Marxism and the philosophy of language*. Cambridge, MA: Harvard University Press.

Volosinov. V. N. (1987). *Freudianism*. Bloomington: Indiana University Press.

Vygotsky, L. S. (1987). *Collected works* (6 vols.). New York: Plenum.

4

The Teaching of Academic Language to Minority Second Language Learners

Guadalupe Valdés

Within the last several years, individuals working with English language learners have focused increasingly on the development of the types of language proficiencies that are required to perform successfully in academic contexts. Most practitioners and researchers agree that, in order to succeed in American schools, such learners must be given the opportunity to acquire *academic*, rather than everyday, language.

Unfortunately, in spite of the growing interest in the kind of language that will result in school success, we currently lack a single definition or even general agreement about what is meant by *academic language*. Although this has been discouraging and problematic for a number of practitioners, what is significant is that many more groups and individuals are now engaging in the examination of what they understand to be academic language and inquiring about its role in the school success of language-minority children. It is my position that it is both useful and productive to try to unravel and examine what different individuals mean by the various terms used to refer to academic language and particularly to understand the dialogic nature of the discussion itself – a discussion held at professional meetings, at conferences, in articles published in journals, and in entire books written by scholars as they consciously or unconsciously respond to other voices in the dialogue. These voices include those heard through the popular media, those of political activists of various types and backgrounds, and those of everyday citizens who want to inform themselves before voting on now-popular propositions that directly focus on language.

In this chapter, I am concerned with voices in two types of dialogue. First, I am concerned with the voices in the dialogue surrounding the development of academic language among diverse learners. I argue that, as the Bakhtin Circle[1] demonstrated, the context for all discussions, including academic

---

[1] I use the term Bakhtin Circle following Duranti and Goodwin (1992) and Moraes (1996) in order to avoid the debate concerning the specific authorship of the works of Voloshinov and Medvedev that have been attributed to Bakhtin.

debates, encompasses the surrounding voices that help shape, reconfigure, and constantly change the multivoiced utterances of the various speakers. The discussion of academic language is no exception. The various existing approaches to the definition of academic language have developed and evolved in communication with a particular set of voices that are part of specific professional worlds. I describe these various definitions as well as the voices to which these various perspectives primarily speak. I point out, however, that, given the various boundaries of academic professions, the dialogue on academic language is unfortunately made up of a series of parallel dialogues that often fail to be heard by scholars who are members of other closely related professions.

My second concern in this chapter is with the voices available to second language learners in both their communities and their schools. Although I agree that English language learners must be given the opportunity to acquire and master the kind of language that will allow them to succeed in school, I have many questions about the kinds of academic language that can be taught and learned in classrooms. I suggest that what is missing from a number of professional and scholarly discussions focusing on academic language is a Bakhtinian view of the types and range of experiences and interactions that must surround minority youngsters if they are to acquire the kinds of language proficiencies considered desirable by educational institutions.

THE SCHOLARLY DIALOGUE ON ACADEMIC LANGUAGE

Scholarly discussions do not take place in a social vacuum. Even without the insights offered by the Bakhtin Circle about the nature of intertextuality, it is very generally accepted that scholars engage in an ongoing dialogue with other members of their academic communities and their professional organizations. Scholars respond to each other's papers, engage in polemical debates about theories and their implications, and write dense scholarly tomes, sometimes understandable exclusively to other members of the same inner scholarly circle.

Within recent years, however, the recognized isolation of scholars in their ivory towers and the perceived irrelevancy of their opinions to public debates has given way to a view in which scholarly "experts" have taken on the role of providing information and background to the courts, to media organizations and to the public in general. As was made evident by the recent Ebonics controversy, the opinions of university researchers and scholars often become very much a part of national debates on issues about which the public has strong interest. As members of professional media organizations seek both to provide background for their audiences and a balance of differing opinions, scholars are sought after to present their views and to participate in what Tannen (1998) calls the "argument culture."

Scholars are expected not to engage in a discussion of the complexity of issues, but to take one of two diametrically opposed sides. Television news programs, for example, regularly offer their viewers the perspective of a single "resident" expert who interprets a controversy for the public, or they present two scholars who take on opposing views on the issues in question. As was made evident by the California campaign opposing Proposition 227, public exchanges where journalists required that bilingual education scholars and second language acquisition experts engage in debates with political activists were very different from academic exchanges among professional colleagues. Often, individuals engaged in the discussion of Proposition 227 had strong opinions and little knowledge of and respect for scholarly evidence.

In the case of academic English, the discussion of many significant and important issues is taking place in a context in which the response of *both* the community of scholarly specialists *and* members of the public (including special interest organizations, news media, parents, teachers, administrators, and policy makers) are anticipated. The dual realms of public context and academic orbit surrounding scholarly discussion result in a discourse that is made up of utterances that are a link in the chain of speech communication in *two* very different types of spheres. Scholarly utterances, then, particularly on topics that are of public interest, attempt to refute, affirm, supplement, rely, presuppose, and take into account as Bahktin ([1986] 1990) maintains, the "echoes and reverberations" (p. 91) of two very different discourse communities. The context for the current dialogue on academic language is depicted in Fig. 4.1.

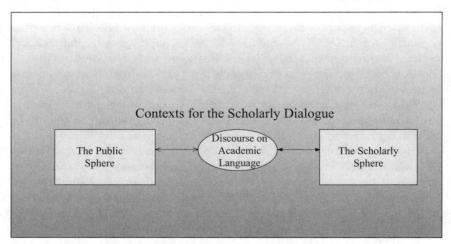

FIGURE 4.1. The scholarly dialogue on academic language.

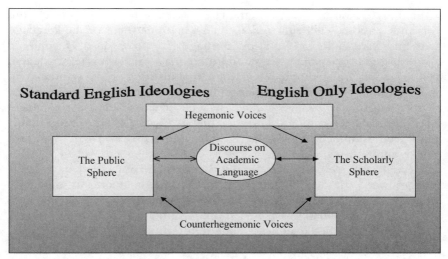

FIGURE 4.2. The ideological context.

The Ideological Context

All public discussions relating to academic language, no matter how neutral, are currently taking place in a context that is influenced by ideologies about the standard language. In the United States, for example, discussions of academic English are informed by ideologies about standard English as well as by ideologies about the place of English in multilingual America. To those concerned about the erosion of standard English, any mention of the teaching of academic language necessarily refers to the teaching of the "correct" language to all students, but especially to students who are speakers of nonstandard varieties of English. To those concerned about maintaining and protecting the status of English as the language of education in the United States, however, discussions of the teaching of academic language necessarily focus on the use of English as the *only* language in which instruction is offered, especially to newly arrived immigrant students.

Researchers and practitioners, then, who enter into the discussion of academic English in this country engage in a dialogue with both hegemonic and counterhegemonic voices that are part of the discourse surrounding both standard English and English only, as illustrated in Fig. 4.2.

THE PUBLIC SPHERE

The Dialogue about Standard English

The various voices that have taken part in the dialogue surrounding standard English have been well described by numerous scholars both in the

United States and in Great Britain. The voices are heard at times of conflict over national curricula and at times when guardians of the language march forward to defend a glorious heritage (J. Milroy, 1999). Hegemonic voices argue for teaching the standard language to the underprivileged, whereas counterhegemonic voices argue that insisting on the standard will only continue to maintain the position of the powerful who already speak the privileged variety of the language. The particular beliefs about language that are known as "standard language ideology" with reference to English have been examined by Lippi-Green (1994, 1997), L. Milroy (1999), and Milroy and Milroy (1999).

Recently, the debates surrounding the Ebonics controversy once again foregrounded the deeply engrained beliefs among Americans about the importance of teaching standard English. As Baugh (2000, p. ix) pointed out, the Ebonics debate "launched another round in a continuing national discussion on how best to educate students for whom standard English is not native." This discussion, as Wolfram, Adger, and Christian(1999) maintain, once again involved the voices of those who oppose the teaching of standard English and favor the acceptance of all varieties of English. It also involved the voices of the proponents of teaching standard English who argue that all students, in order to succeed in school and in the workplace, must master standard English.

As is the case in all public debates and discussions of standard English, the Ebonics debate involved both the hegemonic and the counterhegemonic positions depicted in Fig. 4.2. The ever-present voices of what Milroy and Milroy (1999) term "language guardians" and Bolinger (1980) calls "language shamans" were very much in evidence. Also present among the supporters of the teaching of standard English were African American conservative pundits whose views Baugh (2000, p. 113) attributes to a "uniform sense of linguistic shame about their heritage." These individuals were joined in their condemnation of Ebonics by other opponents of "bad" and "incorrect" English, prescriptivists, and those fearful about the future of English in America. Countering these views – perhaps with little success – were the declarations of academic specialists who focus on the study of African American varieties of English, including Baugh, Rickford, and Smitherman.

The Dialogue About English Only

Like standard English ideologies, ideologies of English monolingualism underlying the English-only movement are protectionist and view English as fundamentally threatened by the current state of affairs. In the case of English only, the threat is seen to involve, not merely the incorrect use of the language by particular groups of people, but the increasing use of non-English languages by rapidly growing immigrant communities. The various voices that have taken part in the debates surrounding English only have been well described by Barron (1990), Crawford (1992), and Daniels (1990). These include the voices of patriotic citizens whose parents or grand-parents did not maintain their immigrant languages and who are afraid that the United States will lose its common language as well as the very strong voices of nativists who fear that, because this country is being overrun with foreigners, Americans are being made to feel like strangers in their own land. Supporters of English only oppose the use of bilingual ballots, bilingual edu-cation, the use of non-English languages in the workplace, and special assis-tance to non-English speakers. Like individuals who support only allowing standard English in classrooms populated by African American children who speak African American English vernacular, many well-intentioned teachers who oppose bilingual education worry that newly arrived immigrant chil-dren will not acquire enough English to succeed both in school and in the workplace. Proponents of the use of non-English languages in addition to English, however, include cultural pluralists, supporters of bilingual educa-tion, supporters of immigrant language maintenance, and political activists supporting the rights of newly arrived immigrants.

Standard English as a Highly Charged Notion

Within the public sphere, then, the voices that enter into a discussion of standard English express deeply held views about education and particu-larly about the education of children who arrive in school speaking either non-English languages or nonstandard varieties of English. The voices of academic scholars involved in public sphere conversations, respond to and refute or affirm the utterances of both informed and uninformed others – all of whom have strong opinions about academic language.

THE PROFESSIONAL AND SCHOLARLY SPHERE

Communities of Professional Practice

In comparison with the public voices engaged in dialogue surrounding the discussion of academic language, scholarly conversations attending to the definition and investigation of the kind of language required for academic success embrace perspectives that differ depending on the particular focus of the professional practice or research community in question. Figure 4.3 depicts the different communities of professional practice that are currently focusing on academic language.

As is evident from Fig. 4.3, discussions of academic language have fo-cused on two very different groups of students. The first group attends to those individuals whose first language is English, whereas the second group attends to students who have learned or are learning English as a second lan-guage. Although the concerns of the different professional groups focusing

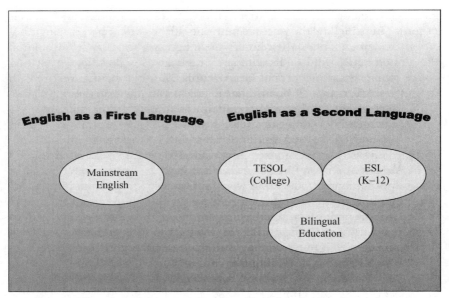

FIGURE 4.3. The scholarly context: Communities of professional practice.

on these two types of students may be similar at some levels, the specific focus of attention and the definitions of academic language used by one professional group and another vary significantly.

For example, in the case of what I have called here *Mainstream English*, which includes the teaching of literature, the teaching of writing and composition at the secondary and college levels, and the teaching of what is known as language arts in the elementary school, the focus on academic English development centers on the development of proficiencies in both oral and written text production. Perspectives within the profession differ, and there are both hegemonic and counterhegemonic voices involved in the conversation within the profession. I will limit my discussion here to the perspective of the field of composition studies within which discussions about academic language and discourse have focused primarily on written language (see also Bazerman, this volume). Responding to the pedagogical needs of teaching English composition to both mainstream and nonmainstream cultural groups within the United States, examinations of the characteristics of academic discourse (e.g., Elbow, 1991, 2000) within writing and composition studies have sought to describe both the intellectual practices of written academic discourse and its surface features. These intellectual practices have been described as involving a particular reading of the world, a way of thinking and of presenting oneself and one's thinking to other members of the same discourse community. Some researchers (e.g., Flower & Hayes, 1981) point out that academic discourse involves writing for an

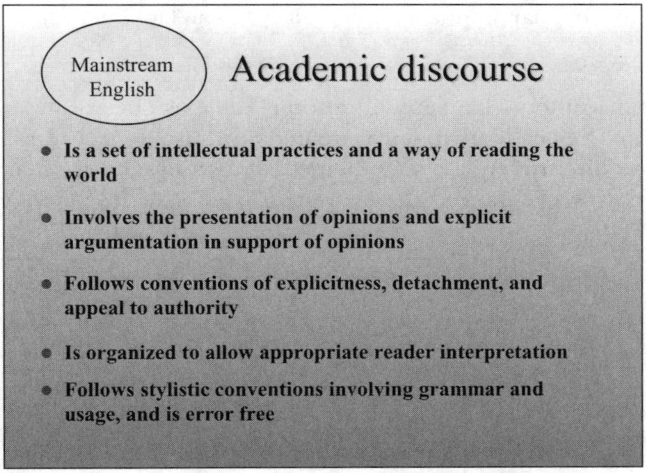

Academic discourse

Mainstream English

- **Is a set of intellectual practices and a way of reading the world**

- **Involves the presentation of opinions and explicit argumentation in support of opinions**

- **Follows conventions of explicitness, detachment, and appeal to authority**

- **Is organized to allow appropriate reader interpretation**

- **Follows stylistic conventions involving grammar and usage, and is error free**

FIGURE 4.4. Views of the mainstream English profession.

imagined community of peers for a specific purpose. For other researchers, academic discourse also involves writing to think through genuine problems and issues.

From this perspective, as I have illustrated in Fig. 4.4, academic discourse is considered primarily to involve the presentation of reasons and evidence as opposed to feelings and opinions. It also involves the development of explicit logical arguments, the detachment of the writer or speaker from his or her topic, the communication of authority and, to some degree, the display of knowledge or erudition. Academic discourse is also described as following particular stylistic conventions including the use of standard English.

In part because of the concern about students known as "basic writers," discussions of academic discourse have attempted to take a position about both the organizational patterns and the "errors" that characterize the oral and written text production of students who enter the academy from non-mainstream backgrounds. Walters (1994) captures the challenges facing these nonmainstream students who enter the academy in his following conceptualization of academic discourse:

Academic discourse clearly represents the stage of hyperliteracy. Education at the college and university level is overwhelmingly dedicated to teaching students to inhabit textual worlds, hypothetical worlds created and sustained through the language of academic discourse. . . . Undergraduate students are encouraged to hold their own in class discussion by stating their opinions and supporting them with acceptable textual evidence, and postgraduate students in seminars and oral examinations are required to participate in the discourse of their discipline, assuming a kind of authority they do not, in fact, possess. In order to succeed, they must learn to "speak in paragraphs," using a register inappropriate for most daily face-to face interactions. (p. 641)

What stands out in Walters's conceptualization is the existence of hypothetical worlds within the academy that are created and sustained through language and that require students to state their opinions and support them with textual evidence in registers considered appropriate for such academic exchanges.

Some members of the writing and composition profession, however, focus their attention primarily on correct usage, grammar, and spelling, especially in the oral and written texts of students who do not come to school speaking the varieties of language valued by academic institutions. For these individuals, academic language is primarily understood to mean language that is free of nonstandard or stigmatized features.

By comparison, the communities of professional practice that focus on students who are speakers of English as a second language have a related but somewhat different perspective on academic discourse/language. In this country, the college-level Teachers of English to Speakers of Other Languages (TESOL) profession is concerned primarily with international students at the postsecondary level. As I point out in Fig. 4.5, for this group of practitioners, academic language, then, is that language used to carry out academic work at the university level as well as the language used within particular disciplines and professions to carry out communication within the field. Much attention has been given by this group to the analysis of academic genres (Swales, 1990), that is, to describing the particular conventions of texts produced by members of professional discourse communities.

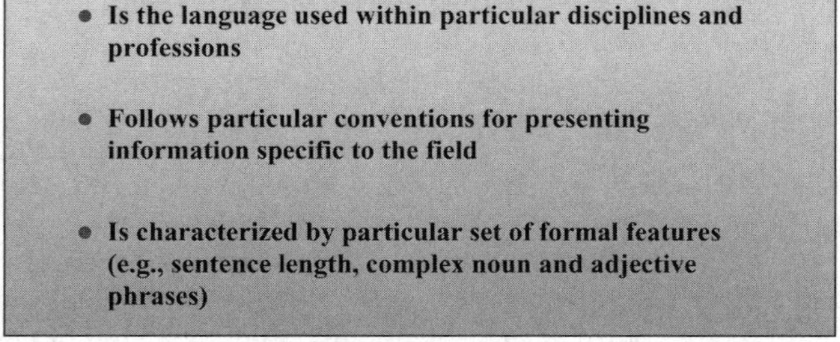

> **TESOL (College)** — **Academic language**
>
> - Is the proficiency required for tertiary study in English
> - Is the language used within particular disciplines and professions
> - Follows particular conventions for presenting information specific to the field
> - Is characterized by particular set of formal features (e.g., sentence length, complex noun and adjective phrases)

FIGURE 4.5. Views of the TESOL (College) profession.

The definition of academic language, although not expressed in the same terms as by the writing and composition community for L1 writers, has many elements in common with it. The TESOL profession also sees academic languages as a set of intellectual practices. Primarily, however, at the college level, this profession is particularly focused on stylistic conventions that are part of that practice (within particular professions), including text organization, presentation of information, and grammar and usage. Importantly, the TESOL college profession views its students as competent both academically and linguistically in their first language and considers that the profession's role is to help them to avoid discourse accent (i.e., the transfer of rhetorical styles from the L1 to English writing, Kaplan [1966, 1988]), as well as other nonnative features that are likely to interfere with communication.

The English as a Second Language (ESL) profession that works with K–12 students, by comparison focuses on non-English background, immigrant students who enter American schools. Much of the activity of this profession has been directed at the teaching of the structure of English to such youngsters as a preliminary to their learning subject matter through English. More recently, however, the pre-K–12 ESL profession has become increasingly committed to content-based approaches to language teaching and to describing the kinds of English language proficiencies needed to succeed academically as illustrated in Fig. 4.6. The *ESL Standards for Pre-K–12 Students* (TESOL, 1997), for example, define this English as (1) the English used to interact in the classroom; (2) the English used to obtain, process, construct, and provide subject-matter information in spoken and written form; and (3) the appropriate learning strategies to construct and apply academic knowledge. It is important to mention that there are competing conceptualizations and definitions of academic language within the

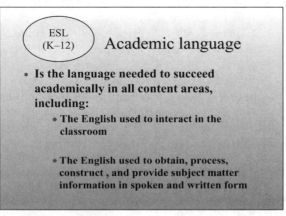

FIGURE 4.6. Views of the TESOL (K–12) profession.

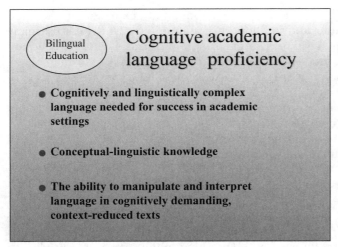

FIGURE 4.7.   Views of bilingual education profession.

profession. I say more about the very different voices in the conversation within the ESL K–12 profession in the second part of this chapter.

Finally, the bilingual education profession is the only group that has been concerned with the development of academic language in both English *and* the first language of arriving immigrant students. Nevertheless, this group of practitioners has focused almost exclusively on the development of what has been called *cognitive academic language proficiency* (CALP), which is considered to be fundamentally different from *basic interpersonal communication skills* (BICS). CALP, as illustrated in Fig. 4.7, was defined initially by Cummins (1979) as "conceptual-linguistic knowledge" and later (Cummins, 1984) as the ability to manipulate and interpret language in cognitively demanding, context-reduced texts. This conceptualization has met with much criticism by researchers (Edelsky et al., 1983; Hawson, 1996; Mac-Swan, 2000; Martin-Jones & Romaine, 1986). However, most practitioners who encountered BICS and CALP in their teacher preparation courses accepted it uncritically.[2] The view presented in Fig. 4.7, then, reflects the original conceptualization of CALP. I talk further about more current conceptualizations of academic language, including those proposed by Cummins himself.

My point in contrasting these different perspectives (which are in several cases only the most well-known, but not universally accepted, positions

---

[2] It is important to point out that a number of researchers carried out research that, to some degree, supported the BICS and CALP conceptualization. Saville-Troike (1984), for example, in a provocatively titled article, "What really matters in second language learning for academic achievement," reported on research carried out on English language acquisition by minority youngsters. She distinguished between the language acquired in social interactions and language measured by the *Comprehensive Test of Basic Skills* (CTBS) in English.

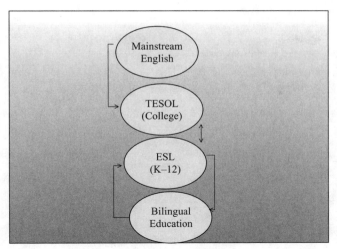

FIGURE 4.8. Dialogues between professions.

within the profession discussed) is to emphasize the multivoiced nature of the academic discussion surrounding academic language as well as the boundaries between speech communication spheres. The professional and academic sphere involved in the discussion of academic language that I have depicted in contrast to the public sphere in Fig. 4.1, rather than a single communication sphere is made up of, what I have called elsewhere (Valdés, 1992), distinct compartments that necessarily assume and imagine different addressees, different conversations, and different arguments and that result in various levels and degrees of dialogism among these similar but very diverse professional communities.

As is evident in Fig. 4.8, the various communities of professional practice may have little to do with one another. Experts in literacy and writing that are part of what I have called here the mainstream English profession, for example, although depicted here as a single profession, may miss many opportunities for dialogue with experts within the same field that work at different levels and with different age groups. In addition, moreover, mainstream English-teaching professionals may rarely interact with TESOL college specialists. ESL K–12 practitioners, however, may participate only as a small and peripheral segment of the bilingual education community but may view themselves as sharing many of the same concerns. Both groups may have little or no communication with the mainstream English profession.

RESEARCH COMMUNITIES

As is evident from Fig. 4.9, the problem of dialogism among the members of related but separate communities of professional practice that have approached the description of academic language becomes even more

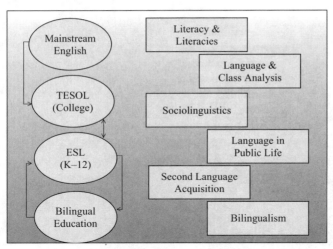

FIGURE 4.9. Research communities and communities of professional practice.

complex when one considers the various research perspectives that have informed their views and positions. Figure 4.9 lists several research perspectives that have directly influenced discussions of academic language in the various communities of professional practice. As is noted, these research communities themselves overlap in significant ways, and researchers that could be classified as working within one research area can often be placed in one or several other related fields. My point here is that in defining academic language, the various communities of professional practice, have looked to and been informed by different dialogues and different voices within the *research* segment of the scholarly domain, which have themselves been informed a variety of different disciplines, for example, anthropology, sociology, literary theory, or psychology.

The work in variationist sociolinguistics, for example, in its study of dialect (e.g., Labov, 1966, 1972) or in its study of register (Biber, 1994, 1995) have influenced the thinking of the mainstream English community not only in professional statements such as *Students' Right to Their Own Language* (Conference of College Composition and Communication, 1974), but also in its approach to the writing of students who do not speak standard English (e.g., Ball, 1998; Farr, 1993; Farr & Daniels, 1986; Lee, 1993). Work on world Englishes (e.g., Kachru, 1992; Pennycook, 1994, 1998), even though less influential in the ESL K–12 and in bilingual education, is increasingly being seen as important by practitioners and researchers working with college-level TESOL (e.g., Rodby, 1992) who argue strongly against single standards of British and American English in the teaching of second language learners.

Other sociolinguistic research, by comparison, has primarily influenced practitioners who work with young children. The work of Heath (1983), for example, has had lasting impact on the language arts and the bilingual education fields. Investigations of classroom interactions and classroom language conducted by Cazden (1988) and Mehan (1979) is also well known to practitioners in both areas. Bilingual educators have also been deeply influenced by the work of Phillips (1972) on the rules governing speech and silence in the classroom among Native American children. Similarly the work of Au and Jordan (1981) is frequently referred to by both mainstream early reading researchers and by bilingual educators. Other work on literacy development in young children, however, (e.g., Daiute, 1989; Dyson, 1989, 1993; Graves, 1983) is not well known by second language practitioners and researchers.

Work on literacy and literacies, including research in reading as well as in writing and composition has primarily been carried out within the mainstream English profession. Classic works, for example, on the oral and literate continuum (Chafe, 1984; Tannen, 1984a, 1984b), on process writing (Britton, 1972; Emig, 1971; Flower & Hayes, 1981), on teachers' responses to writing (Brannon & Knoblauch, 1982; Freedman, 1987; Freedman & Sperling, 1985), on writing and learning (Langer, 1986; Langer & Applebee, 1987), and on peer response groups (Gere, 1987) are sometimes cited by TESOL college researchers. However, few ESL K–12 researchers or researchers focusing on bilingual education refer to them. When this literature is reviewed by TESOL college researchers (e.g., Johns, 1990; Raimes, 1985, 1987; Santos, 1992; Silva, 1993), it is often to point out the difficulties of theory development in L2 writing and the lack of applicability of research findings in first language writing to the teaching of writing in a second language.

Little attention has also been given by the L2 communities to the extensive work that has been carried out on literacy as a social and cultural practice (Cope & Kalantzis, 2000; Delpit, 1988; Edelsky, 1991; Gee, 1990; Rose, 1989; Street, 1984; Walsh, 1991). The view that there are multiple literacies rather than a single literacy, and that these literacies depend on the context of the situation, the activity itself, the interactions between participants, and the knowledge and experiences that these various participants bring to these interactions, is distant from the view held by most L2 educators who still embrace a technochratic notion of literacy and emphasize the development of decontextualized skills. It is important to point out that there are a number of researchers who do work on both literacy and the education of linguistic minority children at the elementary school level (e.g., Bartolomé, 1994, 1998; Bartolomé & Balderrama, 2001; Diaz & Flores, 2001; Edelsky, 1986, 1991; Flores, 1990; Flores, Cousin & Diaz, 1991; Gutierrez, 1992, 1993, 1995; Gutierrez et al., 1999; Reyes, 1992, 2001). These individuals provide one of the few important and exciting links between L1 and L2 research.

The TESOL college research community has examined literacy practices from a somewhat different perspective, although it has not directly taken part in the dialogue on literacy as a sociocultural practice. Focusing on what is known as language and public life or language for special purposes (i.e., Swales, 1990), it has drawn on work in sociolinguistics, especially on the sets of features that characterize registers (Biber, 1994, 1995). It has also drawn on work that has examined the ways that language and discourse function in the construction of science, profession building, the shaping of scientific communities, the process of construction of scientific knowledge, and the role that scientists play in such endeavors (e.g., Gunnarsson, 1998; Gunnarson, Linnell, & Nordberg, 1997). This conceptualization, although similar to those presented by others (e.g., Gee, 1990), has been found useful by the TESOL college profession for examining how the development of proficiencies in academic language relate to socialization processes within particular professions, established traditions in expressing particular views of reality, and the ways in which relations to other related knowledge domains are conveyed.

The language and class analysis literature – including the work of Althusser (1969, 1971); Bernstein (1964, 1977); Bourdieu (1977, [1982] 1995, 1988); Bourdieu and Passeron (1977); Bowles and Gintis (1977); Giroux (1983); Gramsci (1971); and Persell (1977) – and what Pennycook (2001) recently referred to as the "critical applied linguistics literature" (e.g., Fairclough, 1989, 1992; Lankshear & McLaren, 1993; Pennycook, 1990, 1994, 1998, 2001; Tollefson, 1991, 1995) have recently begun to influence the discussion of academic language in both the mainstream and the TESOL college professions. However, they have had much less impact on the ESL K–12 and bilingual education fields. Within the mainstream English profession, these views have been especially influential for researchers concerned about cultural and linguistic diversity such as Guerra (1997) and Reyes (1992). Segments of TESOL college profession, particularly outside the United States (e.g., Canagarajah, 1999; Roberts, Davies, & Jupp, 1992; Wallace, 1992) have also been deeply influenced by this work. Within the U.S. TESOL profession, only a few researchers (e.g., Auerbach, 1989, 1993, 1995) have drawn attention to the fact that the teaching of language is an inherently political process. Similarly, only a few voices within the K–12 public education communities (e.g., Darder, 1991, 1993; Darder, Torres, & Gutierrez, 1997; Walsh, 1995) have called for a critical bilingual and bicultural pedagogy as a foundation for bilingual education.

Finally, as might be expected, with occasional exceptions, research on bilingualism (to include both societal and individual bilingualism) and second language acquisition has not directly influenced the mainstream English community. Research on second language acquisition and bilingualism has primarily informed conceptualizations of academic language within the TESOL college, the ESL K–12, and the bilingual education communities. The research on second language acquisition/learning that is best known to second language practitioners and teacher educators is primarily psycholinguistic in orientation and is often interpreted as emphasizing the acquisition of grammatical structures.

Similarly, the research on bilingualism that has been most influential in the teaching of second language learners is the work of psycholinguists and second language acquisition researchers such as Cummins (1973, 1976, 1977a, 1977b, 1978, 1979, 1981, 1984a, 1984b); Genesee (1988); Genesee, et al. (1978); Hakuta (1986); Hakuta and Diaz (1984); Hakuta, Ferdman, and Diaz (1986); Krashen (1985); Lambert (1955, 1966, 1969, 1972a, 1972b, 1977); Lambert, Havelka, and Gardner (1959); Larsen-Freeman and Long (1991); Long (1981, 1983); Peal and Lambert (1962); and Wong Fillmore (1982, 1985, 1991, 1992). Many of these scholars have examined the cognitive consequences of bilingualism. Interestingly, little attention has been given to the voices within the research community on bilingualism that argue against a monolingual bias and a monolingual norm (e.g., Cook, 1997; Grosjean, 1989; Mohanty & Perregaux, 1997; Romaine, 1995; Woolard, 1999) and that maintain that it makes little sense to compare children raised in bilingual communities with children raised in settings in which only one language is spoken.

In sum, positions about academic language in diverse learners that are held by the different professional communities have developed and evolved in communication with particular sets of voices that are a part of specific professional worlds. In Bakhtinian terms (Bakhtin, [1986] 1990, p. 91), utterances within each professional world "must be regarded primarily as a response to preceding utterances of the given sphere.... Each utterance refutes, affirms, supplements, and relies on the others, presupposes them to be known and somehow takes them into account." Unfortunately, existing boundaries between professional fields have not allowed related dialogues to become a part of ongoing conversations within particular communities. As a result, there has been little opportunity for refutation or affirmation of highly relevant utterances that take place in parallel but unconnected conversations. My focus in this section has been to suggest that, because there may be important consequences when highly relevant dialogues do not enter professional and scholarly conversations, it is critical for us to study not only what does enter into these conversations, but also what does not.

ACADEMIC LANGUAGE AND SECOND LANGUAGE LEARNERS: WHICH VOICES AND WHICH COMMUNICATION SPHERES?

As a result of the uneven intertextuality among the various voices engaged in the discussion of academic language, it should perhaps not surprise us that, like the blind men hoping to describe the elephant, each of the different communities of professional practice tends to see but a small part of the larger reality. The different existing perspectives about academic language and discourse bring into focus the complexities of the challenge

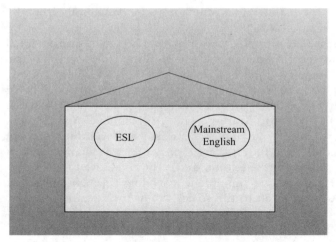

FIGURE 4.10. Professional communities in school settings.

involved in establishing objectives for the acquisition of academic English by minority second language learners. The examination of the various communications spheres allows us to see, perhaps, why it is that within school settings, it is difficult for educators who focus on L2 learners and for mainstream English professionals to work toward the same agreed-upon goals. As I attempt to illustrate here, there is no agreement about what each of the groups means by the terms *academic English, academic discourse, or academic language.* There is only assumed agreement and the expectation by mainstream English-teaching professionals that ESL practitioners can and will deliver second language learners who are "well prepared." As Fig. 4.10 illustrates, ESL practitioners and mainstream English-teaching professionals are in very separate worlds within the same schools.

Unfortunately, as I argue in this section, the results of the limited communication between professions and the emphasis on different elements of the academic language construct have serious consequences for young second language learners. To make matters even more complex, discussions about academic language and its definition *within* the ESL and bilingual professions are different for English Language Learners (ELLs) at different levels. At the elementary level, researchers are most directly concerned with identifying the number of years that it takes students to acquire the kind of language needed to achieve in school, that is, to do well on standarized tests. They argue that this question is especially important given the debates concerning the type of support that is needed by non–English-speaking students in the elementary grades. A great deal of attention, then, is given to "reclassification," that is, to the time that it takes for English language learners to be reclassified as fluent English speakers. As might be expected, definitions of academic language underlying assessment procedures used in the reclassification process are of particular concern.

In contrast, researchers working beyond the elementary school years, have become increasingly concerned about the opportunities available to middle school and high school ELLs. They argue (e.g., Valdés, 2000; Valdés & Geoffrion-Vinci, 1998) that in many high schools across the United States, second language students – whether reclassified or newly arrived – are locked into ESL ghettos from which they seldom exit. They are placed in a series of ESL classes throughout their 4 years of high school, as well as in sheltered subject-matter classes within which content is taught by adapting the English language and the mode of presentation in order the make the subject-matter content more accessible to language learners. As illustrated in Fig. 4.11, movement between regular and college prep classes and ESL/sheltered classes is generally limited. In some schools, however, it *is* possible for students to move out of, for example, sheltered general science and move into regular biology, or to move from sheltered algebra to regular geometry. What is particularly rare is for second language learners to move into regular, college-prep, mainstream English literature courses. In far too many schools, mainstream English teachers continue to insist that second language learners have not yet developed the kind of English that they need in order to do well in their classes. They worry about the errors ELLs make in written English, about their ability to read the texts they assign, and about their ability to engage in discussions about literature at the level that they require.

Once again, it is easy to place blame and to argue that mainstream English teachers want to pretend that the world is made up exclusively of

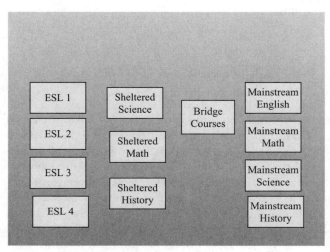

FIGURE 4.11. Enrollment options in high school.

English monolingual, native-speaking students. I am arguing, however, that what may be involved is the result of the very different understanding that ESL teachers and mainstream teachers have about academic English. The students who, from the perspective of the ESL teacher may have acquired academic English as this professional community has defined it, may nevertheless be very distant from the minimal level at which the mainstream teacher imagines her students must begin. The problem, then, may one of definition, one of belonging to distinct communication spheres and to attending to very different voices.

Unfortunately, until there is increased communication between mainstream teachers and ESL practitioners, there will be little progress. ESL practitioners will continue to define the objective of their instruction on their own terms and continue to blame mainstream teachers for rejecting the students that they have carefully prepared to be mainstreamed. There will continue to be two schools in one as administrators become increasing clever at making certain that second language learners are tracked into so-called, college-prep English courses designed especially for them and taught by not-quite-mainstream English teachers who are willing to work with them. Unfortunately, if these students manage at some point to move beyond high school, they will once again enter the ESL ghetto at the community college level where they will be placed into a long sequence of even more ESL classes, all of which are a prerequisite for entry into the credit-bearing composition course for basic writers. Once again, the problem is absent voices in the essential conversations of two professional fields. The highly relevant dialogues of the mainstream English-teaching profession take place in a different communication sphere. ESL practioners cannot respond to – that is, affirm, refute, presuppose or take into account – utterances that are part of a very different conversation.

THE FIRST STEP

Academic English, whether it is referred to as academic language or academic discourse, is central to the school achievement of all learners in the United States. The parallel unconnected conversations that have been carried out by the various professional communities, however, have emphasized different characteristics of the type of language that is needed to succeed in school. The first step in changing the current state of affairs is for communities of professional practice to learn about the work of other professional communities so that dialogues taking place in varied conversations can begin to be part of the same communication sphere. In the sections that follow, I outline the challenges of taking such a first step for individuals who are concerned about the education of English language learners and who are often members of the ESL and bilingual education communities. Including myself as a member of this community, I point out that we can benefit immensely from examining our now-expanding conceptualizations of academic language against existing definitions within the mainstream English profession. I argue, moreover, that in engaging in a dialogue with research perspectives that suggest that the type of academic language that really counts in academia is part of an identity kit that is acquired as a result of participating legitimately in the practices of the dominant, we begin to examine the ways in which language, social class, and dominance and power are related to the acquisition of particular ways of speaking. This examination, in turn, may cause us to seriously question whether "academic language" can be easily taught and learned.

Moving Beyond BICS and CALP

To our credit, there are many encouraging signs of movement in the second language teaching profession. Researchers and an increasing number of practitioners are moving beyond the early notions of BICS and CALP within which contextualized vs. decontextualized uses of language were considered to be fundamental. Even Cummins (2000), while still defending the appropriateness of the distinction, has to some degree moved away from describing academic language abstractly and now describes academic proficiency as "the extent to which an individual has access to and command of the oral and written academic registers of schooling" (p. 67). The new ESL Standards (TESOL, 1997), moreover, include precise descriptors and progress indicators that can help teachers evaluate students' progress toward the acquisition of the kind of English that will allow them to succeed in school. In the Standards document, for example, we are told that to achieve academically students will use English to follow oral and written directions both implicitly and explicitly, request and provide clarification, request information and assistance, explain actions, negotiate and manage interactions, and ask and answer questions. They will also use English to obtain, process, construct, and provide subject-matter information in written form. They will retell information, compare and contrast information, persuade, argue, and justify, analyze, synthesize, and infer from information. They will also hypothesize and predict, understand, and produce technical vocabulary and text features according to content area.

For other practitioners, the definition of academic language is much less elaborate. It is seen simply as subject-matter English, the kind that will automatically be acquired through content-based instruction. Whether programs involve immersion as in the Canadian model, two-way immersion, content-based ESL, or sheltered instruction, the sense is that in these contexts students will automatically acquire "academic language." For practitioners who take this view, academic language is simply the language used in biology, mathematics, and social studies. They consider the specificity of the Standards to be unnecessary, and they take the position that special attention need not be given to teaching students to hypothesize, predict, persuade, or attend to text features according to content area.

Still other voices in the profession, unfortunately, continue to attend to form and to follow the original conceptualization of CALP. The Linguistic Minority Research Institute Newsletter, which is widely distributed to both practitioners and researchers in California, reported on work carried out by Scarcella (2003) that defines academic English as a language that

- Makes more extensive use of reading and writing
- Makes more accurate use of grammar and vocabulary
- Is cognitively demanding and must be learned without contextual cues
- Requires a greater mastery and extensive range of linguistic features than ordinary English

As is noted, the notion of cognitive demands and the view that such language has few contextual cues are still prevalent in this definition. Many researchers, of course, reject this view. Bartolomé (1998), for example, argues that the dichotomy between decontextualized and contextualized discourse is false because, as Gee (1990) maintains, no discourse exists without context. She argues that the use of such terms hides the fact that what is really being discussed is the description of different varieties of language.

Bartolomé (1998) specifically criticizes the misteaching of academic discourse in a bilingual English/Spanish classroom and argues that students will only acquire this type of discourse if teachers create discourse events that require these students to "practice" by producing what she terms "linguistically contextualized language." Examining three opportunities for requiring such production from students – (1) oral vocabulary and definition lessons, (2) classroom presentations, and (3) individual writing – she maintains that these events must be structured so that students address real or imaginary distant audiences with whom they can assume little shared knowledge. Students' perception of the lack of shared knowledge, she maintains, will result in the need to "elaborate linguistic messages explicitly and precisely to minimize audience misinterpretation" (p. 66). In the case of the classroom in which she carried out her research, Bartolomé found that students did not see the need to produce clear and overtly explicit texts. She attributes students' behavior to the teacher's tendency of not insisting on formal language in the classroom and argues further that academic language will only be acquired if direct attention is given to its acquisition. It is important to note that Bartolomé's definition of academic discourse comes closer to the definitions used by mainstream English professionals in that it includes explicitness and the use of formal language.

The emphasis on direct attention or direct teaching of academic language has increasingly been directed at instruction on writing by Bartolomé and other researchers. It has become evident to a number of administrators and practitioners that many students could be reclassified as fluent

English speakers and mainstreamed if only they were able to write well enough to pass the writing portions of existing standardized language examinations. Sadly, it has also become evident that secondary ESL professionals have not been prepared to develop the writing proficiencies of second language learners. As traditional language teachers who are concerned especially about grammatical accuracy, when they attempt to teach writing, they tend to focus on controlled composition (Valdés, 1999, 2000; Valdés & Sanders, 1998) in order to control students' errors. In an attempt to move beyond such practices, some school districts are bringing in L2 writing experts to conduct to workshops in order to prepare teachers to work with ESL writers. Unfortunately, all too often such workshops focus primarily, if not exclusively, on organization and mechanics. Teachers are being encouraged to expect that the presence of topic sentences, body paragraphs, introductions, and conclusions, coupled with the absence of major mechanical and grammatical errors, equal good writing.

What is often missing entirely from discussions of the teaching of academic discourse to L2 learners in both high school and the upper grades is the notion that writing is about ideas, that presentations are about ideas, and that, when one engages in writing and speaking, one also engages in a dialogue with others. Unfortunately, all too often, second language pedagogy and so-called pedagogical support for second language learners does not take into account what we know about dialogue from the perspective of Bakhtinian theory. It does not consider that second language writers, as is the case for all other writers, want "to be heard, understood, responded to, and again to respond to the response" (Bahktin [1986] 1990, p. 127). For example, as compared with discussions about minority college writers (e.g., Severino, Guerra, & Butler, 1997), within discussions about L2 students in the secondary school, teacher response to student writing has not been problematized. Teachers have not been encouraged to enter into a dialogue with students as interested readers of their students' ideas. The reading and writing connections described in the recent volume *The Best for Our Children: Critical Perspectives on Literacy for Latino Students* (Reyes & Halcon, 2001) are seldom made by most teachers of L2 learners. The discussion of texts and students' relationship to texts – indeed their interaction in rich dialogues with the writers of many types of texts – is not part of the conversation in the majority of schools.

The position of both researchers and practitioners concerned about L2 students is understandable. The lack of academic success experienced by such youngsters, especially in the light of increased standardized testing is a national scandal. It is tempting to believe that if teachers can bring students to the point that they can learn *through English,* that is, that they can understand classroom explanations, participate in group discussions, read academic material, and produce written texts that are correctly structured and organized and free of mechanical errors, much will have been accomplished. I have no quarrel with this view. Getting students to such levels is indeed a major accomplishment.

I am also not arguing that students should not be taught the conventions of academic language. I am not even entering into the discussion of whether students should also be made aware of the nature of powerful discourses, or of their social locations in the broader world. What I am questioning is whether academic language can, in fact, be taught or learned effectively in the self-contained, hermetic universes of ELL classrooms. I am arguing that, in order for students to eventually engage as writers in what Guerra (1997, p. 252)calls "the arduous act of struggling with a clash of voices," the class-room must be opened to multiple texts and multiple voices. Students must be encouraged to see themselves as having something to say, as taking part in a dialogue with teachers, with students in their classroom, with students in their school, with members of their communities, and with other writers who have written about issues and questions that intrigue them. I maintain that students should not be encouraged to merely pretend to talk to distant audiences so that their teacher can correct their vocabulary and syntax. They should be made aware of other voices, of how they speak, how they write, of the ways they say and do not say what they mean, of the resources they use to gain attention, to persuade, and to explain, and then, they should be encouraged to respond. From the perspective of Bakhtinian theory, students should invited to see themselves as being active participants in a "social dialogue" and to see their writing as a "continuation" and "rejoinder to that same dialogue (Bakhtin [1981] 2002, p. 277).

Unfortunately, as is evident to those who work with linguistic minority students, that is, with both second language learners and speakers of non-standard varieties of the language, the increasing residential and academic segregation in which these students find themselves offers few possibilities for their participation in communication spheres where academic language is used naturally and comfortably by those who, as Gee (1992, p. 33)suggests, have acquired it by "enculturation (apprenticeship) into social practices through scaffolded and supported interactions with people who have already mastered the Discourse."

In the best of situations, L2 students will have teachers who are themselves speakers of academic varieties of English and who will use these varieties in numerous ways to model the use of such discourse. In a greater number of cases, however, such students will have either nonnative speakers of English as their teachers (whom Wong Fillmore [1992] characterizes as interlanguage speakers of English) or teachers who, while competent in academic varieties of English, must use the language in very constrained ways in order to "shelter" content instruction.[3] In the case of bilingual classrooms, it may also be the case that teachers have developed a very limited range of

---

[3] I am indebted for this insight to George Bunch who is an experienced ESL and social studies teacher and a doctoral student at Stanford University.

proficiencies in the heritage or minority language of the students. Spanish bilingual teachers, for example, are often second- and third-generation Mexican Americans who have themselves been schooled entirely in English and have not mastered the academic varieties of Spanish, or are second language learners of Spanish who may also have had few opportunities to hear academic Spanish outside of university literature classrooms. As I have pointed out elsewhere (Valdés & Geoffrion-Vinci, 1998), for Mexican American bilinguals, the class position of their families in Mexico as well as the diglossic nature of their communities may have provided little access to the higher-level registers of Spanish. To date, discussions about the acquisition of English by minority second language learners (except for the work of Wong Fillmore) have not seriously examined teachers' proficiency and ease in the target language or target discourse.[4]

Interestingly, in her critique of the misteaching of academic discourse, Bartolomé looks to the production of such language by the ELLs themselves as important linguistic input for the further development of their proficiency in academic discourse. Bartolomé appears to be relying on language that what would surely be a learnerese variety of academic discourse that, as is the case with other spoken interlanguage varieties (Wong Fillmore, 1992), would not provide students with nativelike models of standard academic language. In her prescription of good teaching of academic discourse, she does not emphasize the need for exposure to a large variety of oral and written texts or the modeling of the target discourse by a teacher who has him- or herself acquired this discourse. I would argue, moreover, that what is important from the perspective of Bahktinian theory is that teachers command a variety of speech genres as members of various larger communication spheres. They must see their jobs as helping to acquaint their students with the "authoritative utterances that set the tone – artistic, scientific, and journalistic works . . . which are cited, imitated and followed" (Bakhtin [1986] 1990, p. 88). They must understand that second language students need to be given an opportunity to shape and develop their speech experience in "continuous and constant interactions with others' individual utterances" (p. 89).

IMAGINING OTHER POSSIBILITIES

In examining the discussion taking place among L2 educators, it is clear that where we are now and what we are saying about academic language is the

---

[4] The recent work of Bartolomé (1998), however, because it focuses on the misteaching of academic discourse in bilingual classrooms, does discuss the language proficiency of the teacher with whom she worked. She states that the teacher (a second language speaker of Spanish) is highly proficient in this language as well as English, but, except for pointing out that the teacher has taught in Mexico, she offers no details supporting her high evaluation of the teacher's proficiency.

product of what we see in schools today and of our knowledge of the barriers facing minority students. I believe that what we need to do is to imagine other possibilities. Like Guerra (1997, p. 258), we too must envision language minority L2 writers who develop what he called "intercultural literacy," that is, "the ability to consciously and effectively move back and forth among as well as in and out of the discourse communities they belong to or will belong to." Even in middle school, we should want minority L2 writers to understand that they too have something to say. They may choose to say it only to their communities using the conventions appropriate for those communities, but they may also choose to say what is important to them to those who will only listen if the appropriate conventions are followed. We must find ways of giving them the resources and tools to use in multiple discourse communities and communication spheres, while helping them to value their own voices.

From my perspective, the first step in getting ourselves – that is, those of us who work in K–12 ESL and in bilingual education – to a point where we move beyond minimal possibilities for our students is to open the discussions about academic language and discourse to the voices of the mainstream English profession and to invite them to solve the problem with us. We must also engage in a broader dialogue with the voices of the research communities that can guide us beyond our sometimes narrow focus on the acquisition of grammar and lexis and contextualized and decontextualized language. Finally, we must continue to struggle to make accessible to our second language students the textual worlds that are now beyond their reach. They too must hear and respond to other voices and to be "filled with echoes and reverberations of other utterances" (Bakhtin, [1986] 1990, p. 91) that are part of, not just a few, but many spheres of speech communication.

References

Althusser, L. (1969). *For Marx*. New York: Vintage Books.

Althusser, L. (1971). Ideology and the ideological state apparatuses. In L. Althusser & B. T. Brewster (Eds.), *Lenin and philosophy, and other essays*. New York: Monthly Review Press.

Au, K. H., & Jordan, C. (1981). Teaching reading to Hawaiian children: Finding a culturally appropriate solution. In H. Trueba, G. Gutherie, & K. H. Au (Eds.), *Ethnographies of communication in multiethnic classrooms* (pp. 83–130). New York: Garland.

Auerbach, E. (1989). Toward a social-contextual approach to family literacy. *Harvard Educational Review, 59*(2), 165–81.

Auerbach, E. R. (1993). Reexamining English only in the ESL classroom. *TESOL Quarterly, 27*(1), 9–32.

Auerbach, E. R. (1995). The politics of the ESL classroom: Issues of power in pedagogical choices. In J. W. Tollefson (Ed.), *Power and inequality in language education* (pp. 9–33). Cambridge, UK: Cambridge University Press.

Bakhtin, M. M. ([1986] 1990). The problem of speech genres. In C. Emerson & M. Holquist (Eds.), *Speech genres & other late essays* (pp. 60–102). Austin: University of Texas Press.

Bakhtin, M. M. ([1981] 2002). Discourse in the novel. In M. Holquist (Ed.), *The dialogic imagination: Four essays by M. M. Bakhtin* (pp. 259–422). Austin: University of Texas Press.

Ball, A. F. (1998). Evaluating the writing of culturally and linguistically diverse students: The case of the African American English speaker. In C. R. Cooper & L. Odell (Eds.), *Evaluating writing* (pp. 225–48). Urbana, IL: National Council of Teachers of English.

Barron, D. (1990). *The English-only question*. New Haven, CT: Yale University Press.

Bartolomé, L. (1994). Beyond the methods fetish: Toward a humanizing pedagogy. *Harvard Educational Review, 64*(2), 173–94.

Bartolomé, L. (1998). *The misteaching of academic discourse: The politics in the language classroom*. Boulder, CO: Westview Press.

Bartolomé, L., & Balderrama, M. (2001). The need for educators with political and ideological clarity. In M. d. l. L. Reyes & J. Halcon (Eds.), *The best for our children: Critical perspectives on literacy for Latino students* (pp. 48–64). New York: Teachers College Press.

Baugh, J. (2000). *Beyond ebonics: Linguistic pride and racial prejudice*. New York: Oxford University Press.

Bernstein, B. (1964). "Elaborated and restricted codes: Their social origins and some consequences." In J. Gumperz & D. Hymes (Eds.), *The ethnography of communication*. Special Issue. *American Anthropologist, 66* (6 part 2), 55–69.

Bernstein, B. (1977). Social class, language and socialization. In J. Karabel & A. H. Halsey (Eds.), *Power and ideology in education* (pp. 473–87). New York: Oxford University Press.

Biber, D. (1994). An analytical framework for register studies. In D. Biber & E. Finegan (Eds.), *Sociolinguistic perspectives on register* (pp. 31–56). New York: Oxford University Press.

Biber, D. (1995). *Dimensions of register variation: A cross-linguistic comparison*. London: Cambridge University Press.

Bolinger, D. (1980). *Language: The loaded weapon*. London: Longman.

Bourdieu, P. (1977). *Outline of a theory of practice*. Cambridge, UK: Cambridge University Press.

Bourdieu, P. ([1982] 1995). *Language and symbolic power*. Cambridge, MA: Harvard University Press.

Bourdieu, P. (1988). *Homo academicus*. Stanford, CA: Stanford University Press.

Bourdieu, P., & Passeron, J. C. (1977). *Reproduction in education, society and culture*. Beverly Hills, CA: Sage.

Bowles, S., & Gintis, H. (1977). *Schooling in capitalist America*. New York: Basic Books.

Brannon, L., & Knoblauch, C. H. (1982). On students' rights to their own texts: A model of teacher response. *College Composition and Communication, 33*, 157–66.

Britton, J. (1972). *Language and learning*. Hardmondsworth, Middlesex, UK: Penguin.

Canagarajah, S. (1999). *Resisting linguistic imperialism in English teaching*. Oxford, UK: Oxford University Press.

Cazden, C. B. (1988). *Classroom discourse: The language of teaching and learning.* Portsmouth, NH: Heinemann.

Chafe, W. L. (1984). Integration and involvement in speaking, writing and oral literature. In D. Tannen (Ed.), *Spoken and written Language: Exploring orality and literacy* (pp. 35–53). Norwood, NJ: Ablex.

Conference on College Composition and Communication. (1974). Students' right to their own language. *College Composition and Communication, 25* (special issue), 1–32.

Cook, V. (1997). The consequences of bilingualism and cognitive processing. In A. M. B. de Groot & J. F. Kroll (Eds.), *Tutorials in bilingualism: Psycholinguistic perspectives* (pp. 279–99). Mahwah, NJ: Erlbaum.

Cope, B., & Kalantzis, M. (Eds.). (2000). *Multiliteracies.* London: Routledge.

Crawford, J. (1992). *Hold your tongue.* Reading, MA: Addison Wesley.

Cummins, J. (1973). A theoretical perspective on the relationship between bilingualism and thought. *Working Papers on Bilingualism, 1,* 1–9.

Cummins, J. (1976). The influence of bilingualism on cognitive growth: A synthesis of research findings and explanatory hypotheses. *Working Papers on Bilingualism, 9,* 1–43.

Cummins, J. (1977a). Cognitive factors associated with the attainment of intermediate levels of bilingual skill. *Modern Language Journal, 61,* 3–12.

Cummins, J. (1977b). *Metalinguistic development of children in bilingual education programs: Data from Irish and Canadian Ukranian-English programs.* Paper presented at the The Fourth Locus Forum, Columbia, SC.

Cummins, J. (1978). Bilingualism and the development of metalinguistic awareness. *Journal of Cross-Cultural Psychology, 9,* 139–49.

Cummins, J. (1979). Linguistic interdependence and the educational development of bilingual children. *Review of Educational Research, 49,* 222–51.

Cummins, J. (1981). The role of primary language development in promoting educational success for language minority students. In California State Department of Education, Office of Bilingual Bicultural Education (Ed.), *Schooling and language minority students: A theoretical framework.* Los Angeles: California State University, Evaluation Dissemination and Assessment Center.

Cummins, J. (1984a). *Bilingualism and special education: Issues in assessment and pedagogy.* San Diego: College Hill Press.

Cummins, J. (1984b). Wanted: A theoretical framework for relating language proficiency to academic achievement among bilingual students. In C. Rivera (Ed.), *Language proficiency and academic achievement* (p. 10). Clevedon, Avon, UK: Multilingual Matters.

Cummins, J. (2000). *Language, power and pedagogy.* Clevedon, Avon, UK: Multilingual Matters.

Daiute, C. (1989). Play as thought: Thinking strategies of young writers. *Harvard Educational Review, 59*(1), 1–23.

Daniels, H. A. (Ed.). (1990). *Not only English: Affirming America's multilingual heritage.* Urbana, IL: National Council of Teachers of English.

Darder, A. (Ed.). (1993). *Bicultural studies in education: The struggle for educational justice.* Claremont, CA: Institute for Education in Transformation, The Claremont Graduate School.

Darder, A. (1991). *Culture and power in the classroom: A critical foundation for bicultural education.* New York: Begin & Garvey.

Darder, A., Torres, R. D., & Gutierrez, H. (Eds.). (1997). *Latinos and education.* New York: Routledge.

Delpit, L. D. (1988). The silenced dialogue: Power and pedagogy in educating other people's children. *Harvard Educational Review, 58*(3), 280–98.

Diaz, E., & Flores, B. (2001). Teacher as sociocultural, sociohistorical mediator. In M. d. l. L. Reyes & J. J. Halcon (Eds.), *The best for our children: Critical perspectives on literacy for Latino students* (pp. 29–47). New York: Teachers College Press.

Duranti, A., & Goodwin, C. (Eds.). (1992). *Rethinking context: Language as an interactive phenomenon.* New York: Cambridge University Press.

Dyson, A. (1989). *Multiple worlds of child writers.* New York: Teachers College Press.

Dyson, A. (1993). *Social worlds of children learning to write in an urban primary school.* New York: Teachers College Press.

Edelsky, C. (1986). *Habia una vez: Writing in a bilingual program.* Norwood, NJ: Ablex.

Edelsky, C. (1991). *With literacy and justice for all: Rethinking the social in language and education.* London: Falmer Press.

Edelsky, C., Flores, B., Barkin, F., Altwerger, B., & Jilbert, K. (1983). Semilingualism and language deficit. *Applied Linguistics, 4*(1), 1–22.

Elbow, P. (1991). Reflections on academic discourse: How it relates to freshmen and colleagues. *College English, 55*(2), 135–55.

Elbow, P. (2000). *Everyone can write: Essays toward a hopeful theory of writing and teaching writing.* New York: Oxford University Press.

Emig, J. (1971). The composing process of 12th graders. Urbana, IL: National Council of the Teachers of English.

Fairclough, N. (1989). *Language and power.* London: Longman.

Fairclough, N. (Ed.). (1992). *Critical language awareness.* London: Longman.

Farr, M. (1993). Essayist literacy and other verbal performances. *Written Communication, 10*(1), 4–38.

Farr, M., & Daniels, H. (1986). *Language diversity and writing.* Urbana, IL: National Council of Teachers of English.

Flores, B. (1990). The sociopsychogenesis of literacy and biliteracy. *Proceedings of the first research symposium of the Office of Bilingual Education and Minority Language Affairs* (pp. 281–329). Washington, DC: U.S. Department of Education.

Flores, B., Cousin, P., & Diaz, E. (1991). Transforming deficit myths about language literacy, and culture. *Language Arts, 68*(5), 369–79.

Flower, L., & Hayes, J. R. (1981). A cognitive process theory of writing. *College Composition and Communication, 32,* 365–87.

Freedman, S. (1987). *Response to student writing.* Urbana, IL: National Council of Teachers of English.

Freedman, S., & Sperling, M. (1985). Teacher–student interaction in the writing conference: Response and teaching. In S. Freedman (Ed.), *The acquisition of written language: Revision and response* (pp. 106–30). Norwood, NJ: Ablex.

Gee, J. (1990). *Social linguistics and literacies: Ideology in discourses.* London: Falmer Press.

Gee, J. (1992). Socio-cultural approaches to literacy (literacies). *Annual Review of Applied Linguistics, 12,* 31–48.

Genesee, F. (1988). Neuropsychology and second language acquisition. In L. M. Beebe (Ed.), *Issues in second language acquisition: Multiple perspectives* (pp. 81–111). Rowley, MA: Newbury House.

Genesee, F., Hamers, J., Lambert, W., Mononen, L., Seitz, M., & Stark, R. (1978). Language processing in bilinguals. *Brain and Language, 5,* 1–12.

Gere, A. R. (1987). *Writing groups: History, theory and implications.* Carbondale: Southern Illinois University Press.

Giroux, H. A. (1983). Theories of reproduction and resistance in the new sociology of education: A critical analysis. *Harvard Educational Review, 53*(3), 257–93.

Gramsci, A. (1971). *Selections from prison notebooks.* New York: International Publishers.

Graves, D. (1983). *Writing: Teachers and children at work.* Portsmouth, NH: Heinemann.

Grosjean, F. (1989). Neurolinguists, beware! The bilingual is not two monolinguals in one person. *Brain and Language, 36,* 5–15.

Guerra, J. (1997). The place of intercultural literacy in the writing classroom. In C. Severino, J. C. Guerra, & J. E. Butler (Eds.), *Writing in multicultural settings* (pp. 248–60). New York: Modern Language Association.

Gunnarsson, B.-L. (1998). Academic discourse in changing context frames: The construction and development of a genre. In P. E. Allori (Ed.), *Academic discourse in Europe* (pp. 19–42). Roma: Bulzoni Editore.

Gunnarson, B.-L., Linell, P., & Nordberg, B. (1997). *The construction of professional discourse.* London: Longman.

Gutierrez, K. (1992). A comparison of instructional context ins writing process classrooms with Latino children. *Education and Urban Society, 24,* 224–62.

Gutierrez, K. (1993). How talk, context, and script shape contexts for learning: A cross-case comparison of journal sharing. *Linguistics and Education, 5,* 335–65.

Gutierrez, K. (1995). Unpackaging academic discourse. *Discourse Processes, 19,* 21–37.

Gutierrez, K., Baquedano-Lopez, P., & Tejada, C. (1999). Rethinking diversity: Hybridity and hybrid language practices in the Third Space. *Mind, Culture and Activity, 74*(5), 286–303.

Hakuta, K. (1986). *Mirror of language: The debate on bilingualism.* New York: Basic Books.

Hakuta, K., Ferdman, B. M., & Diaz, R. M. (1986). *Bilingualism and cognitive development: Three perspectives and methodological implications.* Los Angeles: University of California, Los Angeles, Center for Language Education and Research.

Hakuta, K., & Diaz, R. (1984). The relationship between bilingualism and cognitive ability: A critical discussion and some new longitudinal data. In K. E. Nelson (Ed.), *Children's language* (Vol. 5). Hillsdale, NJ: Erlbaum.

Hawson, A. (1996). A neuroscientific perspective on second-language learning and academic achievement. *Bilingual Review, 21*(2), 101–22.

Heath, S. B. (1983). *Ways with words: Language, life and communication in communities and classrooms.* Cambridge, UK: Cambridge University Press.

Johns, A. M. (1990). L1 composition theories: Implications for developing theories of L2 composition. In B. Kroll (Ed.), *Second language writing* (pp. 24–36). Cambridge, UK: Cambridge University Press.

Kachru, B. B. (1992). *The other tongue: English across cultures* (2nd ed.). Urbana: University of Illinois Press.

Kaplan, R. B. (1966). Cultural thought patterns in intercultural communication. *Language Learning, 16,* 1–20.

Kaplan, R. B. (1988). Contrastive rhetoric and second language learning: Notes toward a theory of contrastive rhetoric. In A. Purves (Ed.), *Writing across languages and cultures* (pp. 275–304). Newbury Park, CA: Sage.

Krashen, S. (1985). *The input hypothesis.* Oxford, UK: Pergammon.

Labov, W. (1966). *The social stratification of English in New York City.* Washington, DC: Center for Applied Linguistics.

Labov, W. (1972). *Language in the inner city: Studies in black English vernacular.* Philadelphia: University of Pennsylvania Press.

Lambert, W. E. (1955). Measurement of the linguistic dominance in bilinguals. *Journal of Abnormal and Social Psychology, 50,* 197–200.

Lambert, W. E. (1966). Word-association responses: Comparison of American and French monolinguals with Canadian monolinguals and bilinguals. *Journal of Personality and Social Psychology, 3,* 313–20.

Lambert, W. E. (1969). Psychological studies of interdependencies of the bilingual's two languages. In J. Puhvel (Ed.), *Substance and structure of language.* Los Angeles: University of California Press.

Lambert, W. E. (1972a). Language-acquisition contexts and bilingualism. In A. S. Dil (Ed.), *Language, psychology and culture.* Stanford, CA: Stanford University Press.

Lambert, W. E. (1972b). *Language, psychology, and culture: Essays by Wallace E. Lambert.* Stanford, CA: Stanford University Press.

Lambert, W. E. (1977). Effects of bilingualism on the individual. In P. A. Hornby (Ed.), *Psychological, social and educational implications.* New York: Academic Press.

Lambert, W. E., Havelka, J., & Gardner, R. C. (1959). Linguistic manifestations of bilingualism. *American Journal of Psychology, 72,* 77–82.

Langer, J. A. (1986). Learning through writing: Study skills in the content areas. *Journal of Reading, 29,* 400–6.

Langer, J. A., & Applebee, A. N. (1987). *How writing shapes thinking: A study of teaching and learning.* Urbana, IL: National Council of Teachers of English.

Lankshear, C., & McLaren, P. (Eds.). (1993). *Critical literacy: Politics, praxis and the postmodern.* Albany: State University of New York Press.

Larsen-Freeman, D., & Long, M. H. (1991). *An introduction to second language acquisition research.* London: Longman.

Lee, C. (1993). *Signifying as a scaffold for literacy interpretation: The pedagogical implications of an African American discourse genre.* Urbana, IL: National Council of Teachers of English.

Lippi-Green, R. (1994). Accent, standard language identity and discrimination pretext in the courts. *Language in Society, 23,* 163–98.

Lippi-Green, R. (1997). *English with an accent.* London: Routledge.

Long, M. (1981). Input, interaction and second language acquisition. In H. Winitz (Ed.), *Native language and foreign language acquisition. Annals of the New York Academy of Sciences, 379,* 279–278.

Long, M. (1983). Native speaker/non-native speaker conversation in the second language classroom. *Applied Linguistics, 4,* 126–41.

MacSwan, J. (2000). The threshold hypothesis, semilingualism, and other contributions to a deficit view of linguistic minorities. *Hispanic Journal of Behavioral Sciences, 22*(1), 3–45.

Martin-Jones, M., & Romaine, S. (1986). Semilingualism: A half-baked theory of communicative competence. *Applied Linguistics, 7*(1), 26–38.

Mehan, H. (1979). *Learning lessons.* Cambridge, MA: Harvard University Press.

Milroy, J. (1999). The consequences of standardization in descriptive linguistics. In T. Rex & R. Watts (Eds.), *Standard English: The widening debate* (pp. 16–39). London: Routledge.

Milroy, J., & Milroy, L. (1999). *Authority in language: Investigating standard English* (3rd ed.). London: Routledge.

Milroy, L. (1999). Standard English and language ideology in Britain and the United States. In T. Rex & R. Watts (Eds.), *Standard English: The widening debate* (pp. 173–206). London: Routledge.

Mohanty, A. K., & Perregaux, C. (1997). Language acquisition and bilingualism. In J. W. Berry, P. R. Dasen, & T. S. Saraswathi (Eds.), *Handbook of cross-cultural psychology: Basic processes and human development* (Vol. 2, pp. 217–53). Boston: Allyn and Bacon.

Moraes, M. (1996). *Bilingual education: A dialogue with the Bakhtin circle.* Albany: State University of New York Press.

Peal, E., & Lambert, W. (1962). The relation of bilingualism to intelligence. *Psychological Monographs, 76*(546), 1–23.

Pennycook, A. (1990). Towards a critical applied linguistics for the 1990s. *Issues in Applied Linguistics, 1,* 8–28.

Pennycook, A. (1994). *The cultural politics of English as an international language.* London: Longman.

Pennycook, A. (1998). *English and the discourses of colonialism.* London: Routledge.

Pennycook, A. (2001). *Critical applied linguistics: A critical introduction.* Mahwah, NJ: Erlbaum.

Persell, C. H. (1977). *Education and inequality: The roots and results of stratification in American's schools.* New York: The Free Press.

Phillips, S. (1972). Participant structures and communicative competence: Warm Springs children in community and classroom. In D. Hymes, C. Cazden, & V. John (Eds.), *Functions of language in the classroom* (pp. 370–94). New York: Teachers College Press.

Raimes, A. (1985). What unskilled ESL students do as they write: A classroom study of composing. *TESOL Quarterly, 19*(2), 229–58.

Raimes, A. (1987). Language proficiency, writing ability, and composing strategies: A study of ESL college writers. *Language Learning: A Journal of Applied Linguistics, 37*(3), 439–468.

Reyes, M. L. (1992). Challenging venerable assumptions: Literacy instruction for linguistically different students. *Harvard Educational Review, 62*(4), 427–46.

Reyes, M. L. (2001). Unleashing possibilities: Biliteracy in the primary grades. In M. L. Reyes & J. Halcon (Eds.), *The best for our children: Critical perspectives on literacy for Latino students* (pp. 96–121). New York: Teachers College Press.

Reyes, M. L., & Halcon, J. (Eds.). (2001). *The best for our children: Critical perspectives on literacy for Latino students.* New York: Teachers College Press.

Roberts, C., Davies, E., & Jupp, T. (1992). *Language and discrimination: A study of communication in multi-ethnic workplaces.* London: Longman.

Rodby, J. (1992). *Appropriating literacy.* Portsmouth, NH: Heinemann.

Romaine, S. (1995). *Bilingualism* (2nd ed.). Oxford, UK: Blackwell.

Rose, M. (1989). *Lives on the boundary.* New York: Penguin Books.

Santos, T. (1992). Ideology in composition: L1 and ESL. *Journal of Second Language Writing, 11*(1): 159–72.

Saville-Troike, M. (1984). What really matters in second language learning for academic achievement. *TESOL Quarterly, 18*(2), 199–219.

Scarcella, R. (2003). *Academic English: A conceptual framework.* Technical Report. Santa Barbara, CA: Linguistic Minority Research Institute.

Severino, C., Guerra, J. C., & Butler, J. E. (Eds.). (1997). *Writing in multicultural settings.* New York: Modern Language Association.

Silva, T. (1993). Toward an understanding of the distinct nature of L2 writing: The ESL research and its implications. *TESOL Quarterly, 27*(4), 657–75.

Street, B. V. (1984). *Literacy in theory and practice.* New York: Cambridge.

Swales, J. M. (1990). *Genre analysis: English in academic and research settings.* Cambridge, UK: Cambridge University Press.

Tannen, D. (Ed.). (1981). *Analyzing discourse: Text and talk.* Washington, DC: Georgetown University Press.

Tannen, D. (1984a). The oral-literate continuum in discourse. In D. Tannen (Ed.), *Spoken and written language: Exploring orality and literacy* (pp. 1–33). Norwood, NJ: Ablex.

Tannen, D. (1984b). *Spoken and written language: Exploring orality and literacy.* Norwood, NJ: Ablex.

Tannen, D. (1998). *The argument culture.* New York: Random House.

TESOL. (1997). *ESL standards for pre-K–12 students.* Alexandria, VA: TESOL, Inc.

Tollefson, J. W. (1991). *Planning language, planning inequality: Language policy in the community.* London: Longman.

Tollefson, J. W. (Ed.). (1995). *Power and inequality in language education.* Cambridge, UK: Cambridge University Press.

Valdés, G. (1992). Bilingual minorities and language issues in writing: Toward profession-wide responses to a new challenge. *Written Communication, 9*(1), 85–136.

Valdés, G. (1999). Incipient bilingualism and the development of English language writing abilities in the secondary school. In C. J. Faltis & P. M. Wolfe (Eds.), *So much to say: Adolescents, bilingualism and ESL in the secondary school* (pp. 138–75). New York: Teachers College Press.

Valdés, G. (2000). *Learning and not learning English: Latino students in American schools.* New York: Teachers College Press.

Valdés, G., & Geoffrion-Vinci, M. (1998). Chicano Spanish: The problem of the 'underdeveloped' code in bilingual repertoires. *Modern Language Journal, 82*(4), 473–501.

Valdés, G., & Sanders, P. A. (1998). Latino ESL students and the development of writing abilities. In C. R. Cooper & L. Odell (Eds.), *Evaluating writing* (pp. 249–78). Urbana, IL: National Council of Teachers of English.

Wallace, C. (1992). Critical literacy awareness in the EFL classroom. In N. Fairclough (Ed.), *Critical language awareness* (pp. 59–92). London: Longman.

Walsh, C. (Ed.). (1991). *Literacy as praxis: culture, language and pedagogy.* Norwood, NJ: Ablex.

Walsh, C. E. (1995). Critical reflections for teachers: Bilingual education and critical pedagogy. In J. Fredrickson (Ed.), *Reclaiming our voices: Bilingual education, critical pedagogy and praxis* (pp. 79–88). Ontario: California Association for Bilingual Education.

Walters, K. (1994). Writing and education. In H. Hunther (Ed.), *Schrift und Schriftlichkeit; Ein interdisziplinares Handbuch internationaler Forschung/Writing and its use: An interdisciplinary handbook of international research* (pp. 638–45). Berlin: Walter de Gruyter.

Wolfram, W., Adger, C. T., & Christian, D. (1999). *Dialects in schools and communities.* Mahwah, NJ: Erlbaum.

Wong Fillmore, L. (1982). Language minority students and school participation: What kind of English is needed? *Journal of Education, 164*(2), 143–56.

Wong Fillmore, L. (1985). When does teacher talks work as input. In S. Gass & C. Madden (Eds.), *Input in second language acquisition* (pp. 17–50). Rowley, MA: Newbury.

Wong Fillmore, L. (1991). Second language learning in children: A model of language learning in social context. In E. Bialystok (Ed.), *Language processing in bilingual children* (pp. 49–69). Cambridge, UK: Cambridge University Press.

Wong Fillmore, L. (1992). Learning a language from learners. In C. Kramsch & S. McConnell-Ginet (Eds.), *Text and context: Cross-disciplinary perspectives on language study* (pp. 46–66). Lexington, MA: D.C. Heath.

Woolard, K. A. (1999). Simultaneity and bivalency as strategies in bilingualism. *Journal of Linguistic Anthropology, 8*(1), 3–29.

Voices in Dialogue

Dialoguing About Dialogism: Form and Content in a Bakhtinian Dialogue

Allison Weisz Brettschneider

In his essay, *Discourse in the Novel*, Bakhtin claims that all kinds of discourse are "oriented toward an understanding that is 'responsive'" (Bakhtin, 1981, p. 280). This is one of his core ideas: that the meaning of any utterance, whether spoken or written, can only be understood in a particular context and "against the background of other concrete utterances on the same theme" (p. 281). Although he acknowledges the importance of studying external dialogue, or spoken exchanges between people, he also introduces the concept of "internal dialogism." Bakhtin explains that words are shaped by the answer their speaker anticipates, so they are in a constant internal dialogue with their imagined rejoinder. Words are also internally dialogic because they can never fully encompass the object to which they refer, so they are in constant dialogue with the "alien word that is already in the object" (p. 279). Finally, words are in constant internal dialogue with "the subjective belief system of the listener" (p. 282). They cannot create meaning without this context.

Early in our course on Bakhtin, I came to recognize the presence of these forms of dialogism in spoken and written language, and I began to wonder how forms of academic writing might better capture or acknowledge them. I was excited to participate in e-mail exchanges with the authors in this section because the form of these exchanges seemed to reflect the content of Bakhtin's ideas so well. Rather than reading a collection of published essays and dialoguing with myself about them, I could read drafts and engage in multiple levels of dialogue with and about them – internal dialogue with my own belief system as I first read them on my own, oral dialogue with classmates and professors who each came to them with backgrounds and understandings different from my own, and written dialogue with their authors, based on the issues raised in these classroom conversations. This multilayered dialogue seemed especially authentic to me because the authors' "final word" on the issues we discussed was not yet on the printed page. As a result, our e-mail exchanges reflected another aspect of internal dialogism: the struggle against "alien words" in an object, that is, the attempt to find words that truly encompass the meaning the speaker intends. Through private reading, class discussions, and e-mail exchanges, we seemed to be engaged in a series of dialogues that, through their varied forms, laid bare the dialogic nature of language.

DIALOGUES IN ACTION

In Chapter 1, Sarah Freedman and Arnetha Ball share accounts of opportunities they have had to watch and learn from effective communication as it occurs. They also tell of their efforts to understand how effective communication leads to the development of language, literacy, and learning in diverse and sometimes global new contexts. In seeking this understanding, they have found the theories of Mikhail Bakhtin, and particularly his concept of "ideological becoming," very helpful. This and other Bakhtinian concepts were the central focus of a course designed to incorporate the voices of graduate students in dialogues with a number of the chapter authors who have contributed to this volume concerning the authoritative words of the academy and their own evolving internally persuasive discourses. These discussions pushed us to move beyond the comfortable topics we so often embrace to consider some of the more difficult challenges facing education today.

Our dialogues about Charles Bazerman's chapter, Chapter 3, touched on a number of issues related to authorship and agency. Because of my continuing interest in the relationship between form and content in academic writing, I asked him about the shift in the chapter from a theoretical discussion of intertextuality to a personal story about the evolution of his research on intertextuality. His responses showed that this decision was linked to a central argument of the chapter: that the dissolution of authorship is not a natural consequence of intertextuality, as Kristeva's work suggests. In choosing to structure the chapter as he did, Bazerman was foregrounding his own subjectivity and agency as an author. As an alternative to Kristeva's vision, Bazerman suggested the following conception of authorial agency in an e-mail message: "I see us as acting within circumstances, though the circumstances are not of our own making. Authors are not dissolved, although they may be orchestrating complex resources that have origins outside of themselves, but that have met within them and their purposes" (Charles Bazerman, personal communication, March 5, 2002).

Our exchanges about Bazerman's chapter also dealt with an issue closely connected to Ball and Freedman's discussion of ideological becoming. Midway through his chapter, Bazerman distinguishes between Volosinov and Vygotsky's view of dialogism as "a fact of social development" and Bakhtin's view of it as "a moral imperative" (Chapter 3, this volume). We were interested in Bazerman's decision to focus mainly on Volosinov and Vygotsky in framing his discussion of intertextuality, so we asked him to say more about how or if Bakhtin's view might also have impacted his notions about intertextuality. Bazerman rewarded our class with a fascinating explanation of how his own thoughts about the importance of "paying attention to the voice of the other" (Charles Bazerman, personal communication, February 24, 2002) have evolved over time. He concluded that, as a teacher of writing, he had difficulty adopting the view he attritubes to Buber and Bakhtin, that one should listen to diverse voices because of a kind of "golden rule of ethical fairness" (Charles Bazerman, personal communication, March 5, 2002). Instead, he focused on the benefits that both students of writing and people in general could gain from such listening: "As one realizes the importance and variety of the words of others, there is a consequent awakening to the importance of taking those words seriously and attempting to understand them. One comes to see their value more deeply, even if you remain apart from them" (Charles Bazerman, personal communication, February 24, 2002). Thus, Bazerman concluded, dialogism that arises, as it does for Volosinov and Vygotsky, "from an understanding of human development, growth, life" (Charles Bazerman, personal communication, March 5, 2002) is most effective in shaping meaningful encounters with others in the world.

Our dialogues about Mark Dressman's chapter, Chapter 2, focused on the nexus between Bakhtinian theory and pedagogy. We were fascinated by the alternative pedagogical map he constructed with help from Dewey and Bakhtin, but as teachers ourselves we wondered how well this map might be used to teach popular texts, as Dressman suggests. Pointing out that one such text, the Harry Potter book, is "little more than a quilt of images and scenes appropriated from other books" (Mark Dressman, personal communication, February 27, 2002), Dressman wrote that the Harry Potter series would be ideal material for a Bakhtinian analysis. However, he acknowledged that many popular texts lack the multiple layers of language that make *Huckleberry Finn* such a rich work to teach:

You're absolutely right, I think, about the lack of linguistic complexity in Sweet Valley High and other books of that sort, and that's the reason, frankly, that I might not want to teach them in a classroom. From an academic/cultural studies point of view, pulp fiction like Sweet Valley High is enormously attractive because such works teem with ideological significance. I guess that an argument could be made that this is precisely why they should be taught – to expose to young readers how such books prey on them in terms of their consumerism, images of female attractiveness, relations with males, etc. But what's fascinating to you and me could be terribly dry to kids. (Mark Dressman, personal communication, March 10, 2002)

In this discussion about pulp fiction like Sweet Valley High, Dressman suggests some ways he might try to engage students in exploring these ideological issues, but admits that it would be "hard work" because these texts lack the linguistic complexity and multiple layers of language that make *Huckleberry Finn* such a rich work to teach.

In keeping with our focus on pedagogy and theory, we also asked Dressman whether he believed Bakhtin's emphasis on dialogism might have led him to sacrifice any important aspects of literary analysis, such as the New Critics' approach to close reading. He suggested that Bakhtin would see the value of the New Critics' message that interpretations must be grounded in the text, but explained that for Bakhtin, "the text is something a lot more inclusive than what's on the page" (Mark Dressman, personal communication, February 27, 2002). He also proposed an alternative to the New Critics' conception of the teacher as "master reader." In his view, a teacher who sought to involve his or her students in Bakhtinian analysis of texts should act as a "master conversationalist," enagaging students in ideas while modeling "real listening as well as speaking" (Mark Dressman, personal communication, February 27, 2002). In Chapter 4, Guadalupe Valdés takes this notion one step further when she says,

I believe that what we need to do is to imagine other possibilities. Like Guerra (1997, p. 258), we too must envision language minority L2 writers who develop what he called "intercultural literacy," that is, "the ability to consciously and effectively move back and forth among as well as in and out of the discourse communities they belong to or will belong to." . . . We must find ways of giving them the resources and tools to use in multiple discourse communities and communication spheres while helping them to value their own voices. . . . They too must hear and respond to other voices and to be "filled with echoes and reverberations of other utterances" (Bakhtin, 1986 [1990], p. 91) that are part of, not just a few, but many spheres of speech communication.

DIALOGUES AND IDEOLOGICAL BECOMING

In Chapter 1, Sarah Freedman and Arnetha Ball discuss Bakhtin's concepts of ideological becoming and internally persuasive discourse. Two of their quotations from Bakhtin's (1935) *Discourse in the Novel* are worth revisiting here:

The ideological becoming of a human being . . . is the process of selectively assimilating the words of others. (p. 341)

Internally persuasive discourse – as opposed to one that is externally authoritarian – is, as it is affirmed through assimilation, tightly interwoven with "one's own word." In the everyday rounds of our consciousness, the internally persuasive word is half ours and half-someone else's. Its creativity and productiveness consists precisely in the fact that such a word awakens new and independent words, that it organizes masses of our words from within, and does not remain in an isolated and static condition. It is not so much interpreted by us as it is further, that is, freely, developed, applied to new material, new conditions; it enters into interanimating relationships with new contexts. (p. 346)

In many ways, the process of engaging in dialogues about the chapters in this section was a means of lifting the words of the authors – and of Bakhtin – off of the page and into the living discourses of all the participants. For those of us who were new to Bakhtin, it helped to make his language – often inscrutable at first glance – become more "internally persuasive" so that we could develop and apply it in meaningful ways. As we reflected on the authors' reactions to and uses of Bakhtin's ideas, we were involved in our own processes of "ideological becoming," determining for ourselves which of Bakhtin's concepts – and which of the authors' concepts – were most helpful to us in generating new ideas about reading, writing, and teaching.

Woven through all these chapters is the core Bakhtinian concept of dialogism. Ball and Freedman discuss how the creation of dialogic classrooms can facilitate the ideological becoming of students and teachers. Bazerman explains how intertextuality – an outgrowth of Bakhtin's and Volosinov's notions of dialogism – can be can used by readers and writers to improve their practice and strengthen their agency. Dressman builds a new map for literature pedagogy by joining Dewey's ideas about aesthetic transactional experience to Bakhtin's model of reading as a dialogic process. Valdés explores the academic dialogue around how English language learners acquire academic language. She also considers the importance of the dialogues available to English language learners. Such dialogues provide a view of their opportunities to learn. It is clear that dialogism, in its many permutations, is an internally persuasive concept for all the contributors to this section. If the content of these chapters were not enough to demonstrate the generativity of this concept, the form of our interactions with the chapters showed the participants in this process the power of dialogism first hand. After participating in dialogues about dialogism and the many related topics raised in these chapters, we can now engage in more meaningful interactions with Bakhtin's texts and with the work of those who draw on his ideas.

References

Bakhtin, M. M. (1981). Discourse in the Novel. In *The Dialogic Imagination*. Ed. by Michael Holquist, Trans. by Caryl Emerson and Michael Holquist. Austin: University of Texas Press.

Bakhtin, M. M. ([1986] 1990). The problem of speech genres. In C. Emerson & M. Holquist (Eds.), *Speech genres & other late essays* (pp. 60–102). Austin: University of Texas Press.

PART II

VOICED, DOUBLE VOICED, AND MULTIVOICED DISCOURSES IN OUR SCHOOLS

5

Performance as the Foundation for a Secondary School Literacy Program

A Bakhtinian Perspective

Eileen Landay

> Nothing is so practical as a good theory.
>
> – James Britton

The theories of M. M. Bakhtin, philosopher of language, literary critic, and social theorist, have had wide influence in and beyond the academy. Writing in Russia in the years between 1920 and 1960, the period of the Russian Revolution and the rise of the Soviet state, and deeply influenced by those events, Bakhtin's project was to explore and challenge the formalist theories developed by the linguists and literary critics like Saussure and Jakobson. Language, Bakhtin argued, is never a fixed and closed system. Instead, it is a living, ever-changing entity, "social throughout its entire range and in each and every of its factors, from the sound image to the furthest reaches of abstract meaning" (Bakhtin, 1981, p. 259).

If Bakhtin's formulations are useful – and the extent to which they have been taken up and explored in the West since the 1980s suggests they are – there are relevant questions to be addressed: how do these formulations apply in settings whose explicit purpose is to support students' language and literacy development (i.e., schools)? To what extent do school settings promote learning through social interaction? What sorts of social interaction take place in those settings? How can we use Bakhtin's insights to provide a richer, more equitable environment for literacy teaching and learning?

I use these questions, and Bakhtin's (1981) framework, specifically that part of it laid out in "Discourse in the Novel", and the work of several other theorists, including Lave and Wenger (1991), to explore key elements of a specific secondary school literacy program, the ArtsLiteracy Project (ALP), begun in 1997, and currently under development at Brown University. The ALP combines work in literacy and the performing arts for secondary school students at all levels of literacy proficiency, and incorporates both a professional development program for teachers and professional actors and model curriculum for adaptation in secondary school classrooms.[1]

The first section of this chapter provides a summary of four core concepts in Bakhtin's work: *heteroglossia, dialogism, social languages,* and *authoritative discourse/internally persuasive discourse.* The second looks at classroom applications of these concepts. The third offers an overview of a specific literacy project, the ALP, examining it from a Bakhtinian perspective. The fourth suggests a summary set of characteristics for language/literacy learning in classrooms, and discusses issues of implementing and assessing a program like ALP in schools.

A word about terminology: as numerous critics have noted, Bakhtin's work is, in Holquist's words, a "baggy monster" (Holquist, 1981a, p. xviii), often critiqued for lacking systemization. Although this imprecision adds a literary richness to the text and encourages repeated re-readings, it also adds difficulty to using terminology with accuracy. So, for example, there are overlaps in the way Bakhtin uses terms like *word, utterance, discourse, language, voice,* and *social language.* Those who have followed after him have attempted to clarify and systematize. Holquist provides a glossary that addresses each of these terms, and others (cf. Gee, 1992, 1996) have continued to unpack and clarify. In the section below, I briefly gloss these four key concepts.

BAKHTIN: FOUR KEY CONCEPTS

As described above, Bakhtin's work focuses on the social nature of language. Alive and always active, language moves in multiple directions simultaneously: in perpetual tension between centripetal and centrifugal forces – the tendency to unify, centralize, fix, formalize, privilege, and create norms – and the tendency to invent, innovate, vary, expand, and specialize. Bakhtin terms the locus of those forces heteroglossia. The meaning of any utterance is never fixed, but differs in rich and complex ways according to the context and conditions within which it is used. "Every concrete utterance of a speaking subject serves as a point where centrifugal as well as centripetal forces are brought to bear" (Bakhtin, 1981, p. 272).

Further, all aspects of language are dialogic. True to his belief in the fusion of language and the social world, Bakhtin (1981) uses both utterances and individual speaking subjects as his units of analysis. Utterances, in his famous phrase "are populated – even overpopulated with the intentions of others" (p. 294). They contain within them multiple possible meanings that "speak" to one another, create linguistic richness and depth as well as tension and conflict. Traces of past dialogues are embedded in every utterance an individual has at his or her disposal.

---

[1]   For a full description of the project, see www.artslit.org.

Dialogism is also central to all interactions between speaking subjects. Every utterance a person speaks is oriented toward an anticipated response. Individuals frame what they say by a foreknowledge of who will hear it, what they imagine listeners are thinking and might reply. Thus, dialogism is embedded in all meaning; and constant interactions between meanings affect and shape a single instantiation of meaning in a given utterance or word.

Individual persons participate in numerous social languages, which consist of "social dialects, characteristic group behavior, professional jargon, generic languages, languages of generations and age groups, tendentious languages, languages of the authorities, of various circles and passing fashions, languages that serve the specific sociopolitical purposes of the day, even of the hour (each day has its own slogan, its own vocabulary, its own emphases)" (Bakhtin, 1981, pp. 262–3).

These social languages are deeply embedded in the context and consciousness of individuals and groups:

In any given historical moment of verbal-ideological life, each generation at each social level has its own language; moreover, every age group has as a matter of fact its own language, its own vocabulary, its own particular accentual system that, in their turn vary depending on social level, academic institution (the language of the cadet, the high school student, the trade school student are all different languages) and other stratifying factors. (Bakhtin, 1981, p. 290)

One cannot simply adopt the words and utterances of a given social language because each is – to repeat the classic phrase – "populated – overpopulated with the intentions of others. Expropriating (a social language), forcing it to submit to one's own intentions and accents, is a difficult and complicated process" (Bakhtin, 1981, p. 294). Any given individual speaks in multiple languages, many of which are in conflict with one another, and among which, at every given moment, a person must choose.

On issue of power relations, Bakhtin (1981) distinguishes between major categories of social language. Authoritative discourse is the discourse of tradition, generally acknowledge truths, the official line, the voice of authority. Internally persuasive discourse is the discourse of our personal beliefs, the ideas that move us, that shape us and create the stories we tell ourselves about the world and who we are. Bakhtin spends a considerable portion of his essay exploring the definitions of and the interplay between authoritative and internally persuasive discourse. First, he points out that there are not one but many authoritative discourses. These are the unitary languages, or system of linguistic norms that "work toward a concrete verbal and ideological unification and centralization" (Bakhtin, 1981, p. 271).

However, as he takes pains to point out, these are not fixed and real but "always in essence posited ... guaranteeing a certain maximum of mutual understanding and crystalizing into the real although still relative ... unity of the reigning conversation" (Bakhtin, 1981, p. 270). These authoritative discourses – like all discourses – "are specific points of view on the world, forms for conceptualizing the world in words, specific world views, each characterized by its own objects, meanings and values" (pp. 291–2). Discourses are never neutral. Instead,

(l)anguage has been completely taken over, shot through with intentions and accents. . . . All words have the "taste" of a profession, a genre, a tendency, a party, a particular work, a particular person, a generation, an age group, the day and hour. Each word tastes of life; all words and forms are populated by intentions. (p. 293)

These concepts, heteroglossia, dialogism, social languages, and authoritative discourse/internally persuasive discourse represent important features of Bakhtin's theory of language, and provide a powerful lens for analyzing environments, programs, and organizational structures for language teaching and learning.

FOUR KEY CONCEPTS: CLASSROOM APPLICATIONS

As educators in the United States try to make good on a national commitment to support the learning of *all* students, and as the backgrounds of our nation's students grows increasingly diverse, Bakhtin's theories become more and more relevant, providing a useful foundation on which to design and measure teaching and learning environments. If, as Bakhtin argues, heteroglossia (in the original Russian, literally "different speech-ness") is the fundamental condition within which meaning is constructed, then classrooms where didactic instruction is the norm and the teacher the primary speaker are not likely to be effective instructional environments, particularly for those whose background, perspective, and knowledge base differ substantively from the speaker's.

Not merely on command or by rote can or will students appropriate a discourse. It cannot be transmitted from one person to another unaltered like a product sent unchanged from one end of a pipeline to another (Reddy, 1993). Instead, as the concept heteroglossia reminds us, every utterance is embedded in a particular set of social circumstances, shaped by the particular context in which it occurs, and therefore, most clearly understood only by those who most completely share the speaker's understanding of the circumstances and contexts. As Bakhtin (1981) notes,

language is not a neutral medium that passes freely and easily into the private property of the speakers' intentions. . . . Language, for the individual consciousness, lies on the borderline between oneself and the other. . . . It becomes "one's own" only when the speaker populates it with his own intention, his own accent, when he appropriates the word, adapting it to his own semantic and expressive intention. Prior to this moment of appropriation, the word does not exist in a neutral and impersonal language . . . , but rather it exists in other people's mouths, in other people's contexts, serving other people's intentions: it is from there that one must take the word, and make it one's own. (p. 294)

Even this formulation of appropriating language from others through use is complicated by the fact that each individual speaking subject is not the site of one unitary language but rather of multiple competing languages. Embedded in the consciousness of us all are multiple languages, each reflecting a different aspect of our lives. Within one consciousness, these languages are not necessarily compatible and harmonious, but often at odds and in conflict.

How, then, as the locus of numerous competing languages, is an individual identity formed? Bakhtin (1981) argues it happens when these discourses come into dialogic relationship with one another or what he terms "critical interanimation" (p. 296). As we speak, we continually transmit and interpret the words of others, sometimes repeating them directly, sometimes reporting and commenting on them:

In the everyday speech of any person living in society, no less than half (on the average) of all the words uttered by him will be someone else's words (consciously someone else's), transmitted with varying degrees of precision and ... partiality. (p. 339)

In choosing the utterances we want to appropriate and precisely what meaning we want to attribute to them, we choose the stance we want to take. It is in the choices one makes toward these discourses that ones' identity is formed. "The ideological becoming of a human being ... is the process of selectively assimilating the words of others" (p. 341).

Applied to educational settings, then, heteroglossia suggests that in a productive language-learning environment, the learner is subject to a rich and varied range of utterances and is encouraged to participate in the discourse. In this setting, the speaking subject both absorbs and works with language, putting it to use, then interrogating it through interpretation, analysis, reflection, and revision.

Literacy activities promote dialogism, both internal – within one individual consciousness – and external – between two or more speaking subjects (Holquist, 1981b). Writing can serve as a form of dialogism between an earlier and later self. Many writers describe the experience of coming upon a piece of their own writing and wondering over its strangeness, its sense of having being composed by someone other than themselves, in which the ideas seem vaguely familiar, but at the same time distant and external to their reality. A dialogue with those distant texts or with texts closer to one's present self can be a powerful component of ideological becoming. E. M. Forster said it famously: How can I know what I think until I see what I say? But perhaps this aphorism misleads by assuming a preexisting self that is uncovered by writing. It can be much more: it can be an act in which the self is formed. Joseph Harris, cited in Lensmire (2000, p. 62), notes, "Writing is not simply a tool we use to express a self we already have; it is a means by which we form a self to express."

Reading – especially fiction and the biographical forms – promotes several sorts of dialogues: within one's self, between the self and the author, and when the text is shared, between readers. In *The Call of Stories: Teaching and the Moral Imagination,* Coles (1989) describes how a reader's moral imagination is formed through exemplars provided in stories. In *You Gotta Be the Book,* Wilhelm (1997) identifies the differences between readers who can and those who cannot – to return to Bakhtin's phrase – critically interanimate the contents of text with the concrete experiences of their own lives; he then turns this knowledge into a method of instruction that uses drama and visual art to animate texts.

Many recent instructional approaches are designed to promote dialogism. The idea of classrooms as reading/writing workshops, for example, was popularized by Atwell (1998), Calkins (1986), and Graves (1983), in primary, elementary, and middle schools, and later in secondary schools first as an approach to writing instruction, and applied more recently across the grades as reading pedagogy. In workshops, students are asked to replicate the processes and apply the strategies of those who read and write because it is central to their personal and professional identity. As it applies to writing, this instructional model generally has a three-part structure: brief direct teacher presentations in the form of modeling or minilessons, extended opportunities for students to initiate and practice literacy activities, and a time for sharing their work among peers followed by some form of publication. Ideally, students write for real audiences and real purposes.

Students engage in internal dialogues when they keep journals, revise their own writing, develop and maintain portfolios, and ultimately return to and reflect on and gloss these written records through subsequent written responses. Dialogue among people in classrooms takes place in the many current approaches to collaborative learning and groupwork (Cohen, 1986; among many others); in structured discussions such as Socratic or Paideia seminars (City, 2000); book clubs (McMahon & Raphael, 1997); literature circles (Daniels, 1994); or debate programs (Ericson, Murphy, & Zeuschner, 1987). Reading strategies suggest students *question the author, mark up* and *talk back* to the text, and work with a wide range of graphic organizers (Allen, 2000; Blachowicz & Ogle, 2001; Harvey & Goudvis, 2000).

This work takes place in the tradition of what Willinsky (1990) and others have called New Literacy studies. The central goals of these practices are to afford students the chance to participate actively rather than being passive recipients of an information delivery system; to create environments where they have increased choice and control over their work; to give teachers methods for honoring and supporting students' intentions; to make the work personally meaningful; to provide increased interactions among students; and to minimize the existing hierarchy of power. In this mode, "everything *means* (emphasis mine), is understood as a part of a greater whole – there is a constant interactions between meanings, all of which have the potential of conditioning others. . . . Which (meaning) will affect the other, how it will do so and in what degree is what is actually settled at the moment of utterance. A word, discourse, language or culture undergoes 'dialogization' when it becomes relativized, deprivileged, aware of competing definitions for the same thing. Undialogized language is authoritative or absolute" (Holquist, 1981b, p. 426–7).

How, when, and under what circumstances adolescents willingly enter into and wholeheartedly engage with the work of dialogization is an important issue for educators. As numerous writers and researchers (Delpit, 1995; Heath, 1983; Kohl, 1994; to name just a few) remind us, many adolescents enter secondary school literacy classrooms knowing they are in a world where an alien language is being spoken, a language that is not their own.

For adolescents, engaged as they are in identity development, this may be dangerous territory, particularly for those whose forming identities are at odds with the norms of mainstream society. A deep gulf often exists between the authoritative discourse of the schoolroom and the discourses Bakhtin identifies as internally persuasive. Authoritative discourses or what Delpit (1995), Gee (1992, 1996), and others have termed *the languages of power* encode *cultural capital* (Bordieu & Passeron, 1977). Internally persuasive discourses, on the other hand, are often "denied all privilege, backed up by no authority at all, and frequently not even acknowledged in society . . . not even in the legal code" (Bakhtin, 1981, p. 342).

This distinction becomes important in thinking about literacy development among youth, given that they are one of the primary social groups within our society that create what Bakhtin refers to as the "language of the hour." Adolescents constantly coin new terms that characterize and define youth culture, and set it at odds with authoritative discourses. To students for whom school has not been a friendly place and in which they have not been deemed proficient or successful, the discourses they have found internally persuasive, and the identity they have crafted with and around those discourses, are not those privileged in schools (Cook-Gumperz, 1986; Gilmore, 1987; Heath, 1983; Michaels, 1981).

Other students appropriate the authoritative discourse, but only in the most superficial ways. These students read and write correctly, and complete tasks dutifully, but without being genuinely engaged either with the ideas or the process. These same students often find ways to passively resist efforts to draw them into more substantive engagement with the work.

Gee (1996) writes persuasively about the extent to which language and literacy are social practices, closely tied to one's identity. *Discourses* in Gee's formation are ways of displaying through words, actions, values, and beliefs, one's membership in a particular social group or social network. A Discourse (always capitalized by Gee to differentiate this meaning of the term from many possible others) is a sort of identity kit that comes complete with the appropriate costume and instructions on how to act, talk, and often write, so as to take on a particular social role that others will recognize. Discourses are ways of being in the world, or forms of life that integrate words, acts, values, beliefs, attitudes, and social identities, as well as gestures, glances, body positions, and clothes. Not everyone is comfortable enough with the dominant discourse, confident or willing to participate, to commit wholeheartedly to serious learning even in a classroom that uses workshop methods.

Not all words for just anyone submit easily to this appropriation, to this seizure and transformation into private property; many words stubbornly resist, others remain alien, sound foreign in the mouth of the one who appropriated them and who now speaks them; they cannot be assimilated into his context. (Bakhtin, 1981, p. 294)

Many activities in the most progressive classrooms are based on the idea that reading and writing a wide range of texts – within which are embedded a wide range of social languages – will contribute to an individual's cognitive, intellectual, and moral development, especially if the work is carried out in a social setting where students are encouraged to talk about texts. But among the students in our classes, not all are in a position to see the value of – or seriously engage in – these activities.

A reading of Bakhtin suggests that in the most comprehensive sense, a person cannot put on and take off a discourse like a garment of clothing. To a preview an argument I will make shortly, though, it may be that by engaging in substantive performance activities within a community of practice, students may "try on" a discourse and perhaps even "borrow" it, an appropriation that offers the possibility of future thoughtful and selective assimilation.

Further, this interpretation of Bakhtin suggests that to help *all* students reach high levels of literacy, educators need to think beyond the workshop model and beyond the even newer practices of helping students attend to processes of reading and writing through direct instruction in comprehension strategies (cf. Tovani, 2000). Although both approaches work well for individuals already convinced of the value of appropriating a discourse, for other students, prior conditions must exist. Those conditions are best described as engaging students as valued apprentices in a community of practice that requires high levels of literacy.

"Discourses are not mastered through overt instruction but by enculturation (apprenticeship) into social practices through scaffolded and supported interaction with people who have already mastered the Discourse" (Gee, 1996, p. 139).

In the following section, I describe one literacy program whose primary emphasis is on developing a community of practice that calls on and helps students develop strong literacy skills. In this performance program, the ALP, students work collaboratively to share their internally persuasive discourses, explore authoritative discourses, and subsequently learn to compare discourses and develop metaknowledge about them all (Gee, 1996).

THE ARTSLITERACY PROJECT

The ALP is a program for secondary school students aimed at literacy development through the performing arts. The project involves students working with one or more core texts to bring them to performance. It is not a traditional drama program that replicates plays for audience consumption. Neither is it *process drama* (Wagner, 1999), which uses role play to deepen participants' understanding of content or develop skill in perspective taking. Although it combines elements of both approaches, ALP's major focus is to construct a classroom community in which adolescents develop the skills and habits of mind to convey meaning through – and recover meaning from – a range of symbol systems, most explicitly, print text.

In the seven years since the program's inception, core texts have included challenging works by Shakespeare, Shaw, Garcia Lorca, and Sophocles; children's books, such as *Where the Wild Things Are,* used with a class of new English speakers; and *The Bill of Rights,* used in a American history/American literature class. Students are introduced to the text, work with it in a variety of ways, and produce an original work in response. Their final performance, which is presented publicly to an audience, incorporates sections of the core text, other relevant texts, and their own original work, combined and organized to respond to a central theme.

In each ALP classroom, a teacher works collaboratively with a professional actor. After joint professional development in which teacher/actor partners incorporate planning, teaching, feedback, and reflection, they design and teach a unit using a curriculum framework called the performance cycle (Fig. 5.1). [2]

Classes include students at all levels of proficiency and have included students identified as gifted, honors, English language learners, and special education. The work is done within the schedule of the school day in ordinary classroom spaces.

Key features of the program are its:

- Design that incorporates a high-quality final public performance
- Pairing of teachers and professional actors with ongoing mentoring by experienced mentors
- Focus on a building sense of community between and among students and faculty
- Emphasis on creating conditions in which students become increasingly receptive to – and capable of – bringing their own interests and ideas to bear on challenging texts.

The goals of the program are both socialization and skills. The first segment of the cycle focuses on building a community of practice in a classroom; the final segment on one or more performances by an ensemble

[2] Developed by ALP project director Kurt Wootton and faculty director, Eileen Landay.

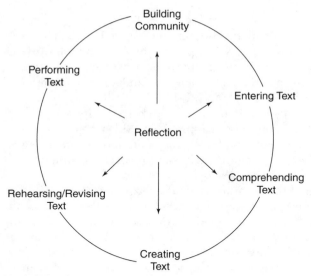

FIGURE 5.1. The performance cycle.

that includes all members of the class. The performance is a culmination of all the work done during the course of the cycle, an artistic presentation of students' original work created in response to the many texts they have encountered. In creating this performance, students' knowledge is transformed and displayed; they *use* what they know and demonstrate what they have come to understand (Wiske, 1998).

Although most literacy programs begin at either step three or step four of the cycle (comprehending text or creating text), a major emphasis in the ALP are steps one and two (building community and entering the text).[3] In so doing, the project takes into account how closely literacy practices are tied to identity, especially for adolescents who do not count school literacy activities as a central part of their identities.

Through work in performance, students enter the richly dialogic world of multiple discourses and critically interanimate its texts, exploring and practicing in order to choose which of them will become internally persuasive. The discourses are presented through the lives and language of speaking subjects. Students "try on" and "practice" a discourse in a provisional way. Do you want to know and feel what it is like to be driven mad by jealousy in an uncertain world, mad enough to destroy what you most prize? Try on the discourse of Othello. Want to tell Othello a story of your own or a story of someone you know? Want to wrest an explanation from Iago beyond his final and infuriating, "From this time forth I never will speak word"?

---

[3] Nancy Hoffman, a major contributor to the project's development of ALP, clarified this important point, which has become central to both the project's theory and its practice.

(Shakespeare, 1997, p. 1239). Work in the ALP offers just those opportunities for every participant. In this work, students are supported by all other members of a carefully constructed community of practice.

CREATING A COMMUNITY OF PRACTICE

In looking carefully at what constitutes the kind of community of practice where rich, substantive language and literacy learning go on, we imagine with Bakhtin a site where the social life is vital and full of energy, where participants move about, talk, and listen to one another to share ideas, where official and unofficial discourses "interpenetrate." We have to look beyond Bakhtin for a more precise description of such a community and the mechanics of how it develops. Here the work of Lave and Wenger (1991) is helpful. As they describe it, being a member of a community of practice implies

participation in an activity system about which participants share understandings concerning what they are doing and what that means in their lives and for their communities. (p. 98)

A classroom as a community of practice then, has a shared purpose, one that everyone involved understands clearly and believes has real meaning for him/her, and for others who are important to them. The specific attributes of the community shape the kinds of learning its participants do.

"Learning is a process that takes place in a participation framework, not in an individual mind. ... Learning is, as it were, distributed among coparticipants, not a one-person act. While the apprentice may be the one transformed most dramatically by increased participation in a productive process, it is the wider process that is the critical locus and precondition for this transformation" (Lave & Wenger, 1991, p. 15).

This wider process is a picture of how the whole community works. How apprentices (in our case, students) develop depends at least in part on how clear a vision they have of the purposes and workings of the community.

"Apprentices gradually assemble a general idea of what constitutes the practice of the community. This ... sketch of the enterprise might include who is involved; what they do; what everyday life is like; how masters talk, walk, work, and generally conduct their lives; how people who are not part of the community of practice interact with it; what other learners are doing; and what learners need to learn to become full practitioners. It includes an increasing understanding of how, when and about what old-timers collaborate; collude and collide, and what they enjoy, dislike, respect, and admire. In particular, it offers exemplars (which are grounds and motivation for learning activity), including masters, finished products, and more advanced apprentices in the process of becoming full practitioners. Such a general view, however, is not likely to be frozen in initial impressions. Viewpoints from which to understand the practice evolve through changing participation in the division of labor, changing relations to ongoing community practices, and changing social relations in the community" (Lave & Wenger, 1991, p. 96).

Effective communities of practice look at themselves as learning systems for all participants. Their purposes are clear to all. They take special care of apprentices, offering them a view of the whole enterprise and access to all participants, especially those slightly more advanced than themselves. They are, by definition, active systems. They also provide a combination of challenge and safety that permits apprentices to grow and develop into full participants.

A community of practice built around performance work supports and encourages dialogism throughout. And it is in dialogism, Bakhtin tells us, that identity develops. Modeling, discussion, transformation of text to gesture, text to talk, text to text, repeated retellings, reflection of numerous sorts and at numerous levels: all are present throughout ALP for all participants. Elements of the community include making the work purposeful, social, active, visible, and explicit. Students report feeling a strong positive sense of membership in an ensemble, being engaged with the work and receptive to new ideas, and experiencing tangible personal and social development.

Membership in an Ensemble

From the outset, students know that they will be working in an ensemble, that they are expected to know their fellow ensemble members, capitalize on their talents and strengths and, in a phrase introduced by one of the project's teachers, "take care of one another." A class activity frequently used early in the program is called *Common Ground*. Students line up on one side of the classroom and the teacher asks questions of the students, such as "How many of you speak Portuguese?" "How many regularly look after younger brothers and sisters?" Those who can answer the question in the affirmative cross to the other side of the room. Through a carefully designed series of questions, the ArtsLiteracy teacher "introduces" students to one another, and foregrounds their talents, skills, and interests, particularly in relation to the themes of the core text they are about to encounter.[4]

Students in ALP classes contrast the classroom climate created by an initial focus on community building with their experiences in other classrooms in large schools where they may go through an entire year without knowing one another's names. Dominique[5], a student in a 4-week ArtsLiteracy class

---

[4] For a comprehensive description of ArtsLiteracy activities in each component of the performance cycle, go to www.artsliteracy.org/handbook.

[5] Student names are all pseudonyms.

designed around the life and work of Federico Garcia Lorca (1994), specifically his play, *Blood Wedding*, commented that in other school situations, group work is undermined "because we don't really take a long time getting to know each other – it's like [...] 'I do not like you, so don't even talk to me!'" In contrast, a strong sense of community, structured by real interpersonal relationships, underlies and enables all the other features of ensemble membership, including "getting things done" at the most basic level.

ArtsLiteracy instructors work hard to model and create a classroom climate in which students can put aside their fears of judgment or scorn – formidable obstacles for all of us, and more so for adolescents – and delve into the work at hand. The results are tangible. On the last day of one class, an instructor has just finished thanking the students for their final performance. The speech ends in rousing applause. Just as the students begin to resume activity, Ashley's voice rings out: "Wait, wait, can I say something?" The classroom goes quiet as Ashley, a girl who cried on the first day because she didn't want to perform, stands up on a chair and begins to speak. In her comments, echoed by several students after her, she expresses how much she enjoyed the class, emphasizing the uniqueness of a classroom atmosphere in which "you don't have to be afraid to look like an idiot because people will still like you."

In addition to an emphasis on a positive classroom climate, teaching partners work hard to establish a clearly defined sense of purpose. Desiree describes her response to their efforts:

Everybody's into it. Everybody's into it because the teachers, they give you the energy to get into it, and you feel like there's a purpose, that you need to fulfill a purpose, and that's why everybody's serious about what they're doing, like "Come on, let's get this done." And everybody's cooperating, and everybody cares.

Melissa further establishes the link between purpose – specifically the sense of purpose generated by the expectation of performance – and accountability:

You actually have to act, and like, with the other things, you don't actually have to do anything; you just kind of put in your input and sit around and you talk about it. But with this you actually have to *do* something. If you make a suggestion you have to follow through on that and actually act it out or something.

As Melissa implies, accountability is possible because, when working on performance activities, everyone's work is active and visible. Adults model giving explicit directions and asking for explicit and precise feedback. Teachers, actors, and students demonstrate and discuss what good work looks like, and who is doing it. Because accountability exists not as the purview of individuals, but within the bounds of the community values described above, it does not devolve into individual competitiveness. Although directions are explicit and the work of individuals is visible, like any good team with a collective sense of purpose, the accountability focuses largely on the effectiveness of the ensemble.

Beyond accountability for the successful completion of the task at hand, ensemble members are also, as Jori Ketten (2002) writes in her paper on the ALP, "accountable with others for the welfare of the group." As ensemble members, students balance their behavior, learning when to take the lead and when to take a less dominant role, when to give and receive criticism, to voice their own ideas convincingly and to listen carefully to those of others. Monica humorously describes the way in which the ArtsLiteracy class has modified the role she takes in group work:

Well, I'll be serious. I don't like listening to other people's opinions. I want what I want. But like, in this class, it taught me to be more, more . . . appreciating other peoples' opinions. Because before, I guess I was just so used to always doing everything; I always wanted everything to be perfect. But then, like now, it's not like that anymore.

In a successful ensemble, students build intellectual as well as social relationships, learning to see each other not just as friends, but also as "good school minds," with insights and resources to contribute to the task at hand. Peter expresses his understanding of the give-and-take of ensemble membership:

I love group work. Because . . . it gives me a chance to help other people out and also gives me – me the same benefit, like, people helping me out with something that, that I may not know or understand.

Isaiah is more specific:

Cause sometimes . . . you have to learn how to . . . incorporate different people's opinions into the acting. Remember, you remember that Southern accent? That was, like, my idea, you know, and they, like, accepted it. So it was, like, cool, you know? And . . . they, I . . . I learned how to accept criticism and stuff.

Implicit in their comments is an understanding and appreciation of the flexibility necessary to effective group work, as well as a respect for their peers' – and their own – judgment and intelligence. Student perceptions of each other as talented and serious thinkers/actors/writers is another benefit of ensemble membership. A class that conceives of itself as an intellectual community is primed for substantive learning.

Receptivity

Although community building continues throughout the performance cycle, teacher/actor partners quickly introduce activities intended to help students "enter the text." The types of activities they use contrast with those used in more traditional settings where teachers will give a brief context-setting explanation, if they do anything at all, then assign students to read a segment of a text – *The Great Gatsby*, for example – for homework, and follow up the next day with a quiz to see if students have read and understood. As one teacher put it, "Students who can't or won't read an extended text independently are very quickly 'put out of the game.'"

In ALP classrooms, the point is to support students in staying in the game. Teacher partners do this by making initial connections with the text in a social setting where students can work with peers to get a sense of the text's content and style, to raise questions about the text, to identify possible personal connections, and to get the maximum possible help in working with assigned material. Much like watching a movie's coming attractions, entering the text activities are intended to introduce students to the material and to pique their interest. For example, in the Museum of Texts activity [6] students browse through brief relevant excerpts of texts and look at related visual materials placed throughout the room. Using a previously prepared records form, they address one or more questions having to do with the contents of the texts and their connection to it. After some time, they gather in performance groups to discuss and compare their findings. This activity prepares them to do some introductory improvisational work, to begin working together in ensemble, and to begin working with the core text.

Working with a challenging and unfamiliar text, students were increasingly open to its themes and language. In ArtsLiteracy classrooms, students are frequently out of their seats, performing. As a natural and necessary part of the process, they read and discuss written work and become active participants in the invigorating multisensory process of bringing a text to life:

It's not what you think, like, "Oh gosh, I can't understand the language," because they bring life to it ... the reason why I think they bring theatre to it is to get you excited about what you're doing and to ... to think differently ... to think that "Oh yes, Shakespeare can be fun" ... all these things that we thought were boring can be fun.

In these activities, the normally invisible act of reading becomes visible, and people's interpretations and reasons for making those interpretations become explicit. Frequent discussion and reflection on every aspect of the work supports students like Monica in asking questions about the contents of the text *Blood Wedding* and her classmates' responses to it:

We – every time we would finish doing our skits ... we would sit down, in the circle, and we would all talk about it and say, "How do you think Girl feels about marrying Boy?" And we would talk about it like that, and it made me think "Oh, yeah" – and it kinda makes the story better, too. Because it leaves you with questions and you wanna find the answers, so you'll keep reading to find the answers.

As they continue work of this sort, students begin to demonstrate increasing openness to new ideas, an increased ability to focus, willingness

---

[6] See a complete description of this activity at www.artslit.org/handbook.

to participate, take risks, and learn, and a general state of being "into" the happenings of the classroom. Not all students are completely comfortable initially, but after the first several days, even the shyest students participate willingly. For example, when asked to describe her general feelings about the class, Melissa responded:

Ok, um, the class is really fun . . . but sometimes it's hard for me because I'm so shy that it's hard to just get up there and do something. Like, they want us to dance in front of people, and I really can't dance. . . . But it's really helping to like overcome some of that stuff and just get out there. Like on the first day, we were all like, "Oh, this is so stupid." But now, we're like more comfortable with each other . . . I like the class.

Personal and Social Development

As they participate in ArtsLiteracy activiites, students report being aware of many different aspects of personal development. Allison speaks of overcoming shyness.

(I)t's been different, and a little bit hard for me cuz, I'm really shy and like, can't, I don't like to like, talk a lot? I'm more like a inner person, I don't say anything – I like to write things, and I don't tell anybody anything about . . . but it's helping, been helping me a lot, cuz I've been, all my life I've been wanting to be more open and talk more. And I – I think I'm getting it.

Desiree mentions having increased confidence in expressing her own opinions.

Being able to get up in front of people without being scared. Saying what I feel, not being scared to share my opinions. Because before in school, I'm so like scared, I'm so paranoid. Kind of the kids . . . but over here, you know, they teach you . . . because you know, you're practicing for a performance, so you have to get out there and you have to. . . . It really does help me to be louder and more open.

Dominique identifies the goals of the class as "trying to show you a way to say what you believe in." Drawing on the material of the course, which had to do with the life and work of Federico Garcia Lorca, she said,

It's gonna be controversial cause everybody doesn't have the same beliefs, but like, through poetry . . . [Lorca] was a poet – even though he got executed in the end, he still said and fought for what he believes in.

Referring to expectations articulated by Ricardo, the actor in his class, Peter describes how he is learning to apply those same expectations in other areas of his life:

Um, just like, Ricardo saying, "I won't accept failure," and "I don't want you to accept failure either." And . . . it's even, like, helped me in doing, like stuff with my band, like I'm not going to half-ass this, you know? I'm gonna do it so it's right. And, and I'm gonna do it, so that way I feel good about it, knowing that people who are listening to us, or watching us is going to feel the same way. And they're gonna say like, "Wow. They're, like, giving it their all." And then I'm saying, "I'm giving this my all, I'm doing it like, the best possible."

Finally, Lily, a recent immigrant from Vietnam, describes increased comfort with the language and the resulting sense of confidence that has brought:

I can do more what I want to do, right? So I can speak up . . . speak up.

CONCLUSION

By using Bakhtin's four key concepts – and specifically the master trope *heteroglossia* – to explore and analyze a particular approach to literacy teaching and learning such as the ALP, do we stray too far afield from the circumstances for which these concepts were developed? After all, Bakhtin worked principally as a literary theorist, and the essay in which these concepts are most clearly explicated is titled "Discourse and the *Novel*" (emphasis added). Or, as the foregoing pages suggest, are these theoretical constructs a helpful lens through which to look at language learning in school settings?

Holquist (1981a) provides these grounds for generalizing from a study of the function of language in a novel to the function of language in the classroom:

At the heart of everything Bakhtin did is a highly distinctive concept of language . . . an almost Manichean sense of opposition and struggle . . . a ceaseless battle between centrifugal forces that seek to keep things apart and centripetal forces that strive to make things cohere. This Zoroastrian clash is present . . . in the specificity of individual consciousness. . . . The most complete and complex reflection of these forces is found in human language . . . and stresses the fragility and ineluctably historical nature of language and the best transcription of language so understood is the novel. (p. xviii)

Like the world of the novel, the world of an active, purposeful, reflective classroom, is by definition a place described by Bakhtin where "several languages established contact and mutual recognition with each other" to create "a dialogue of languages" (Bakhtin, 1981, pp. 294–5).

As soon as a critical interanimation of languages (begins) to occur in the consciousness . . . then the inviolability and predetermined quality of these languages (comes) to an end, and the necessity of actively choosing one's orientation among them begins. . . . Consciousness finds itself inevitably facing the necessity of *having to choose a language*. With each literary-verbal performance, consciousness must actively orient itself amidst heteroglossia, it must move in and occupy a position for itself within it. (pp. 295–6)

In both the world of the novel and the world of the active, purposeful class-room, the dialogue of languages is ongoing, and the participants' position open to modification, a condition I have called receptivity.

"The more intensive, differentiated, and highly developed the social life of a speaking collective, the greater is the importance attaching, among other possible subject of talk, to another's word, another's utterance, since another's word will be the subject of passionate communication, an object of interpretation, discussion, evaluation, rebuttal, support, (and) further development" (Bakhtin, 1981, p. 337).

In describing what he terms a *speaking collective,* Bakhtin identifies atti-tudes, activities, and forms of learning in a community of practice. By ap-plying this theory in developing a specific school literacy program, the ALP, we have arrived at the following organizing principles:

- Create opportunities for students to do shared purposeful work that cul-minates in public *performances of understanding.*
- Embed the work in a community of practice that includes peers and adults, where expectations are high and the climate is positive.
- Establish an environment in which students and their discourses are re-sources rather than liabilities, in which they work productively on the boundaries between the canonical and the vernacular.
- Support students in bringing their own interests and ideas to bear on challenging texts, producing their own texts in response, and combining multiple, rich, and varied forms of discourse to shape a final performance that demonstrates their understanding of a significant issue illuminated by those texts.
- Design activities that create visibility through modeling and demonstra-tion, explicitness through clear directions and continual feedback and re-sponse, and reflectiveness by jointly establishing standards and discussing means to achieve those standards.

In pursuit of more fine-grained program principles and specific practices, I raise issues and suggest questions in three categories. First are questions of effectiveness. For whom and under what circumstances will programs such as the ALP be internally persuasive? Given that many schools – particularly those that serve students who live in poverty – have dropout rates frequently in the range of 60 percent, it is crucial to look as honestly and unflinchingly as possible at what it will take in school and out to create circumstances that will lead to improved student literacy not as an end to itself but as a means of improving students' chances to lead a more productive life. Anthropologists, sociologists, and organizational theorists (cf. Heath & McLaughlin, 1993; McLaughlin, Irby, & Langman, 1994) look at literacy development as socially situated in circumstances that include but go well beyond students' lives in school. This perspective suggests that schools, especially as they presently exist, are one small and often insignificant aspect of shaping students' lives.

On the other side of the issue is evidence that power relations are established and shaped in the microinteractions of discourse in everyday life and that students' experiences with social languages in schools are significant aspects of those microinteractions (Bloome, Puro, & Theodorov, 1989; Gee, 1996; Heath, 1983; Mehan, 1979; Michaels, 1981). This perspective leads us to ask how to create a school environment that recognizes the distinction between the internally persuasive and the authoritative, and finds ways to productively merge the two.

A second set of questions has to do with the environment of schools and the extent to which, as the keeper of the authoritative discourse, it can be shaped around recognizing and honoring students' goals rather than its own drive toward efficiency, order, and conformity. Numerous studies (cf. Minick, 1993) have shown how classroom discourse acts to socialize students to follow orders literally, and not to ask questions, and punishes them for interpreting, questioning, or taking initiative. Although the adoption of workshop or New Literacy practices is aimed at altering those practices, it is not clear how genuine or effective these efforts are and how they function within the larger school setting. Can work in one classroom alone alter the negative effects of an overall environment that is repressive? What kinds of active, social, purposeful work will the institution tolerate? Will large secondary schools, especially those who serve poor students ever be able to treat their students as "resources"? Given the other demands on resources, will such a program – and its requirements of time, space, and human energy – be viewed as cost effective?

Finally, there are questions about the efficacy of the language practices in an environment such as the ALP. Assuming that work in such classrooms supports students' developing engagement with language and literacy, what amount and type of practice and skill development will students need to move to and demonstrate proficiency? Under what conditions does practice with "skills" contribute to creating internally persuasive discourse? Exactly what are those "skills," and under what circumstances are they best practiced? Although some answers are beginning to emerge that are consistent with the theories laid out by Bakhtin and Lave and Wenger (cf. Heath, 1999), strong pressure exists to measure success almost exclusively through students' scores on standardized achievement tests.

It is clearly unrealistic in the present climate to expect test scores as a measure of student literacy achievement to vanish or even to diminish any time soon. However, it may be possible to sharpen general awareness that test scores are designed to support and to measure only authoritative discourse, and that only in the extremely specialized and narrow context of multiple choice or short-answer responses. Further, it is hard to refute the point that these highly circumscribed circumstances are created for the sake of efficiency and intended to serve institutions and not learners. To expand the idea of assessment to include performance work is to enrich it in ways that may serve individual learners within strong communities of practice.

It is important to acknowledge that critiques of the New Literacy practices come from several sources and deserve serious attention. How rigorous is the work undertaken and produced? To what extent are students genuinely engaged? How do we define substantive and productive learning, and to what extent are students achieving it? Theoretical frameworks such as Bakhtin's and practical applications such as the ALP help us to frame the questions, and continue to seek the answers.

ACKNOWLEDGMENTS

A version of this chapter was first presented at the National Council of Teachers of English Research Assembly, Berkeley, California, February, 10, 2001. Support was provided by a grant from the Mimi Sherman Stearns Memorial Research Fund at Brown University and the Spencer Small Research Grants Program.

I gratefully acknowledge the assistance of Amanda Goldstein, Sarah Kwon, Laura Rubin, and Maythinee Washington in the data collection and preliminary analysis, supported by the Undergraduate Teacher Research Program and the Mimi Sherman Stearns Memorial Research Fund at Brown University, summer 2001, under the direction of Professor Nancy Hoffman. Thanks also to Keri Hughes, Dmitri Seals, and Heather Sofield for the interviews and case studies in summer 2000; to Jori Ketten for all contributions, especially her thoughts on constructing a community of practice; and to Nancy Hoffman, Michael Baron, Nancy Safian, John Holdridge, Reif Larsen, Liz Parrott, Megan Sandberg-Zakian, Kurt Wootton, and the many actors, teachers, and administrators in Central Falls and beyond for their myriad contributions to the developing ALP community of practice.

References

Allen, J. (2000). *Yellow brick roads: Shared and guided paths to independent reading, 4–12.* Portland, ME: Stenhouse.
Atwell, N. (1998). *In the middle: Writing, reading, and learning with adolescents* (3rd ed.). Portsmouth, NH: Heinemann.
Bakhtin, M. M. (1981). *The dialogic imagination: Four essays.* (Ed. M. Holquist) (Trans. C. Emerson & M. Holquist) Austin: University of Texas Press.
Blachowicz, C., & Ogle, D. (2001). *Reading comprehension: Strategies for independent learners.* New York: Guilford Press.
Bloome, D., Puro, P., & Theodorov, E. (1989). Procedural display in classroom lessons. *Curriculum Inquiry, 19,* 265–91.
Bordieu. P., & Passeron, J. C. (1977). *Reproduction in education, society and culture.* London: Sage.

Calkins, L. (1986). *The art of teaching writing.* Portsmouth, NH: Heinemann.

City, E. (2000, November). *Conversation is essential: The Paideia Seminar in a working thinking classroom.* Paper presented at The Coalition of Essential Schools Fall Forum, Providence, RI.

Cohen, E. (1986). *Designing groupwork: Strategies for the heterogeneous classroom.* New York: Teachers College Press.

Coles, R. (1989). *The call of stories: Teaching and the moral imagination.* Boston: Houghton Mifflin.

Cook-Gumperz, J. (1986). *The social construction of literacy.* New York: Cambridge University Press.

Daniels, H. (1994). *Literature circles: Voice and choice in the student-centered classroom.* Portland, ME: Stenhouse.

Delpit, L. (1995). *Other people's children.* New York: The New Press.

Ericson, J., Murphy, J., & Zeuschner, R. (1987). *The debater's guide.* Carbondale: Southern Illinois University Press.

Garcia Lorca, F. (1994). *Blood wedding.* (Trans. Langston Hughes & W. S. Merwin) New York: Theatre Communications Group.

Gee, J. P. (1992). *The social mind: Language, ideology, and social practice.* New York: Bergin & Garvey.

Gee, J. P. (1996). *Social linguistics and literacies: Ideology in discourses.* Bristol, PA: Taylor and Francis.

Gilmore, P. (1987). Sulking, stepping and tracking: The effects of attitude assessment on access to literacy. In D. Bloome (Ed.), *Literacy and schooling* (pp. 98–120). Norwood, NJ: Ablex.

Graves, D. (1983). *Writing: Students and teachers at work.* Portsmouth, NH: Heinemann.

Harvey, S., & Goudvis. A. (2000). *Strategies that work: Teaching comprehension to enhance understanding.* York, ME: Stenhouse.

Heath, S. B. (1983). *Ways with words: Language, life and work in communities and classrooms.* New York: Cambridge University Press.

Heath, S. B., & McLaughlin, M. W. (Eds.). (1993). *Identity and inner-city youth: Beyond ethnicity and gender.* New York: Teachers College Press.

Heath, S. B. (with Roach, A.). (1999). Imaginative actuality: Learning in the arts during the nonschool hours. In E. Fiske (Ed.), *Champions of change: The impact of the arts on learning* (pp. 19–34). Washington, DC: The President's Committee on the Arts and the Humanities.

Holquist, M. (1981a). Introduction. In M. M. Bakhtin. *The dialogic imagination: Four essays.* Austin: University of Texas Press.

Holquist, M. (1981b). Glossary. In M. M. Bakhtin. *The dialogic imagination: Four essays.* Austin: University of Texas Press.

Ketten, J. (2000). Unpublished paper, Brown University.

Ketten, J. (2002). *The community behind the curtain: Unpacking ArtsLiteracy pedagogy.* Unpublished thesis. Providence, RI: Brown University.

Kohl, H. (1994). *"I won't learn from you": And other thoughts on creative maladjustment.* New York: The New Press.

Lave, J., & Wenger, E. (1991). *Situated learning: Legitimate peripheral participation.* New York: Cambridge University Press.

Lensmire, T. J. (2000). *Powerful writing, responsible teaching.* New York: Teachers College Press.

McLaughlin, M. W., Irby, M., & Langman, J. (1994). *Urban sanctuaries: Neighborhood organizations in the lives and futures of inner-city youth.* San Francisco: Jossey-Bass.

McMahon, S., & Raphael, T. (Eds.). (1997). *The book club connection: Literacy learning and classroom talk.* New York: Teachers College Press.

Mehan, H. (1979). *Learning lessons.* Cambridge, MA: Harvard University Press.

Michaels, S. (1981). "Sharing time": Children's narrative style and differential access to literacy. *Language in Society, 10,* 423–42.

Minick, N. (1993). Teachers' directives: The social construction of "literal meanings" and "real worlds" in classroom discourse. In S. Chaiklin & J. Lave (Eds.), *Understanding practice: Perspectives on activity and context* (pp. 343–76). New York: Cambridge University Press.

Reddy, M. (1993). The conduit metaphor: A case of frame conflict in our language about language. In. A. Ortony (Ed.), *Metaphor and thought* (2nd ed., pp. 164–201). New York: Cambridge University Press.

Shakespeare, W. (1997). The tragedy of Othello, the moor of Venice. In G. B. Evans (Ed.), *The Riverside Shakespeare* (2nd ed., pp. 1246–96). New York: Houghton Mifflin.

Tovani, C. (2000). *I read it but I don't get it: Comprehension strategies for the adolescent reader.* Portland, ME: Stenhouse.

Wagner, B. J. (1999). *Dorothy Heathcote: Drama as a learning medium.* (rev. ed.) Portland, ME: Calendar Islands Publishers.

Wilhelm, J. (1997). *You gotta be the book.* New York: Teachers College Press.

Willinsky, J. (1990). *The new literacy: Redefining reading and writing in the schools.* New York: Routledge.

Wiske, M. (1998). *Teaching for understanding.* San Francisco: Jossey-Bass.

6

Double Voiced Discourse

African American Vernacular English as Resource in Cultural Modeling Classrooms

Carol D. Lee

Language is a powerful mediator of learning. It is the dominant medium through which communication occurs, and it provides humans with symbolic resources through which to manipulate ideas and solve problems. The study of literature is directly situated on the plains of language use. Literary texts are themselves multilayered. Readers stand in dialogic relationship to the multiple layers of potential meaning that the language of literature conveys. In this chapter, I describe an apprenticeship into literary response in a high school serving African American students who are speakers of African American Vernacular English (AAVE).

Bakhtin provides a set of constructs through which to analyze the role that AAVE discourse norms played in socializing students into a complex literate practice. The focus on AAVE with these students is important for several reasons. First, a majority of the students had standardized reading scores well below the 50th percentile. The high school had a history of underachievement. The students learned to tackle challenging problems of interpretation in very difficult literary texts within a short period of time, despite their low reading scores. In addition, the variety of English that served as their primary medium of communication (i.e., AAVE) has been denigrated in the academy and viewed more as a detriment than a resource (Bereiter & Engelmann, 1966; Orr, 1987; Stotsky, 1999). Because these student attributes are more often than not viewed as detrimental, it is useful to understand how the students' language resources supported learning. Bakhtin is very useful in this regard (Lee & Slaughter-Defoe, 1995).

Bakhtin (1981, 1984a, 1986; Volosinov, 1986) argues that language is inherently dialogic in nature. That is, when we speak, we take up the social languages and genres that are already in existence in the language and cultural communities in which we actively participate. On a macro level, one could argue that African American English stands in a dialogic relationship with so-called "standard" English of Wider Communication. We also respond to propositions, beliefs, and values that are already in currency, whether we are using inner speech to talk to ourselves and internally direct our problem solving, or whether we are in direct dialogue with others. In dialogue, Bakhtin argues – as does Goffman (1981) – that we craft our utterances in dialogue in anticipation of the response of those with whom we are in dialogue. Our response stances are influenced by others. In classrooms, students' responses anticipate the official scripts of traditional schooling. These scripts define who can initiate ideas, what language is appropriate, what ideas are acceptable, and when it is appropriate to respond.

Sociolinguists have argued that participation in any social language involves an appropriation of identity (Gee, 1996). In many underachieving schools, students are led to believe that participation in disciplinary literacy demands that they reject the social and national languages of their home communities. Some students respond with discourses of resistance, exerting effort to redirect the official scripts of their teachers (Gutierrez, Rymes, & Larson, 1995). The challenge in many classrooms has been how to apprentice students into disciplinary identities that do not diminish existing identities that students bring both individually and as members of different cultural communities.

Some have argued that classroom discourse communities that employ hybrid language practices provide spaces in which students can negotiate and be apprenticed into the new social languages of the disciplines (Gutierrez et al., 1995; Lee, 1997). How such opportunities are constructed through language requires both conceptual tools and microgenetic analyses (Erickson, 1992) of instructional discourse to understand both the hybrid language practices and the consequences of those practices.

As students engage in the act of interpreting works of literature, they invariably use both indirect discourse and reported speech to communicate what they understand about the internal states of characters, characters' goals, and actions. Of particular interest is how students disentangle the voice of the author, the narrator, and those of the characters. In some cases, these voices represent the same perspective; in other cases, they do not. Bakhtin (Voloshinov, 1986) proposes that reported speech has a double edge. On the one hand, reported speech attempts to capture the truth value of activity, of the plot for example. On the other hand, according to Bakhtin, reported speech and indirect discourse also capture the perspective of the reportee. This subjective quality of the speech is embodied in the stylistic variation of the talk. The stylistic character of language use has both a private and a public face. The private face is individual. The public face involves speech genres and norms for discourse that are community based and historically inherited. The interaction between the private and public face of language use is dynamic. A speaker does not only inherit stable ways of using language, but also contributes to the tradition. For speakers of AAVE, the inherited norms of the language demand both fidelity to traditional principles as well as individualized distinctiveness. When these students enter traditional classrooms, they are often stepping into tripartite territory where they must negotiate the official disciplinary language (which itself is doubled voiced according to Bakhtin), the community-based language through which they communicate, and their individual ways of crafting language use.

In the case of students who speak AAVE, it is possible, even likely, that two social languages are at least relevant to their talk about literature in classsrooms: AAVE and discourse based on literary reasoning. It is often assumed that the invocation of these two social languages are at odds, particularly in the context of the academy. Gutierrez (Gutierrez, Baquedano-Lopez, & Tejeda, 1999) makes a case for the value of hybrid language practices in classrooms. The idea of hybrid language practices resonates very much with Bakhtin. In Gutierrez's argument, hybrid language practices often involve strategically drawing on the resources of two national languages, such as English and Spanish, and/or finding ways to bridge the scripts/goals of teachers as well as those of students. The argument I make is related, but slightly different. In this case, we are looking at two social languages (Bakhtin, 1981), both in the national language of English, but used in very different contexts and for very different purposes, presumably. Within AAVE (which may be defined as a dialect of English), there are many speech genres. These genres include, but are not limited to, signifying, loud talking, marking, and testifying (Mitchell-Kernan, 1981). In expository genres, Ball (1992) identifies three patterns that characterize preferred styles among the cohort of African American adolescents in her study. Ball also notes the oral foundations of these expository patterns. Smitherman (1977, 1994) describes the African American rhetorical tradition whose patterns may be seen in oral as well as written narrative and expository genres. That tradition includes

1. Rhythmic, dramatic, evocative language
2. Reference to color-race-ethnicity
3. Use of proverbs, aphorisms, Biblical verses
4. Sermonic tone reminiscent of traditional Black church
5. Use of cultural referents and ethnolinguistic idioms
6. Verbal inventiveness, unique nomenclature
7. Cultural values – community consciousness
8. Field dependency (involvement with and immersion in events and situations; personalizing phenomena; lack of distance from topics and subjects) (Smitherman, 2000, p, 186)

How these oral genres and rhetorical patterns are appropriated in pursuit of literary reasoning is one goal of this chapter. That is, from a Bakhtinian perspective, how two social languages, reflecting different relationships of power, come into dialogic relationship with one another is the question.

Literary reasoning involves attending to the layers of possible meaning that rich literature makes available, and in fact, invites. It requires that the reader (and the reader speaking about his or her understanding of the literature) pay close attention to language play as an aesthetically pleasing end in itself, and as medium for double entendre, for layers of meaning that may either add on to the literal (i.e., metaphoric), or contrast with the literal (i.e., ironic or satiric) (Winner, 1988). Literary reasoning also requires that the reader take on a historical stance, actively looking for connections with other texts by the author and by other authors, and perhaps most important, to look for connections with cultural and cross-cultural scripts of the human experience (i.e., local and archetypal themes). Literary arguments are almost always grounded in evidence from the texts, and that evidence is warranted through intertextual appeals and through appeals to the lived experiences of the reader. Although the academy assumes such literary reasoning is best communicated through the English of Wider Communication (Smitherman, 1999), literature often belies such academic assumptions. This unraveling of dominant discourses by other social languages, this constant pregnant retort to official utterances, is very much at the heart of Bakhtin's argument.

Literature, from almost any historical or national tradition, quite often involves hybridity. In the midst of Medieval fourteenth-century England, Chaucer used the vernacular English, instead of Latin, and created characters who critiqued the dominant discourses of his era (e.g., the Pardoner of the *Canterbury Tales*). Toni Morrison (1984) says that she tries to create a language stage that invites the reader to stand up and shout, to get the Holy Ghost, just as the parishoner answers the preacher's call with an emphatic response in the Black church:

There are things that I try to incorporate into my fiction that are directly and deliberately related to what I regard as the major characteristics of Black art, whatever it is. One of which is the ability to be both print and oral literature. . . . It should try deliberately to make you stand up and make you feel something profoundly in the same way that a Black preacher requires his congregation to speak, to join him in the sermon, to behave in a certain way, to stand up and to weep and to cry and to accede or to change and to modify – to expand on the sermon that is being delivered. (p. 341)

She says she wanted the opening of *The Bluest Eye* – "Quiet as it's kept, there were no marigolds in the fall of 1941" – to sound like the intimate conversation that two Black women have over the phone. Alice Walker (1982) holds an undermining conversation with the epistolary novel when Celie, the protagonist of *The Color Purple*, says

Dear God,
I am fourteen years old. I have always been a good girl. Maybe you can give me a sign letting me know what is happening to me.

. . . He never had a kine word to say to me. Just say You gonna do what your mammy wouldn't. First he put his thing up against my hip and sort of wiggle it around. Then he grab hold my titties. Then he push his thing inside my pussy. When that hurt, I cry. He start to choke me, saying You better shut up and git used to it. But I don't never git used to it. And now I feels sick every time I be the one to cook. (p. 3)

Her voice wrenches with both vulnerability as well as almost ancestral wisdom. Walker (1988) writes that Celie speaks in the voice of her great-grandmother:

Celie speaks in the voice and uses the language of my step-grandmother, Rachel, an old black woman I loved. Did she not exist; or in my memories of her, must I give her the proper English of, say, Nancy Reagan?

And I say, yes, she did exist, and I can prove it to you, using the only thing she, a poor woman, left me to remember her by – the sound of her voice. Her unique pattern of speech. Celie is created out of language. In *The Color Purple*, you see Celie because you "see" her voice. To suppress her voice is to complete the murder of her. And this, to my mind, is an attack upon the ancestors, which is, in fact war against ourselves. (pp. 63–4)

Gayl Jones (1991) makes an impressive case for the oral language foundations of the African American literary tradition: Paul Laurence Dunbar, Langston Hughes, Sterling Brown, Sherley A. Williams, Zora Neale Hurston, and Jean Toomer, to name a few. These authors create texts that are double voiced, reporting on and critiquing the contradictions of the American experience, and the deep insights and contradictions in the African American experience. Thus, the seeds of African American English and Literary Discourses are ripe resources for a hybrid garden of wild flowers that do not look very much like the staid gardens of traditional classroom settings.

One final idea from Bakhtin (1984b) that seems relevant to this discussion is that of carnival. Bakhtin introduces the idea of carnival in his analysis of the work of Rabelais. Bakhtin states that carnival has served historically as a ritualized response to authoritative structures. It is a site in which humor serves to undermine authoritative relationships of power and critiques dominant discourses. I will illustrate in this chapter how the hybrid language practices of Cultural Modeling classrooms take on both the character and the function of carnival as described by Bakhtin.

My interest in the Cultural Modeling Framework is to understand how adolescent speakers of AAVE, who are also low achieving in reading comprehension (as measured by standardized assessments) learn to engage in hybrid language practices that involve both the strategic use of AAVE and the tools of literary reasoning. In both a Vygotskian (Vygotsky, 1987) and a Bakhtinian sense, I want to understand how these students used multiple mediational means as resources. The challenge of translating the symbolic language and discourses of academic disciplines into everyday language is perhaps the biggest difficulty that schools face. Conceptualizing the demands of the symbolic language and discourse of the discipline and the resources of particular everyday languages and experience is no simple matter. Robert Moses and Charles E. Cobb (2001) in their important book documenting the evolution of the Algebra Project quote from noted philosopher W. V. O. Quine. Moses and Cobb state "Quine insisted that elementary arithmetic, elementary logic, and elementary set theory get started by what he called the 'regimentation of ordinary discourse, mathematization *in situ*" (pp. 197–8). Thinking about these questions in mathematics with speakers of AAVE is very different than thinking about them with literature and speakers of AAVE. At the same time, I must say it was precisely Robert Moses' work with the Algebra Project that helped to formalize my own line of reasoning about Cultural Modeling as a framework for thinking about this question of transfer across academic disciplines and across different language communities.

The study reported here is of an intervention in an underachieving urban high school. Fairgate High School is in a large urban district with a long history of low achievement, particularly within its high schools. Sixty-nine percent of its students are from low-income families. In 1995, the average "American College Test" (ACT) score was 15.4 in reading for all students who took the exam and 13.7 for students who completed a core high school course of study. The intervention took place over a period of 3 years. The intervention involved the redesign of the English Language Arts curriculum for all students in the school based on the principles of the Cultural Modeling Framework. The school continues to use the Cultural Modeling curriculum, although some amendments have been made in response to new district mandates. As part of the project, this author taught one class each of the 3 years. This study reports on a class of high school seniors I taught during the last year of the intervention.

I report here on a unit of instruction that focused on symbolism. Students interrogated what I call cultural data sets in preparation for reading John Edgar Wideman's short story "Damballah"; Toni Morrison's novel *Beloved*; short stories by Amy Tan and William Faulkner; poetry by Dante and Emily Dickinson; Shakespeare's *Macbeth*; and finally Ralph Ellison's *Invisible Man*. The analysis in this chapter addresses students' analysis of a cultural data set in preparation for their work with these canonical texts. The students were high school seniors. Most students had reading scores on standardized assessments in the bottom quartile. I have demonstrated their high levels of reasoning about the canonical texts in other publications (Lee, 1992, 1993, 1995a, 1995b, 2000, 2001; Lee & Majors, 2000).

The transcript analyzed here is from a larger corpus of data. I videotaped my teaching every day for 3 years. In addition to the videotapes, I also have samples of student work, videotapes of other teachers in the Fairgate English department, interviews with students and teachers, and quarterly assessments our project developed given over the 3 years. Our project used discourse analysis to try to understand the quality of reasoning in which students routinely engaged and how they came to be able to carry out such performances. That protocol involves dividing transcripts into episodes, where an episode is defined as an interchange of a string of utterances around a common question or claim. We looked at who poses the question, what kind of literary question it is, how questions and claims are picked up and by whom, and what belief systems are invoked through the utterances. We analyzed the structure of the arguments, based on structures described by Toulmin (Toulmin, Rieke, & Janik, 1984) and Kuhn (1991). Across these areas of focus, we analyzed how AAVE was used, in particular, how it aided or constricted student reasoning. For the purposes of this chapter, we looked for evidence of Bakhtinian concepts: multiple perspective taking or voice, ventriloquation, invocation of multiple social languages, and dialogic responses among students.

DOUBLED-VOICED DISCOURSE

Bakhtin says that all our utterances are double voiced. We speak both in response to utterances that precede our turn in a chain of conversation. We speak in response to our perceptions of the perceptions of those to whom we are directly responding – which includes both ratified and non-ratified participants (Goffman, 1981). However, we also carry forward ideas, perspectives, and belief systems that we inherit from prior historical conversations, whether we accept or reject those propositions. We carry these voices forward along with our individual responses and perspectives. According to Bakhtin, these multiple voices are dialogically linked. In the examples that follow, I will illustrate how multiple dialogic voices animate the responses of students in an exchange.

In Cultural Modeling, cultural data sets are used to provide students with practice in using discipline-specific modes of reasoning (Lee, 1999). These data sets are drawn from the everyday experiences of students and thus represent unofficial texts in the academy. In our literature curriculum, these data sets may be stretches of talk involving African American English speech genres, such as signifying (i.e., "Your mother's so fat, she has to use a satellite dish as a diaphragm" [Percelay, Ivey, & Dweck, 1994, p. 42]). They could be rap lyrics, rap videos, or clips from films. In this example, students have watched a 5-minute film that appeared on an HBO series called "Subway Stories." "Sax Cantor Riff" was written and directed by Julie Dash, noted filmmaker and director of the acclaimed film "Daughters of the Dust." In the film, a young African American woman enters a New York subway station, picks up the phone, and begins to sing resonantly to her mother who is in the hospital. The girl sings the African American spiritual "Soon I will be done with the troubles of the world, going home to be with

God." A jazz saxophone player is on the platform and plays a jazz riff. The girl drops the flowers she is carrying, drops the phone, and walks out of the subway, while a train passes by and you see the sign Church Avenue. As the girl leaves, a Jewish Rabbi enters the subway and sings a religious song in Hebrew. The sax player who is African American plays a jazz riff as background to the rabbi's song. Upon the completion of the rabbi's song, the sax player and the rabbi bow heads to one another. The film is ripe with symbols. Our assumption is that the students would likely watch this series on HBO and would have some understanding of the symbols. The goal of discussion about "Sax Cantor Riff" is to help the students make public to the teacher and to one another the strategies they use to come up with their interpretations of what's going on.

Students were divided into small groups to discuss the film. The transcript in Appendix A captures the discussion of one group.

I make the claim here that there are multiple voices speaking through the utterances of these students: (1) cultural models (D'Andrade, 1987) regarding death, regarding what gives people power in life and cultural scripts (Schank & Abelson, 1977) for what happens when one dies that are rooted in traditional African American (and by extension African) ontology; (2) literary modes of reasoning that privilege the figurative over the literal; and (3) AAVE discourse norms that privilege ways of speaking and entering conversation (Smitherman, 1977).

Although the dialogue in the film never directly states that the girl's mother has died, students easily make the inference that when the girl drops the phone, her mother has died. They also recognize that the girl singing the song has a certain power that other people in the subway station recognize. That effect is clear and literal in the film. However, in turns 8, 11, and 13, the students attribute the impact of the girl's singing to the girl's faith and the fact that she sings "from her heart." The power of music that embodies a deep emotional immersion in the delivery is very much a part of the sacred and secular lives of most African Americans. Smitherman (1977) states that African American discourses exist along a secular-sacred continuum. It is interesting that they do not attribute the impact to the words of the song, but rather to the girl's delivery. This is also consistent with norms for African American English. That is to say, how you deliver is as important as what you say.

When the teacher (who is the author of this chapter) asks in turn 14, "Is there any history to this song?", she is looking for a response that picks up the historical significance of African American spirituals as a tool in political activity (i.e., its use as a medium of communication regarding times to escape during the African Holocaust of Enslavement or as a rallying force during the Civil Rights Movement). In many respects, the teacher is here invoking an IRE (initiate-respond-evaluate) script, anticipating an "official" response to her question. The students, in contrast, invoke an "unofficial" script, and construct a narrative to warrant their claims. In turns 15 and 16, the students claim, "That's her mother's favorite song, so it had to be an old one" or "Her mama probably sang it to her, and her grandmother sang it to her, and her grandmother's grandmama sang it to her." The responses of these two students carry forward an African/African American ontology in which family is most important, and where the role of the mother and the lineage of the mother are the line that brings knowledge, wisdom, and values forward. The transcript does not do justice to the delivery of any of the exchanges. When K says turn 16, she repeats the parallel structure of each clause with loud, rhythmic, and dramatic prosody, and uses her hand to point as a way of emphasizing the importance of her words.

When the teacher in turn 19 asks about the train, the students need no scaffolding to reach a symbolic interpretation of the function of the train. The three students who respond in turns 20–22 complete and elaborate one another's responses, as if together they were making one statement. There is virtually no pause between their responses. Consistent with Bakhtin's argument, the students actually use phrases that are routinely used in the Black community to describe death – "Her mother passing on" – and what happens after death – "the train is on its way home." That is, the students ventriloquate the oral texts they have heard before. You will also note the lack of copula in turn 21, a distinct feature of AAVE (Rickford et al., 1991; Smitherman, 1977). The teacher revoices (O'Connor & Michaels, 1993) the students ideas in turn 23, but adds another dimension when she says, "You all are getting deep." Gee (1996) describes how people show their membership in particular communities by knowing how and when to speak. The word "deep" here is from the Black lexicon and means profound. One pronounces it by elongating the long vowel: d**eeeee**p. That use and pronounciation of "deep" signals to the students that the teacher has entered and values African American English discourse, and it is an appropriate medium of communication in this classroom. It is less of an invitation to use AAVE syntax features and more of an invitation to continue to explore the cultural model that explains death's transition. The longest student to student exchange follows the teacher's remark.

The turns of talk from turn 24 through turn 28 are culturally rooted elaborations of the original claim that the train signifies that the girl's mother has died. The double-voiced nature of the utterances are very stark at this point. They are without doubt reasoning analogically, privileging the figurative over the literal. This is literary reasoning, and it is precisely the kind of inferencing, using intertextual links, and elaborating metaphorically that reading canonical works of literature require. Although the students, unknowingly at this point, invoke literary norms for reasoning, they couch their utterances in ways privileged by the counter language of AAVE. When CT delivers turn 24, he moves his head from side to side, mimicking the movement of the train. He smiles as he says this, as though he is mocking himself and the enterprise in which he is engaged, very much like the spirit of carnival that Bakhtin discusses. K says turn 25 as though she were singing. There is a satiric tone to K's utterance. She is referring to the scene where the train is presumably/metaphorically carrying the girl's mother to heaven. That has been the students' interpretation. That is a very sad event, but the tone of turn 25 is not sad, as though K is mocking the representation of the mother's passing on. It is also ironic that K seems to reverse the roles of the mourner and the person who has passed on when she says, "There go my baby." Again, note the lack of copula in her response. One would expect the mother to say that about her dead daughter, rather than the daughter to have said that about her dead mother. We know from the earlier conversation that K is not confused over who has died. It is as though K has become swept up in the drama of the group's portrayal of the scene that she superimposes a reversal of roles for the characters. It is as though through double-voiced discourse that CT and K are both invoking and critiquing an African/African American worldview and signifying on the playful act of literary interpretation. Indeed, interpreting literature is a playful act, seeing just how far you can push the edges of the way language is used. This playful signifying is picked up again in turn 30, where CT says, "It was a sad little subway story. I can feel it all the way here, and make me want to cry and stuff." CT is smiling when he says this. He points to his throat when he says, "I can feel it all the way here," as though the pathos of the story has literally got caught in his throat. He uses a metaphor – the story getting caught in his throat – to satirize the very literary quality of the story.

This carnival-like double-voiced discourse uses both the norms it critiques. It both uses African American discourse and critiques the worldviews embedded in it. It engages in literary reasoning while satirizing the very playfulness of such reasoning. The talk must also be seen in its historical context. These are high school seniors, many of whom have experienced repeated failure in the official world of schooling. More often than not, critique of the disciplines into which they are being apprenticed (at least theoretically) requires a resistance that leads to problems, low grades, discipline referrals, etc. In this case, the discipline itself invites a playful resistance and the social language of AAVE privileges such playfulness. It is an interesting marriage, or at least courting, that I had not considered before.

In turns 27–30, students turn their attention to explaining the function of the girl's scarf and her flowers in the film text. They bring to bear cultural scripts about funerals: "Like when people die, they put flowers on they grave and stuff" (turn 28). (Note the lack of possessive pronoun, another feature of AAVE). In the film, the girl carries flowers. Shortly after she begins singing, "Soon I will be done with the troubles of the world," the camera zooms in on the flowers she dropped. There is an almost slow-moving image of her scarf waving, and you can see images of flowers on the scarf. In turn

28, D says, "That scarf represents flowers and stuff. Like when people die, they put flowers on they grave." The shared cultural script around funerals serves as an anchor around which a distributed argument evolves. SH initiates attention to the scarf in turn 26. In turn 27, K begins an elaboration of the scarf's significance and D in turn 28 completes K's utterance. The clear dialogic relationship between K and D's line of reasoning becomes evident in K's uptake in turn 29 where she elaborates in detail on the scarf's signification. However, at this point, K adds another dimension to the double-voiced discourse. The shared cultural scripts reflect an African American ontological perspective or voice. These include the reference to the flowers and also the spiritual beliefs about death as "passing on" to an afterlife, signified by the train.

However, there is also a new perspective involving literary reasoning coming on the floor. K's utterance in turn 29 invokes the question of authorial intent. Julie Dash, the director and writer of "Sax Cantor Riff," is analogous to the author of a literary text. K questions why Julie Dash decided to focus the camera on the flowers falling to the floor and the scarf flowing in the winds of the tunnel. She interrogates the causal link between the attention in the text to the scarf falling and the last scene where the girl is talking on the phone with the scarf around her neck. K says, "I didn't see her take that scarf off." By implication, I read K's statement to reason that there must be some additional importance to the camera zooming in on the scarf. She then goes on to critique the author's choice when she says in turn 29, "She should have had the girl take the scarf off." Her intonation in that turn is very authoritative (//She **shoudda** have the girl take the scarf off//). Students had been asked what questions they had about the film. Another small group of students in the same class asked why the scarf was blowing. Students in that group came up with the same perspective, namely, the fact that the camera zoomed in on the camera suggests it was intended to be significant. In these series of exchanges, double-voiced discourse surfaces in the style of African American discourse and syntax, reflecting the perspectives of African American ontology, literary reasoning, and the perspective of the literary critic who questions authorial intent.

The last series of exchanges takes place between turns 32 and 42. The teacher has asked whether there are any other associations that students might make with the train. One student, C, has been sitting through this group work with her head buried along the back of the chair. She has not said a word throughout. As background, this young lady did not speak AAVE. She articulated her words in a very "standard" manner and did not talk with the lilt and prosody that characterized the way virtually all other students in the class talked. As her teacher, I recognized that she did not want to be a part of this group. The students in this group were not high achievers and would generally not be seen as "top" students in the class. I believe C saw her presence in this group as a put down and chose not to participate.

However, at the end of the group work, she was the one who responded in turn 32, "Does it have anything to do with the underground subway or underground railroad where everybody is trying to get away from?" C has made a very powerful intertextual link between the train and a historical symbol from African American history. It introduces what could be a contradicting explanation of where the train was headed, or could be construed as a complementary extension to the idea of home as heaven (i.e., heaven as a place where one is free). In this interchange, the multiple voices emerge from different perspectives of the students, and the double-voiced discourse takes on new layers of tensions within discourses, but specifically between students.

The same CT who had said earlier in turn 24, "Spiritually, she could be on that train watching her daughter . . . ," now says in turn 33, "Well, the train could have just been coming." That last statement suggests a literal interpretation of the train, where his earlier statement suggests a figurative interpretation of the train. D, K, and SH all ignore C's allusion to the underground railroad. They offer no uptake of C's intertextual link to the underground railroad until after turns 39, 43, and 44, where the teacher imputes importance to C's assertion. Ironically, it is CT in turn 47 who elaborates a way to reconcile what could have been conflicting interpretations of the signification of the train passing by. CT says, "Free from worries. She ain't got no more worries." In the interim between turn 33 and 42, the other members of the group continue to elaborate on the idea of the mother going to heaven on the train. In a set of moves characteristic of AAVE discourse, the students both narrativize and dramatize the symbolic interpretation of the train taking the mother on to heaven. They coconstruct their memory of a religious song, "Let's Get on Board," as another intertextual link in the exploration of the figurative space of the train. In turn 42, CT begins to sing the song, again reminiscent of the carnival-like atmosphere that this performance of AAVE discourse norms in instructional conversation invites. In turn 34, D says, "The train going away to the main spot."

Smitherman (1977) notes how AAVE discourse spans a sacred-to-secular continuum. The phrase "the main spot" is a ventriloquation. It is a phrase commonly used in the Black community to talk about a lounge or bar where folks hang out to party. D in double-voiced discourse invokes a blasphemously secular allusion to talk about a sacred space. Keep in mind that I have been arguing that students in this group have been signifying – engaging in a form of subtle ritual insult – on the very act of literary signification throughout this group work. The irony is that their acts of signifying more deeply than they imagine thrust them into the very world they are inadvertently critiquing. I as the teacher am very aware of this. It is, in fact, the rationale behind the very design of the Cultural Modeling Framework. I am playing with them, and they are playing with me.

CONCLUSION

There are fascinating links between these African American adolescents and Bakhtin, a minority struggling with his radical politics and subject to the political restrictions of the authoritative voices of his day. Bakhtin's analyses provide a structure through which to articulate the presence of the African American voice that the academy tries so hard to silence. Noting a similar relationship to African American literature, Peterson (1995) quotes Bakhtin on speech acts:

Our speech, that is, all our utterances (including creative works) are filled with others' words, with varying degrees of otherness or of "our own-ness," with varying degrees of familiarity and alienation. These words of others bring with them their own expression, their own intonational value, which is assimilated, reworked, and reaccented by us. (p. 97)

Peterson (1995) comments on Bakhtin:

Given this understanding, the very language by which "we" would articulate our being is experienced as an occupied zone. While this depiction may seem theoretically acute or even generally valid, it certainly applies, practically speaking, to the situation of literary discourse in Russian and the African American language communities. Literature itself, in cultural-historical terms, was introduced as a European institution that was both alien and central as an exclusionary norm of articulate identity. Under these circumstances, Russian and African American literary texts were, from their inception, bound to be performative and contestatory speech acts. It is not accident that Russian and African American literary texts tend toward formal anomaly and "hidden polemic." (pp. 97–8)

Our goal in the Cultural Modeling Project was to apprentice students who were speakers of AAVE into the community of literary readers. The contested language, AAVE, and the contested literature, African American literary works (both canonical and popular literary works such as rap and the popular media) were the seeds to be watered in this garden. The speech acts through which students pushed themselves above the underground were performative, contestatory, and indeed tended toward hidden polemic.

Bakhtin invites explorations of hybridity and of contested perspectives. The constructs of ventriloquation and double-voiced discourses inherently deconstruct the language lines drawn by traditional views in the academy. With the increased diversity of the student population in U.S. schools, attention to the multiple language resources that students bring from their family and community experiences is more important than ever. In the Cultural Modeling Project, we have endeavored to design a framework through which to take up these resources in systematic ways that recognize the generative intersections between disciplinary and community-based discourses. Bakhtin has provided invaluable assistance in these efforts.

APPENDIX A

"SAX CANTOR RIFF" – Directed by Julie Dash

(1) **T**: Does the song have any effect on the trouble of the world that's represented down there in that church?

(2) **D** : Yeah.

(3) **T**: So what do you think Julie Dash might be trying to say?

(4) **SH**: I know that girl got them girls' attention.
(5) **D**: And one person can get everybody's attention, and maybe one person can change one of the people's that stole that magazine. They probably wanted to know what she was singing about.
(6) **SH**: Those people who screamed, they thought she was crazy after she started singing.

(7) **T**: So what was the power of this girl on these other girls. What do you think gave her that power?

(8) **D**: She sung from her heart and her mother being sick.
(9) **CT**: They could feel it.

(10) **T**: Why do you think those girls could feel that song? Have you heard that song before?

(11) **SH**: She was singing it from her heart, you know.

(12) **T**: You think if she was singing any old song from her heart it would have had the same impact?

(13) **K**: No, she had faith in that song.

(14) **T**: She had faith. She certainly had strong feelings about it. Is there any history to this song? Did she just make this song up off the top of her head or something?

(15) CT: That's her mother's favorite song, so it had to be an old one.

(16) K: Her mama probably sang it to her, and her grandmother sang it to her, and her grandmother's grandmama sang it to her.

(17) T: In fact, it might have gone back to when?

(18) CT: Slave days.

(19) T: In fact it did. Now, does that train fit in there any where?

(20) CT: I think it means . . .
(21) SH: . . . Her mother passing on.
(22) K: The train is on its way home.

(23) T: The train could be symbolic of her mother passing on, just like the train was passing on. You all are getting deep.

(24) CT: Spiritually, she could be on that train watching her daughter like . . . (he moves his face from side to side)
(25) K: (emotionally) There go my baby.
(26) SH: I don't know . . . like that scarf.
(27) K: That's what that scarf's about. When she takes that scarf off . . .
(28) D: That scarf represents the flowers and stuff. Like when people die, they put flowers on they grave, and stuff.
(29) K: . . . And flowers on the floor, and stuff, and they was flowing, and then all of a sudden the scarf was off, and I didn't see her take that scarf off. So something's wrong with that. She should have had the girl take the scarf off.

(30) CT: It was a sad little subway story. I can feel it all the way here, and make me want to cry and stuff. (smiling)

(31) T: Are there any other associations you can make with this train? (C raises her hand)

(32) C: Does it have anything to do with the underground subway or underground railroad where everybody is trying to get away from?

(33) CT: Well, the train could have just been coming.

(34) D: The train going away to the main spot, and her mother passing away to heaven.

(35) SH: But there's a church song.

(36) K: Yeah.

(37) SH: Get on the train, or something.

(38) CT: Get on board.

(39) T: Which was associated with what?

(40) SH: With the underground railroad?

(41) K: . . . . church and let's go home. [K begins to sing lines from a song]

(42) CT: What's that song my mama be playing – just get . . .

(43) T: Could there be any relationship between that song you're thinking about, this train passing, and C's point about the underground railroad? (pause)

(44) T: What was the function of the underground railroad?

(45) D: To take the slaves away from all that.

(46) T: And what might that have to do with her mother and . . .

(47) CT: Free from worries. She ain't got no more worries.

References

Bakhtin, M. M. (1981). *The dialogic imagination: Four essays by M. M. Bakhtin.* (Ed. M. Holquist). Austin: University of Texas Press.

Bakhtin, M. M. (1984a). *Problems of Dostoevsky's poetics.* (Trans. C. Emerson). Minneapolis: University of Minnesota Press.

Bakhtin, M. M. (1984b). *Rabelais and his world.* (Trans. H. Iswolsky). Bloomington: Indiana University Press.

Bakhtin, M. M. (1986). The problem of speech genres. In C. Emerson & M. Holquist (Eds.), *Speech genres and other late essays.* Austin: University of Texas Press.

Ball, A. F. (1992). Cultural preferences and the expository writing of African-American adolescents. *Written Communication, 9*(4), 501–32.

Bereiter, C., & Engelmann, S. (1966). *Teaching disadvantaged children in pre-school.* Englewood Cliffs, NJ: Prentice Hall.

D'Andrade, R. (1987). A folk model of the mind. In D. Holland & N. Quinn (Eds.), *Cultural models in language and thought* (pp. 112–47). New York: Cambridge University Press.

Erickson, F. (1992). Ethnographic microanalysis of interaction. In M. LeCompte, W. Millroy, & J. Preissle (Eds.), *The handbook of qualitative research in education* (pp. 201–26). New York: Academic Press.

Gee, J. P. (1996). *Social linguistics and literacies: Ideology in discourses.* New York: Taylor and Francis.

Goffman, E. (1981). *Forms of talk.* Philadelphia: University of Pennsylvania Press.

Gutierrez, K., Baquedano-Lopez, P., & Tejeda, C. (1999). Rethinking diversity: Hybridity and hybrid language practices in the Third Space. *Mind, Culture, and Activity, 6*(4), 286–303.

Gutierrez, K., Rymes, B., & Larson, J. (1995). Script, counterscript, and underlife in the classroom: *James Brown versus Brown v. Board of Education. Harvard Educational Review, 65*(3), 445–71.

Jones, G. (1991). *Liberating voices: Oral tradition in African American literature.* New York: Penguin.

Kuhn, D. (1991). *The skills of argument.* New York: Cambridge University Press.

Lee, C. D. (1992). Literacy, cultural diversity, and instruction. *Education and Urban Society, 24*(2), 279–91.

Lee, C. D. (1993). *Signifying as a scaffold for literary interpretation: The pedagogical implications of an African American discourse genre* (Research Report Series). Urbana, IL: National Council of Teachers of English.

Lee, C. D. (1995a). A culturally based cognitive apprenticeship: Teaching African American high school students' skills in literary interpretation. *Reading Research Quarterly, 30*(4), 608–31.

Lee, C. D. (1995b). Signifying as a scaffold for literary interpretation. *Journal of Black Psychology, 21*(4), 357–81.

Lee, C. D. (1997). Bridging home and school literacies: A model of culturally responsive teaching. In J. Flood, S. B. Heath, & D. Lapp (Eds.), *A handbook for literacy educators: Research on teaching the communicative and visual arts* (pp. 330–41). New York: Macmillan.

Lee, C. D. (1999). *Supporting the development of interpretive communities through metacognitive instructional conversations in culturally diverse classrooms.* Paper presented at the annual conference of the American Educational Research Association, Denver, CO. \leaflong{4pt}

Lee, C. D. (2000). Signifying in the zone of proximal development. In C. D. Lee & P. Smagorinsky (Eds.), *Vygotskian perspectives on literacy research: Constructing meaning through collabative inquiry* (pp. 191–225). New York: Cambridge University Press.

Lee, C. D. (2001). Is October Brown Chinese: A cultural modeling activity system for underachieving students. *American Educational Research Journal, 38*(1), 97–142.

Lee, C. D., & Majors, Y. J. (2000). *Cultural modeling's response to Rogoff's challenge: Understanding apprenticeship, guided participation and participatory appropriation in a culturally respnsive, subject matter specific context.* Paper presented at the annual meeting of the American Educational Research Association, New Orleans.

Lee, C. D., & Slaughter-Defoe, D. (1995). Historical and sociocultural influences on African American education. In J. Banks & C. Banks (Eds.), *Handbook of research on multicultural education* (pp. 348–71). New York: Macmillan.

Mitchell-Kernan, C. (1981). Signifying, loud-talking and marking. In A. Dundes (Ed.), *Mother wit from the laughing barrel* (pp. 310–28). Englewood Cliffs, NJ: Prentice Hall.

Morrison, T. (1984). Rootedness: The ancestor as foundation. In M. Evans (Ed.), *Black women writers (1950–1980): A critical evaluation* (pp. 339–45). New York: Doubleday.

Moses, R. P., & Cobb, C. E. (2001). *Radical equations: Math literacy and civil rights.* Boston: Beacon Press.

O'Connor, M. C., & Michaels, S. (1993). Aligning academic task and participation status through revoicing: Analysis of a classroom discourse strategy. *Anthropology and Education Quarterly, 24*(4), 318–35.

Orr, E. W. (1987). *Twice as less: Black English and the performance of Black students in mathematics and science.* New York: Norton.

Percelay, J., Ivey, M., & Dweck, S. (1994). *Snaps.* New York: William Morrow.

Peterson, D. E. (1995). Response and call: The African American dialogue with Bakhtin and what it signifies. In A. Mandelker (Ed.), *Bakhtin in contexts: Across the disciplines* (pp. 89–98). Evanston, IL: Northwestern University Press.

Rickford, J. R., Ball, A. F., Blake, R., Jackson, R., & Martin, N. (1991). Rappin' on the copula coffin: Theoretical and methodological issues in the analysis of copula variation in African-American English. *Language Variation and Change, 3*(1), 103–32.

Schank, R. C., & Abelson, R. P. (1977). *Scripts, plans, goals, and understanding: An inquiry into human knowledge structures.* Hillsdale, NJ: Erlbaum.

Smitherman, G. (1977). *Talkin and testifyin: The language of Black America.* Boston: Houghton Mifflin.

Smitherman, G. (1994). The blacker the berry, the sweeter the juice: African American student writers and the NAEP. In A. Dyson & C. Genishi (Eds.), *The need for story: Cultural diversity in classroom and community* (pp. 80–101). Urbana, IL: National Council of Teachers of English.

Smitherman, G. (1999). CCCC's role in the struggle for language rights. *College Composition and Communication, 50*(3), 349–376.

Smitherman, G. (2000). *Talk that talk: Language, culture and education in African America.* New York: Routledge.

Stotsky, S. (1999). *Losing our language: How multicultural classroom instruction is undermining our children's ability to read, write, and reason.* New York: Free Press.

Toulmin, S., Rieke, R., & Janik, A. (1984). *An introduction to reasoning.* New York: Macmillan.

Volosinov, V. N. (1986). *Marxism and the philosophy of language.* Cambridge, MA: Harvard University Press.

Vygotsky, L. (1987). *Thinking and speech* (Ed. & Trans., N. Minick). New York: Plenum.

Walker, A. (1982). *The color purple.* New York: Harcourt Brace Jovanovich.

Walker, A. (1988). Coming in from the cold. In A. Walker (Ed.), *Living by the word.* New York: Harcourt Brace Jovanovich.

Winner, E. (1988). *The point of words: Children's understanding of metaphor and irony.* Cambridge, MA: Harvard University Press.

7

Narratives of Rethinking

The Inner Dialogue of Classroom Discourse and Student Writing

Christian P. Knoeller

These students are changing their minds right and left. I remember, years later, precisely when and where this thought first occurred to me: sitting outside a sidewalk café on the outskirts of Berkeley, sorting through a stack of compositions from twelfth graders, their papers brightly colored by coding highlighters. I still remember the heat of the sun that morning in early summer. The class had written three times about a book they themselves had decided to read together: *The Autobiography of Malcolm X*. As I reread what each student had written before and after discussing it in class, it dawned on me. Discussing this controversial work together had led many students in the class to reconsider their assumptions. Some also began to reconsider their previous views about whether such books – and issues – belong in public high school English classes in the first place. Most remarkable of all, several virtually reversed their initial positions, in part to acknowledge the views of their classmates – above all, those who held opposing opinions about the work.

Perhaps all this will come as little surprise to teachers and English educators in the era of reader response theory. It has become almost a truism that the reading experience is a highly individual one. Whether we speak in terms of *transactions, interactions,* or *connections,* each student reader forges his or her own relationship with a work. And multiple perspectives are a given when interpreting any text in the classroom. Formal, classroom literature study, in this view, naturally involves not only articulating but also *negotiating* interpretations.

Influenced by reader-response approaches, a generation of English teachers commonly assigns informal writing about literature, such as response logs, reaction papers, and dialogue journals. These methods legitimize, at least implicitly, developing interpretations incrementally over time. Some teachers routinely ask students to revisit earlier entries and to revise them as their appreciation of a work grows, informed by discussion and, particularly, the "readings" of their classmates. I believe that many of us adopt such practices largely on faith. Yet what, exactly, do students gain in the process?

This question hit me, that morning years ago, with the force of revelation. I had witnessed students explaining *how* they had changed their minds, in ways that seemed important, even profound. How had that happened, I wondered? What I had glimpsed, although I had no name for it at the time, were their *narratives of rethinking*.

Narratives of rethinking can be oral or written, as students test perspectives and recount turning points in their understanding. In class discussion, they convey persuasive appeals to classmates by tracing the process by which one arrives at a particular point of view. Students can thereby express their own evolving interpretations *dialogically*, often juxtaposing several different perspectives in the process. Students might, for example, voice ideas that they once, but no longer, subscribe to – contrasting their previous positions with new ones. Such contrasts are the basis of narratives of rethinking: an account of *how* one's own views have changed over time. Alternatively, they can attribute similar rethinking to others, such as authors and characters.

The inner dialogue represented in narratives of rethinking can involve reconciling multiple perspectives internalized from both texts and class discussions. Consider how Eva, the focal student for this study, explained in an interview her evolving response to a reading, describing first her rethinking while writing, and then her rethinking afterward, in response to class discussions. Here, Eva demonstrates that she is well aware of how her interpretations change across time, what Iser (2000) refers to as "a recursive undercurrent in the very process of interpretation itself" (p. 84). She finds that both writing and discussion provide opportunities for such rethinking. The process she describes is clearly a dialogical one. Note that to depict this process involves recalling – and restating – previous thoughts (*italicized* here)[1]:

I kept on arguing with myself. . . . Well, I just had conflicts with my own – every time I'd write something or, I'd start putting it down on paper and then I'd read it. And then I'd go, *well wait a second, do I really think this?*. . . . I like doing that because then, you know, at least then I don't feel like I've got a closed mind about it at all. But, I don't know, sometimes I just want, I wish things were simpler. . . . But when I'm talking [in class discussion], you know, someone else brings up a point and I'm like *Well wait a second*, you know, and then I change my mind about something.

This chapter examines specific instances of rethinking that reveal *inner* dialogue and suggest the interaction between classroom talk and subsequent student writing. To do so, I draw on Bakhtin's theories of appropriation and dual-voicing (1981, 1986) as a framework for analyzing classroom language and its relation to interpreting texts. Textual interpretation, in light of Bakhtin, is seen to involve a process of internalizing words – or *voices* – of

---

[1] Transcription conventions are detailed in Appendix A.

others, including those encountered in written works such as authors, narrators, and characters. Indeed, it is striking to see the degree to which student readers explicitly recall perspectives from texts – including those that they would question – accepting some while rejecting others, expressing a mix of imitation and resistance. The analysis of classroom talk and student writing, taken together, can in fact reveal much about the ways in which internalized dialogue and voicing contribute to textual interpretation.

By incorporating multiple speech events, written texts, and even previous thoughts, narratives of rethinking reveal the dialogical nature of classroom language and textual interpretation. Yet, what does voicing reveal about the inner dialogue that underlies rethinking? And how, exactly, does voicing contribute to such narratives? In this chapter, my own narrative of rethinking, I examine the role of inner dialogue and voicing in classroom interpretation of text.

BAKHTIN'S THEORIES OF VOICING

Bakhtin's theories of dual-voicing (1981, 1986) offer a powerful tool for analyzing narratives of rethinking as well as classroom discourse generally. Dual-voicing – *voicing* hereafter – refers to utterances, or parts of utterances, that are attributable to two speakers at once (indicated by *italics* throughout this chapter). During discussions of literature, for example, a student might paraphrase from memory a statement attributed to an author. Such an utterance is clearly the student's words, yet it also simultaneously still belongs, in a sense, to the author. In narratives of rethinking, it is often such *voicing* that allows students to juxtapose two or more related perspectives.

Voicing is part and parcel of interpreting texts in the classroom. When students respond to a work, they naturally voice the language of others, including authors and characters. Such voicing turns out to be an important feature of instructional conversation about literature (Knoeller, 1998a). Especially when discussion allows for sustained student conversation, echoing and answering perspectives expressed by classmates and texts, interpretation proves a highly social process. Voicing the words of others is an essential element of such negotiation – perhaps even a *necessary* one. Such voicing effectively extends dialogue by incorporating the words and perspectives of others into one's own thought, speech, and writing. To appreciate its role in negotiating interpretations, it is useful to view voicing in terms of *whose* words are being represented. Elsewhere I have proposed a typology that distinguishes varieties of voicing present in the classroom during student-led discussions (Knoeller, 1993, 1994, 1998a, 1998b).[2] This chapter focuses on the role of such voicing in narratives of rethinking.

---

[2] The first category, *textual*, refers to voices drawn from specific written works under discussion. The second, *interactional*, refers to voices of those individuals present and participating in the discussion itself. The third, *contextual*, refers to all voices not derived from the text or the discussion itself.

Narratives of rethinking often incorporate one of two types of voicing. One type is *textual,* when students voice the language of authors or characters, whether read verbatim or paraphrased from memory. When quoting or paraphrasing authors and characters, students may seek to illustrate specific perspectives while calling others into question.[3] Such textual voicing can also allow students to attribute rethinking to an author. The other type of voicing in narratives of rethinking I term *interactional:* voices of those actually present and participating in the discussion – such as when voicing recapitulates what students themselves have *already* thought and said.

Although interactional voicing can involve the words of *other* readers (i.e., the speaker's classmates), narratives of rethinking, as we will see, often involve voicing one's *own* language as well. Students readily use voicing to reiterate and develop what they have personally said, written, or thought *previously.* In fact, representing one's own previous thought or speech in this way typically involves voicing. By recounting a *prior* position, such voicing often provides the linguistic device in narratives of rethinking for representing inner dialogue. Accordingly, a student narrative of rethinking will frequently voice a previous utterance or understanding, for example, in order to signal a subsequent shift in perspective.

Overall, narratives of rethinking can be classified according to who does the rethinking: student readers vs. textual authors or characters.

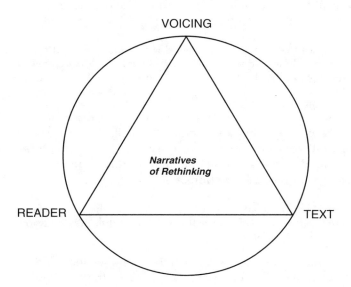

---

[3] Bakhtin termed such relationships *directionality,* differentiating between unidirectional and varidirectional voicing (see Morson and Emerson, p. 146–56). Directionality characterizes the dialogical relation of the current speaker to a voiced utterance. Unidirectionality involves voicing to illustrate or concur with a previous utterance. Varidirectionality involves voicing to question, contest, or qualify.

In the first case, the student recounts personal rethinking; in the second, the student attributes rethinking to others. (Occasionally, student narratives couple the two, attributing rethinking to both the reader and a text.) For the purposes of this study, then, analysis addresses these two types of voicing, distinguishing between the *text* and the *reader*, respectively: that is, rethinking attributed to authors and characters in a work vs. rethinking attributed to students themselves.

ORAL NARRATIVES OF RETHINKING

Narratives of rethinking most often, although not always, involve voicing. The examples below – all of which do include voicing – are drawn from student interviews as well as class discussions relating to the works of several authors, including Baldwin, Didion, and Woolf. These narratives recount rethinking that occurred previously when either speaking or writing about readings.

Reader/Student Voicing

An oral narrative of thinking that Eva offered during an interview describes her writing processes. In this instance, she voices the sort of questions that routinely went through her mind while writing, depicting inner dialogue:

Well, I just had conflicts with my own – every time I'd write something or, I'd start putting it down on paper and then I'd read it. And then I'd go, *well wait a second, do I really think this?* You know, because I just kept on, I was just confused about exactly how I felt about it.

Similarly, Eva described in the same interview how class discussion, in general, could dramatically alter her impression of a work. Here, she voices her opinion before and after discussion to contrast the two. Although she has apparently "invented" the example spontaneously, this narrative of rethinking again voices Eva's own *previous* thinking:

It's like something that if I had just read it and someone asked me what did you think of the book? I'd be just like, *Oh God, don't read it.* But, you know, after the discussion, I would say, *Well, yeah, I learned from it.*

In contrast to the inner dialogue illustrated in the examples above, narratives of rethinking can also be derived from *social* dialogue. In the following instance, for example, Eva generalized in an interview about her rethinking processes *during* discussions. Specifically, this narrative of rethinking refers to a previous class discussion of Virginia Woolf's *A Room of One's Own*. Here, Eva again uses voicing, this time to contrast her reactions to the work privately while reading, with how they changed later when talking to classmates about the book. Notice how she repeatedly voices her own previous inner speech, three times in this brief excerpt alone, incorporated into an overall narrative of rethinking.

When I'm talking, you know, someone else brings up a point and I'm like *Well wait a second*, you know, and then I change my mind about something. I don't know. It, you know, a lot of people to me get really, really strong opinions about things and sometimes I can't decide whether I really like a book or whether I don't. Like when I, like when I read *Room of One's Own*, when I was reading it, I hated it. That was just like, *God this is so boring. I hate this. I hate this.* And then I got into class and I had a lot of stuff to say about it. And I think, *Well, wait a second. Do I hate it that much*, you know. It was more like I didn't really enjoy reading it. I guess you could say that. Cause it's not really an enjoyable thing to read, but when you bring things up [during discussion] you learn a lot from it.

In this way, voicing can represent previous inner speech and one's own perspective *at another point in time* (e.g., "while I was reading, I thought *so and so*"), thereby recounting a student's internal dialogue to depict rethinking.

As a final example for this type of voicing, consider the following case, drawn from a class discussion of another work, Didion's essay, "Some Dreamers of the Golden Dream." Eva explains how her interpretation has changed since writing her initial response. The voicing in this narrative of rethinking represents Eva's own previous *writing*:

I don't know where, somewhere I put in the paper I said, *I started to get in myself. I (nearly) felt sorry for [the character]* and I, I sort of said that *Joan Didion did too*, but it's, she doesn't. I don't think [Didion] feels sorry for this [character] *at all*.

Although referring to how the author may have "felt" about a character, the rethinking is attributed to the student herself. Voicing her own previous writing in this way allowed Eva to recount her rethinking process.

TEXTUAL VOICING

In the preceding section, all examples illustrate narratives where the rethinking is attributed to the student herself. *Textual* narratives, in contrast, voice rethinking attributed to others. When discussing literary works, after all, a student can attribute rethinking to both authors and characters, as shown below.

Textual/Author Voicing

In the following case, drawn from a student-led discussion in class, Eva's narrative voices rethinking attributed to an *author*: Virginia Woolf from *A Room of One's Own*.

I thought that was, yeah, because when she was talking about that, I thought that was really good, because when she realized, *Well, wait a second. And all of these women, they they don't have a complete character. All they are is how they are in relationship to men, in relation to men, in relationships with men. . . .* Well, I think a lot of what she was saying, I think a lot of what she saying was that, *Okay, so these, these men wrote about these women that were suddenly, you know,* brave . . . *but they weren't whole. They weren't really complete characters. What it was was images, I think, in the books, that they weren't completely real. That the writers didn't, that the authors didn't, didn't give them complete characters.* /I think/ I think that was a lot of what she was saying.

Textual/Character Voicing

In the next example, again drawn from class discussion, Eva's narrative voices rethinking attributed to a central *character*, John, from Baldwin's *Go Tell it on the Mountain*:

I felt bad for him, he was 14 years old and everyone had his future planned for him. And that's kind of scary. What is he's supposed to be this, you know, a preacher and he never, what if he never had the experience that he had at the end of the book. I mean I think that was like a question that he, I mean he didn't, I think that's partly why he rejected the religion was because, *Well, wait a second. Right now I don't believe in it. And what if I have to start preaching and I still don't believe in this?*

Narratives of rethinking can also be found in student writing. Oral narratives of rethinking, as we will see, readily provide a basis for subsequent writing, including exposition and argument, such as when a student uses such a narrative to organize a composition. Rhetorically, this strategy can resemble a traditional concession: acknowledging counterarguments or alternative perspectives. In contrast to oral narratives, such written accounts of rethinking take a different form. Although oral narratives of rethinking frequently use voicing to depict turns in dialogue, a student's written exposition is more likely to subsume such propositions as unattributed arguments. A student composition, therefore, might summarize discussions without voicing per se, offering generalizations about rethinking instead. In such unvoiced, written narratives, rethinking can be said to have been "thematized."

SETTING FOR THE STUDY

To examine how such narratives of rethinking function in the classroom, I draw on the classroom language – both oral and written – of an Advanced Placement (AP), twelfth-grade English class in an ethnically and socioeconomically diverse urban school grappling with *The Autobiography of Malcolm X*. Since students were allowed to enroll for the class on a self-selected basis, the group was diverse academically; twenty-one students (in a class of twenty-four) agreed to participate in the study.

The teacher, Joan Cone, has taught English in a public, secondary setting for more than 30 years, instructing a mixture of ninth- to twelfth-grade classes, including sections of AP Language/Composition such as this one. She is an accomplished researcher and tireless advocate of educational equity. At a student's request, Cone's class had elected to read *The Autobiography of Malcolm X* together.

I focus on an individual student, Eva, one of five "student voices" case studies reported on previously (Knoeller, 1998a). Eva's oral and written narratives of rethinking reveal how such voicing comes into play when students negotiate the interpretation of text. The following case study is organized chronologically, encompassing the instructional unit devoted to *The Autobiography of Malcolm X*. Accordingly, the analysis will trace this unit's sequence of compositions and discussions, focusing on Eva's use of narratives of rethinking.

Primary data sources include (1) transcripts for two full periods of student-led discussion of the book, (2) Eva's three written compositions, and (3) transcripts of her year-end interview. Secondary data sources include (1) transcripts for class six, full-period, student-led discussions of other works; and (2) transcripts of interviews with the teacher.

Overall, activities for this instructional unit were sequenced as follows:

>First Composition → First Discussion →
>>Second Composition → Second Discussion →
>>>Third Composition →

CASE STUDY ANALYSIS

First Composition

Students read *The Autobiography of Malcolm X* outside of class and were asked to write an informal "reaction" to the book for homework. Eva's initial "reaction paper" revealed multiple and conflicting emotions. Indeed, *emotions* were central to Eva's view of responding to literature. In an interview, Eva explained that she saw more to reading literature than explication. Rather, she believes readers engage texts in personal ways, a view compatible with reader-response theories of textual interpretation. Asked, "Do you think this class has always just analyzed the book?" Eva replied, "It seemed to me my own feelings get into it, and that's inevitable." Her first composition about the book reflected this belief, cataloging her initial reactions in just such emotional terms (e.g., *proud, happy, mad*, etc.).

Importantly, her composition is a chronological, incremental account, a *narrative* of the reading process, reminiscent of Wolfgang Iser's (1971, 1978) early phenomenological accounts of the reader's interaction with a text. Structurally, each of her four paragraphs address specific "moments" in the autobiography – and thereby in the reading process: (1) "in the beginning of the book," (2) "his life in the ghetto," (3) "throughout the rest of the book," and (4) "after he had gone to Mecca." The third paragraph addresses a series of *contradictions* Eva perceives in the author. Although compact, this paragraph actually probes issues of race, gender, and religion. Notice the sharp contrast – between "respecting" and "rejecting" – suggesting Eva's rethinking while reading.

I really respected Malcolm for education and disciplining himself. But throughout the rest of the book, I found myself rejecting things he said. He was as bad as the white man. [Malcolm X] called himself open minded. But he wasn't. He said women wanted to be weak and to be protected by strong men. He was anti-Semitic, though he often said he wasn't. He said, "*In Islam we were taught that as long as one didn't know the truth, he lived in darkness.*" Why is his truth any better than what others had found to be truths?

The final paragraph builds on the third by *answering*, dialogically, specific views Eva attributes to the author. Although critical of some of the author's apparent contradictions, she introduces the *theme* of "change," both in the author's mind and in society at large, in a favorable light. Here, in written form, rethinking attributed to the author is unvoiced and treated implicitly, or "thematized."

Even after he had gone to Mecca, I didn't accept all of his ideas. I did agree that the "white man" mentality in America did exist and should be fought against. I admire Malcolm for not being stuck in his ways – for being able to change. But I still felt he discriminated against people – Jews, women, even non-whites (who weren't black either), and, of course white people. While I do think that black people need to be strong within their own people to be strong in fighting racism, I don't agree with his seclusion of any non-black from his Black Nationalist organization. I believe that to eliminate racism, people have to think differently about each other. Whites have to respect blacks and get it out of their minds that blacks are "lower" than they are. And blacks have to respect whites.

As an antidote to discrimination and intolerance, Eva called for reciprocity and mutual respect between blacks and whites – based on *rethinking* existing prejudice. Importantly, because Eva was writing before the class began discussing the book, her composition provides a kind of baseline: her initial "take" on the work. Moreover, it addresses a number of themes – such as "change" – that would be developed at length during subsequent discussions.

I would argue that the organizing principle for this composition, beyond its chronological account of reading, is implicitly a narrative of rethinking delivered in its last two paragraphs. After all, as Eva revealed in an interview, "every time I'd write something or, I'd start putting it down on paper and then I'd read it. And then I'd go, *well wait a second, do I really think this?*"

First Discussion

After turning in their initial written reactions to the teacher at the beginning of class, students discussed the book. The first of two student-led discussions took an entire class period, facilitated by students who had volunteered, including Eva. She was an active, even avid, participant in class, frequently volunteering to help lead discussions of readings. Her confidence at speaking adamantly in class is in keeping with Eva's academic history – as a student in gifted and honors classes since elementary school – and her extracurricular aspirations, such as acting.

Because Eva helped facilitate the class discussions of *The Autobiography of Malcolm X*, she was in a position to initiate topics. She viewed these discussions of reading as extremely valuable, describing the importance that she and other students in the class placed on questioning and rethinking. Eva acknowledged that the book had stirred up "a lot of emotions," including allegations of racism at the school. Asked what she had valued about those discussions, Eva cited the differences in interpretation among her classmates, that "so many people felt so many things about it." During those class discussions, Eva repeatedly explained her ideas in terms of how they had changed – incrementally and dialogically.

Eva especially appreciated the breadth and flexibility she perceived in student-led sessions to explore many facets of a text, as opposed to a narrowness she associated with writing conventional literary analysis. In her estimation, discussions allowed students to zero in on what interested them most about a work: to interpret and respond and to "analyze all aspects of the book." Indeed, she had come to value discussion itself as a vehicle for such exploration and rethinking, describing how her views about the book had been reshaped by class discussion.

As a facilitator, Eva opened the discussion with an extended plot summary. Her introductory remarks attribute rethinking to the author. Like her first, compact composition, Eva's oral account in class again addressed issues of race and religion. Note how she concludes this extended turn, excerpted below, with textual voicing of the author ("Look, I was wrong"):

And then he went to Mecca where he had a revelation that, he realized that, you know, the white people there were no different. Color of skin did not matter. It was the religion that brought them together. And so he came back, you know, very different. And he was, he was confused and he was, you know, which was understandable because he, he really changed his ways. And he wasn't quite sure what he believed in when what he believed in before was falling apart. I mean, because he realized that all white men are not the devil. That Elijah Mohammed is not as great as he thought he was. . . . Yeah, that's one thing /. . . . / that I admire about Malcolm is that he he could say, *Look, I was wrong* and that he had a change.

Perhaps because students had written reactions in advance of talking together about the book, Eva sometimes summarized rethinking, as she had in her composition. Although Eva has clearly offered an account of rethinking here, one attributed to the author, it is generalized because his *previous* positions are apparent only by implication. As in her composition, rethinking attributed to the author has been thematized. (In contrast, the second discussion, to be analyzed later in the chapter, includes more examples of *voiced* narratives of rethinking).

As the discussion continued, another topical strand was carried across from Eva's initial composition: the author's apparent contradictions. The class puzzled over whether Malcolm X had actually progressed in his thinking, as opposed to merely contradicting himself repeatedly. This theme is relevant to the analysis of narratives of rethinking because Eva's own evolving interpretation hinges on this point – contingent on how to "read" shifting perspectives encountered in the text.

Vera: Excuse me. Excuse me. He also said, he also said, another point he made, that I thought was interesting that, was that [citing text]: *Instead of fighting for our civil rights in this country we should be fighting for our human rights before the United Nations.* /yeah/ So you've been putting out what he said about violence and everything, but you have to also look at other theories that he had, other things that he promoted.

Eva: No, I understand that. I think he has to, you know, decide what he's going to do. What it is.

Byron: He wasn't totally sure.

Eva: And he had so many conflicting ideas, and he should have, it doesn't all work out like that, you know. I think that in order to have a peaceful coexistence, what you have to do, what you had to do, is change the mind's of these people who look at these black people as being below them.

Vera: How are you going to do that?

Byron: How are you going to do that?

Pamela: Nobody's figured that out yet.

Eva: Do you realize that perspectives don't just change?

Later in this discussion, when Eva returned to the same topic at greater length, she ultimately relied on an explicit narrative of rethinking. She and her classmates wrestled, in a sense, with a narratological question: the reliability of the narrator. Notice how Eva describes her own rethinking as contingent on the author's. In her turn, that concludes the following episode from the discussion, Eva's textual voicing attributes rethinking to Malcolm X:

Pamela: He was very confused because he /laughter/ when you guys were talking, I didn't know what part in the book you're talking about, because he like changed *drastically*, you know. And that's why he

/ . . . . / also in the epilogue, I think you see him more as a real person, he's like, he's like *yes, this I want, you know, racism to stop, but I don't how to do it, you know.* He's more like human . . . and we're reading about him because he tried it. Even though all his ways weren't correct or his thoughts or anything. I mean he, you have to admire, you know, his commitment, you know, to try and change the world.

Vera: It's kind of like the paper we had to write, you know the little thing we read, *is a man truly what his actions are, or is he something deeper?*

Pamela: Yeah.

Byron: I think he was something deeper. I think we're something deeper because I don't really feel like he was, I didn't really feel like he was, I felt that he was peaceful person at heart, but that he felt that violence was the only way to get things done. Violence was the only way to get things done on the street. And doing things, real violence, you know, to get people's attention.

Eva: I think in a way, I think in a way he didn't completely know, exactly what he believed in. Because, oh his, I feel so many conflicting, I mean, at first what really helped him, I think, was that he believed in the Black Muslim "cult," if you can call them that. He believed in them so strongly, he knew exactly what he believed in: not to be poor, not to smoke. I mean it gave him a really good foundation and a sense of security that he knew exactly what he was fighting for. But then he started changing, and it was really really hard for him, because he was thinking, *Well, maybe this is not the way, probably this is not the way to win our struggle.* And so for a while I really didn't like him because he kept on saying, *Oh yes, I'm very open minded. I hate all white people,* you know. /laughter/ I just said, *Wait a second,* I couldn't stand, you know, it really made me mad. But then while seeming very close minded, he was open minded enough to see that he was wrong, and then change. I mean then change his thoughts. And, you know, it's really hard to know from one page to the next whether to admire him or to really disagree with him.

In this single turn, Eva recapitulates a number of the central concerns that had emerged during the first discussion. Her ideas touch on sophisticated interpretive issues, bordering on hermeneutics as Iser (2000) defines it: "hermeneutics marks the stage at which interpretation becomes self-reflective" (pp. 41–2). Impressively, students had arrived at such insights on their own, using vernacular language not laden with the conventional terminology of literary criticism. Instead, voicing is the linguistic device that enables such complexity in her narratives of rethinking.

Second Composition

Eva's second composition in response to *The Autobiography of Malcolm X* was especially concise – barely half the length of her first "reaction paper." When serving as cofacilitator for the first full-period, student-led discussion, Eva had already engaged classmates in intense dialogue. Yet, writing in response to that discussion, she made important concessions, acknowledging the discussion explicitly and, in a sense, extending the classroom dialogue in written form. Remarkably perhaps, given its brevity, her composition still addressed rethinking repeatedly. Much like her first paper, this one also summarized and thematized rethinking.

Importantly, this assignment emphasized responding to class discussion. Pedagogically, linking writing to both previous and upcoming discussion might well be viewed in Bakhtinian terms. As Allen (2000) observes, Bakhtin's view of language emphasizes just such sequences of dialogical relationships: "all language responds to previous utterances...and seeks to promote further responses...all utterances are dialogic, their meaning and logic dependent upon what has previously been said and on how they will be received by others" (p. 19). In the classroom, such sequences of assignments can readily place writing dialogically in response to classroom talk. As Freedman (1994) notes, "For Bakhtin, each piece of writing will be composed of the writer's past interactions with the thoughts of others and of anticipated future interactions" (p. 5), such as student writing informed by its relationship to ongoing classroom discourse.

Specifically, Cone instructed students to write for homework both in response to this discussion and in anticipation of *further* discussion. In an interview, she paraphrased the prompt for that second composition as "what happened to you today in class – and now what do you think." She gave this assignment orally in class at the end of the first of the two student-led discussions of the book as follows:

So tonight I want you to go home and write, you know, what you got out of [the discussion], did you change your perceptions....I want you to think tonight in terms of tomorrow's discussion. Where is he when he's telling the story. And how does the epilogue fit in? Because I think if you're going to talk about his transformation....Where in the book, if the book is 400 pages long, it's longer than that, at what page does the transformation take place....I think that may help us in our discussion.

Eva's written response traced how her thinking about the book had continued to progress, relating how her initial view of the autobiography had been altered by those expressed by her classmates: "After I read the epilogue, I started to like Malcolm X. He seemed much more human. But in the discussion, I realized how much I disagreed with him." Despite her vehemence during that discussion itself, Eva had clearly been moved to rethink her initial reactions. Here is that composition in its entirety:

After I read the epilogue, I started to like Malcolm X. He seemed much more human. But in the discussion, I realized how much I disagreed with him. Then I saw him as a very afraid man – exactly opposite of what he seemed. He clung to a religion to feel secure. He completely devoted himself to that religion – and he was strong in doing so. Which is why it is hard to believe that, in a way, he was weak.

After Malcolm X went to Mecca, he kept contradicting himself. I felt sorry for him – looking back on it. I admired him for being able to change a bit. He saw that he was wrong, but his practices didn't change that much.

In the epilogue, Haley showed the real Malcolm – who got upset very easily; who was scared to trust anyone (besides Elijah Mohammed & Allah); he was afraid to love anyone; he was afraid of being ridiculed by people more educated than he was. He educated himself and he made himself very strong, he hid his fears.

His bark was worse than his bite. He preached violence, but didn't practice it. He preached against the white man at first, but he let there be exceptions. He became very confused and my feelings about him change all the time.

As with the first composition, Eva's account covers a lot of territory. And like the earlier piece, it achieves its breadth by compression. Accordingly, rethinking is again thematized (e.g., "in the discussion, I realized how much I disagreed with him"). Although devoid of voicing and lacking the specificity of full-fledged narratives of rethinking, such summary statements still make the same claim: the reader reporting a change in her thinking. She alludes to her reasons in the commentary that follows, including contradictions attributed to Malcolm X ("opposite of what he seemed" and "he kept contradicting himself"). Yet, importantly, Eva acknowledges that the author's apparent contradictions might instead evidence "change." And as she had during the first class discussion, Eva again explicitly links her own rethinking to the author's: "He became very confused and my feelings about him change all the time." In this way, the composition effectively presents the very argument rehearsed orally the day before, although now in "capsule form." I would argue that this compressed written narrative evokes the whole of the argument echoed from the classroom, narratives of rethinking and all.

Perhaps it is Eva herself who best explains her reluctance to reiterate discussions more fully in her writing. During an interview, she explained that while tempted to derive ideas from discussions, she also strove for originality when she wrote:

If we have a discussion, and then afterwards I have to write a paper, I don't want to write the same things that came up in the discussion because I feel, you know, we already did this, why I am writing about it again. Once I really should not, I *should* write it down, because, you know, then it'll be good. But, I don't know, I like to bring up new things all the time. Because I feel like it's my own thought. Because if I bring out something from the discussion, or something, somebody else might have brought it up. And it's totally valid and maybe now I understand so I should write it, but, but I don't like to do that. I like to think that this is my own thought and I made this up myself.

Setting the oral narratives of rethinking beside her subsequent writing reveals how the two are intertwined. Eva told her classmates that "its really hard to know from one page to the next whether to admire him or to really disagree with him." During the discussion, she spelled out specific contradictions, and offered several narratives of rethinking attributed alternately to the author or herself. Her written argument effectively summarized those oral narratives, ending on precisely the same note: "He became very confused and my feelings about him change all the time." Clearly, as a reader Eva was continually adjusting her interpretation to reflect the author's seemingly indeterminate identity – the mark of ongoing rethinking that connects her composition to class discussions.

Second Discussion

As was the custom in this classroom, the same group of students facilitated every discussion of any given work. So Eva was again a discussion leader. In this capacity, she took a number of extended turns. Several involved narratives of student rethinking.

The first of these actually refers back to the previous discussion as the *occasion* for rethinking. At issue again is the appearance of contradictions in the author. Specifically, Eva wondered whether Malcolm X was actually as strong as he made himself out to be. Although this narrative of rethinking at one point voices the author, the rethinking is attributed to Eva herself:

Eva: In the first discussion, I thought that, I, I started thinking of
         Malcolm X's activity, being afraid and not as strong as he seemed
         because . . . and he was afraid of being opposed to anyone. He was
         afraid of being hurt by anyone, of trusting anyone. I suddenly got
         this because he wasn't clinging onto, clinging onto, you know, he
         clung onto his religion, and it was his whole life, and that's what
         made him feel strong was because *[speaking emphatically in altered
         voice] I'll finally have something, I'll get the rules down in front of me of
         what I'm supposed to believe. There are no exceptions. White man is the
         devil*, stuff like that, you know. So that, that's when he started, you
         know, he looked very, very strong. But then, then I got the sense
         that, you know, that in his, in the epilogue and stuff he was really
         very afraid that he would have a bad day. And he would start
         snapping out and having outbursts and stuff like that because, you

know, things started toppling beneath him. And, you know, I just
felt he was very insecure, where he *seemed* so secure.

Vera: Do you think that knowing his past, like when he talks about his
childhood, does that help you understand his philosophies?

Eva: Well, yeah. I mean he had a very hard life and lot of it or most of it
was because of this society . . . I mean, I understand that.

Helen: You have to, you have to base your, your opinions of people on
your own, I mean, your own experiences that you've had.

Here, several discourse markers (e.g., "I started thinking," "I suddenly
got this," and "But then, then I got the sense") signal rethinking. Although
Eva does not voice her own previous perspectives, the contrast is explicit,
and so it is clearly an example of rethinking framed in a slightly different
way linguistically.

In the classroom, such oral narratives of rethinking do not occur in isolation, of course, but in the context of ongoing dialogue and interaction. I
believe it is worth examining just how such narratives can contribute to ongoing discussion. To illustrate, consider the following episode, one initiated
by the teacher. Although Cone spoke only infrequently during student-led
discussions, and always with exceptional discretion, preferring to let students guide their own conversations in an unmediated way, occasionally she
was moved to speak. At issue is how Malcolm X viewed the role of violence
as a political tool. Late in this episode, Eva seeks to resolve the question in
a single, complex turn, one that couples several instances of voicing with a
narrative of her own rethinking:

TEACHER: Well you know it's interesting when you said *Well did he need to
do more* and Byron said and a lot of you said, you know, *Martin
Luther King didn't accomplish anything.* I guess what really
concerns me is that we don't know what, you know, it doesn't
come up in our history what he accomplished, but Martin
Luther King really relied on the press it seemed. And I think
that changes really happened. . . . I'm not saying *he was
perfect*, but I think we don't understand how much Martin
Luther King really accomplished. But as difficult as I have,
problematic as this book is for me, even now, on second
reading 20 years afterwards, I think that Malcolm X had a
tremendous effect on our society today. /right, I mean/ But I
guess because Martin Luther King is my hero.

Bonita: And I was kind of angry because, no one really acknowledges
Malcolm X like they acknowledge Martin Luther King.
/Yeah, like VERA already said that/ You know, everyone
acknowledges the connection there with Malcolm X, and the
positive part of what they're doing. And I was really angry for

	that, because I think that we should acknowledge Malcolm X because it would give a lot of pride, pride and self esteem. [multiple voices]
Byron:	always on how life, the press, you know, how he changed they kept on saying the same things.
Nicholas:	. . . he wanted violent change. So if he wanted change by violence probably because he has said, you know, *we can change but you can't do it peacefully.* And the people over here would say, *Let's have a peaceful kind of change,* you know. /Vera: But, but, I mean/ You're not going to praise Malcolm X for saying, *Yes, we want violent change.*
Vera:	He didn't say *We want violent change.* He said, *We want change.*
Nicholas:	Yeah he did. He said, Yeah, I mean that's the way /if he glorifies it/ He even said *Use violence to change.*
Bonita:	But did he use violence though?
Nicholas:	No, I'm just saying, I was saying . . . *people have remembered him for saying **If we have to, let's use violence to get change**.* And then I feel crazy for saying or believing in that.
Vera:	Well, what about the brave people who believe in, in that the change should be, right, the change should be better.
Nicholas:	Yes, but [they] didn't remember the violent part.
Vera:	Should they? /. . . . /
Eva:	Yeah, that's a big problem. Obviously people didn't. Because at least the people don't really think about Malcolm because, I mean even with preaching all of this violence, did he ever do a violent act?
Byron:	No.
Eva:	No. He didn't. So that's why I think in part I think, *Well, did Malcolm really change at all? Because wait a second, he was preaching violence and there was no violence, and therefore it wasn't Malcolm X.* That's what people don't realize. He, he. . . . he grabbed people's minds in a lot of ways. None of them said, *Look what I'm doing. I'm uniting with Blacks.* He said, *We're uniting in violence, or we should unite in violence.* And just, just kind of sifting that out.
TEACHER:	. . . she says that he says. /laughter/ She says, you know, *that he matured.* You're right.

The apparent "disconnect" between word and deed for Malcolm X troubled students. Eva's narrative of rethinking attempts to address such vexing questions in the text. Characteristically, she frames the issue in terms of changes attributed to the author – where the term "change" had become a kind of code in this classroom for rethinking. Ironically, Cone even quips about Eva voicing the author here ("she says that he says"), yet takes her point that Malcolm X had in fact "matured" in his thinking about social and political progress – and the place of violence in achieving them. Yet, perhaps Cone has in fact grasped only *part* of Eva's nuanced narrative. The question Eva had actually raised here is how to "read" changes attributed to the author. She calls into question whether the most strident positions commonly associated with Malcolm X had *ever* been accurate. Perhaps it is the public perception of the man, she suggests, that has changed instead. Still, this is clearly a narrative of Eva's *own* rethinking. As she has repeatedly, Eva wrestles with uncertainties in the text, especially shifting and seemingly indeterminate aspects of the author's presentation of "self" as well as his historical "moment." Linguistically, the narrative of rethinking brings just such complexity to a single utterance.

In anticipation of the third and final composition, Cone directed students toward the end of the second discussion to again consider how Malcolm X's thinking had changed and its relationship to the importance of the book. In the same discussion, she reiterated the significance of the book's epilogue in rhetorical terms: "in terms of literature you have to look at is that from what point of view is this guy telling the story. And what's his purpose in telling the story? Because I think his purpose changes. And, and then the epilogue changes things too." Cone had already described to the class her own assessment of the book over time ("on second reading 20 years afterwards, I think that Malcolm X had a tremendous effect on our society today") and, implicitly, how her own perspectives about it have continued to evolve – especially regarding the work's enduring impact and significance:

It's a diatribe on white people – and you see this *shift*. I think maybe that's why people think it's such an important book – that this is the sort of a real change in a man's life for all kinds of reasons. Let me ask you this. Well, I'm going to ask you to write tomorrow. . . . So I want you to think about, you know, what do you admire about him? And what do you, what do you hate about him? Okay. So, tonight I'd like you to think about those things. And tomorrow I'm going to give you an in-class essay that I hope will pull it all together.

Third Composition

The last written response to *The Autobiography* took the form of a letter directed to the school district's "English Chairman," arguing for or against adopting the book.

When composing her letter, Eva took the occasion to comment on the success of discussions. When it came to evaluating the value of the work, and whether it is worthy of adding to the school district's list of required, senior reading, Eva cited the dialogue during discussions, as well as how the book had challenged students – precisely because it demanded them to come to terms with uncertainties in the text. Eva, who had wrestled with her own emotions throughout the unit, ultimately favored the book's adoption, due in part to the "strength" of class discussions – especially dialogue and rethinking. Central to Eva's rationale for adopting the book is that the text provides a vehicle for essential, albeit difficult, dialogue about racial relations, acknowledging that it should probably be assigned with discretion. Despite having been embroiled in some of the most contentious discussion herself, Eva's letter opens by recounting the importance of such dialogue. In the end, Eva valued dialogue and difference, and, as always, the chance for everyone to rethink their perspectives.

Eva's opening paragraphs offer a conditional endorsement of adoption, contingent on the "maturity" of groups of future students. Although recognizing the possibility of discord, her endorsement hinges on an appraisal of the discussions her own class had held. Eva's compact letter (279 words), clearly draws on her previous thinking. In fact, it seems at moments to echo her second composition intertextually. Eva's letter opens this way:

Dear English Chairman,

My Advanced Placement English class read The Autobiography of Malcolm X. Our class discussions had a lot of participation and opposing views. I think we had more students participate than we had in any other discussion. Everyone had to examine their feelings about the book very carefully. I would like you to put Malcolm X on the suggested reading list for seniors with the advise [sic] for only classes who would be mature enough to respect the feelings of everyone in the class.

I warn that some classes may not be able to handle the book. It can muster up a lot of anger and some people aren't good at dealing with these feelings.

Eva acknowledges the difficulty of such dialogue (i.e., "a lot of . . . opposing views" and "a lot of anger"). Although she only hints at rethinking – that she and her classmates "had to examine their feelings about the book very carefully" – I believe that the possibility of rethinking is implicit here. In an interview, Eva elaborated on this idea:

I think I said, *It should if the teacher, it's the teacher's choice, though, that she should know her class and make sure they can handle it.* /because/ Because it could bring up a lot of tension, and then you have to be mature enough to understand, you know, try and figure out your own feelings and stuff like that. /right/ Because some people couldn't handle it, you know.

For Eva herself, the notion of "figuring out your own feelings" had been central to her interaction with this book all along. Why should students be required to read such a book? For Eva, the answer boiled down to how Malcolm X seemed to embody an intellectual stance – a capacity for rethinking. As we have seen, that process was by no means a simple one for her – particularly given the indeterminacy of the text – one that continually involved rethinking.

Incidentally, Eva's letter also offered a telling disclaimer: "A problem our class had was that we sometimes strayed from talking about the book and started arguing about our own solutions to end racial problems." Not everyone would agree that this is problematic, of course. At issue, from the standpoint of interpretive theory, is whether formal, classroom study of literature should be limited to textual explication and analysis (akin to the tenets of New Criticism), or open into a wider realm of discussion associated with reader-oriented theories: that is, extrapolating from a text in ways that connect to students' lives. In Bakhtinian terms, such questions can be framed in terms of dialogue and response (1986). To the extent that classroom interpretation involves both reading a work and discerning the responses of others, rather than merely "explicating texts," differing interpretations must be negotiated. As Todorov (1984) suggests, while conventional approaches to textual interpretation emphasize either the text's authority or the reader's contribution, "the third kind would be the dialogue advocated by Bakhtin, where each of the two identities remains affirmed . . . where knowledge takes the form of dialogue" (p. 108). Indeed, what Eva characterizes here as digression might to others represent a sign of success during such discussions: evidence of genuine student engagement with their classmates about a text and its implications.

But it is in the letter's close that Eva finally *thematizes* rethinking, this time in service of her overall argument for adopting the book:

But we also discussed our feelings about Malcolm X and found that we had a hard time deciding what we thought of him. I think, though, that that added to the strength of our discussions. We had to keep trying to figure out who Malcolm X really was. His changes in the book were a new experience to all of us. We have been reading books that have already been planned at the beginning. This book's tone changed before our very eyes and our feelings, in turn, changed as well.

Consider this: the closing paragraphs of Eva's third composition represent in a sense her "last word" on the subject, at least in this classroom. Not that she will not go on thinking about the book – and rethinking things. Referring to another work in an interview, Eva said, "in the discussion we brought up a lot of questions and they're still not quite answered. . . . Maybe one of these days I'll read it again when I get older and maybe I can figure it out."

I am left with a feeling of considerable awe at the complexity of interpretive discourse reflected in Eva's writing and her contributions to discussions. I would argue that such "classroom language" is every bit as rich and nuanced as the works of literature it is purported to serve. Like Eva, I hope in time to comprehend more fully just how such "texts" are to be read.

DISCUSSION

In closing, let me offer a brief, personal narrative of rethinking. Returning to the transcripts of classroom discourse and sets of student compositions, I had anticipated certain types of findings. Having been present during these discussions in class, I remembered well several of the most emotional exchanges. I recalled also the surprise of discovering that the oral language of the classroom had been carried forward in writing: in a Bakhtinian sense, that what had been internalized and appropriated proved to be part of an ongoing "inner" dialogue. What had impressed me above all, however, was the willingness students ultimately had shown to accommodate perspectives expressed by classmates that differed, sometimes dramatically, from their own.

As I reread their writing, there was often evidence of such accommodation: some students who on first reading had given the book their almost unqualified endorsement, later acknowledged that it could offend classmates, and consequently should be assigned with discretion. Others, who had taken exception to the author's arguments and actions from the start, came to recognize the value of dialogue that discussing the book had allowed. I am reminded of how Geertz (1983) speaks of difference, reciprocity, and dialogue: "The problem of the integration of cultural life becomes one of making it possible for people inhabiting different worlds to have a genuine, and reciprocal, impact upon one another. . . . And for that, the first step is surely to accept the depth of the differences; the second is to understand what these differences are; and the third to construct some sort of vocabulary" (p. 161).

These students ultimately embraced such rethinking as the very point of talking and writing about what they read in school. Debating perspectives on racial relations, the students had wrestled with beliefs – each other's, of course, but also with their own. What did *not* emerge upon close re-reading of the data, however, were any neat patterns of reciprocal accommodation. Instances, yes, each singular and moving in its own right. Yet, such concessions still strike me as enormously important in an ethical sense, since they inevitably led in the direction of respect and tolerance.

I had also underestimated the teacher's role – how effectively Cone had coaxed the class to return to and reassess the text, as well as to reconsider their own responses. She had systematically framed assignments in ways that linked talk and writing. Making such connections explicitly, of course, contributed complexity to their thinking, in keeping with Bakhtin's linguistic theories. "According to Bakhtin, our internal conversations, the dialogues that make up our texts, will inevitably be richer if they occur in sociocognitive and cognitive spaces where multiple voices and multiple ways of voicing are welcomed" (Freedman, 1994, p. 227). And, repeatedly, Cone admonished students to engage respectfully in dialogue with one another and, in a sense, with themselves, responding to ideas and issues that reading this work had raised.

Given the student-led format for discussions, it would be easy to underestimate the teacher's role. Yet as we have seen, Cone had still participated, albeit with considerable discretion, contributing to student-led discussions in strategic ways. In addition, she repeatedly framed discussions and writing assignments in terms of rethinking and admittedly invited – even "prompted" – student rethinking; occasionally, she even seemed to model it. Talking and writing about rethinking were thereby legitimized, but the outcome of this process was not scripted in any formulaic way. There were no reductionistic "right answers" operating here. In fact, the whole dynamic of rethinking seems the antithesis of classrooms where students please the teacher by regurgitating specific information or by parroting particular perspectives. Indeed, at moments this class seemed to approach an ideal described by Lawrence-Lightfoot (1999): "Respect creates symmetry and empathy, and connection in all kinds of relationships, even those, such as teacher and student . . . embedded in classroom dialogue as [a teacher] helps students learn how to ask good questions, value inquiry, listen to each other, and begin the habit of thoughtful reflection" (pp. 9–12). Importantly, teachers can guide students to enter into dialogue with classmates, and perhaps to view their own learning and development in ongoing, collaborative, and even social-constructivist ways.

From a social-constructivist perspective, the overall "discourse history" of this class is reflected in the ways that specific issues were returned to and built upon over time, whether within a single instructional unit or even across an entire school year. Although exploring complex themes repeatedly is not easily scripted by formal curriculum, it suggests how classroom learning is ultimately socially situated, especially when ongoing instructional conversation allows for connections among multiple texts. Classroom learning, I would argue, is rooted in such sustained social and inner dialogue, and reflected in student narratives of rethinking.

Such negotiation of perspectives and interpretations is precisely the sort of dialogue envisioned by composition theorists interested in instructional practices informed by Bakhtinian theory. Farmer (2001), for example, argues that "In our class discussion, in our assignments, in our responses to student work, as well as in every other aspect of our pedagogies, we pitch camp on *borderlines*, for there and only there are we able to meet our twin obligations to mutual inquiry, to dialogue" (p. 148). When such ideals are realized in practice, as we have seen, students can engage texts with both passion and insight.

Witnessing how articulately students such as Eva recount rethinking – during class discussions and implicitly in writing afterward – suggests how profoundly classroom language can contribute to developing increasingly complex perspectives on texts. What is more, students had spoken openly about the most vexing issues, including the legacy of racial relations, and their own place in a pluralistic world. In the end, theirs is a complicated and recursive story, a narrative with multiple voices that each and every student engages individually, drawing on texts and talk, as their own narratives of rethinking unfold.

APPENDIX A

Transcription Conventions

Transcription of discussions and interviews were generally punctuated in the manner of written language, excepting "sentence fragments," for which periods separate intonation units.

Name:	Speaker's turns labeled by pseudonym, excepting the teacher.
Italic	Voicing: Speakers representing – explicitly or implicitly – words attributed (or attributable) to others or read from written text.
Bold Italic	Multiple "levels" of embedded voicing, akin to quotes within quotes.
Underscoring	Emphatic stress signaled by intonation, unless otherwise noted.
/—/	Back channel cues.
[—]	Notes and commentary.
. . . .	"Text" of talk deleted.

References

Allen, G. (2000). *Intertextuality: The new critical idiom*. London: Routledge.

Bakhtin, M. (1981). Discourse in the novel. In M. Holquist (Ed.), *The dialogical imagination* (pp. 259–422). Austin: University of Texas Press.

Bakhtin, M. (1986). The problem of speech genres. In C. Emerson & M. Holquist (Eds.), *Speech genres and other late essays* (pp. 60–102). Austin: University of Texas Press.

Farmer, F. (2001). *Saying and silence: Listening to composition with Bakhtin*. Logan: Utah State University Press.

Freedman, S. W. (1994). *Exchanging writing, exchanging cultures: Lessons in school reform from the United States and Great Britain*. Cambridge, MA: Harvard University Press.

Geertz, C. (1983). *Local knowledge: Further essays on interpretative anthropology*. New York: Basic Books.

Iser, W. (1971). Indeterminacy and the reader's response in prose fiction. In J. Miller (Ed.), *Aspects of narrative* (pp. 1–46). New York: Columbia University Press.

Iser, W. (1978). *The act of reading: A theory of aesthetic response*. Baltimore: John Hopkins University Press.

Iser, W. (2000). *The range of interpretation*. New York: Columbia University Press.

Knoeller, C. P. (1993). *How talking enters writing: A study of 12th graders discussing and writing about literature*. Unpublished doctoral dissertation, University of California, Berkeley.

Knoeller, C. P. (1994). Negotiating interpretations of text: The role of student-led discussions in the understanding of literature. *Journal of Reading, 37* (7), 572–80.

Knoeller, C. P. (1998a). *Voicing ourselves: Whose words we use when we talk about books.* Albany: State University of New York Press.

Knoeller, C. P. (1998b). Negotiating interpretations of text: The role of student-led discussions in the understanding of literature. In M. Opitz (Ed.), *Literacy instruction for culturally and linguistically diverse students* (pp. 105–14). Newark, DE: International Reading Association.

Lawrence-Lightfoot, S. (1999). *Respect: An exploration.* Reading, MA: Perseus Books.

Morson, G. S., & Emerson, C. (1990). *Mikhail Bakhtin: Creation of a Prosaics.* Stanford: Stanford University Press.

Todorov, T. (1984). *Mikhail Bakhtin: The dialogical principle.* Theory and History of Literature Series, Volume 13. Minneapolis: University of Minnesota Press.

8

Ever Newer Ways to Mean

Authoring Pedagogical Change in Secondary Subject-Area Classrooms

Cynthia L. Greenleaf
Mira-Lisa Katz

> The semantic structure of an internally persuasive discourse is not finite, it is open; in each of the new contexts that dialogize it, this discourse is able to reveal ever newer ways to mean.
>
> —(Bakhtin, 1981, p. 346)

The texts of educational research are replete with descriptions of teachers resistant to the pedagogical changes that others prescribe or mandate (Pajares, 1991; cf. Richardson, 1990). In the large body of research devoted to educational reform, teachers are often depicted – positioned – as unable, unwilling, unknowing, and/or unskilled. In this chapter, we aim to describe, instead, a professional learning environment in which teachers, who are seen as knowledgeable experts in their disciplines, are invited to engage in collaborative inquiry and to adaptively design classroom innovation.[1] We describe the discourses that shape this learning environment and show how teachers, as a result of their collaborative experiences and exchanges, take up social and dialogical tools for imagining and authoring new pedagogical selves. We illustrate how, in the process, teachers begin to offer new possibilities for their diverse, urban students – themselves often positioned as unable, unwilling, unknowing, and/or unskilled – to enact new literate identities and practices in the classroom.

Bakhtin's key theoretical constructs of "dialogism" and "authoring" provide us with a theoretical framework for reflecting on the power and potential of inquiry-based professional development for teachers. "Dialogism" conveys Bakhtin's understanding of the omnipresent and dialogical social contexts in which human beings are always "in a state of being 'addressed'

---

[1] And here we align ourselves with advocates of professional learning opportunities in which teachers take, or are offered, subject positions as agents of their own learning and change (Bissex, 1994; Buchanan, 1994; Carroll & Carini, 1991; Cochran-Smith & Lytle, 1992; Florio-Ruane, 1990; Freedman et al., 1999; Fullan, 1993; Goswami & Stillman, 1987; Smith, 1996).

and in the process of 'answering'" (Bakhtin, 1981; Holland et al., 1998; Holquist, 1990). From such a perspective, individuals, including those in professional development and teaching situations, are always in the act of responding to the social world, and in making meaning through their responses to that world, they are also reshaping or "authoring" it. This, we suggest, is what teachers had an opportunity to do in the context of a professional development program, the Strategic Literacy Network (SLN); take the words and ideas available to them through the professional development discourse and culture, and "populate them with their own intentions" (Bakhtin, 1981, p. 294) thereby making them their own.

The examples we share in this chapter illustrate what can happen as teachers interact in dialogical learning environments with colleagues, students' voices, and texts. To illustrate the dynamic process of self-authoring, we draw from the voices of participating teachers themselves, from the ways in which they frame their own classroom practices and reconstruct positions and identities for and with their students. By looking closely at the particular opportunities teachers encountered through participation in this inquiry-based professional development, we explore how the settings and activities of the professional learning environment served as a "dialogic space of authoring" for the teachers. This space provides a helpful, and we think hopeful, lens for reconceiving of teachers' professional growth over time. In concluding this chapter, we consider the data's implications for the design and practice of professional development and suggest that professional development that offers an invitation to teachers to engage in such self-refashioning reaches, in powerful and promising ways, into the lives and literacies of their students.

A BAKHTINIAN FRAMEWORK FOR REFLECTING ON INQUIRY-BASED PROFESSIONAL DEVELOPMENT

For Bakhtin (1981), language is inherently dialogic, populated by social history and ideologies, understood not only as a system of abstract grammatical categories, but also better conceived as ideologically saturated – "language as world view" (p. 271). Individuals must wrestle, in appropriating language that is inevitably preshaped by prior histories and ideologies, to convey their own meanings and nuances through and against the meanings and forms of utterances available to them:

The living utterance, having taken meaning and shape at a particular historical moment in a socially specific environment, cannot fail to brush up against thousands of living dialogic threads, woven by socio-ideological consciousness around the given object of an utterance; it cannot fail to become an active participant in social dialogue. (p. 276)

In this sense, even the language of thought is characterized by internal dialogism, populated, in Bakhtin's view, with the intentions of others. In exploring Bakhtin's dialogism, Holquist foregrounds the way individuals are always responding to this dialogic social world in order to make sense of it:

Existence is addressed to me as a riot of inchoate potential messages. . . . Some of the potential messages come to me in the form of primitive physiological stimuli, some in the form of natural language, and some in social codes, or ideologies. So long as I am in existence, I am in a particular place, and must respond to all these stimuli either by ignoring them or in a response that takes the form of making sense, of producing – for it is a form of work – meaning out of such utterances. (Holquist, 1990, p. 47, cited in Holland et al., 1998, pp. 169–70).

As individuals recognize and work to make meaning through this "primordial dialogism of discourse," the creative possibility in language can transform their thoughts and actions, assisting in their "ideological becoming" (Bakhtin, 1981, p. 275). Bakhtin characterizes this process of active and engaged understanding, and the new conceptions that emerge from it, as follows:

. . . an active understanding, one that assimilates the word under consideration into a new conceptual system, that of the one striving to understand, establishes a series of complex interrelationships, consonances and dissonances with the word and enriches it with new elements . . . it is in this way, after all, that various different points of view, conceptual horizons, systems for providing expressive accents, various social "languages" come to interact with one another. (p. 282)

Dialogism then, once engaged, offers a space of authoring new meanings and conceptual systems. In dialogical, heteroglossic, polyphonic interactions, " . . . several consciousnesses meet as equals and engage in a dialogue that is in principle unfinalizable" (pp. 238–9). Although for Bakhtin language is stratified, dynamically diverse, constructed of speech belonging to and shaped by social groups, there is also a contrary and powerful impulse in individuals and society to deaden and "monologize" thought and language, to close off the possibility inherent in the dialogic nature of human life, to "fall out of the dialogue" (Bakhtin, 1979, p. 168, cited in Morson & Emerson, 1990, p. 56). In other words, even though language itself is inherently and potently dialogic, social situations are frequently not. This monologic impulse is closely related, in Bakhtin's writings, to singularity of viewpoints, transmission, and recitation rather than meaning making, and didactic and authoritarian discourses that have ceased to be "internally persuasive" to the thinking being. He laments that:

. . . an individual's becoming, an ideological process, is characterized precisely by a sharp gap between . . . the authoritative word (religious, political, moral; the word of a father, of adults and of teachers, etc.) that does not know internal persuasiveness, and . . . [the] internally persuasive word that is denied all privilege, backed up by no authority at all, and is frequently not even acknowledge in society. (Bakhtin, 1981, p. 342)

There are many parallels in Bakhtin's descriptions of the monologic impulse within human discourse and life and the schooling of young people, as well as the ongoing development of their teachers. Classrooms and professional development settings are most often characterized by monologic forms of discourse, participation structures (see Philips, 1974) that deny learners roles and valid voices in these settings. In the following pages, we describe how dialogical modes of discourse and learning were supported in the professional development setting and subsequently emerged in teachers' classrooms as teachers worked to engage their students in collaborative work to make sense of difficult, course texts.

An Inquiry-Based Learning Environment for Secondary Teachers

Since 1994, we and our teacher colleagues have been engaged in designing, implementing, and studying a program of professional development to enable teachers to build more complex conceptions of reading and student learning, as well as a repertoire of classroom practices that support students' reading development.[2] This program, known as the Strategic Literacy Initiative, involves networks of interdisciplinary school teams of teachers in California's Bay Area in inquiry activities designed to help them recognize, articulate, further develop, and *teach* their own subject-area literacies.[3]

Underlying this work is a conception of reading as a sociocultural practice that is at once the orchestration of meaning by individual readers – Graves' *composing* act – and the shaping of meaning by individuals' membership in interpretive communities that are part of complex, social worlds (Bakhtin, 1981; Cope & Kalantzis, 1993; Graves, 1990; Greenleaf et al., 2001; Moje, Dillon, & O'Brien, 2000; Rabinowitz & Smith, 1998; Scribner & Cole, 1981; Smagorinsky, 2001; Street, 1995). This understanding of reading illuminates our view of the situated social and cognitive work that is necessary for learners to participate successfully in academic literacies across the typical

---

[2] The study reported here was supported by a 3-year grant from the Spencer and MacArthur Foundations' Program in Professional Development Research and Documentation.

[3] Since its beginnings as a teacher-research collaborative in 1994, the Strategic Literacy Initiative has convened over twenty networks of teacher teams to engage in inquiry-based professional development of the kind described in this chapter. Over time, the inquiry tools and practices of the Strategic Literacy Initiative have grown to include many that are not described in these pages. Here, we draw from a study of the inquiry practices and teacher participants of a single network, known as the Strategic Literacy Network (SLN), which met during the 1997–1998 and 1998–1999 school years.

secondary curriculum (see Bartholomae, 1985; Courts, 1997; Gee, 1992, 1996).

Across the academic disciplines or domains of learning commonly taught in school, reading and literacy practices can differ strikingly, as can the epistemologies, historical discourses, and conventional practices of the disciplines (e.g., Applebee, 1996; Bartholomae, 1985; Eeds & Wells, 1989; Grossman, 1990; Lee, 1995; Lemke, 1990; Rabinowitz, 1987; Rex & McEachen, 1999; Stodolsky, 1988; Wineburg, 1991). Secondary teachers often interpret student performance with reference to the customary practices and discourses of their disciplines (including the epistemologies and ways of reading valued in these disciplines, which are hidden from view), yet do not often explicitly teach students how to participate in these practices (Bartholomae, 1985; Freedman et al., 1995; Hull & Rose, 1989; Hull et al., 1991). Helping secondary teachers and their students to access and extend their own literate practices is the complex problem to which we have addressed our work (Greenleaf et al., 2001; Schoenbach et al., 1999). To do so, we invite teachers to engage in inquiry activities designed to access and problematize their conceptions of reading, academic reading tasks, and students' reading performances.

Central to the professional development of the SLN during the 1997–1999 school years were literacy learning cases of students reading a variety of texts. These tools give teachers practice analyzing how students understand and approach academic literacy, and help teachers think about what students are already bringing to these tasks. These literacy learning cases are based on case studies of individual students conducted in collaboration with teachers, and are informed by prior work to develop a set of literacy learning cases as a part of a research study of remedial learners in postsecondary settings (Greenleaf, Hull, & Reilly, 1994). In working with these cases, teachers repeatedly encounter and engage in inquiry practices – specific routines and discourse structures that support them in surfacing and articulating reading processes. Such practices include analyzing texts, interpreting student talk and reading performances, adaptively implementing instructional ideas in their classrooms, and reflecting on their classroom practices in preparation for further refinement and adaptation.

The student case materials – video and text-based "close-ups" of ninth-grade students struggling with and making sense of various texts – give teachers a chance to hear students talking about their reading histories and habits, and to see students reading a variety of academic and recreational texts and responding to an interviewer's questions about their reading. These cases not only provide teachers with a window into students' reading "errors" and challenges, but also provide a closer look at the strengths and theories about reading that students use to make sense of school texts and reading practices. Across the varied cases, teachers have the opportunity to see that students approach and read various texts quite differently, reading is shaped by many situational factors, and students' reading of one text will not demonstrate the full range of reading strategies and competencies they may actually have at their disposal.

The professional development approach of the Strategic Literacy Initiative is based on a *generative* model of teacher learning (e.g., Hillocks, 1995); inquiry activities are designed to assist teachers in building the internalized knowledge and experience base necessary to carry out the long-range planning, refinement, and on-the-spot classroom problem solving that expert teaching of reading within a subject-area classroom demands. The case materials and inquiry processes themselves are designed to be generative thinking tools facilitating the knowledge growth and practical expertise of teachers. Inquiry activities with these cases are designed to unsettle teachers' first impressions of students, drive them to look more deeply at how students are thinking and what resources and voices they are bringing to reading tasks, and help them recognize what Rose (1989) calls "the incipient excellence" that characterizes many underperforming students in our classrooms. The dialogic learning environment of the SLN provides teachers access to discursive tools and resources that help them reconceive literacy and student performance. In what follows, we use excerpts from an inquiry discussion about a student's reading to explore the ways teachers refashion their thinking and begin to imagine new pedagogical selves.

Talking and Learning Through Case Inquiry: Teachers
Voices in Dialogue

As a living, socio-ideological concrete thing, as heteroglot opinion, language, for the individual consciousness, lies on the borderline between oneself and the other. The word in language is half someone else's. It becomes "one's own" only when the speaker populates it with his own intention, his own accent, when he appropriates the word, adapting it to his own semantic and expressive intention. (Bakhtin, 1981, pp. 293–4)

In the following account of a day in the SLN, we share how teachers begin to take words and meanings that, in Bakhtin's view, "lie on the borderline between oneself and the other," and make the ideas of the professional development community their own by appropriating its discourse (language, ways of interpreting student performance, conceptions of literacy) and adapting new understandings to their own pedagogical intentions and designs. Throughout this account, we show how these teachers' voices provide examples of Bakhtin's claim that people move from being respondents to "externally authoritative discourse" toward building "internally persuasive discourse" by recasting others' ideas in the process of making sense of them:

Internally persuasive discourse – as opposed to one that is externally authoritative – is, as it is affirmed through assimilation, tightly interwoven with "one's own word." In the everyday rounds of our consciousness, the internally persuasive word is half-ours and half-someone else's. Its creativity and productiveness consist precisely in the fact that such a word awakens new and independent words, that it organizes masses of our words from within, and does not remain in an isolated and static condition. It is not so much interpreted by us as it is further, that is, freely, developed, applied to new material, new conditions; it enters into interanimating relationships with new contexts. More than that, it enters into an intense interaction, a struggle with other internally persuasive discourses. (Bakhtin, 1981, pp. 345–6)

Significantly, this process of assimilation is one of *integration* and *reconfiguration*; such growth is both creative and improvisational and relies fundamentally on teachers' agency in developing such new pedagogical ways of being. That is, teachers' shifts in thinking, doing, and interacting in the professional development context – their "ideological becoming" – seem reflective of the struggles between multiple internally persuasive discourses – preexisting beliefs and ideas about students, literacy and texts, and the discourses they encounter in the company of colleagues in this context. Below, teachers' articulations of these new ideas reveal how understanding occurs at the heart of this linguistic and ideational wrestling match – at the very point of utterance.

It is a rainy Saturday morning in February. Twenty-nine middle and high school teachers from five urban schools are gathered in San Francisco for a professional development session focused on reading. This morning, they are engaging in an inquiry focused on Nyala,[4] a ninth-grade African American girl, reading several pieces of literature: *Mama*, a novel by Terri MacMillan who is a writer Nyala had chosen for her own recreational reading; a segment of *Romeo and Juliet*, which Nyala was currently reading in her English class; and a short story by James Thurber, which had been given to the class as part of a collection of short stories from which students were to choose and read independently for a literature project.

With this inquiry, teachers have an opportunity to closely analyze the many language features of literary texts, as well as to surface their own use of these features to draw inferences and understandings about the literary world being constructed by the author. As they view the videotape of Nyala's reading, teachers have frequent opportunities to reflect and discuss – in small-groups and in the network as a whole – the observations and interpretations they are making of Nyala's reading of these texts. They are drawn to the puzzle of Nyala's very different readings, and drawn by her articulate complaint to explore possible explanations for why Nyala cannot hear or feel the Thurber story.

The day begins with teachers carrying out their own close reading of "The Catbird Seat" by James Thurber, an inquiry that deliberately focuses them on the signals in the text they are using to draw inferences and begin to construct a fictional world. After this small-group work, the teachers share

---

[4] All student and teacher names in this manuscript are pseudonyms.

their thoughts and observations. From a Bakhtinian point of view, we see these teachers appropriating their collaborative experience and employing it to reimagine classroom interactions with students and texts:

Karen: One of the things at the beginning that kind of frustrated me, and I was wondering how we might think about this in the classroom, is, we were really being pretty literal, "This is what I know," and to support how you know from the text was really the same thing that we were saying that we knew. . . . Once we got to more in the text to play with and sort of shifting interpretations, basically, then it got more interesting, and it was more important to go back to the text, I thought, at that point. So I thought that there were two levels of things going on, and I'm wondering if we should do this with both, all at the same time, or if we should sort of . . . tailor it a bit. . . . The other thing that I've come away with sort of embedded in my head which could be reinforced through this, is the question answer relationships because a lot of what we're saying is, "Well, it's right there." Or, it's me and the – y'know, [Facilitator: That's a nice] like Broadway, New York, theater district, it's me and then y'know, the text. [Facilitator: That's a nice connection, yeah.] And I can see the two sort of as companion structures . . .

Leah: Just thinking about my own students, I think I'd have to do a lot of modeling about that because . . . I find that they really struggle with figuring out the subtext a lot of times. So I think that this may be useful, especially if they're doing it in a group because other people's interpretations sort of built on. Like I said something, and then Mary said something, and then Krista said, "Oh, I hadn't thought about it that way but since you mention it now I'm wondering if she's kind of coming on to him."

Aaron: When you're reading fiction, there's a certain amount of sense making that takes place at the beginning where you fix the world the author's making, the time and place, and where you come to understand the nature of that world. . . . So I think this would be a particularly useful exercise. You pointed out it would take forever to do this through a whole story, but if you can take the time to do it for the first page of the story . . . then once everyone is in the same place, in the same point, then you can go on and they can read it.

In this exchange, we see these teachers drawing on their own experiences in the reading inquiry to think about instruction, linking their reading with colleagues to their observations of students. They connect these reading experiences as well to the pedagogical ideas they have encountered in this professional development network, such as the Question-Answer-Relationships (QAR) (Raphael, 1982) that Karen recognizes she has been using in the inquiry as she locates her own interpretations of the Thurber piece "right there" and in "me and, you know, the text." Similarly, Leah refers to modeling invisible reading processes as a mode of teaching, an idea that has been key to conversations in this professional community. The social resources of the professional development context – in the form of ideas and talk – become the material resources individual teachers use to reflect on their own experiences and begin to construct new pedagogical ideas and practices.

The teachers' collaborative reading experiences and inquiry lead seamlessly into pedagogical problem solving and instructional design, literally an authoring of new pedagogies. We see this process reflected in Karen's lengthy utterance. Here, Karen wonders if the process of identifying text signals enforced a more literal reading of the Thurber short story than she would like her students to construct. (Later, we'll see how she revises her thinking about this.) She sees this process as similar to the "right there" questions in QAR. She reports that once she and her colleagues got further into the text and had more to work with, however, they were engaged in more interpretive work and drew on background knowledge, which she understands as "me and, you know, the text" responses. She is, in a Bakhtinian sense, appropriating social resources – both QAR pedagogical practices and the collaborative reading experience – and mentally tailoring her classroom use of the close reading inquiry based on this experience, linking it to QAR as a companion structure to support students in their reading of literature.

Similarly, Aaron muses aloud about when in the process of reading a piece of literature it might be most beneficial to engage students in collaborative, close readings focused on drawing inferences from signals in the text. For Aaron, close reading may be a way to assist students in stepping into a literary world as they first begin a piece of literature (Langer, 1995). Like Karen, Aaron is designing, or authoring, imagined classroom practice in this discursive space. Leah recalls the way each of the teachers' interpretations of the text built on one another's to enrich the reading. She mentally transposes this experience to the classroom environment, envisioning her students as resources to one another in the endeavor to construct literary understandings, just as she and her colleagues enriched one another's readings. In this short exchange, these teachers take positions as theory builders and classroom orchestrators, metaphorizing and appropriating from their own collaborative reading as interpretations build on one another to imagined classrooms, where students are able to experience a similar building of interpretations and entry into the world of the author's making.

After this close reading inquiry, the teachers read the beginning of *Mama* and analyze the similarities and differences in the two texts. Having prepared by explicitly articulating their own reading processes and comprehension puzzles with these texts, the teachers then begin an inquiry into Nyala's reading of these texts. After meeting Nyala through excerpts from a literacy history interview, teachers watch a segment of a videotaped reading interview in which Nyala talks about the first several paragraphs of *Mama*. They see Nyala read and discuss *Mama* with ease, picturing the characters and interpreting the social world MacMillan draws in this novel. The teachers make some notes and begin to share their observations about Nyala's reading. They find Nyala's rapid summary of the gist of the text to be especially impressive evidence of her comprehension abilities. Below, we excerpt from the discussion after the teachers share observations of the impressive way Nyala has created detailed images of the character Mildred, drawn key inferences about the troubled relationships at the heart of the novel, and expressed her concern for the central character. In the following exchanges, we see teachers exploring the role of talk in comprehension, the possibility of comprehending at the point of utterance, the possible ways that "the process" of talking about text can actually shape what is seen and what is remembered about it:

Karen: I have kind of a question. What strikes me about these interv –
             or say just this interview is that there's a lot of sort of
             stumbling, you know, 'stuff' and 'like', 'y'know', this imprecise
             stuff. 'Stuff', I just used it. So, you could say that as she talks,
             she's trying to, in that moment, comprehend what she's read.
             And my question is, in fact, with, with her level of reading, is
             that really what she's doing? And is it only when she's talking
             about it that she's comprehending? What's happening when
             she's just alone with the text and reading it?

Facilitator: So, where is the actual meaning making? [Karen: Right.]
             When is that happening? [Karen: Right.]

Lynn: I tended to look at it as, because obviously she reads the text
             and understands it, but when she talks to us, she drops
             grammar, slurs words, whatever. And there I am doing the
             same thing she did. I think all these 'y'knows' and 'likes' are
             just like 'whatever'. It's a padding that teenagers use when
             they talk, and she gets the meaning. She knows. And if you
             disregard all those other paddings, what she says are the
             nuggets that she's already understood. To me.

Carla: I was thinking the same thing when we were doing the James
             Thurber story. We tended to read a paragraph but then as we
             began talking about it, we would go back and find other stuff
             that we hadn't remembered. . . . [Usually] When I'm reading
             fiction, I'm just sort of absorbing the sense of it as it goes
             along and some of the detail, but I miss probably a lot of the
             detail. And so I've noticed with these interviews often that – I
             mean, in terms of your question – how much do we actually
             retain and how much does the process sort of force us to go
             back and find it?

Linda: But she talked about how she talks about books with her
             sister. . . . I know that I, and maybe she does, you know, get it

> when she talks about it, and we know that she talks about it
> when she's doing recreational reading with her sister, so . . .

The teachers are watching a videotaped interview in which the interviewer's questions and the student's responses interact to shape next questions and next responses, just as teachers' collaborative close readings "built on" each other to create shifting meanings of Thurber's story. Clearly, talk has an impact on comprehension, but what role does talk play? Again, these teachers are offered, and taking up, positions as theorists, exploring possible accounts for a phenomenon of interest they have identified in Nyala's reading interview. Karen's question – What happens when she's just alone with the text and reading it? – calls these teachers to answer, to consider the ways the form and the content of Nyala's talk can mean. In answering, they position Nyala metaphorically as illustrative of readers, in general, as well as of the students in their own classrooms. In the process, Nyala's voice becomes text and data for these teachers, a voice that itself calls from them a dialogic response.

As they did while reading "The Catbird Seat," these teachers are collaboratively building on one another's interpretations to construct and refute different understandings or "readings" of Nyala's talk. They are also exploring what kind of evidence students' talk about texts can provide: does the kind of linguistic "imprecision" in the case show a reader groping to form and express meaning? Someone "thinking out loud?" They echo then, in both the form and the content of their talk, Bakhtin's (1981) conception of dialogism: "In the actual life of speech, every concrete act of understanding is active. . . . Understanding comes to fruition only in response. Understanding and response are dialectically merged and mutually condition each other; one is impossible without the other" (p. 282).

After this conversation, the teachers watch the videotaped reading interview as Nyala reads and draws inferences from a scene of *Romeo and Juliet* with relative ease and sophistication, and shares how she reads scenes aloud with her mother in the family kitchen. However, when Nyala faces "The Catbird Seat," she finds the internal and ironic voice of the text increasingly inaccessible, finally exclaiming with some exasperation, "I can't hear what I'm read'n. I like to hear what I'm read'n or feel what I'm read'n. And I can't really feel it or hear it, and I just don't like the story." Nyala's voice compels these teachers to answer. After watching Nyala read and talk about several sections of "The Catbird Seat," they work in small inquiry groups to share and explore the possible meanings and implications of what for them were particularly striking moments in Nyala's reading. Subsequently, in a whole group discussion, they debrief and share their insights.

The case inquiry process has been building to this moment of synthesis. Reporting back from the small-group work, Karen describes to the group a critical insight she came to through the Nyala case:

I loved her [Nyala's] comment when she said, "There's too many people and it doesn't tell the whole story about them," because in fact, she's specifically said what is interesting about this piece, and what you need to fill in as a reader. The other thing is, I'm rethinking what I said earlier about this process, that it was cumbersome because there was too much literal. Once she said what she said here, and watching her reading process, I realized that she's having to make all sorts of inferences, and that it's not literal for her. And that I think it's good to sort of have this firsthand experience of that.

Here, Karen shares her changed understanding of the close reading process and its potential utility for her students, an understanding she has come to through this opportunity to hear Nyala's voice and witness her struggle with "The Catbird Seat." Standing in for students in Karen's classroom, Nyala has helped Karen to rethink what she thought about this process and to realize that students are faced with the need to make a lot of inferences when they do not have the cultural knowledge demanded by particular texts. In this moment, Karen is fundamentally revising her understanding of reading, of teaching reading, and of student performance on reading tasks.

Carla then draws together her colleague's voices from different points in this morning's inquiry work, imagining a design for classroom instruction in which "strategies like what we started out doing this morning," meaning the close reading inquiry, could enable students like Nyala to "read the rest of the story on her own, once she got in, once she was there." Drawing on the voices of her colleagues as they respond to Nyala's compelling call to answer, she designs, or in Bakhtin's terms authors, a novel pedagogy for her students and her classroom:

Carla: What occurred to me as she was struggling with the Thurber piece was when she used the term, "I can't hear it." Linda was talking about being able to hear a narrator's voice. But it's also, I think, what Aaron was talking about earlier about when we read fiction, what we do is we find the time and place and once we get there, and we visualize it, then the story unfolds from there. And that when a reader can't get there, can't hear the voice, can't find the time or place, then the rest of it doesn't make any sense. And so what occurs to me is that in helping students be able to access text that is more difficult than what they're more normally used to or is language that they're uncomfortable with and unfamiliar with or requires background knowledge that they don't have, that using strategies like what we started out doing this morning [can help] . . .

            . . . What I was wondering is that if as a teacher you could go through a process maybe in the beginning of that story, where, to help them find New York, the 1940s, what this company might be like, what Mr. Martin, what kind of a person he was, and what his life might have been like, which is an utterly, totally foreign experience for a teenager today, that then she might be able to read the rest of the story on her own, once she got in, once she was there.

In this inquiry discussion, and the other inquiries into literacy learning cases that they experience as they participate in the SLN, teachers are given experience and support to explore multiple possible meanings of student performance on valued, literacy tasks. From a Bakhtinian perspective, the SLN provides a discourse community in which teachers have access to a new set of cultural resources and tools – the voices of literacy researchers, the SLN facilitators, their colleagues, and the case study students. In this heteroglossic context, students' voices provide new texts to which teachers respond, and in the process, come to understand in new ways. As they engage in the dialogic learning environment over time, teachers have opportunities to understand and appropriate new ways of talking and thinking about the teaching of reading; their access to others' ideas may allow them to, in Bakhtin's words, "make these words and ideas their own." In our view, as the discourse of the SLN becomes "internally persuasive," teachers develop new senses of themselves as teachers of reading, and more generous and hopeful views of students.

The dialogic professional development culture offers, then, a space of authoring new conceptions and new pedagogical ideas. In the following pages, we explore the ways in which SLN teachers began to reconfigure their classroom practices and orientations toward students, to imagine new pedagogical selves, and to offer students new voices and roles in literate activity. We suggest that teachers began to author classroom practices mirroring the dialogical learning environment of the SLN, offering students critical opportunities to engage in dialogue with text and with their classroom communities. Such opportunities to dialogue and engagement have potentially profound consequences for students' abilities to develop literate practices and literate conceptions of self.

TEACHERS' VOICES IN REFLECTION ON STUDENTS, READING, AND CLASSROOM PRACTICES

In a study of teacher development in the SLN, we traced teachers' knowledge growth and change over a period of two years. In addition to the audio- and videotapes of the discursive learning environment of the SLN that we have drawn upon in the preceding pages – teachers engaging in reading process analysis, text analysis, analysis of students' reading processes, and collegial conversations around teaching practice at SLN meetings – we also collected teachers' written reflections and carried out practice-grounded interviews with teachers at the beginning and end of each year. For these practice-grounded interviews, teachers brought a text they planned to use in their classroom, any lesson plans or materials from working with that text in the past, and any related samples of student work that were available. They then gave a detailed walkthrough of their classroom work with the text, describing how they introduced this text to their students, how they structured teaching and learning activities with the text over the period of time it was used, what they were hoping students would learn from their instructional activities, and how they assessed whether they and their students had met these instructional goals. At the end-of-year interviews, teachers were also asked to comment on any changes they had noticed in their own reading processes and teaching.

These interviews were guided by protocols yet gave teachers an opportunity to both display and reflect on their practice and philosophies. In these interviews, teachers positioned texts, literate activity, and students in the daily enactment of subject-area curriculum. Anchored in classroom teaching through the lesson materials and student work samples, they provided us views of the range of reading activities, learning activities, and social roles afforded to students in the teachers' classrooms. Yearly pre- and post-interviews gave evidence, then, of how teachers' conceptions of reading, their instructional practices, and their views of students changed over time as teachers participated in the dialogic inquiry environment of the SLN. In what follows, drawing on teachers' voices from these practice-grounded interviews as well as written reflections, we show how participating teachers' conceptions of students and their literate abilities changed over time, and how such shifts in their views reshaped opportunities for students to learn and to engage with texts in their classrooms.

Teachers' Initial Views of Students and Their Abilities

When we began this work, many of the teachers in the SLN raised doubts about their students' literate abilities, and expressed concern about how to address their students' learning needs around reading. The teachers' voices we excerpt below from practice-grounded interviews and reflective journals demonstrate widely held views of students among the participating teachers and provide clues to how these teachers were conceptualizing student literacy performance at the beginning of their participation in the SLN. Like many of her colleagues, Joanna, an English and History teacher, framed her expectations of students largely in terms of what they lacked:

Joanna: I try to avoid having expectations of where they'll be. Some of the things I've noticed they don't have . . . is summarizing information or restating it in their own words. Whether it's

> reading a paragraph from a history textbook or from a
> novel . . . to actually summarize and pick out main ideas or put it
> into their own words, . . . they just have a tendency to copy. Some
> of that's their reading level. (year 1, fall)

Her colleague, Doug, expressed similar views:

Doug: A significant percentage of the students coming into my class
        are . . . below norm on the CAT test. . . . the students who
        score . . . below norm on the CAT test don't read very well and
        don't like to read . . . reading is not a very pleasurable activity for
        them, and so that's my expectation. (year 1, fall)

At the beginning of their participation in the SLN, Joanna and Doug and
many of their fellow teachers expressed little faith in their students, pointing to students' difficulties with summarizing, identifying main ideas, and
paraphrasing. These same students, they told us, typically scored poorly on
reading tests, and did not like to read. Another teacher, Roberta, described
what she saw as a diminished inner mental landscape, which she believed
was linked to their reading performances:

Roberta: [How can a teacher get] a young adolescent teenager who has
           never been stimulated, who has never been taken places, to have
           a more active sense of creativity, to engage in fantasy and
           dreams? . . . A lot of the students that we have today I don't think
           are creative. They don't have imagination. How do you create
           an imagination in a child who has never had it? (year 1, fall)

Prior to SLN work, then, many teachers saw reading problems as internal
to students. Such appraisals of students echo a public discourse of defi-
ciency – a discourse that characterizes students as lacking skills, as not liking
to read or being very good at it, and as coming from backgrounds (the implication being from families and cultures) where they supposedly haven't
been "stimulated" and therefore lack creativity and imagination.

Teachers' Initial Classroom Practices: Students' Roles, Social Participation, and Interaction with Texts

When we began to look at how the work of literacy was being accomplished
in these teachers' classrooms, that is, how teachers and students were actually engaging with literacy, we were struck by how little contact with text
students actually had. The following quotes are revealing in this regard.
Again, the perspectives here represent many teachers' orientations when
they first began to work with the SLN. Doug lamented that in his classroom,

Doug: [Students are not going to see] a whole lot of novels which is
        distressing, but the reality is it's hard to get them to read

novels . . . and my curriculum is not dependent on being able to have them discuss or write about a passage of the book that most of them probably haven't read. (year 1, fall)

Because of this "reality," Doug frequently excerpted what he felt were key passages from novel-length works, asking students to write journal responses to these key passages, but did not, at this point in time, believe students could manage lengthier texts. Voicing the concerns of many subject-area teachers we work with, Joanna worried about her role in the classroom, and how to approach the very real dilemma of getting critical subject matter across when students seemed unable to read and analyze texts on their own:

Joanna: . . . I find maybe for issues of time, I tend to restate things because I want them to get what the story is telling them. . . . I'm constantly summarizing so that kids don't miss the main points. . . . I wish I didn't have to assume that role as much, but I find I do. . . . Sometimes students read on their own, but that's . . . rare. Most of the time, it's a whole class reading. (year 1, fall)

Similarly, Carla suggested why, in her class, as in Joanna's, reading and discussions tended to be whole-class, teacher-centered activities:

Carla: . . . [O]ne of the hardest things is getting kids to read the textbook with any meaning, and to do something other than simply parrot back the words without any understanding of what they mean. (year 1, fall)

Her solution, like Joanna's, was to read the text to students. Carla read core literature aloud to her students, stopping at points she thought were appropriate to discuss as they were reading. She did not want to give up difficult but worthy texts (she named "A Modest Proposal" by Jonathan Swift as one such text), so she would "lead a group of kids through it step by step," select vocabulary to preteach so students did not lose the thread of the piece as they went through it, and "read it well, with expression" as a "model of fluent reading" for her students.

Similarly, Carla provided guides, such as graphic organizers, to help students skim the history textbook for specific information, to "pick out what these ideas were." She also posed questions to which students were to respond. Carla described the challenge of accessing the textbook in this way:

Carla: . . . students will just write words out of the text without understanding what they mean or even recognizing when they aren't answering the questions posed. (year 1, fall)

Carla hoped these charts and her questions would guide students through the text while "avoiding the trap of simply asking questions that allow them to take sentences out of the text."

These teachers were not alone in doing literate work for their students; another teacher told us that a core literature text assigned in her district was too difficult for her students, and "finally I ended up telling them, they just couldn't get it, they couldn't." These quotes, emerging in teacher interviews over lesson samples and student work, communicate a vision of students as largely unable to work with text. Given such views, it makes sense that teachers' classrooms would have been organized to provide relatively limited opportunities for students to engage directly with texts because they weren't perceived as being able to do so. On the whole, we found that at this point in time, teachers offered students primarily passive roles in relation to text. Interaction and communication between students was minimal, and texts remained largely, and quite literally, untouched by students' hands because the actual reading and interpretation was most often done *by* teachers *for* students. Quite simply, teachers, not students, were doing the actual work of literacy.

However, as we saw in the excerpts from SLN discussions, teachers started to examine their own ways of reading, to rethink what it means to read, and to reconsider students' literacy performances. These teachers had experienced and practiced dialogical ways of learning; they struggled to make meaning with texts and student voices, took risks, displayed uncertainty, appropriated one another's voices and meanings, and authored novel conceptions of texts, student learning, and literacy tasks. In varied ways, they set about re-creating such a dialogical learning environment for their students. An examination of the data illustrates what these developments looked like from the teachers' perspectives as literate life in their classrooms evolved.

Appropriating Discourses, Authoring Change: Apprenticing Students to New Literate Practices

As teachers engaged in the kind of dialogic inquiry we described earlier, they acquired broader, more socially grounded conceptions of literacy and came to see students as more capable. In response, they began to alter the kinds of text-based activities they offered to students, and to develop new pedagogical approaches, which included many more opportunities for students to talk about and interact with text. Carla, for instance, was newly aware of how she typically made sense of text that was difficult for her and as a result of participating in the SLN, had a consciousness of her own processes of reading that she had not had before.

Carla: ...particularly if I'm reading something that's difficult, something that's new to me, I find myself thinking about, conscious of, what

> my process is, you know, what I'm doing in order to understand
> what it is I'm reading. . . . One of the things I've become most
> tuned into, I think, is the importance of the background
> knowledge in understanding something that's difficult . . . and
> dissecting something in terms of what do you need to know in
> order to understand this . . . (year 1, spring)

When something was difficult to read, Carla recognized, "I don't have the picture to be able to understand." This understanding, appropriated from the inquiry practices and cultural resources in the professional learning community, reshaped Carla's teaching practices in specific ways. Now, Carla made much more of an effort to foreground important background information, to do what she called, "scaffolding the reading to make it possible."

Carla: I'm much more conscious now of the need to assist students in
        reading difficult text. I don't just throw stuff at them and expect
        them to read it. . . . understanding how important providing the
        prior knowledge and framework for reading something is in order
        for somebody to read it and read it well, and how much that has to
        be part of the lesson that goes along with it. . . . I can see that
        happening in a lot of different ways. (year 1, spring)

Making reading possible required Carla to design "a lot of different ways" to foster interactions, that is, dialogic interactions, between her students' prior knowledge and experiences and classroom texts. To do so, Carla needed access to her students' knowledge, experience, and thinking. Appropriating new conceptions from the dialogical learning environment of the SLN was only the beginning, then, of a process of dialogical response to students and their learning needs, for Carla and other participating teachers.

SLN teachers described to us how they began to invite their students' voices and perspectives about their own reading experiences into the classroom in a variety of ways. Gen and Roberta asked students to write in journals about how they were approaching reading tasks, what they found difficult, and what they did in response to reading difficulties. In class, these and other teachers began to foster conversations about their own and their students' struggles with meaning. These conversations offered students new roles as problem posers and resourceful problem solvers, and teachers began to capture students' strategies, for example, in "good readers' strategies" posters that became living documents, frequently referred to and updated as reading experiences in the classroom multiplied.

As a result of the new and more powerful roles students began to play in classroom instruction, teachers saw students developing more honest approaches to their own reading. Rather than hiding what they didn't know, which had been fairly standard practice for many students up until this point, as teachers and students began to articulate their thinking about text together, and to develop a language of textual inquiry, students began to display an openness about where things were breaking down in their own reading, which in turn gave teachers a way in – a means for designing a relevant and meaningful map for instruction:

Roberta: One thing I've really appreciated is [that my students will now say] 'Miss J., I can't get past page fifty-eight' and 'that's all I've got'. They're not trying to make me think that they've read the whole book. They are really owning that part if it and I like that. (year 1, spring)

Students' sense of ownership seemed to be linked to how teachers were rethinking their own roles in the classroom, as well as those of their students:

Joanna: I realize that it's such a disservice to walk them through it and summarize for them, . . . because it's not teaching them any strategies to deal with it on their own. And so I don't think they noticed it necessarily . . . but I think [they are now able to use strategies to work with text on their own]. (year 1, spring)

Teachers' abilities to reimagine their own roles was linked to having found ways to successfully apprentice students to the literate practices of their disciplines, in part through new forms of conversation about those practices. Roberta, for instance, integrated literature circles into her English language development classroom. Paul integrated conversation about how students were grappling with difficult reading into discussions of complex literary ideas in Socratic seminars in his ninth-grade English class. Joanna turned literature circles over to her students to structure and carry out, just as she found ways to help her students work together to summarize expository readings in history. From a Bakhtinian perspective, these increasingly dialogical forms of interaction around texts gave teachers access to their students' thinking and reasoning during literacy tasks. As this occurred, teachers responded by constructing new, more generous view of their students' capabilities. They started to talk about students' skills and abilities in new ways, and to link skills with students' sense of empowerment and engagement:

Joanna: This year I've experienced an insight – skills are power, and power brings engagement. My students have changed as readers this year. Reading is less mysterious and they are less daunted . . . (written reflection, year 1, spring)

Teachers began to see how their students' sense of ability with text was also connected to their growing enjoyment of reading, and to their growing sense of themselves as readers:

Gen: I just think we're having more fun reading [laughs] and I've been focusing so much more on skills and on developing power around getting ahold of the text that I didn't think that it would be more fun for them. But I think they feel much more empowered . . . they enjoy that sense of ability. (year 1, spring)

Similarly, Roberta, who initially saw her students as having an impoverished imagination and little creativity, was formulating an entirely different view as she looked over her students' vocabulary work at the end of the year:

Roberta: I think what this says about what we've been doing is that they're not just reading words anymore. No way. . . . They're imagining things. They're using higher order thinking skills to predict, to summarize, and to question . . . (year 2, spring)

Clearly, these teachers were coming to see their students as resourceful and strategic thinkers and readers.

Not surprisingly, as teachers began to see ways to apprentice students to subject-area literacies, in large part through increased dialogue and interaction around text, they observed an increased amount and frequency of student reading, both in their classrooms and at home:

Doug: I had more success getting the assigned books read as homework . . . [and] an amazing percentage of them did finish *The Grapes of Wrath.* (year 2, spring)

Roberta was similarly thrilled with the progress of English language learners in her class:

Roberta: One of the things that we [initially] said is that there is no way that these kids [English language learners] can read the core literature that is selected for the school district. What I'm so proud of is that now they're in literature circles and each group is reading a core literature text independently. (year 2, spring)

Furthermore, in Roberta's view, students were no longer opting for the easy way out:

Roberta: My students are no longer choosing the easy way out [by picking the simplest book for SSR] with the biggest writing or the one with the pictures . . . [Students] chose the books that were about *ideas* that they wanted to read about. (year 2, spring)

Many teachers saw a deepened sense of commitment developing on the parts of students. Students were taking ownership around reading and learning; they considered themselves accountable not only to their teachers, but also to one another. In other words, as students' abilities with text were evolving in the minds of both teachers and students themselves (as students *appropriated* textual practices), social relations around text were shifting in ways that linked students to literacy and to one another more deeply. In the process of describing her work with literature circles, Joanna reflected on how turning work over to small groups encouraged students' accountability to each other and to their own learning:

Joanna: What surprised me the most is how committed they are to it. I give them a calendar and say you need to finish your book within three weeks, and almost all of them finished in two by their own doing. . . . For the most part, that accountability to the group and to a peer rather than a teacher made a big difference. (year 2, spring)

Perhaps most important, however, were the literate identities students were invited to embody in these teachers' classrooms. As teachers saw new pedagogical paths to approach subject-area literacies and developed a new language to work with text, they began to view their students as capable coinquirers and literate practitioners. Teachers saw their students, in turn, welcoming the new social spaces opening up around classroom literacy practices, and embracing, with what was surprising enthusiasm for these teachers, the literate selves they were being invited to enact in these teachers' classrooms. Critically, students' new sense of ownership and their willingness to take responsibility around reading, which resulted in part from teachers' invitations to them to take part in new ways, was connected, in their teachers' minds, to how students viewed themselves as readers:

Paul: I honestly believe my students see themselves as being readers who are competent. I see this in the way they talk about tackling a difficult text. . . . I think that in my literature classes, my students have gained the feeling that they can be good readers [which] I attribute to their increasing ability to sit down with something and not give up after looking at it for the first time. (year 1, spring)

Like Paul, Carla also saw her students' sense of themselves shift as she became more able to turn the work of literacy over to them:

Carla: In their end of the year self-assessments, most . . . of my students said that they thought they were better readers. . . . When students . . . can read well, they are more likely to enjoy reading. When they can read well *and* can read something they enjoy, they are more likely to read. How did I gain this insight? By observing my students and listening to what they said. (written reflections, year 2, spring)

As they walked us through their instructional practices, then, teachers described students as doing more reading, and as engaging more deeply with text. Yet it was clear, from these interviews, that teachers themselves were engaging students in new ways in dialogical meaning-making processes, inviting students to share their thinking and formulate questions, and being pleasantly surprised by the quality of thinking students' questions reflected. As teachers came to see students as resources for one another, they also began to treat students as guides for the teaching process itself, that is, they read students' interactions with texts in ways that informed pedagogical decision making and reshaped practice, including the kinds of roles teachers and students took with one another. Ultimately, what this meant was that students had more support for learning, they were given much more challenging text-based work, and their social roles in the classroom expanded – they were invited to become coinquirers, problem solvers, theorizers and, ultimately, more strategic literate thinkers and practitioners.

In fact, the lines between "teacher" and "learner" became blurred as students were invited into the collaborative textual and discursive problem-solving processes that constitute the heart of academic learning and literacy. Compared to the teacher-centered literacy activities and classroom environments they portrayed early on in the study, over time, teachers came to describe literacy-rich classrooms in which students were deeply engaged in dialogue with texts as well as with their peers and teachers. These practice-grounded interviews with teachers thus not only gave us a detailed vision of the novel ways of interacting with text that were developing in these classrooms, but also revealed new collaborative and dialogical partnerships emerging between the teachers and their students.

Learning from Students, Authoring a New Pedagogical Self: An Illustration

Forming an identity on intimate landscapes takes time, certainly months, often years. It takes personal experience to organize a self around discourses and practices, with the aid of cultural resources and the behavioral prompting and verbal feedback of others (Holland et al., 1998).

The importance of learning from students in order to better facilitate their learning is a cornerstone of constructivist pedagogy. In secondary classrooms, where teachers face up to 160 students per day in short blocks of time, practices that can make such learning from students possible are unfortunately rare. Here, we show how the dialogic practices and cultural resources of the SLN, and critically, the verbal feedback of students as they gained new voices and roles in the classroom, facilitate a teacher's learning from his or her students. Illustrating Bakhtin's notions of dialogism and heteroglossia, we show how offering students new and more powerful voices as learners propelled this teacher's process of pedagogical change.

To do so, we summarize the stances and insights that Carla, a tenth-grade Humanities teacher, offered us as she participated in the SLN for 2 years. Earlier, we saw Carla designing new pedagogies as she listened to Nyala's voice and to the voices of her colleagues and facilitators in the SLN. In the previous section, we also shared how Carla attributed her new insights into student thinking and literacy learning to "observing [her] students and listening to what they said." The dialogic practice of case inquiry in the SLN made students' voices available for teachers to "make sense" with, and the inquiry culture of the SLN treated these voices seriously, granting them prominence and value. Here, we want to highlight how over time Carla appropriated these cultural practices of constructing meaning with student voices; she began to invite her own students' voices into her classroom and increasingly, to offer them new interactions with classroom texts. In turn, these powerful student voices and perspectives compelled Carla to answer, to respond as a teacher in new ways. What is key, here, are the ways that Carla transformed the participation structures (Philips, 1974) of her classroom in response to her students, granting them new roles and responsibilities, new literacy learning opportunities, and ultimately, new identities as literate practitioners.

Initial Pedagogies: Modeling and Carrying Out Literate Practices for Students

In the beginning of her first year in the SLN, Carla did not believe that her students could read most of the things that are part of her curriculum, as we saw earlier. As a result, she read core literature aloud to students, pres-elected vocabulary to teach them, and gave students questions and graphic organizers to guide their interactions with texts, as we saw above. Although Carla wanted her students to generate greater understanding of complex ideas and have access to worthy, if difficult texts, the intellectual work and often the actual reading of the text was Carla's work. Students' work in reading was limited to answering the questions she had posed and to locating the information and ideas to which she guided them.

Evolving Pedagogies: Engaging Students in Literate Practices

In contrast, by the end of her first year in the SLN, Carla had offered her students greater responsibility and agency as well as more powerful, liter-ate roles. She walked us through a unit with the novel, *Buckingham Palace, District Six* that followed a unit on South Africa and the Apartheid system. Structurally, the book is divided into three parts, each introduced autobio-graphically by the novelist. These autobiographical introductions were read as a class. The seven main characters of the book were then introduced in seven chapters. Carla assigned students to read one of these chapters on their own, then work in groups to portray the character of the chapter in a presentation to the class in the form of a skit, a dialogue, or another form of the group's choosing. Some groups chose to read their chapter during class, others for homework.

The core assignment for the unit was a reading log that included the following: notes taken as each group presented on their character, a character chart, responses to questions given by the teacher, quotes and notes (reader response, dual entry journal), a chart of five houses tracking the characters visually, questions that students *themselves* raised about the reading, and vocabulary for which students were asked to use their own prior knowledge and the context of the reading to define. The purpose of these reading logs according to Carla, was "to record what the book was about as well as students' own reflections and responses to the book." The difference in the roles and responsibilities Carla afforded her students at year's end from the circumscribed roles she gave them early in the year is striking. In the company of their peers, students were now expected to orchestrate their own reading of classroom texts, and to engage thoughtfully and responsively (dialogically) to make meaning with them. In a written reflection, she wrote:

My practice began to shift as I deliberately worked to provide the necessary scaffolding (prior knowledge, framework, vocabulary, visualization, organization, etc.) for reading a particular text. My goal is for students to learn these strategies, not to rely on me to provide the scaffolding (written reflection, year 1, spring).

In Carla's descriptions of her changing pedagogical practices, and in her end-of-year reflective writing, we see Carla repositioning her students, over time giving them greater responsibility for their learning experiences as well as tools to assist them in reading more powerfully. We also see her shifting her own goal to encompass this greater agency – voice and power – on the part of her students. This dialogical impulse continued to grow for Carla, and to contribute to her own growth.

Fostering New Literate Selves: Learning as the Appropriation of Dialogic Literacy Practices

In August of the following year, Carla and other SLN teachers were invited to formulate a focus for their year's work in the classroom and for their own professional learning. Carla chose questioning as a focus for her classroom. By September, however, Carla had reformed her goal. Rather than *teach* questioning, she wanted her students to *internalize* questioning *themselves*, as a way of approaching reading tasks. She observed:

In the past, I've approached reading assignments by asking students to respond to my questions. There has always been that feeling like I'm feeding it to them, or that they've responded in a somewhat stifled way to the questions because they're expecting that I'm looking for a particular answer. I often feel like I'm leaving students with my questions and they may get there, but I'm never sure whether they got there because I sort of pushed them down the path that I wanted them to go on.... We all have in our own head what we're thinking when we ask questions. You don't know for sure whether you're getting a spontaneous answer from the kids or the kids are holding back because they're intimidated about saying what's on their mind or because they think you're looking for something in particular (year 2, fall).

In contrast, Carla found that by turning questioning over to the students, she was able to see how well they were grappling with assigned readings. In addition, she saw levels of engagement that were surprising and gratifying to her:

The difference when kids come up with their own questions is that you can tell. The question itself indicates how deeply they've thought about it. In order to ask a question, they have to understand (year 2, spring).

Reimagining her teaching role in terms of coinquirer rather than "spoon-feeder," Carla saw how students were reading more deeply and more independently, and by engaging in new ways, giving her access to their thinking and literate activity:

When I first started asking students to pose questions about their reading, low and behold I got this absolutely incredible group of questions. I thought, "These are better questions that I would have ever asked if I were coming up with questions to lead a discussion." Day after day, I was incredibly impressed with the quality of the questions. The kids seem to be much more engaged in the reading. That's part of what's exciting about it, is their level of engagement. A very different dynamic happens when they're asking the questions than when a teacher does. When they're leading the discussion, leading the answers, the quality of the questions really indicates that they're thinking about what they're reading (year 2, spring).

Carla's descriptions of her classroom, her teaching, and her students demonstrate that a good deal more in the way of literacy practice was offered to students in Carla's classroom over her 2 years of participation in the SLN. She engaged her students in more reading, and in consciously developing comprehension strategies, particularly questioning as a way to engage with difficult text. As importantly, in our view, students' roles and opportunities in the classroom changed as Carla herself took on new roles and enacted new understandings of literacy learning. Based on her own changing recognition of the complexities of reading, and based on "observing my students and listening to what they have to say," Carla created a classroom in which students were invited to take on new roles as readers, as question askers and conversational partners, as discussion leaders, and as thinkers, rather than merely as responders to the teachers' questions.

This brief acount of Carla's changing pedagogy over 2 years illustrates, for us, Bakhtin's conceptions of a dialogical social world in which an individual can author novel practices. Over time, Carla appropriated voices and experiences from the professional development context, populated, as they were, with the ideologies and intentions of other speakers (including those facilitating network sessions), to reform – reauthor – her own classroom practice. In this process of reauthoring, other students' voices (from SLN case inquiries) figured prominently. In turn, Carla began to open dialogical spaces for her own students' voices in her classroom. As she did so, her students responded with new levels of engagement, revealing literate selves Carla had not formerly seen and to which she then responded with new instructional goals and practices. The evolving learning environment of Carla's classroom became increasingly dialogical, and the very process of classroom change was dialogically propelled as she began to make room for, and listen to, her students' voices and perspectives.

AUTHORING PEDAGOGICAL CHANGE IN DIALOGICAL PROFESSIONAL LEARNING ENVIRONMENTS

It is not impossible for people to figure and remake the conditions of their lives. Bakhtin shows that, from the very fact that cultural resources are indelibly marked by social position, people can reassert a point of control through the rearrangement of cultural forms as evocations of position. The equation of the means of expression and social force – the notion of voice – works both ways. It positions persons as it provides them with the tools to re-create their positions. The fields of cultural production that circumscribe perspectives become, in Bakhtin's handling, spaces of authoring (Holland et al., 1998).

In a recent chapter on the importance of learning in and from the practice of teaching, Ball and Cohen (1999) argue that to realize current visions of school reform in which schools are transformed into places where all students learn with understanding and are able to accomplish intellectually rigorous work, teachers must become insightful in listening to and interpreting students' ideas about academic subjects, expand the interpretive frames they bring to their observations of students so they can see more possibilities in what students do, and come to see their students as capable of thinking and reasoning. We concur. Yet, professional development that actually assists teachers to build such knowledge is not commonplace. Rather, most professional development for teachers still focuses narrowly either on telling them about research or instructional practices (rather than engaging them in such practices), or on training them in specific methods of instructional delivery (rather than on developing broad conceptual and pedagogical frameworks for reflecting critically on practice). Many of these professional development practices fail to engage teachers in learning, or to provide them with the support they need as learners to translate new knowledge and beliefs into new pedagogical practices. From a Bakhtinian standpoint, these common practices position teachers as mere recipients of authoritative discourses about "research knowledge," "best practices," or

"teaching techniques." Opportunities for teachers to generate new conceptions or to appropriate literacy and learning practices and translate them
from one context to another, given the prevalence of such professional development practices, is rare.

Yet, as we said at the outset of this chapter, teachers suffer a set of criticisms
similar to those inveighed against their students: like their underachieving students, many teachers, particularly those working in urban schools,
are described as recalcitrant, dense, unwilling, and unable (see Richardson, 1990). Numerous studies have documented the disconnect between
changes in teachers' knowledge or beliefs and changes in pedagogical practice (Alvermann & Moore, 1991; Conley & Warren, 1988; Konopak, Wilson,
& Readence, 1994; Moje & Wade, 1997; O'Brien, 1988), accounting for
this lack of connection in a number of ways, from the personal and disciplinary to the organizational and political. We suggest that an additional,
and more generous explanation for teachers' difficulties in transforming
new knowledge into new practice may stem from the professional training
offered to teachers, which too often fails to provide them with opportunities
to build firsthand, experiential knowledge about reading, and in so doing,
to imagine new roles for themselves in students' literacy learning.

Dialogical and inquiry-based professional development approaches, in
contrast, provide a social context in which teachers are able to construct internally persuasive discourses about student thinking and literacy teaching
and learning (Greenleaf et al., 1994; Moje & Wade, 1997; Risko, McAllister,
& Bigenho, 1993; Risko et al., 1996; Sykes & Bird, 1992). In this chapter,
we demonstrate how the settings and activities of the SLN served as just
such a dialogical space of authoring for a group of secondary subject-area
teachers. Employing a Bakhtinian frame (Bakhtin, 1981, 1986; Holland et
al., 1998), with its attention to how human development is socially mediated
through language, helped us reflect on teachers' pedagogical growth over
time as they participated in a variety of activities and social contexts within
the professional development environment. Specifically, Bakhtin helped us
articulate what happened for a particular group of teachers as they inter-
acted in this discursive setting.

Through dialogic inquiry and intellectual experimentation and improvi-
sation, we saw teachers appropriating one another's voices, engaging with
the theoretical ideas that are shaping the professional development culture, and developing a new set of internally persuasive voices that served
to help them reimagine their professional and pedagogical identities, as
well as reconsider the literate capabilities (and identities) of their students.
Critically, as teachers appropriated new conceptions and understandings
from the dialogic learning environment of the SLN (changing definitions
of literacy, new views of students, new ways of understanding teaching and
learning), they came to offer students a richer and more varied set of learning opportunities, supports, activities, tasks, and roles in the classroom.

In an era in which calls for increased accountability have resulted in increasingly prescribed and scripted programs for teaching, this study demonstrates that teachers can and should be entrusted with the means by which to reflect on and renew their own practice. Our findings thus problematize widely accepted models of professional development (specifically, delivery-based models that focus on techniques) and underscore the importance of professional learning experiences that involve teachers in authoring their own pedagogical change. In these pages, we have shown that when teachers are offered opportunities to engage with colleagues in professional and dialogical inquiry, they benefit from the wisdom of the group, they appropriate and borrow ideas and constructs from one another and from professional development facilitators, and they gain a set of conceptual and pedagogical tools that help them to reconfigure their pedagogical worlds. In turn, they come to offer their students new voices and roles in their classroom communities and novel spaces for authoring literate selves, opening up, in Bakhtin's (1981) terms, "ever newer ways to mean" (p. 346).

References

Alvermann, D. E., & Moore, D. W. (1991). Secondary school reading. In R. Barr, M. L. Kamil, P. B. Mosenthal, & P. D. Pearson (Eds.), *Handbook of reading research* (Vol. II, pp. 951–83). New York: Longman.

Applebee, A. (1996). *Curriculum as conversation: Transforming traditions of teaching and learning.* Chicago: University of Chicago Press.

Bakhtin, M. (1981). *The dialogic imagination.* Austin: University of Texas Press.

Bakhtin, M. (1984). *Problems of Dostoevsky's poetics* (Trans. C. Emerson). Minneapolis: University of Minnesota Press.

Bakhtin, M. (1986). *Speech genres and other late essays.* Austin: University of Texas Press.

Ball, D., & Cohen, D. (1999). Developing practice, developing practitioners: Toward a practice-based theory of professional education. In L. Darling-Hammond & G. Sykes (Eds.), *Teaching as the learning profession: Handbook of policy and practice* (pp. 3–32). San Francisco: Jossey-Bass.

Bartholomae, D. (1985). Inventing the university. In M. Rose (Ed.), *When a writer can't write: Studies in writer's block and other composing process problems* (pp. 134–65). New York: Guilford Press.

Bissex, G. L. (1994). Teacher research: Seeing what we are doing. In T. Shanahan (Ed.), *Teachers thinking, teachers knowing: Reflections on literacy and language education* (pp. 88–104). Urbana, IL: National Council of Teachers of English.

Buchanan, J. (1994). Teacher as learner: Working in a community of teachers. In T. Shanahan (Ed.), *Teachers thinking, teachers knowing: Reflections on literacy and language education* (pp. 39–52). Urbana, IL: National Council of Teachers of English.

Carroll, D., & Carini, P. (1991). Tapping teachers' knowledge. In V. Perrone (Ed.), *Expanding student assessment* (pp. 40–6). Alexandria, VA: Association for Supervision and Curriculum Development.

Cochran-Smith, M., & Lytle, S. (1992). Teacher research as a way of knowing. *Harvard Educational Review, 62*(4), 447–74.

Conley, M. W., & Warren, S. (1988). The development of teacher explanations during content reading lessons. In J. E. Readence & R. S. Baldwin (Eds.), *Dialogues in literacy research* (pp. 259–66). Chicago: National Reading Conference.

Cope, B., & Kalantzis, M. (1993). *The powers of Literacy.* Pittsburgh, PA: University of Pittsburgh Press.

Courts, P. L. (1997). *Multicultural literacies: Dialect, discourse, and diversity.* New York: Peter Lang.

Duckworth, E. (1987). *The having of wonderful ideas and other essays on teaching and learning.* New York: Teachers College Press.

Eeds, M., & Wells, D. (1989). Grand conversations: An exploration of meaning construction in literature study groups. *Research in the Teaching of English, 23*(10), 4–29.

Florio-Ruane, S. (1990). Creating your own case studies: A guide for early field experience. *Teacher Education Quarterly, 17*(1), 29–41.

Freedman, S., Simons, E., Kalnin, J., & Casareno, A., & M-CLASS Teams (Eds.) (1999). *Inside city schools: Investigating literacy in multicultural classrooms.* New York: Teachers College Press.

Freedman, S. W., Flower, L., Hull, G., & Hayes, J. R. (1995). *Ten years of research: Achievements of the National Center for the Study of Writing and Literacy.* Technical Report No. 1-C. Berkeley, CA: National Center for the Study of Writing.

Fullan, M. (1993). *Change forces: Probing the depths of educational reform.* London: The Falmer Press.

Gee, J. (1992). *The social mind: Language, ideology, and social practice.* New York: Bergin & Garvey.

Gee, J. (1996). *Social linguistics and literacies: Ideology in discourses* (2nd ed.). London: The Falmer Press.

Goswami, D., & Stillman, P. (Eds.) (1987). *Reclaiming the classroom.* Portsmouth, NH: Boynton-Cook.

Graves, D. (1990). *Discover your own literacy.* Portsmouth, NH: Heinemann.

Greenleaf, C., Hull, G., & Reilly, B. (1994). Learning from our diverse students: Helping teachers rethink problematic teaching and learning situations. *Teaching & Teacher Education, 10*(5), 521–41.

Greenleaf, C., Schoenbach, R., Cziko, C., & Mueller, F. (2001). Apprenticing adolescents to academic literacy. *Harvard Educational Review, 71*(1), 79–129.

Grossman, P. (1990). *The making of a teacher: Teacher knowledge and teacher education.* New York: Teachers College Press.

Holland, D., Lachicotte, W., Skinner, D., & Cain, C. (1998). *Identity and agency in cultural worlds.* Cambridge, MA: Harvard University Press.

Holquist, M. (1990). *Dialogism: Bakhtin and his world.* New York: Routledge.

Hull, G. A., & Rose, M. (1989). Rethinking remediation: Toward a social-cognitive understanding of problematic reading and writing. *Written Communication,* 8, 139–54.

Hull, G., Rose, M., Fraser, K. L., & Castellano, M. (1991). Remediation as social construct: Perspectives from an analysis of classroom discourse. *College Composition and Communication, 42*(3), 299–329.

Konopak, B. C., Wilson, E. K., & Readence, J. E. (1994). Examining teachers' beliefs, decisions, and practices about content-area reading in secondary social studies. In C. Kinze, J. A. Peter, & D. J. Leu (Eds.), *Multidimensional aspects of literacy research, theory, and practice* (pp. 127–36). Chicago: National Reading Conference.

Langer, J. (1995). *Envisioning literature.* New York: Teachers College Press.

Lee, C. (1995). A culturally based cognitive apprenticeship: Teaching African American high school students skills in literary interpretation. *Reading Research Quarterly, 30*(4), 608–30.

Lemke, J. L. (1990). *Talking science: Language, learning, and values.* Norwood, NJ: Ablex.

Moje, E. B., Dillon, D. R., & O'Brien, D. G. (2000). Re-examining the roles of the learner, the text, and the context in secondary literacy. *Journal of Educational Research, 93,* 165–80.

Moje, E. B., & Wade, S. E. (1997). What case discussions reveal about teacher thinking. *Teaching & Teacher Education, 13*(7), 691–712.

Morson, G. S., & Emerson, G. (1990). *Mikhail Bakhtin: Creation of a prosaics.* Palo Alto, CA: Stanford University Press.

O'Brien, D. G. (1988). Secondary preservice teachers' resistance to content reading instruction: A proposal for a broader rationale. In J. E. Readence & R. S. Baldwin (Eds.), *Dialogues in literacy research* (pp. 237–43). Chicago: National Reading Conference.

Pajares, M. F. (1991). Teachers' beliefs and educational research: Cleaning up a messy construct. *Review of Educational Research, 62*(3), 307–32.

Philips, S. (1974). Participant structures and communicative competence: Warm Springs children in community and classroom. In C. Cazden, V. John, & D. Hymes (Eds.), *Functions of language in the classroom* (pp. 370–94). New York: Teachers College Press.

Rabinowitz, P. J. (1987). *Before reading: Narrative conventions and the politics of interpretation.* Ithaca, NY: Cornell University Press.

Rabinowitz, P. J., & Smith, M. (1998). *Authorizing readers: Resistance and respect in the teaching of literature.* New York: Teachers College Press.

Raphael, T. (1982). Question-answering strategies for children. *The Reading Teacher, 36,* 186–90.

Rex, L., & McEachen, D. (1999). 'If anything is odd, inappropriate, confusing, or boring, it's probably important': The emergence of inclusive academic literacy through English classroom discussion practices. *Research in the Teaching of English, 34,* 65–129.

Richardson, V. (1990). Significant and worthwhile change in teaching practice. *Educational Researcher, 19,* 10–19.

Risko, V. J., McAllister, D., & Bigenho, F. (1993). Value-added benefits for reforming remedial reading methodology course with videodisc and hypercard technology. In T. Rasinski & N. Padak (Eds.), *Inquiries in literacy learning and instruction* (pp. 179–89). Harrisonburg, VA: College Reading Association.

Risko, V. J., Peter, J. J., & McAllister, D. (1996). Conceptual changes: Preservice teachers' pathways to providing literacy instruction. In E. G. Sturtevant & W. M. Linek (Eds.), *Growing literacy: Eighteenth yearbook of the College Reading Association* (pp. 104–19). Harrisonburg, VA: College Reading Association.

Rose, M. (1989). *Lives on the boundary.* New York: Penguin Books.

Schifter, D., & Fosnot, C. T. (1993). *Reconstructing mathematics education.* New York: Teachers College Press.

Schoenbach, R., Greenleaf, C., Cziko, C., & Hurwitz, L. (1999). *Reading for understanding: A guide to improving reading in middle and high school classrooms.* San Francisco: Jossey-Bass.

Scribner, S., & Cole, M. (1981). *The psychology of literacy.* Cambridge, MA: Harvard University Press.

Smagorinsky, P. (2001). If meaning is constructed, what's it made from? Toward a cultural theory of reading. *Review of Educational Research, 71*(1), 133–69.

Smith, M. A. (1996). The National Writing Project after 22 years. *Phi Delta Kappan, 77*(10), 21–31.

Stodolsky, S. (1988). *The subject matters: Classroom activity in math and social studies.* Chicago: University of Chicago Press.

Street, B. (1995). *Social literacies: Critical approaches to literacy in development, ethnography and education.* London: Longman.

Sykes, G., & Bird, T. (1992). Teacher education and the case idea. In G. Grant (Ed.), *Review of research in education* (Vol. 18, pp. 457–521). Washington, DC: American Educational Research Association.

Wineburg, S. S. (1991). On the reading of historical texts: Notes on the breach between school and academy. *American Educational Research Journal, 28*(3), 495–519.

Voices in Dialogue

Multivoiced Discourses in Ideological Becoming

Verda Delp

Mikhail Bakhtin suggests that in the midst of our struggle to interpret and understand the dialogic relationships that exist when two distinct discourses come together, we fight to construct new ways to mean and, at the same time, reconstruct and reconfigure our ideological consciousness:

> Another's discourse performs here no longer as information, directions, rules, models and so forth – but strives to determine the very basis of our ideological interrelations with the world, the very basis of our behavior; it performs here as authoritative discourse, and an internally persuasive discourse.

> Both the authority of the discourse and its internal persuasiveness may be united in one word – one that is simultaneously authoritative and internally persuasive – despite the profound differences between these two categories of alien discourse. But such unity is rarely given – it happens more frequently that an individual's becoming, an ideological process, is characterized precisely by a sharp gap between these two categories.... The struggle and dialogic interrelationship of these categories of ideological discourse are what usually determine the history of an individual consciousness. (Bakhtin, 1981, p. 342)

I believe this notion of ideological becoming is the core of Bakhtinian theory. I have come to think of ideological becoming as an ever-evolving collection of meanings that have been forged upon our consciousness as a consequence of the individual ways we partake of the dialogic offerings that come before us. It is within these dialogic interactions and relationships that we may journey to *think* about ideas, to *interpret* language, to *understand* the intentions persuasive, authority of others, and to *construct* new understandings, perspectives, and ideologies for ourselves. We can imagine these dialogic interrelationships as offering us varied opportunities to come up against the ideological positioning of others and, over time, to bring forth for ourselves newly constructed ways to mean.

In thinking about this notion of ideological becoming in relation to the manuscripts I read for our course on Bakhtinian perspectives, and moreover, in regard to the correspondence I conducted with their authors, I have come to see that our dialogic interactions were indeed evocative occasions for reflection and query for each of us; and in the end, opportunities to for us to reconstruct our ideological consciousness. I imagine these meaning-making occasions for each of us: for the authors, in the writing of their manuscripts, and again, in the answering of my questions; and for me, in interpreting their texts, in responding to their voices with my own voice, and finally, in thinking about their replies to my queries. With our questions and answers moving us even further along on our individual and collective journeys to construct new meanings for ourselves, this grand dialogic has also brought about the reconstruction and reconfiguration of our ideological consciousness.

CORRESPONDING WITH THE AUTHORS: CONSTRUCTING NEW WAYS TO MEAN

To portray this dialogic journey and its nuanced relationships and meaning-making outcomes, I have chosen to quote particular questions and answers from the correspondence I carried out with the authors about their manuscripts. In this way, I hope to emphasize the nature of our distinct discourses and perspectives, and to illustrate the ways they have come together to bring about our responses to each other's texts and the constructions of new perspectives and understandings. Further, I have placed within this text quotations from Bakhtin's writings to honor his voice and to symbolically position his words within and among our dialogic relationships and our ideological consciousness:

...there can be neither a first nor a last meaning; [anything that can be understood] always exists among other meanings as a link in the chain of meaning, which in its totality is the only thing that can be real. In historical life this chain continues infinitely, and therefore each individual link in it is renewed again and again, as though it were being reborn. (Bakhtin, 1981, p. 345)

Cynthia Greenleaf and Mira Katz: Constructing a Professional Discourse

Truth is not born nor is it to be found inside the head of an individual person, it is born *between people* collectively searching for truth, in the process of their dialogic interaction. (Bakhtin, 1984, p. 110, emphasis in original)

For Greenleaf and Katz, teachers in their study "take up social and dialogical tools for imagining and authoring new pedagogical selves" (p. 1). In their chapter, the authors describe what happened to teachers who participated in an inquiry-based professional development series:

Through dialogic inquiry and intellectual experimentation and improvisations, we saw teachers appropriating one another's voices, engaging with theoretical ideas shaping the professional development culture, and developing a new set of "internally persuasive voices" which served to help them reimagine their professional and pedagogical identities and reconsider the literate capabilities and identities of their students. (Greenleaf & Katz)

In reflecting on their ideological positioning and in considering my own perspective regarding the dialogic interrelationships that come about when diverse discourses come together, I decided to ask Greenleaf and Katz about the ways they constructed opportunities for teachers to build a "professional discourse" for themselves and how this might be seen in relation to their developing "internally persuasive voices." I posed the following questions:

In your discussion of the generative nature of inquiry-based professional development, you write: "These case materials and supportive protocols for inquiry comprise a type of 'record of practice' around which participants can begin to build a professional discourse." Can you elaborate on what this professional discourse consists of? It clearly involves teacher talk but does it also include writing? For example, did the teachers keep a journal that reflected their ever-evolving perspectives – which might be seen as the representations/documentations of their internally persuasive discourses. (V. Delp, personal communication, March 2002)

Greenleaf and Katz provided an extensive response to these queries:

[These practices] include a language around and about texts, as well as ways of being, thinking and doing with texts that students in turn had access to. In this sense it was a professional discourse first in the [professional development] context, but also came to live in (and we like to think across) teachers' classrooms.

. . . we viewed the professional development as an activity system in which teachers would experience, practice, and acquire specific knowledge, dispositions, and habits of inquiry and reflection. . . . The SLN discourse around student literacy performance was explicitly designed to support this learning on the part of participating teachers. Inquiry prompts, rituals, individual reflective writing, small group work, and whole group discussions were opportunities to instantiate and shape new ways of reading the world of literacy, classroom practice, and student performance.

As a part of this support for new inquiry practices, we gave teachers journals to use as they worked in sessions and moved from our time together into their own classroom work and inquiry. In addition, we took time in sessions for teachers to capture new insights, questions, or concerns, and to reflect on the implications of the discussions we were having for their own teaching and their own students. We asked teachers to come to sessions ready to share reflections from their work back on site with the professional community, and frequently started the day with that sharing. (personal communication, March 2002)

Reflecting their own distinct discourse, Greenleaf and Katz offer in their response further insights – beyond their chapter – into the ways teachers went about constructing individual and collective professional discourses. In listing particular "opportunities to instantiate and shape new ways of reading the world of literacy . . .," these scholars mark the relationship between such interactions and the developing, "internally persuasive discourses" of these teachers.

Christian Knoeller: Narrative of Rethinking

The semantic structure of an internally persuasive discourse is *not finite*, it is *open*; in each of the new contexts that dialogize it, this discourse is able to reveal ever newer ways to mean. (Bakhtin, 1981, p. 346)

In his chapter, Christian Knoeller revisits his discussion of dual voicing[1] to examine "some of the most compelling yet elusive questions about how we use the language of others to learn." Early in his chapter, Knoeller reflects upon his understanding of the ways in which students appropriate language from others:

Textual interpretations, then, in light of Bakhtin, is seen to involve a process of internalizing words – or *voices* – of others, including those encountered in written works such as authors, narrators, and characters, but importantly the voices of other *readers* also. Indeed, it is striking to see the degree to which student readers explicitly recall perspectives from texts – including those that they would question – accepting some while rejecting others, expressing a mix of imitation and resistance. (pp. 149–50, this volume)

In thinking about Knoeller's perspective concerning language learning and the taking on of the voices of others and my own ponderings regarding the construction of new meanings and ideological consciousness, I sent along a quotation from Bakhtin with my query, hoping to bring forth his interpretation of the ways he envisions the interrelationships of these ideas. My questions follow:

What is your understanding of Bakhtin's notion of ideological becoming? Does ideological becoming relate in any way to your concept of narratives of rethinking? (V. Delp, personal communication, February 2002)

Embedding a quotation from Bakhtin within his response, Knoeller answers my query with a contemplative discussion in which he frankly considers new constructions of meaning for himself:

You have drawn a striking point from a particularly rich essay here. In fact, the sentence you've quoted appears *immediately* before a passage that has been a centerpiece for my own work that begins, "When verbal disciplines are taught in school, two basic modes are recognized for the appropriation and transmission – simultaneously – of another's words" (Bakhtin, 1981, 341). Bakhtin goes on at this juncture to contrast verbatim quotation, such as reported speech, with what I term *interpretive paraphrase*.

I find the idea of "ideological becoming" to be intriguing, but, to be honest, I'm not sure just yet what to make of its relationship to the narratives of rethinking that

---

[1] For discussions on dual voicing, refer to Christian Knoeller (1999). *Voicing ourselves: Whose words we use when we talk about books.* Albany: State University of New York Press.

I've analyzed. In the few pages of the essay devoted to this topic, Bakhtin seems to be interested in the dialogical relationship between (1) "authoritative" (often institutional) public discourses and (2) "internally persuasive" private discourse. While Bakhtin concedes that the two can at times coincide, he also acknowledges that they are prone to diverge.

Do you suppose that the concept of "ideological becoming" intersects with narratives of rethinking in this regard? Could it be that the two describe similar kinds of "inner dialogue" linking public and private discourse? (Knoller, personal communication, March 2002)

Pushing his thinking even further than in his manuscript, and portraying with abandon his reflective-interpretive stance, in sharing his understanding of Bakhtin's notion of ideological becoming in relation to his own concept of narratives of rethinking, Knoeller's response to my query brought forth opportunities for us both to reflect upon our ideological positioning and to construct new ways to mean.

Landay: Literacy Development and the Performing Arts

Language is not a neutral medium that passes freely and easily into the private property of the speaker's intentions; it is populated – overpopulated – with the intentions of others. Expropriating it, forcing it to submit to one's own intentions and accents, is a difficult and complicated process. (Bakhtin, 1981, p. 294)

In her chapter, Eileen Landay discusses Bakhtin's notions of authoritative and internally persuasive discourses and ideological becoming in relation to The ArtsLiteracy Project (ALP), a program for students that offers literacy development through performing arts. Presenting secondary students with opportunities to bring core texts to performance, this project focuses on students "[developing] the skills and habits of mind to convey meaning through – and recover meaning from – a range of symbol systems, most explicitly, print text" (p. 9).

Explaining the ideological positioning that underlies this work, Landay offers her perspective regarding the coming together of authoritative and internally persuasive discourses:

As we speak, we continually transmit and interpret the words of others, sometimes repeating them directly, sometimes reporting and commenting on them. In choosing the utterances of others we wish to appropriate and precisely what meaning we wish to attribute to them, we choose the stance we wish to take. It is in the choices one makes toward these discourses that one's identity is formed. "The ideological becoming of a human being . . . is the process of selectively assimilating the words of others" [341]. (pp. 5–6)

Reflecting on Landay's positioning regarding stance taking and appropriating discourse from another, and my own thinking about dialogic interrelationships and interactions and the resulting constructions of meaning, led me to ask this scholar about the ways ALP students partake of opportunities to appropriate meaning-making skills and practices, and to develop their internally persuasive discourses. I focused my query on students' experiences:

In your chapter, a student says that doing skits about "Blood Wedding" led her group to raise questions about the characters and to look more closely at the play to explore them. In her words, "You'll keep reading to find the answers." Can you explain how students went about finding these "answers" in the text? And, can you explain how these practices might reflect the development of their internally persuasive discourses? (Landay, personal communication, April 2002)

Hereupon, Landay describes the ways in which ALP students participated in discussions within their classroom community:

My sense is that the dialogues students engaged in took numerous forms. Most evident were the discussions themselves. Most frequently these were led by teachers and actors, but students entered with enthusiasm, and more often than is usual in school, there were moments when students took control of the conversation and engaged in lengthy, spirited exchanges with one another. Teachers encouraged and modeled "looking back at the texts," exploring a wide range of possibilities and listening carefully to everyone's ideas. All of this seemed to me a perfect example of Vygotsky's ZPD where students' capacities to comprehend and interpret grew as a result of the collective conversation.

   In the process of slowing down, looking again, listening to a range of possible interpretations, students seemed to understand more deeply. Which aspects of this understanding are "external" and which "internal" becomes difficult to say. (Landay, personal communication, April 2002)

   Interestingly, in describing the ways these students receive support and encouragement to explore text, and to listen to and reflect upon the voices of others, Landay remarks on how difficult it becomes to distinguish between external and internally persuasive discourse. In posing this uncertainty for consideration at this time and in this way, Landay conjures up a renewed opportunity for reflection and for the construction of new ways to mean for us both.

Carol Lee: Cultural Modeling

Powerful and profound creativity is largely unconscious and polysemic. Through understanding it is supplemented by consciousness, and the multiplicity of its meanings is revealed. Thus, understanding supplements the text: it is active and also creative by nature. Creative understanding continues creativity, and multiplies the artistic wealth of humanity. The co-creativity of those who understand. (Bakhtin, 1986, p. 141)

   In her chapter, Carol Lee writes about African American students, who, as part of their "apprenticeships" in cultural modeling classrooms, appropriate interpretive perspectives and learn to participate in the culture of "disciplinary literacy." Early in her manuscript, Lee voices a critical concern regarding classroom discourse communities:

The challenge in many classrooms has been how to apprentice students into disciplinary identities that do not diminish existing identities that students bring both individually and as members of different cultural communities.

Thinking about the cultural modeling approach to teaching students to draw upon their internal linguistic and cognitive resources to find meaning in texts and in the world around them, and my own thinking regarding meaning-making opportunities and relationships, inspired me to ask Lee about the particular practices and strategies student apprentices appropriate and how these skills support them, over time, as they learn to interpret literature of the canon:

You presented one small sample of classroom talk in which your students demonstrated how they "interrogated . . . cultural data sets in preparation for reading . . ." the canonical texts that would follow. As students interpreted the symbolism in the film, what were the salient strategies and approaches they learned and how were they applied to the study of the texts that followed? (V. Delp, personal communication, April 2002)

In her reply, Lee explains exactly what her students learned from their participation in cultural modeling discourse communities:

They learned to pay attention to details in the literary text that signify something important is going on and that a literal interpretation of that text is insufficient. They also learned specific strategies for then reconstructing either a metaphoric, ironic or satiric interpretation above and beyond the literal. These textual markers included placement in an important position (like titles, openings); when something is repeated a lot it's important; when a literal interpretation does not seem sufficient because of the attention drawn to [an image].

Habits of mind included assuming that the details are there for a reason, believing that as a reader you needed to account for all the details, even when they seemed not to have anything to do with one another; being willing to think metaphorically; attending to language play as an aesthetically pleasing end in itself; be willing to engage with complexity and not jumping to a single, simple solution to a question right away, being willing to ask and attend to questions. All of these strategies and habits of mind were explicitly necessary to make sense of the canonical texts that followed. (Lee, personal communication, April 2002)

Lee answers my query with a list of particular strategies and approaches students appropriate when they take on "apprenticeships" in cultural modeling classrooms. In noting these "habits of mind" – the interpretive skills and practices, along with students' existing internal resources – Lee provides occasion to reflect on the role of the student "apprentice," and to think about how we might imagine classroom discourse communities that mediate the "sharp gap" (Bakhtin, 1981, p. 342) between the culture of "disciplinary literacy" and the diverse cultures of our students.

GENERATIONS OF THOUGHT: IDEOLOGICAL BECOMING

The tendency to assimilate others' discourse takes on an even deeper and more basic significance in an individual's ideological becoming, in the most fundamental sense. (Bakhtin, 1986, p. 342)

In quoting my questions and authors' responses to these questions, I have tried to portray the nuanced ways our discourses have come together to bring about particular dialectic relationships and opportunities for reflection and interpretation. Further, I expect that these dialogics have indeed summoned forth the reconstruction and reconfiguration of our ideological becoming. We have each journeyed, farther than before our correspondence, to think about ideas, to understand the intentions of others and, in responding to the ideological positioning of those others, to construct new understandings and perspectives for ourselves. We have intensified and refined our collections of ideas within our consciousness with newly forged meanings and perspectives. Bakhtin writes about the "historical life" of meaning in his notes from 1970 to 1971:

[T]here can be neither a first nor a last meaning; [anything that can be understood] always exists among other meanings as a link in the chain of meaning, which in its totality is the only thing that can be real. In historical life this chain continues infinitely, and therefore each individual link in it is renewed again and again, as though it were being reborn. (Bakhtin, 1986, p. 146)

References

Bakhtin, M. (1981). Discourse in the novel. In C. Emerson & M. Holquist (Eds.), *The dialogic imagination: Four essays by M. Bakhtin* (pp. 259–422). Austin: University of Texas Press.

Bakhtin, M. (1986). *Speech genres and other late essays.* (Trans. V. W. McGee) (Ed. C. Emerson & M. Holquist.) Austin: University of Texas Press.

PART III

HETEROGLOSSIA IN A CHANGING WORLD

9

New Teachers for New Times

The Dialogical Principle in Teaching and Learning Electronically

Jabari Mahiri

INTRODUCTION

Bakhtin's dialogical principle informs and extends our understanding of possibilities for teaching and learning electronically. At the dawn of the twenty-first century, debates over "e-learning" have decidedly shifted from whether it works to how best to take advantage of it. This raises provocative questions about the pedagogical strategies and curriculum designs needed to effectively prepare new teachers for these new times and challenges – particularly in urban, multicultural settings – if schooling itself is not to become obsolete. In this chapter, a web-based, graduate course on urban education for preservice teachers taught by the author in 2001 is used as a "text" for discussion and analysis. Bakhtin's notion of the chronotope as a unit of analysis is extended to a metaphor of the classroom as a chronotopic-like unit (or space) that can provide "X-rays" of important issues in the larger society. It is argued that Bakhtin's ideas about the dialogic, intertextual, heteroglossic nature of meaning-making by human "subjects" prefigure and are highly relevant to the complex issues surrounding teaching and learning generally, as well as electronically.

Techniques and tools for teaching and learning have not changed much in K–12 schooling since its inception in the United States, despite the rapid pace of other societal changes. Yet, the literacy demands of the new century and, consequently, the demands on students after they leave high school are changing radically. In earlier work (Mahiri, 1998), I noted that students must now develop skills to access and evaluate information in overwhelming quantities from global sources. They must be able to analyze and synthesize this information in conjunction with foundational, yet mutable, interdisciplinary knowledge in order to solve problems and potentially contribute to new knowledge. In the workplace, as additional sources of strategic advantage emerge that require sophisticated "process-oriented" technologies, they also require new levels of education and new literacy skills. The most pervasive changes, however, may be in the kinds of demographic and social relationships occurring – especially in urban, multicultural settings.

I have suggested ways that computers, the Internet, digital cameras, video cameras, CDs, and so on can offer new tools for teaching and learning, and I have also argued that twenty-first-century schooling can offer provocative possibilities for transformational interactions to help us more effectively negotiate, if not bridge, our societal and cultural divides (Mahiri, 2000a, 2000b). Yet, it will be our design and implementation of new pedagogy and curriculum, I believe, that will ultimately determine the efficacy of schooling in this millennium and, hence, the future of U.S. schools.

How do we best prepare new teachers to be effective in new-century schools? This chapter argues that Bakhtin's ideas about the dialogic, intertextual, heteroglossic nature of meaning making by human "subjects" prefigure and inform considerations and conceptualizations for preservice programs, as well as subsequent practices of teaching and learning. Essentially, Bakhtin's work can significantly enhance the intellectual and sociocultural work of schools.

NEW TEACHERS FOR NEW TIMES

As the result of a recent California governor's initiative to address severe teacher shortages, teacher education programs in the state's university system were mandated to significantly increase the number of prospective teachers that they admitted and graduated.[1] California, like many other places in the United States, is also experiencing profound demographic change. With a population approaching 35 million, it has also become a state in which whites are no longer the majority. At the same time, whites are the overwhelming majority of K–12 teachers in the United States. In addition, they represent the vast majority of people currently going into teaching as a profession.[2]

To a degree, these demographic characteristics of K–12 teachers were also reflected in the new cohort of candidates admitted into the Multicultural Urban Secondary Education (MUSE) program at University of California, Berkeley, for the 2001–2002 academic year.[3] Specifically, nineteen

---

[1] Teacher education programs in California require candidates to have completed a bachelor's degree before admittance and work toward a teaching credential in either a single subject or multiple subjects.

[2] The National Center for Education Information reported in 1996 that nearly 90 percent of U.S. teachers are white and that "[e]ven in urban schools, which have a high proportion of minority students, 73 percent of teachers identify themselves as white" (*San Francisco Chronicle*, October 17, 1996, p. A2).

[3] The MUSE program offers a Cross-Cultural Language and Academic Development single-subject credential in English, along with a Master's Degree in Language, Literacy, and Culture.

of the twenty-six students in this new cohort were white, although there had been extensive recruitment efforts to attract candidates from diverse racial/ethnic and sociocultural backgrounds. Four people in this cohort were males. There were also four Latina women, and three women of Asian or East Asian ancestry. There were no African Americans, male or female. Four other graduate students, all women who were not preservice teachers, were allowed to take the "Urban Education" class that was designed for these MUSE students and is the focus of this discussion. Of these four, one was Asian, one Latina, one white, and one African American. My teaching assistant, an advanced graduate student in education, and I are both African American males.

With the program's focus on "multicultural, urban" schools, it was paramount to prepare *all* prospective teachers to be effective in these, as well as other, settings of U.S. schools. This cohort's program began in the summer semester of 2001, during which they took a class on bilingual education along with this class on urban education. I devised a number of strategies for learning in and beyond the classroom to contribute to the development of the dispositions, knowledge, and skills needed to be effective in urban schools. Drawing on work done with other Senior Fellows of the Annenberg Institute for School Reform between 1998 and 2000, I framed the class around five lenses that were coded "AEIOU." Through these lenses urban educators are seen as

*A*gents of social change who work to bring about educational
*E*quity in achievement and access through effective and culturally sensitive
*I*nstruction and curriculum to produce desired learning
*O*utcomes within the context of (and with an understanding of)
*U*rban conditions and structures that present both opportunities and constraints

The challenge for the class was to facilitate these prospective teachers in understanding and engaging in educational practices focused through these and other relevant lenses.

Three core strategies for teaching and learning were used to address this challenge – forming the class into a "community of learners," accessing the "perspectives of key stakeholders" in the educational process, and working toward a concept and skill set of "teachers as ethnographers." Throughout the course the instructors, other MUSE faculty and staff, invited guests, and the students themselves were relied upon as learning resources, and we attempted to create a class culture that encouraged dialogue, multiple perspectives, and student-generated learning experiences. Many of the texts, invited guests, and class activities were selected to provide "emic" (authentic insider) perspectives on issues and topics of urban education. Multiple texts were used through the class, including audio, video, visual, animated, film, and web-based texts. The class also worked to position teachers as ethnographers who would facilitate students in developing some of the skills of research and ethnography as a central and powerful way of learning about themselves and others, as well as society and the world.

Another key concern was to help prepare new teachers to take advantage of technological resources for mediating teaching and learning. Clearly, their future students are already highly invested in numerous electronically mediated, popular cultural practices that provide degrees of personal pleasure and power. Working from a number researchers' studies of the variety of ways youth engage in learning and literacy activities beyond school, I have argued that some youth actually use these experiences as alternatives to (or even in opposition to) school-based learning (Mahiri, 2003). This situation will become more pronounced in the near future as technological advances increasingly permit higher levels of multisensory, multidimensional, overlapping cyber experiences with written, aural, and visual texts in digital formats. At the same time, provocative issues surrounding access, authorship, and ownership are all being reconfigured by technology. Teachers should not be positioned to compete with new technologies for the minds of students, but they should be able to use appropriate technological innovations for their own pedagogical purposes.

The web-based education commission – a congressional committee that recently heard testimony from hundreds of teachers, students, and private-sector executives throughout the year 2000 – recommended that "the next administration and Congress make e-learning the center piece of future education policy" (Kirby, 2000, p. B5). The commission's report found "that only 39 percent of teachers' training takes place on paid time, compared with 90 percent for private sector workers" (p. B5).

The MUSE students did, in fact, take a mini course on technology concurrently with their initial classes, but there was also a need for an integrated approach. I received an instructional minigrant[4] about a month before the class began to support the creation of this kind of approach. I designed the class, in part, to introduce new teachers to a variety of strategies and advantages (as well as limitations) of various techniques for mediating teaching and learning electronically. I believed that their exposure to these techniques while being students themselves would enable them to see something of their future students' potential engagement in learning through technology that they could eventually employ in their own teaching.

The strategy for the class was not toward distance learning; instead, it was organized as a series of thematic modules that worked in conjunction with the lecture/discussions of selected texts, presentations by guests (stakeholders) from the field, and student-led activities. This style of organization somewhat modeled the format of a computer with multiple opportunities to "click on" and "drag" a variety of learning experiences

---

[4] The proposal awarded in May 2001, by the Instructional Minigrant Program at UC Berkeley, was titled "Modeling Electronic Mediation of Instruction for Pre-Service Teachers."

and resources into each class. In the summer semester, classes were 4 hours each, twice a week, for 6 weeks. Despite this condensed schedule, elements of the electronic format facilitated students in reading and responding to all or significant parts of more than fourteen books, as well as a wide range of articles and web-based resources with a variety of focuses on urban education.

THE CHRONOTOPE AND THE CLASSROOM

Bakhtin formulated the chronotope as "[a] unit of analysis for studying texts according to the ratio and the nature of the temporal and spatial categories represented" (Todorov, 1981/1984, p. 426). Although he was discussing the reading of literary texts, I believe that the concept of the chronotope is viable for reading classrooms as a kind of "dynamic text" (a "narrative" of teaching and learning revealed and completed through interactions of "characters" in the classroom community). Bakhtin suggested that "[t]he chronotope is an optic for reading texts as X-rays of the forces at work in the culture system from which they spring" (Todorov, 1981/1984, p. 426). This idea is also akin to his discussions of the "carnivalesque," which he applied by synecdoche to the whole of culture. Similarly, classrooms can be optics for reading the social spaces expressed therein in terms of how they replicate and/or illuminate some of the temporal/spatial categories and cultural/structural dimensions of the larger society.

Bakhtin borrowed the term "chronotope" from the natural sciences, but appropriated its use with respect to literary texts in a unique way. This conceptual movement across fields was, in fact, quite common in his work. Originally, the term was introduced in mathematical biology in connection with theories of relativity. Bakhtin noted, however, that "[t]he specific meaning it has come to have there is of little interest to us; we will introduce it here into literary studies, somewhat like a metaphor (somewhat, but not quite) (Todorov, 1981/1984, p. 14). Essentially, he used the term to specify "a literary category of form-and-content" (p. 35) that revealed spatiotemporal models characteristic of every novelistic genre. His notion here was that "[e]very genre that is an essential genre is a complex system of ways and means of apprehending reality in order to complete it while understanding it" (p. 83). In short, in attempting to depict a world that has infinite possibilities, genres make selections from those possibilities, and thereby set out a model of the world. He proposed that this modeling of the world could be seen in terms of two constitutive elements – time and space.

Bakhtin focused on novelistic genre, but his attention was also on the relation between the work and the world, where the work (unlike the world) offered a conditional sense of completion. He recognized also that "[h]owever realistic or truthful it may be, the represented universe can never be chronotopically identical with the real universe where the representation occurs"

(Todorov, 1981/1984, p. 52). Yet, he believed that "[e]very genre has its methods, its ways of seeing and understanding reality, and these methods are its exclusive characteristic" (p. 180). Importantly, as Todorov pointed out,

It must immediately be added that Bakhtin does not use the notion of chronotope in restricted fashion, and does not limit it simply to the organization of time and space, but extends it to the organization of the world (which can be legitimately named "chronotope" insofar as time and space are fundamental categories of every imaginable universe). (p. 83)

This broader application is also linked to what I have in mind regarding notions of the classroom as chronotope. This aspect of my discussion is akin to how Gilroy (1993) proposed the ship as a novel manifestation of Bakhtin's concept of the chronotope. In rethinking modernity via the history of the black Atlantic, Gilroy "emphasised that ships were the living means by which the points within that Atlantic world were joined. They were mobile elements that stood for the shifting spaces in between the fixed places that they connected" (p. 16). Here, Gilroy was working within de Certeau's delineation of the concept of "a space," which offers some illumination to Bakthin's notion of "space" (and time) as key constitutive elements in various genre (or genrelike) models of the world. "A space," de Certeau (1984) notes, "exists when one takes into consideration vectors of direction, velocities, and time variables. Thus space is composed of intersections of mobile elements. It is in a sense articulated by the ensemble of movements deployed within it" (p. 117). So for Gilroy, ships were both constructed by and representative of the political economy and cultural conflicts and intersections of the slave trade and its relationships to modernity. Accordingly, he argued, "[ships] need to be thought of as cultural and political units rather than abstract embodiments of the triangular trade" (p. 17).

Similar to Gilroy's chronotopical conception of ships, I think the classroom offers a chronotopic-like unit (or model) for analysis along space/time and other dimensions of cultural/political interaction. Teaching and learning both involve and reveal an array of micropolitical and microcultural transactions and productions. Classrooms are embedded within society, but they can also represent or constitute some of the movement between societal spaces (its structures, meanings, and forces) in ways that could be seen as models for how the fixed places themselves might be changed or changing. As a chronotopic space, our classroom provided many opportunities to see the inner workings of forces in the larger culture system in terms of how they were partially revealed in the daily dynamics of doing class.

This perspective on the classroom as a chronotope for reading (and also for acting on) society was important for engaging prospective teachers who were often questioning how (and even if) they could actually become "agents of social change" who could "bring about educational equity ... through ... instruction" that produces "desired learning outcomes within the context of (and with an understanding of) urban conditions and structures." Statements posted on student home pages on our website captured some of this early self-questioning, as seen in the following examples:

My entire life has taken place mostly in the suburbs so that is why I am a little anxious going into urban schools...(S26, home page, July 2001)[5]

I am deathly afraid of my first year as a teacher. I frequently wonder if I will permanently damage a student's life forever. (S30, home page, July 2001)

Sleeter (1992) and other researchers showed that many white teachers are unaccustomed, afraid, or uncomfortable in discussing difficult issues of race, nationality, social class, religion, gender, sexual orientation, disability, and school and community violence. I have found that students of color often have similar problems dealing with these same issues with respect to teaching in urban schools. These difficult issues surfaced in the first week of class through our reading and discussion of *Our America* (Jones & Newman, 1997) and in the first student group presentation on *Subtractive Schooling* (Valenzuela, 2000), and continued throughout the semester.

The play of tensions in our classroom surrounding these issues were fluid models of ways these tensions and forces play in the larger society. Our challenge was to effectively read and analyze these dynamic "texts" that we were collectively authoring and enacting through classroom life and learning. The difference, however, between the space of the classroom and the space of society was that we had a greater opportunity (method) to work toward understanding these tensions and forces, and hence, we could actually work toward resolution (completion). This feature of the classroom as a chronotopic space reflected one of Bakhtin's key notions about the relationship between the work (a model text) and the world – the notion that the work could offer a conditional sense of completion or understanding that was difficult to access in the actual world.

Part of our "method" for working toward completion or understanding was the electronic extension of opportunities for discourse on difficult issues. The website offered a key forum for students in the class to express their feelings about what they were thinking and learning. This

---

[5] To document student comments without personally identifying them, each of the thirty students in the class was given a random "student number" (i.e., "S15"). After the student number, the electronic source of the comment is identified as "home page," "discussion board," or "e-mail," and other nonelectronic sources are identified as "verbal communication" or "course evaluation." The date of each comment follows the identification of its source. For comments coming from student home pages, only the month and year may be available (i.e., "July 2001"). Because the identity of students is not known in the course evaluations, the designation for a citation from this source is "S" followed by a slash, plus a different random letter from the alphabet (i.e., "S/Z").

feature of the class is taken up again in the next section of this chapter. For now, however, I discuss one electronic exchange that was posted on the website's "discussion board" at the end of the first week of class, and link it to opportunities for personal and collective transformation and understanding. The first expression captured the spirit of a number of the students' early electronic and verbal communications at that stage of the semester:

. . . class is asking tough questions and, sometimes, I feel awfully small. Is a faith in collaboration just 'romantic possibilitarianism'"? (S5, discussion board, July 7, 2001)

"Romantic possibilitarianism" was a term from one of our readings that this student was using to refer to the notion that when changes in meaning and consciousness are seen as the key aspects of social transformation, there is a risk of reducing complex issues to mere discursive constructions. This student was questioning the ability of the class community to actually transform its members' consciousness of complex social issues through class discourse and collaborative work.

I believe that a key feature in working toward understanding was in the students' abilities to extend the classroom discourse electronically. For example, another student responded to S5 with the following comment:

As far as the smallness thing, YES, I feel that too. And I just finished reading *Made in America* with these kick-ass teachers who cared and fought and organized. . .and 3 out of 4 are outta there at the end of the book, after 2–3 years. Very demoralizing. But I gotta say, for every evening I go to bed with the wind knocked out of me from the reading, every time a teacher like Ms. Hatano or Dr. Cone walks in the door, I puff right back up. And I think, maybe we can each do that, be one of the right-on teachers that puts the wind back in the sails of some of those already out there, and for each other. Romantic possibilitarianism is a FINE approach, as long as you back it up with pragmatic methods and techniques. (S13, discussion board, July 9, 2001)

In conjunction with the extension of discourse in electronic dialogues, significant work had been done to engage the students in classroom dialogues with key people working in urban education. Through these kinds of class scripts, the students were able to see possible answers to problems of individual and social transformation as they could be affected, in part, through schooling. Principal Hatano and Dr. Cone were two of the guest presenters who came to talk about their work in urban schools. Hatano is the coprincipal of a unique urban, charter school in the San Francisco Bay Area, and Dr. Cone is an effective urban high school teacher who has done significant work and writing on untracking advanced placement English classes. These kinds of presentations took place during the third hour of each class, and for that hour, class was open to anyone who wanted to come and hear the presenter(s). During Hatano's presentation, for example, there were more than sixty people present. Because all ten presentations were video-taped, these provocative dialogues that began in person were extended in audio/video texts that were the foundations for the final papers, where students were asked to select and take a stance on the perspectives from one presentation by bringing it into dialogue with relevant ideas from a number of other course readings. Similar to the following comment, every student in the class expressed how valuable they found these presentations to be for helping them deal with difficult issues surrounding urban schools.

As part of this community of learners, I would also include all the presenters. . .invited to our classes because I now feel that I have people to turn to – who are practitioners in the field – with my questions about issues that I will encounter such as racial disparity, tracking and untracking, small schools, charter schools, gender and race relations, incorporating multicultural and pop culture texts into my curriculum, academic literacy, teacher research, student voice, and closing the achievement gap. (S2, home page, August 2001)

Urban students themselves are also principal stakeholders, and some of these students came to class in person, in video clips and documentaries, and in required readings, such as *Our America* (Jones & Newman, 1997) and *Subtractive Schooling* (Valenzuela, 2000). Readings and discussions of these kinds of texts revealed additional aspects of the chronotopical nature of the classroom. For example, *Our America* was selected because it provided personalized youth perspectives on urban conditions that many teachers often do not see. It initially grew out of two radio documentaries, *Ghetto Life 101* and *Remorse: The 14 Stories of Eric Morse* that were created by the two authors, LeAlan Jones and Lloyd Newman, when they were 13 years old. LeAlan and his sisters were being raised by his grandmother because his mother was mentally ill. Lloyd was being raised by his two teenage sisters because his mother had died and his father was an alcoholic. *Ghetto Life 101* chronicled their young lives growing up with violence and poverty in and around the Ida B. Wells Housing Project in Chicago. When 5-year-old Eric Morse was dropped out of a fourteenth-floor window of a building in Ida B. Wells by two other boys who were 10 and 11 years old, LeAlan and Lloyd interviewed the boys involved (the youngest kids ever to be sentenced to prison in the United States), along with a number of family members and residents to create another series of radio specials.

Reading this book was disturbing for many of the prospective teachers. As one class member noted, "taking a walk through the 'ghetto' in South Side Chicago through the eyes of two young kids, LeAlan & Lloyd, is beyond words" (S21, home page, July 3, 2001). During its reading and discussion, there was also a group report on *Subtractive Schooling* done by three of the Latina women in the class. They chose to do the first half of their presentation in Spanish to position and challenge the majority of people in the class as if they were second language learners. Reflective of Fairclough (1992), they were using the discourse of their presentation as "a mode of action, one form in which people may act upon the world and especially upon each other" (p. 63). This activity produced an element of frustration in some of the class members that the three presenters believed that learners of English as a second language experience daily in contemporary schools.

As the prospective teachers encountered these provocative texts, they also had to confront themselves in terms of issues of personal identity and their motives to teach in urban schools. This "turning inward" was consistent with Ferdman's (1990) notion that

A teacher should feel comfortable with his or her own background before attempting to delve into that of others. . . . Before helping others to do so, one must initially explore one's own values and attitudes about diversity as well as one's degree of awareness of the role culture plays in one's own identity formation. (p. 201)

This notion was echoed and extended in many of our class readings, such as Nieto's (1996) call for teaching to be seen as a lifelong journey of transformation. She also notes that teachers need to face their own identities, become learners and identify with students, become multicultural and multilingual, confront racism and other biases in schools, and develop a community of critical friends and colleagues.

The two activities around *Our America* (Jones & Newman, 1997) and *Subtractive Schooling* (Valenzuela, 2000) dramatically brought notions of "the other" into contact with the self for many of the preservice teachers. These dynamic texts of teaching and learning were read and seen by the students as X-rays of larger societal texts on these issues. In addition to considerations of domination and subjugation, these class texts also revealed the intricate ways in which new identities and new cultural categories are being continually formed and negotiated. In essence, the classroom was a place where the dialogue itself around these kinds of texts was a form of social practice through which multiple cultural identities were not only represented, but also negotiated.

The classroom is a chronotopic space where various "mobile elements" of the culture system intersect, but it also allows for conscious orchestration of these elements to create movement toward greater understanding and completion. As key stakeholders in education contributed to the authoring and enactment of the scripts of class, our community of learners was better able to understand how to change in relation to the world in order to effect more productive change in the world – in part, though work in schools.

DIALOGIC TEACHING AND LEARNING

The dialogical principle is the dominant theme in Bakhtin's theory of language that grounds his epistemology. It reflects his belief in the interdependence of history, text, and meaning. For Bakhtin, "meaning" implies and requires community:

The entire verbal part of human existence (external and internal discourse) cannot be charged to the account of the unique subject, taken in isolation; it does not belong to the individual but to his *social group* (his social environment). (Todorov, 1981/1984, p. 30)

Dialogic qualities of meaning making are revealed in interactions between speakers and listeners who are "always already" social beings. An utterance always addresses someone, and the addressee participates in the formation of meaning along with other elements of the social situation in which the utterance occurs. The idea that every utterance is related to previous utterances is key to Bakhtin's dialogism, and another term that has been used for this idea is intertextuality. Meanings, therefore, are not neutral or derived independently; they are heteroglossic in that they are acquired through and marked with multiple prior voices and contexts. Importantly, these prior voices and contexts shape and organize not only meaning, but also experience. According to Bakhtin, "There is no experience outside its embodiment in signs" (Todorov, 1981/1984, p. 43).

All language activities of teaching and learning are inherently dialogic. However, as new teachers work to develop dispositions, knowledge, and skills needed in twenty-first-century schools, I believe conscious considerations of dialogic qualities of meaning-making benefit this process. Because meaning implies community, our attention was toward particular processes of meaning-making available in the specific discourse community of the class. We explored how we were alternately (and simultaneously) speakers and listeners who were "always already" linked in dialogical meaning-making exchanges. One student's comment captured something of the significance of our interactions as a community of learners:

Looking back over the past 6 weeks of classes, I am amazed at the scope and the depth of the issues we have covered. However, besides the textbooks and the lectures, I have found an entire layer of personal experience to reflect on as well. I found the group work and class discussions to be particularly powerful in this respect, and although we never really took notes on what one another said, I still remember distinctly what came out of many of those conversations. So I'd have to say I had 30+ teachers this semester! (S7, home page, August 2001)

In the class, we tried to become conscious of how our attempts to hear other voices and create new meanings were circumscribed by prior voices and received meanings. As I argue further, electronic resources were integral to our access and exploration of other voices, as well as the authoring of our own. We came to see and experience the class as a discourse community in which we learned not only about a wide range of urban education issues, but also about ourselves and others through dialogues stimulated by a variety of texts that were often mediated electronically.

It is important for urban educators to have a broad definition of the kinds of texts through which meanings are made in addition to traditional written texts. This class was grounded in definitions of texts that were used in the teaching standards for English Language Arts of the Interstate New Teachers Assessment and Support Consortium (INTASC).[6] Based on these definitions, a text is any segment of language or symbol that creates a unit of meaning. Texts include printed material, such as stories, poems, essays, books, and newspaper and magazine articles. However, they also can be spoken representations of meaning, such as oral stories, discussions, or speeches. They can be dramatizations, such as live enactments, films, and television; visual representations of meaning, such as paintings, cartoons, sculpture, graphics, and holography; tactile representations, such as Braille; and even lived experiences, such as a day in the park, a conversation with a loved one, or an observation about a social situation.

There were four required books that we all read, and ten selected books (each with an excerpted chapter in our course reader) that were presented to the class by assigned student groups. In addition, each student individually reviewed a book and posted its annotation on the class website. So, beyond the fourteen central books, at various levels we engaged more than forty books on urban education during the semester. As one student noted, "I leave . . . class feeling like a grape leaf: green, somewhat limp, and overstuffed – in a tasty, savory kind of way" (S13, home page, August 2001).

Comments like this reflected the fact that we also used many other texts extensively in class – short video clips from documentaries, movies, and student or teacher productions; music CDs of popular cultural artists; segments of audio recordings, such as National Public Radio Specials that corresponded to readings; visual stills of art, drawings, graffiti, and advertisements; computer-mediated animation and visual/sound presentations; web-based resources like a number of websites connected to class topics, as well as our own website's electronic blackboard, discussion boards, home pages, and course documents; guest lectures and their subsequent video documentation; field trips to urban education organizations such as Kids First and the Bay Area Coalition of Equitable Schools; and live enactments that were often created by the students themselves as parts of group presentations on assigned books. Understandably, some students believed all this was at times a bit rushed, or that we were "trying to pack too much information into one class period" (S/A, course evaluation, September 15, 2001).

---

[6] INTASC is a part of the Council of Chief State School Officers, which is a consortium of thirty-four states. In the case of INTASC, these states work together to, among other things, create model performance standards for evaluating new K–12 teachers in a variety of subject areas.

Productively engaging a wide array of texts into the classroom was facilitated by technology. Our classroom had been recently renovated and provided with a host of electronic text delivery systems, including web connections. The use of multiple texts aided us in seeing or exploring the interdependence of meaning, texts, and history. We were able to experience how different texts allowed us to make meaning differently, and how they had different histories of creation and use. The ability to access a wide array of texts in the classroom also increased the number and nature of voices able to participate in the dialogues on urban education. It helped us to see more clearly how dialogues are always entered from multiple "subject" positions and social spaces, and how some of these may be in conflict with others. Importantly, these conflicts are both represented and negotiated dialogically.

A key conflict for many of the preservice teachers involved coming to understand and make visible ways that white privilege is manifested. Similar to the main point in a class handout on the topic of understanding privilege that we discussed, many students confronted the fact that even if they understood how racism disadvantages many people, they had not understood its other side – white privilege – with its unearned advantages. In this regard, one student noted:

Coming from a background of white privilege, I assumed the canon was there for a reason and the reason was that everyone should learn it. . . . I did see the need for a more broad definition of what was considered canonical, yet I never realized how grounded my pedagogy was in the belief that there are certain texts that every literate person should read. I have to admit that I am still struggling with this. (S15, home page, August 2001)

Through our texts and with each other we were able to critique ways that privileged perceptions and experiences were "received" without us really having perceptions of privilege. For example, I noted on the first day of class that what might affect students more than the preservice training in their conceptions of teaching was the way they themselves had been educated in school. This idea was developed more fully in one of the student-led group presentations on the book *The Teaching Gap: The Best Ideas from the World's Teachers for Improving Education in the Classroom* (Stigler & Heibert, 1999). From this extensive study of teaching practices in three countries – Germany, Japan, and the United States – these authors convincingly demonstrated how extensively teacher perceptions of teaching are already culturally bound. In line with this notion, the student cited above was reflective on how her earlier teaching experiences were shaped by her own education.

I realize that all of my understanding of diversity went out the window once I was in front of 25 seventh graders. I fell into the trap of thinking that there was one way to do everything. While it was against my better judgment and my experience as a teacher, I fell into default mode: the traditional classroom full of teacher centered instruction. I remember thinking, "I was bored with grammar, and, by god, my students will be bored with it too." I exaggerate here to stress the point that I think this class has changed me. (S15, home page, July 2001)

Bakhtin's notion of the heteroglossic nature of utterances reveals the complexity of attempting to speak or think beyond already marked voices from prior contexts. He notes that "[l]anguage is not a neutral medium . . . it is populated – overpopulated – with the intentions of others . . . forcing it to submit to one's own intentions . . . is difficult" (Bakhtin, 1981, 294). In attempting to transform perceptions of self and others, students found that it was not only difficult, but painful. Some of the voices heard in class revealed the asymmetrical power relations in which privilege and difference are rooted. As Sholle and Denski (1993) note, "For those whose lives have benefited through occupying a position of privilege . . . the collapse of these structures, the unmasking of the once absolute and eternal as now arbitrary and transient . . . all of this will most certainly find response in words like *crisis, the end of meaning, the end of history,* and so on" (p. 305).

Although some students thought that as a community we "dealt . . . effectively with [these] sensitive topics" (S/B, course evaluation, September 15, 2001), others noted that "many of the voices heard in the course stirred up emotional issues" (S/C, course evaluation, September 15, 2001), and that "perhaps our class needed more team-building . . . to establish our connections a little more solidly" (S20, home page, July 20, 2001). We had a class picnic at the beginning of the semester and went on a great hike together after the first week of class, but clearly the work of making stronger connections to each other needs to go on throughout the semester.

A key question was how could we deal critically with difficult issues such as white privilege as a community of learners without triggering debilitating feelings of white guilt? The fact is that it was triggered. For example, one student noted:

There is an imposed guilt in me (whether self imposed or imposed from without, I don't know) that I am somehow responsible for the centuries of imperial oppression symbolized by my melanin-deprived skin, or because my ancestors were European, or because I am male. I know that this is an over exaggeration, but it is how I feel sometimes. (S18, home page, August 2001)

Yet, I believe that the sum experience over the semester with these difficult issues was productive as partially reflected in the following student comment:

White guilt. I heard it expressed several times throughout the semester. I think it is almost a natural reaction from a white person who is feeling racialized while exploring all of the deep problems in our country (and planet) around race. . . . Certainly, there is going to be a lot of discomfort around the issues that will be raised in multiculturalism, but I just don't see guilt as being productive in any way. . . . I think we need to accept responsibility for the world, in the sense that we are responsible for changing that world as much as we are capable of. I think this sense of responsibility, as opposed to guilt, is empowering, because it forces us to see ourselves as agents of change, rather than passive vehicles of oppression. (S7, home page, August 2001)

Of course, my own intentions for the class were also marked and muted by prior contexts. I had provided a lot of texts on issues surrounding race and gender, but fewer on considerations of social class and none on sexual orientation. Several students eventually pointed out the lack of treatment given to issues such as sexual orientation and disability in my curriculum, as noted in the following comment:

This is not meant to criticize ANYONE, for if anything it points to how easily groups can slip through the cracks as we attempt to cover the huge range of diversity in our classroom. But this semester for me was marked by a growing personal conscious-ness about gay and lesbian issues in education, mainly as a result of my individual book report book, along with a growing sense of invisibility as I looked at the cur-riculum in both of our classes and saw nothing on those issues in them. . . . [W]ith Jabari's blessing, [two other students] and I were able to assert the importance of our community's needs in the curriculum just this week. But I felt like that experience, more than anything we read or anyone we listened to, really hammered home the importance of creating an inclusive curriculum that reflects the lives and issues of our students. (S7, home page, August 2001)

Clearly, there are muted voices inside the classroom itself that need to be heard. A challenge for pedagogy and curriculum in the new millennium is to create effective and culturally relevant ways to access, amplify, and learn from these voices. In the demographic landscape of contemporary schools and society, new teachers will need highly refined cultural lenses to see the lines of difference and domination as they overlap and intersect, sometimes in subtle or novel ways. The following student comment provides a poignant example:

Growing up in Orange County was growing up in privilege. Coming-out in Orange County was having a portion of that privilege abruptly and unequivocally stripped from me. . . . There is no faster way to "unpack the knapsack of privilege" than to have it abruptly ripped open and emptied of some of its contents. . . . I went from being a part of the majority to identifying with a highly stigmatized minority. Going through this transformation changed my life in more ways than one: it allowed me to see the world from two VERY different perspectives; it illuminated how much I had not seen or understood before; it began to reveal how my views, my beliefs, my LOGIC, my interpretation of the universe, and my most carefully guarded and closely held values were filtered through the very powerful lenses of race, class, gender, ability, age, religion, nationality, culture, sexuality, language, and life experience. It challenged me to step outside – to attempt to remove – these invisible lenses and look for meaning anew. To question. To think critically. To be open. To check myself. To acknowledge my own privilege. To seek out difference and demystify it in order to disarm my own fear and ignorance. To build bridges. To reach out. To take risks. To work toward change. To make my life about learning and love. And, here I am. (S4, home page, August 2001)

In our classroom, dialogues on complex, difficult issues in society were social practices through which diverse cultural identities were made visible and negotiated. Providing the substance of these practices does not necessarily require electronic mediation. Indeed, as Haas (1995) argues, technologies are not merely tools for individual use, they are themselves culturally constructed systems that manifest ideology and values marked by prior histories and contexts. They can, in fact, work to inhibit some voices from being heard. As one student noted, "I'm not comfortable, as yet, meditating on things in such a public place as a web page" (S6, home page, August 2001). Nevertheless, I believe that the variety of communication technologies did offer dynamic resources to help us achieve some of our goals for new, urban teachers that were partially reflected in the "AEIOU" lenses. A key additional goal was to help prepare these new teachers to take advantage of technological resources for mediating teaching and learning.

The use of varied, communication technologies changed the nature of the learning experiences in the class. The fact that technology so easily captured and made permanent many aspects of how the students were using it was itself significant. The electronic record of communication going back and forth between students as well as between students and the instructor captured both incremental and global ways that the students were changing their perceptions and skills. It provided records of the students' work in process on assignments and offered new opportunities to influence that progress toward completion. In grading assignments, the available technology allowed me to respond to student texts in a unique form of dialogue affected through the "comment" feature in the word processing program. I could embed a comment that ranged from a single word or symbol up to several paragraphs "behind" any word that I highlighted in a student's text. When the text was returned to the student it would look exactly the way it did when it was handed in electronically, with the exception that the returned text would have selected words highlighted. When the student clicked on this highlighted word, a dialogue box would pop up. This feature was more akin to actual dialogues with students about their ideas than any form of writing comments on an actual student paper. It also meant that no actual paper changed hands. Students submitted their final papers electronically and received them back electronically with my comments embedded in dialogue boxes that "spoke" only at appropriate points in the text, and only when "asked" with a mouse click.

Features of technology also provided the class with multiple and fluid points of access into the discourse on urban issues. For example, we read *Our America* (Jones & Newman, 1997), but we also heard LeAlan and Lloyd tell parts of their stories in their own voices. We heard the voices of the young boys charged with murder in the death of 5-year-old Eric Morse, and we heard the voice and story of the father of one of the boys who was charged, even while the father himself was in prison. The dialogues started by these and other voices were able to continue in and beyond the class – not only orally, but electronically in web-based discussion boards, electronic blackboards, student home pages, e-mails, website documents, and other web links. The students' voices in this chapter (with the exception of comments from course evaluations) came from these electronic sources. So, students had increased access to other voices in forms that might be argued to be more authentically representative than many forms of written texts.

The students also had increased opportunities through technology to speak in their own voices to other members of the class. Like access, authorship is reconstituted through technology. Opportunities and ease for students to speak and write themselves into the discourse influenced the flow of information and ideas, as well as some of the dynamics of power in the class. Students had power to direct aspects of their learning and the learning of other members of the class, including the instructor. This power culminated perhaps in the student-led presentations on selected texts. As I noted earlier regarding the presentation on *Subtractive Schooling* (Valenzuela, 2000), these group reports sometimes took the forms of live enactments and also became forums for student displays of their mastery of electronic text delivery systems. They became sites for demonstrations of skills with technology that students could also use in their own instruction in the future. The student's group presentation on *Inside City Schools* (Freedman, 1999), for example, incorporated dramatic enactment and technology in a short film production that helped set the stage for more intensive discussions and critical considerations of multiculturalism. The clip was funny, but more important, it captured an aspect of this emotionally charged topic electronically in a way that helped to dissipate the tension that some people experienced around these issues.

In addition to access and authorship, the use of technology in conjunction with other pedagogical strategies helped foster a greater sense of ownership for learning by the students. For their group presentations, the challenges in using technology were really challenges to find more potent and engaging ways to communicate their ideas. What they came to see through their work in preparation for presentations, as well as in small-group work inside the classroom, was that they themselves were powerful resources for the learning and social transformation of others. As one student noted, "I found the presentations by members of the class to be eye opening and informative" (S2, home page, August 2001). Similar comments permeated the course evaluations in which students emphasized the significance of the group presentations with respect to "the role of the students as teachers" (S/X, course evaluation, September 15, 2001). Students found through their social/intellectual work in shifting groups that they could be increasingly honest with each other. As one student noted, "I had been chewing on something someone at my table said weeks ago and finally had the courage to say, 'What did you mean by that!?!'" (S5, home page, August 2001).

Students found that these dialogic relationships surrounding their small-group readings and subsequent "writings" of class texts helped them change their perceptions of themselves and others. For example, one student noted her "completely changed view" from reading Freire (1993) in conjunction with "the 20+ something hours spent talking with . . . [the other two women in her group] on how far I'm willing to go to change" (S11, home page, August 2001). Another women from the same group spoke to the significance of this process of dialogical learning and personal change as follows:

I would just like to acknowledge my fellow *Pedagogy of the oppressed* group members. . . . Y'all crack me up! My brain cells are still reeling from the mental marathons we traversed together in dissecting this book. Thank you for being willing to talk about the book in terms of your own personal experiences and struggles. I gained so much from our discussions. (S4, home page, August 2001)

Meanings are marked with prior voices and contexts, but meanings can change and new identities can be forged through critical dialogues that take place in dynamic societal spaces. Language is not a mere medium of social exchange; it is a central form of social exchange. Electronically mediated teaching and learning can create valuable opportunities for personal and social transformation inside and beyond the space of classrooms, and teachers must be able to apprehend these possibilities of technology while being aware of its constraints.

NEW-CENTURY SCHOOLING

Technology offers new tools for teaching and learning. However, the efficacy of schooling in this millennium is ultimately tied to new pedagogical designs. The notion of the class as a community of learners was at the center of this design for preparing new teachers to teach in diverse school and societal settings. Concepts from Bakhtin facilitated understanding how members of this learning community engaged ideas and each other in the "writing" of a dynamic text of triumphs and conflicts in learning about provocative issues of schooling and society. I argued that this dynamic text of the class was a chronotopic-like optic for reading some of the larger cultural/structural and political dimensions in society. In other words, the play of actions and tensions collectively authored in the spatial/temporal settings of class provided partial models of ways that similar tensions and actions played in the larger society. One value in our reading of a model text, following Bakhtin, is that in contrast to the actual world it is easier to arrive at a conditional sense of completion or understanding.

Community in the classroom as in society does not occur automatically or spontaneously; it has to be created. In this chapter, I describe how our community of learners was created dialogically. Specific uses of technology helped to extend our dialogic engagements through a variety of textual mediums, and I believe these uses of technology also revealed important considerations for teaching and learning in new-century schools.

References

Bakhtin, M. (1981). *The dialogic imagination.* Austin: University of Texas Press.

de Certeau, M. (1984). *The practice of every day life.* Berkeley and London: University of California Press.

Fairclough, N. (1992). *Discourse and social change.* Oxford, UK: Blackwell.

Ferdman, B. M. (1990). Literacy and cultural identity. *Harvard Educational Review, 60*(2), 181–204.

Freedman, S. (1999). *Inside city schools: Investigating literacy in multicultural classrooms.* New York: Teachers College Press.

Freire, P. (1993). *Pedagogy of the oppressed.* New York: Continuum.

Gilroy, P. (1993). *The black Atlantic: Modernity and double consciousness.* Cambridge, MA: Harvard University Press.

Haas, C. (1995). *Writing technology: Studies in the materiality of literacy.* Mahwah, NJ: Erlbaum.

Jones, L., & Newman. L. (1997). *Our America.* New York: Scribner.

Kirby, C. (2000, December 20). Politicians ponder how best to use web in education. *The San Francisco Chronicle*, pp. B1, B5.

Mahiri, J. (1998). *Shooting for excellence: African American and youth culture in new century schools.* New York: Teachers College Press and Urbana, IL: National Council of Teachers of English.

Mahiri, J. (2000a). Pop culture pedagogy and the ends(s) of school. *Journal of Adolescent & Adult Literacy, 44*(4), 382–5.

Mahiri, J. (2000b). What will the social implications and interactions of schooling be in the next millennium? *Reading Research Quarterly, 35*(3), 420–4.

Mahiri, J. (Ed.) (2003). *What they don't learn in school. Literacy in the lives of urban youth.* New York: Peter Lang.

Nieto, S. (1996). *Affirming diversity: The sociopolitical context of multicultural education.* White Plains, NY: Longman.

San Francisco Chronicle, October 17, 1996, p. A2.

Sholle, C., & Denski, S. (1993). Reading and writing the media: Critical media literacy and postmodernism. In C. Lankshear & P. L. McLaren (Eds.), *Critical literacy: Politics, praxis, and the postmodern.* New York: State University of New York Press.

Sleeter, C. (1992). *Keepers of the American dream: A study of staff development and multicultural education.* London: Routledge Falmer Press.

Stigler, J., & Heibert, J. (1999). *The teaching gap: The best ideas from the world's teachers for improving education in the classroom.* New York: The Free Press.

Todorov, T. (1981–1984). *Mikhail Bakhtin: The dialogical principle.* (Trans. W. Godzich). Minneapolis: University of Minnesota Press. (Original work published 1981).

Valenzuela, A. (2000). *Subtractive schooling: U.S.-Mexican youth and the politics of caring.* New York: State University of New York Press.

10

Is Contradiction Contrary?

Melanie Sperling

> ...it's apparent...that the theories (people) employ change, flexibly and of necessity, from moment to moment in conversation, (and) that the notion of limiting conversation to a rigid rule of theoretical constancy is an absurd denial of what conversation is.
>
> – (Gopnik, 2000, p. 96)

> On all its various routes toward the object, in all its directions, the word encounters an alien word and cannot help encountering it in a living, tension-filled interaction.
>
> – (Bakhtin, 1934–35/1981, p. 279)

When it comes to beliefs, attitudes, and values, as humans we may all be defined as much by contradictions as by consistencies. Everyday experience is enough to confirm this observation and, in fact, to give it the status of a truism. How it plays out for English teachers as they discuss their students' engagement with and achievement in literacy is the focus of this chapter. This chapter is about a group of secondary English teachers at the cutting edge of classroom practice, and about their holding of sometimes contradictory theories about engagement and achievement that get played out in their classrooms as part of writing and literature instruction. Rather than view such contradiction as problematic, I see it as ordinary and necessary in the dialogue forged of everyday classroom experience. Similar to essayist Adam Gopnik, cited at the opening of this chapter, I argue that teachers' shifting theories reveal the multiple and sometimes conflicting realities of their dialogic existence in the world of school or, put another way, their shifting identities as they relate to one another, to students inside the classroom, and to outside others, such as policy makers, who influence classroom life. Ultimately, such multiple relationships shape what teachers perceive and do.

In offering my own perspectives on teachers' shifting theories, I draw primarily on Bakhtin's accounts of the social genesis of discourse and thought, and the notion that discourse and thought are born of multiple and sometimes opposing forces. For Bakhtin, discourse and thought are always in a process of becoming, in the interactive, dialogic contexts that give them shape and meaning. In this respect, as indicated by the citation from Bakhtin at the opening of this chapter, discourse and thought exist in the "tension-filled interaction" of the living moment. This chapter argues that, as researchers, we need to focus on such moments if we are to fully understand teachers and students in classrooms.

A BAKHTINIAN ACCOUNT

The Social Genesis of Discourse and Thought

Bakhtin's account of discourse and thought is captured by Morson (1986) in his explanation of discourse's social dynamic:

Bakhtin understands discourse to be not an individual writer's or speaker's instantiating of a code but, instead, the product of a complex social situation in which real or potential audiences, earlier and possible later utterances, habits and "genres" of speech and writing, and a variety of other complex social factors shape all utterances from the outset. (p. 83)

For Bakhtin, then, discourse and thought are composed of the individual's past interactions with the thoughts of others and of anticipated future interactions. In fact, Bakhtin reminds us that "social dialogue reverberates in all aspects of discourse, in those (aspects) relating to 'content' as well as the 'formal' aspects themselves" (1934–35/1981, p. 300), and that in everyday dialogue, "the listener and his response are regularly taken into account." (p. 280).

In this respect, discourse and thought *ipso facto* are, to use Bakhtin's term, heteroglossic. That is, the word, the utterance, the verbal moment are multivoiced, infused with "shared thoughts, points of view, alien value judgments and accents" (Bakhtin, 1934–45/1981, p. 276) that reflect what Holquist (1981) calls "a matrix of forces practically impossible to recoup" (p. 428).

Key to the notion of heteroglossia for Bakhtin – and to thinking about the English teachers' discussions that I later present – is the nature of the voices that comprise heteroglossia. According to Bakhtin, these voices can be parceled into two oppositional forces, those that seek to unify or homogenize thoughts, actions, beliefs, and values, and those that seek to decenter or upend them. Bakhtin calls these forces, respectively, "centripetal" and "centrifugal," the latter exemplified for Bakhtin by the novel, which in its finest heteroglossic form serves to decenter.[1] In the way that Bakhtin sees the creative force of the novel as centrifugal or decentering, I believe that we can think of such force at work in teachers' discussions of engagement and achievement, and in the sometimes contradictory notions that teachers hold as these decentering forces come up against the more homogenizing or unifying ones that also comprise their experience.

Moreover, I believe we need to think of the teachers' discussions about engagement and achievement as dynamic themselves, conceptualized and enacted in the moment and thus responsive to the dynamic forces, both unifying and decentering, of the moment's conversation. If one's discourse and thought are seen as dynamic in this way, it follows that discourse and thought can be seen to reflect multiple and sometimes conflicting theories gleaned from a multiplicity of dialogic experience. In the case of English teachers, such experience encompasses the ways of the English classroom, including its students, its purposes, and its place in a broader school and civic culture.

I emphasize that this dynamic is not problematic, but rather *the way things are*. And to understand the way things are, we can profit by analyzing the moment as an instantiation of forces rather than as some kind of molded product that, like concrete, is transportable across moments and places. This chapter aims, then, not so much for "getting," or clarifying, or depicting a teacher's singular point of view as if there were such a thing,[2] as if there were, as Bakhtin says, a force for overcoming heteroglossia. Rather, it aims more for unpacking the multiple points of view that inform teachers at given moments and that show, through the dynamics evident in the moment, *the person in front of us now*.

RESEARCH PERSPECTIVES

Research, especially research rooted in sociocognitive and sociocultural theories, uncovers the contradictions by which individuals involved in the enterprises of schooling appear to be defined, motivated, and constrained.

---

[1] In "Discourse in the Novel," Bakhtin (1934–35/1981) analyzes novelistic discourse by focusing on the kinds of authorial strategies – for example, the separation of author from characters, narrator from author (revealed especially through parody and irony) – that show novelistic discourse as multivoiced and therefore tension filled. He backs up his observations on the novel with accounts of the discourse of everyday life, which he describes as "contradiction-ridden and tension filled" (p. 272), much as we see fiction to be. Indeed, in the field of education, Bakhtin is taken up by researchers to explain, not a fictional layering of voices to create artistic discourse and meaning, a central focus for Bakhtin, but the very nonfictional layering of voices that comprise discourse and meaning for teachers and students day to day.

[2] Therefore, point of view may best be regarded as a fiction in the way that the notion of objectivity is in a postmodern world.

Such research emanates from a range of domains, and approaches contradiction at a number of levels, from that of concrete teaching and learning experience to that of belief, attitude, and value. It also tends to approach contradiction as a temporary condition that should be resolved, for example, through negotiation (a cognitive resolution) or the choosing of sides (a social and political resolution).

Familiar to literacy researchers and educators, for example, are recent sociocognitive theories of composing, one of the better known, perhaps, being Linda Flower's (1994), which recognizes often-hidden contradictions among the in-school and out-of-school experiences that influence writers. This kind of work contributes to theories of literacy that not only allow for contradiction as part of a literate meaning-making process, but also that privilege it. Writers are influenced by, and develop style and identity through, layers of experiences – with family, in school, in the community – which Flower suggests they negotiate as part of the writing process.

Brandt's (2001) case studies of the literacy practices of dozens of Midwesterners emphasize from a sociocultural perspective the often mismatched approaches that individuals bring both to writing and to reading, approaches that change within individuals over time (one's approach to writing at age 16, for example, is not the same as one's approach at age 60) and across generations. Brandt exposes the dialogic or relational roots of individuals' literacy in her analysis of these readers' and writers' intimate connections with what she calls the various "sponsors" of their literacy: book publishers, calendar makers, libraries, family traditions, and workplace resources, for example. Each sponsor shapes a person's literacy in particular ways, sometimes compatibly with one another but often not. Although Brandt's chief point is that literacy changes historically, over time, as sponsors of literacy (read relationships between literate self and others) change or receive differing emphases in different historical periods, I believe we can extrapolate from this point to understand that such shifts or changes should also be able to occur within moments of time, so that inconsistent beliefs and attitudes may undergird reading and writing processes at any given moment as multiple "sponsors" bear on that moment.

The layering and jigsawing of what appear to be inconsistent beliefs and attitudes about literacy are also seen in the processes of teaching and learning, as teachers and students construct multiple ways of being with one another around text. The teacher may be at once guide, authority, and collaborator; the student, compliant doer, also authority, also collaborator, all appropriate if apparently inconsistent ways of doing reading and writing in school (Sperling, 1995). Supporting this point and focusing on students as writers, Cazden (1988) observes how students construct multiple and sometimes contradictory ways of enacting classroom learning roles as they stand in different relationships to teachers as opposed to peers. Dyson (1993) similarly analyzes beginning writers' varied and sometimes contradictory "social spheres of interest" (p. 13), including what she calls the official world of school, the unofficial peer world, and the sociocultural community of the classroom. It has been argued that such varied influences (or relationships, or dialogues) need somehow to be perceived as cohesive – or okay together – in order for teachers and students to get on well with the business of the classroom (Sizer, 1985). I suggest that we take them to be okay together because the constellation of classroom roles and relationships get constructed in classrooms by teachers and students as they take shape in contingent contexts. Put another way, the multiple relationships that get shaped in the classroom reflect and are appropriate to contextual shifts within the pressing moment.

INSIGHTS FROM ASSESSMENT

Much insight on contradiction as a facet of classroom experience can be gleaned from research on assessment. Shepard (2000), for example, analyzes teachers' contradictory ways of knowing in the domain of achievement testing. She discusses how teachers often think about and approach teaching from social-constructionist perspectives while they think about and approach achievement testing like behaviorists. Shepard's thesis is that such apparently contradictory stances or theoretical mismatch can be troubling. Focusing on the system of teacher assessment developed for the National Board for Professional Teaching Standards, Delandshere and Petrosky (1998) explore assessment mismatch in terms of "the conflicting demands often placed on an assessment system" (p. 15). They give as an example the demand that assessment support learning and teaching vs. the demand that it rank and sort individuals. They also point out that, whereas theoretical discussions of assessment include both quantitative and qualitative summaries, when discussions turn to concrete evidence they focus only on numerical scores or ratings. "How reasonable is it," they ask, "to think of complex teaching performances as quantities of properties?" (p. 16). Yet, of course, not only experts in assessment, but also classroom teachers and other educators do so, often with no apparent second thought.

The ironies that seem to be inherent in assessment practice may in no small part both reflect and condition the limits of the very language we use when we discuss learning. In a reflection on two metaphors for learning, what she calls the "acquisition metaphor" (learning as accumulation of goods) vs. the "participation metaphor" (learning as apprenticeship in thinking, a concept drawn from Rogoff, 1990), Sfard (1998) argues that "different metaphors may lead to different ways of thinking and to different activities" in the classroom (p. 5).[3] Surely, thinking about the learning

[3] Sfard draws heavily on linguists who have made this same point (in particular, Lakoff & Johnson, 1980; Reddy, 1978; Sacks, 1978).

of reading and writing as the acquisition of something (information, skills, and so on) inspires different types of teaching and assessment than does thinking about such learning as ongoing participation in a broader social or cultural system (see Sperling, 1994, on this distinction as it is made by preservice teachers). The question is whether these ways of thinking can live side by side.

It is to issues such as these that this chapter is addressed. In this chapter, I discuss the topics about which I sought teachers' perspectives: students' engagement in reading and writing, their reading and writing achievement, and the place of assessment in the achievement–engagement relationship. The focus is both on how a group of English teachers perceived these topics and on the language they used when they discussed them. As I listened to these teachers and studied what they said to me, I was reminded how much these topics are infused for these teachers with multiple ways of knowing and being in the world of the English classroom. Although these ways are contradictory at times, and therefore can be viewed as troubling, I suggest that they are ordinary in a Bakhtinian sense and therefore revealing, not only of the many social contexts in which these teachers find themselves, but also of their exquisite sensitivity to encountering the forces, sometimes homogenizing, sometimes decentering, of their work.

THE STUDY

Last year I met with fourteen English teachers from middle schools and high schools in the southern California region that lies between Los Angeles and Palm Springs known as the Inland Empire. The Inland Empire is largely a working class region in the high desert. It enjoys a great deal of population diversity, with plentiful representation of east and southeast Asians, Latinos, African Americans, and whites, many of them transplants from the Midwest or from other parts of southern California. All the teachers with whom I spoke teach in schools that, demographically, look like the Inland Empire. Some of the teachers were teacher-consultants with the National Writing Project and came highly recommended to me by Inland Area Writing Project directors from a longer list representing the best teachers of that project. Some were recommended by university faculty and local school district administrators. I selected the initial fourteen on the basis of these recommendations and for the differing academic contexts in which they taught – from middle through high school; from relatively affluent to relatively impoverished student populations; from schools with mostly Latino and African American students to those with mostly white students; and from suburban to semirural locations. I was able to observe some of them in their classrooms and schools. I was able to interview all of them and spoke with each for about an hour, some in my office and some on site in the teachers' classrooms. None of the teachers had met me before we talked, but they all appeared open and willing to talk to me about their classrooms and their teaching. They divulged faults and successes both, and of the fourteen teachers who talked with me for around an hour each, I invited back six, four high school and two middle school teachers, for a second interview. I invited these six as a way of reducing the larger group to what the first interview suggested were the "cream of the crop," teachers who were conscious of current research in reading and writing, who were leaders in their schools and, in one case, who was in the process of being certified by the National Board of Professional Teaching Standards. These second interviews were held in my office and lasted for at least two hours, in some cases, close to three. They were tape-recorded and later transcribed. In all, approximately twelve hours of interview tapes were transcribed verbatim. For the limits of this chapter, I focus on the four teachers who taught at the high school level.

We covered a lot of territory in these interviews, but everything we talked about can be summed up as follows: the teachers' approaches to teaching writing and reading, the nature of students' engagement with writing and reading that year in their classrooms, the nature of students' writing and reading achievement that year in their classrooms, and, integral to these topics, the kinds and uses of writing and reading assessment used in their classrooms that year. To address these topics, I asked each teacher to focus on one of their current classes, the one in which the most reading and writing was being done. For some teachers, this meant focusing on honors classes. For others, it meant classes that were regular track.

I worked with two graduate students at the University of California, Riverside, to study these interviews.[4] We coded them for what teachers talked about (topic) and for how they talked (stategies). That is, coded topics all centered on reading and writing, and were suggested by the focus of the study itself. Coded topics included: reading and writing (kinds, uses, teacher role in, student role in); student achievement (high, low, teacher role in, student role in); student engagement (high, low, teacher role in, student role in); and assessment (kinds, uses, teacher role in, student role in). (See Table 10.1 for topic categories and examples.) Coding for these broad categories involved bounding off chunks of interviewer–interviewee conversation at points of topic-shift and then coding each chunk. When appropriate, chunks were multiply coded.

To try to capture teachers' perspectives on these topics, I further analyzed the chunks for key discourse strategies, that is, key ways the teachers conveyed their perspectives within each category. I focused on discourse strategies believed to reflect perspective (e.g., Bakhtin, 1934–35/1981),

---

4 PhD students David Livingston and Guy Trainin conducted initial coding of interview transcripts and computer input of coding. David Livingston continued to work on the data in later stages of analysis. My thanks and appreciation to them both.

TABLE 10.1. *Teachers' Topics of Conversation*

Topic	Example
Reading and writing	"Well this year we worked on preparing them for the reading comprehension section of the STAR Test." *Kind* of reading: reading for comprehension; *use*: to take a test; *teacher role*: to coach or train; *student role*: to be coached or trained.
Student achievement	"I would love to take credit for it [student's achievement], but I think it's already there, you know . . . " *Achievement level:* high; *teacher role*: to observe and nourish; *student role*: to bring gifts to the table.
Student engagement	"Westin turned in something that was not even a page, I think, in response to this book. . . . And that was sort of my first introduction to what I would say is much more a laziness issue rather than an ability [issue] . . ." *Engagement level:* low; *teacher role*: to interest student in participating in the work; *student role*: to participate at ability level.
Assessment	"I do feel that my means of assessment [i.e., in the classroom] gives the students an opportunity to shine and to show their achievement . . ." *Kind*: informal, tailored to each student; *use*: formative; *teacher role*: to provide opportunity for student to display their best; *student role*: to excel within own zone of ability.

including use of reported speech; mimicked speech; borrowed language; inference of others' experience, beliefs, and values; hypothetical situation; and appeal to authority, norm, or ideal (see Table 10.2).

This coding process allowed us to derive descriptive themes about students' literacy engagement and achievement and led us to discover teachers' theoretical contradictions. I discuss the contradictions below, using the coding as a kind of language to help in this discussion, focusing on what the teachers said and the voice or force that appeared to be operating as they said it. I have not calculated correlations between the what and the how of the teachers' discourse because each chunk of talk is saturated with both explicit and implicit voices or forces, impossible, as Holquist has indicated in discussing Bakhtin's work, to "recoup" or in any sense meaningfully trace. It is important, however, to understand and perceive their existence.

The next section, then, is devoted first to an example from the interviews through which I illustrate the great extent of voices – and forces – reflected in the teachers' talk, that is, the extent of voices coexisting. I explicate the example guided by Bakhtin's (1934–35/1981) approach to explicating the discourse of the novel. I next present the core findings from the analysis, the contradictory theories that we derived from studying the interviews.

TABLE 10.2. *Teachers' Discourse Strategies*

Discourse Strategy	Example
Reported speech	[*She says to her class*] . . . when your boss asks you to read this article on plastics and see what the main idea is and if it's useful for what your purposes are at your job, you're going to have to learn to summarize, pull out the main idea. (Patricia)
Mimicked speech	Now they can go out and interview people . . . [mimicking a student's paper] " . . . recently I interviewed 10 people and I posed these question to these people, and I went in and I talked about the people and they talked about their answers. And in conclusion, after doing these ten people, [I] found that . . . " (Hank)
Borrowed language	I have them [students] do *a dialectic journal* . . . where they're responding to parts of the texts that they find interesting. . . . (Bette)
Inference of others' experience, beliefs, values	*I know there are kids that have read the book, and care about it,* . . . but then they just don't do the essay . . . (Bette)
Hypothetical situation	*If you were doing a college class* and you were going to discuss a text, the first thing you have to do after you read the text is to be able to summarize it and know what the point was . . . (Sharon)
Appeal to authority, norm, or ideal	They [students] have to present it [their paper]. They read it to the class. . . . *This is what research is. You find out this stuff; you present it.* (Hank)

I discuss them in terms of voices or forces. I aim, with this sequence of presenting an explicated example before presenting the broader themes, to convey through the example the kind of cultural-linguistic saturization endemic to the themes. Doing so helps to establish the themes as representing teachers' multilayered "responses" in the moment, which reflect the moment and those who populate it in part by reflecting past responses and anticipated future responses as well.

Voices Coexisting

In my interview with Sharon,[5] we discussed reading assessment at length. Sharon explained to me her usual assessment routines for the class that she focused on in this interview, an eleventh-grade honors English class. The following example comes from this discussion. In the example (which

5 All teachers' and students' names are pseudonyms.

is a chunk of talk as I have described chunks above, and is coded for the topic "assessment, kinds and uses"), Sharon's begins by talking about the quizzes that she gives her students in order to assess their knowledge of the literature they are reading in class, which is plentiful. The students need to know the content of the literature, she says, in order to participate in the class seminar. She finishes this chunk of talk by explaining to me what she means by seminar, and reiterating how students need to be fully prepared when they participate in it. (Sharon is "S"; the interviewer [myself] is "I"; conversational turns are numbered. Italics are mine; italicized portions are the focus of the following explication.)

¹S: Well, *we would do quizzes* for content. *That's standard.*
²I: Yeah.
³S: And if you don't do that they [the students] get lax and don't do their reading. Seminar forced them to read and think before they came to class, so it is rather demanding. Those that did it–
⁴I: 'Seminar' meaning [in] this particular honors class or–
⁵S: I do seminar with all my classes but–
⁶I: Would you explain that?
⁷S: Yeah. *If you were doing a college class and you were going to deeply, going to discuss a text, the first thing you have to do, after you read the text, is to be able to summarize it and know what the point was and then to determine, well, how did the author support that main point and how does it connect to other things we've read and what supports will I bring in. So it's actually very challenging.*
⁸I: Yes.
⁹S: And if they prepare, they do well, and there is very definitely higher order thinking going on. But if they choose not to prepare and to not participate, they're accepting a low grade but they're also not growing and they need, I think, more structure, forcing them to do that preparation.

In turn 1, the first italicized portion represents, I would argue, *three* differing assertions about quizzes, or three differing voices. Certainly, the inclusive pronoun "we" encompasses what one would presume are the *two* differing voices of the teacher, on the one hand, and her students, on the other hand. One might surmise that these two voices are real enough, even though they are only implicit in Sharon's talk, in the sense that they are grounded in actual teacher and student experiences with quizzes. However, "we" also encompasses a third voice, which is a melding of the first two, the plural voice ("we") that Sharon actually articulates. I would argue, following Bakhtin, that this articulated voice is not grounded in the same reality as the first two are. That is, this third voice synthesizes the experiences of the teacher, on the one hand, and her students, on the other hand, conflating the experiences for the purpose of the moment. In this respect, "we" is a convenient fiction, lumping the teacher and students together as if they were one and the same. Much inference takes place in this assertion. That is, Sharon infers that the students' experience with quizzes can – and may – be lumped with hers to convey something meaningful to *me*, her interlocutor. The moment of talk itself, then, works on and conditions her message. The second italicized portion of turn 1 represents yet another voice that of the authority or classroom norm into which quizzes fit, the "standard." In the space of this one short turn, then, Sharon represents at least four voices, and experiences past and present.

To see how voices feed one another, I skip to turn 7 (although I could really use any one of the other turns to illustrate my point) because this turn dramatically illustrates shifting perspectives. Sharon's shifts in perspective are marked by steady pronoun shifts ("you" to "we" to "I"), as well as by intermixing of assertions and questions. This language marks key discourse strategies representing a range of "hidden" voices. The first italicized portion of turn 7, "If you were doing a college class" and so on, represents the language of hypothesis. Sharon presents a situation that has not taken place although it could take place, and that therefore lends authority, the authority of the "typical" case of being in college, to her ensuing explanation. It is marked as a hypothetical by the words "If you were," and I would argue that the "you" is both a hypothetical other as well as the "you" of the moment of this interaction, or Sharon's interlocutor. Infiltrating this hypothetical example are words, phrases, and commonplaces, taken from the conventionalized language associated with the reading of literature – "be able to summarize," "know what the point was," "how did the author support that main point," and so on. These words represent yet another layer of voices, these not hypothetical but real, therefore making the hypothetical situation all the more realistic itself. Sharon's shift into direct questioning – "how did the author support that main point and how does it connect to other things we've read" represents yet another voice, perhaps that of textbook author or instructor questioning or guiding students through a critical reading of literature. Here the "we" seems to represent both the hypothetical, continuing the hypothetical scenario posed at the beginning of Sharon's turn, as well as the real – the "we" of this teacher and her students in honors English. This double-voiced "we" is prepared for in earlier turns, in which Sharon discusses the "we" of teacher and her students in turn 1. It is also conditioned by what follows, "and what supports will I bring in," as Sharon shifts into first person, speaking hypothetically in the voice of the student in the hypothetical example, representing herself perhaps as well (the real first-person "I" of this turn, and perhaps mimicking the "I" of her students). This second "I" prepares her interlocutor (me) for her next assertion, that what actually (not hypothetically) occurs in her classroom between herself and her students is "actually very challenging." This assertion represents the authority of Sharon's first-person experience and judgment. It may also represent an answer to an anticipated but unspoken question about the value of seminar in reading literature. Ultimately, then, Sharon's discourse interacts within the moment, with me her interlocutor, and with likely future interlocutors like me.

In sum, a number of voices or forces are represented in Sharon's discourse. No doubt some are, in the Bakhtinian sense, homogenizing (I would say that the conventionalized voice of the literary reader is one of these). Others, also in the Bakhtinian sense, may be decentering (although without more evidence it is impossible to guess which these might be). Given the above explication, it is not surprising to me that the exploration of teachers' perspectives on reading and writing that I undertook in the study reveals teachers' theoretical contradictions. It is to these that I now turn.

Findings on Contradiction

Three salient contradictions appeared in the interviews across teachers. The first was the idea that *literacy ability is innate* vs. the idea that *literacy ability is socially constructed.* The second was the idea that *literacy achievement is reflected in assessment* vs. the idea that *literacy achievement sits apart from assessment.* And the third was the idea that *assessment is an impartial gauge of literacy achievement* vs. the idea that *assessment is a constructed (and in that sense partial) gauge of literacy achievement.*

These three sets of stances are clearly interrelated. If ability is constructed, for example, it may not be tapped by assessment if assessment is differently constructed. However, to efficiently address each set, I focus on each, one at a time.

Innate ability/social construction
In accounting for students' literacy engagement and achievement, the teachers all tended to differentiate between what they discussed as students' innate literacy ability compared with literacy ability constructed in the social-cultural contexts inside and outside of school. Yet the distinction between the two split along student ability lines. That is, for all teachers, high ability tended to be accounted for by invoking a stable societal ideal (e.g., the ideal of "brilliance"), whereas low ability was always accounted for by inferring about students' experiences and beliefs as they played out in social contexts (e.g., "begging off from reading"). Yet, while the teachers presented what amounted to two differing theoretical stances on the genesis of student achievement and engagement, they seemed not to be conscious of the distinction they were making.

Examples of how they talked about their high-ability readers and writers follow (emphases are added to draw attention to talk of innate ability):

1. She would read and write in such a manner that constantly astounded me and I mean it's hard to describe you kind of feel it's one of those people you kind feel that you almost can't do a very good job of teaching them because they are *probably beyond you* even, you know. And so, *she was kind of*

a difficult one, she's another where she would, could always be counted on to come up with the insights or lead the discussion in a really interesting way or point things that I hadn't even thought of, or and her *writing was just phenomenal, I mean, amazing, amazingly sophisticated.* I mean technically, *practically perfect. Imaginative* beyond belief... and she is going to go into science.... I was like, I'm going to kill you please don't.... I mean she was one who, every single prize at the end of the senior year went to her because there is just nobody else that could compare to her. *She is just a super super gifted person* I think in general.... *She's just one of those people who's pretty much brilliant....* (Bette)

2. I don't know, it almost seems like *he has the ability* and a lot of it is cultural too because you know his family really enriches his environment at home and they have standards about going on to college and education being important. He buys into that totally, so he's already on his adventure to educate himself. I think a lot of it has to do with the enrichment he has at home. I love would to take credit for it too, saying I gave him some good pieces to read and think about, but I *think it's already there you know.* (Patricia)

3. You know, I think *self-assurance* would be the first one [way to describe the student], he's really *self-assured,* he *is confident in himself.* And I would say *self-starter. Coachable.* [If] there's a mistake and I say well, maybe we can try it this way and he doesn't get mad and say, I did try it. He listens, he'll alter his approach. (Patricia)

4. I told her at the beginning of the year, that *she was a thoroughbred,* but her writing, that *thoroughbreds are very hard to handle and they run away from you,* so you really have to discipline them, and then if you do, then you're going to have an excellent race horse. You're going to have *an undisciplined powerful horse* and you're going to be hanging on for dear life as it runs away with you. (Sharon)

5. [The student was] *Generous,* and *she was interested in what other people say.* (Sharon)

That's that's really lovely, isn't it, goodness gracious. What accounted for her motivation and engagement? (Interviewer)

This I don't know, I could have done a greater study about where she came from and so forth, but *she came that way.* (Sharon)

All italicized portions represent the teachers' appeal to the authority of societal definitions or norms – brilliance, self-confidence, self-assurance, and so on. The voice influencing their perceptions is, then, that of society at large, with its conventional ways of naming competence. And the students embody these norms ready-made, prior to or despite the life of the classroom. I do not mean to imply that the teachers ignored how they worked with these students, or that they did not also at times describe influences molding students' ability, as Patricia does in Example 2 when she talks about the cultural influence of home being "much of it." However, the approbatory societal voice pervades their representations of high-achieving, highly engaged students.

This way of accounting for achievement did not extend to lower achievers. For lower achievers, the teachers' perspective encompassed the students' own perceptions of themselves as students and of their visible behaviors in class. Through this inferencing of students' experiences, beliefs, values, and so on, and through mimicking students' voices as they talked to me (much as Bakhtin sees authors playing with characters' voices in order to complicate their own authorial stances), their discourse represented the student's voice as key to their own perspective on lower-achieving students. In the examples below, I emphasize language that points up this voice:

6. I guess I would classify her as low achieving because she consequently because of *her reluctance to write, she would end up with drafts that weren't corrected,* you know, she didn't practice as much as some of the others, so I think that you know it made her writing problematic a lot of the times. *If she didn't see something as immediately useful,* you know which I try to impress upon them, that your writing skills are useful and *even though they like grudgingly acknowledge that, it's like they show you by what their choices are, you know, that they make what's important to them or what they believe is important,* and I don't think I ever convinced her of that. (Bette)

7. And they [students] would come in and read it with *me so they could say, right there, I don't get it.* That would help. Or just to even annotate the text. Place a question and *then in class raise your hands and say, what does he mean when he says . . . if something was too challenging for this kid he just wouldn't . . . and he seemed very tired,* like I said . . . (Patricia)

Tired. (Interviewer)

Tired. All the time, *I want to go to sleep,* that kind of [thing] . . . (Patricia)

8. He was the one that didn't want to read and *he was always begging off from reading.* (Hank)

9. I set it up on purpose so that those who like to write could excel in writing, so those who liked to talk could excel in talking. And there are those who are very good on paper who hate to talk and there were times that *they would deliberately take a D- on a seminar because they didn't prepare. But they knew that* – that was the ground rules and they *if wanted the grade they would sweat to prepare and when they realize how much sweat it took, they didn't always want to do it. So yeah they would choose.* (Sharon)

Note how in Example 6 Bette represents the students' voice by inferring the students' experiences and values (e.g., seeing things as immediately useful, showing you what's important to them). Hank in Example 8 does the same (the student is "begging off"), as does Sharon in Example 9 (students would deliberately choose their fate in class). In Example 7, Patricia represents the students' voice by mimicking it ("I don't get it," "I want to go to sleep").

For these lower-achieving students, their difficulties as writers and readers tended to be more visible in the teachers' *language* about them than was any stable characteristic. It is not incidental that the process of poorly achieving can also be highly visible in the classroom. As teachers, we can often feel the sweat of a student's striving, whereas we may ascribe to the realm of mystery a student's being a "thoroughbred." I want to make the point here, though, that these teachers appeared to live peaceably with these different ways of representing the two groups of students, just as I believe many of us do in the world outside of school. All this is to say that in characterizing their students, the teachers, I believe unwittingly, fit their students differentially into the achievement dynamic. Doing so, they revealed contradictory theories about learning and achievement for the two groups.

Assessment reflects achievement/assessment sits apart from achievement
The teachers' representations of the assessment–achievement relationship were rife with implied theories of assessment and learning contradictory to one another. Each statement below reflects such contradictions in its own way. I present the examples first and follow them with discussion:

10. *I do feel* that my means of assessment [i.e., in the classroom] gives the students an opportunity to shine and to show their achievement. Because for one thing, I do a variety of assessment techniques. . . . *I'm not one of the teachers who gets excited when somebody fails or I try to trick them with trick questions or something like that.* . . . I just want to know what the students know . . .
. . . *reading comprehension done in preparation for the SAT test, I did do that.* . . . I just gathered materials from teacher resources and so unfortunately their reading wasn't related to what we were studying in class, but you *know I know that they need practice with that.* So, I would give them practice, you know, reading comprehension passages and then they would answer the questions on the passages . . . (Bette)

11. *One of the things that I know is true about students that age* is that every day is a new adventure, and they are either attentive or not attentive. And some days my best students would have no idea how to approach the text, and other days they would be real astute, very scholarly. So, you know, I don't really think the factors are so much what do they know as the availability of their mind on that given day . . .
And we don't give freshman grade placement tests, as far as what grade they're reading on. We don't do that . . . but that would be a good assessment tool, and I felt that should be something that we should do, *check their vocabulary, comprehension level and their reading levels to see where they stack up.* But we don't do that. (Patricia)

12. [Regarding STAR test] They have each item that the kids performed on, so I will have scores on how they did on grammar, how they did on reading . . . and that will tell me where I need to work a little more

intensively. . . . *But I think a lot of kids this age are just not capable of capturing grammar . . . or the overall picture of vocabulary.* . . . So I don't know, it gets a little frustrating and I think part of my philosophy is they'll get it when they get it. So when we're dealing with a standardized test. . . . I don't know, I'm not sure I totally believe in what I'm doing 100% of the time but I do it because I know I probably should. (Patricia)

13. The SAT 9, that's bragging rights for the principal, that's all it is. . . . I would rather have had the test in October; then I could've seen what I really needed to teach. . . . *A lot of assessment is in the eye of the beholder.* (Hank)

Example 10 shows a teacher who designs her own assessments to be fair to students and to try to tap what they really know, while at the same time preparing them for an assessment that may not be fair to them in the same way but that she believes they nonetheless need to master.

The teacher in Example 11 portrays students as products of context, shaped by the exigencies of the day. Yet, at the same time she appears to value understanding how students "stack up" to their peers, two stances about students that are conceptually in conflict but that seem to live together nonetheless within the teacher's system.

This same teacher, in Example 12, says variously that test scores indicate students' needs, that they indicate nothing, and that they indirectly stand for what is expected of her by unnamed higher-ups vs. what she expects of herself, which are here two different things entirely.

Example 13 shows how assessment accomplishes contention, in this case a teacher in contention with his principal – a kind of commonplace of teacher-administrator relationships. However, the contention here spawns two conceptually contradictory stances on assessment. On the one hand, the test means nothing; it is simply "bragging rights for the principal," its value "in the eye of the beholder." On the other hand, the test could mean everything if only administrators could deliver the test results at the beginning of the academic year, giving the teacher a good opportunity to base his teaching on them. In either case the teacher–administrator dialogue shapes his stances, but the stances do not match conceptually.

The fact that these teachers each express their own contradictions implies their representation of conflicting voices or forces. When Bette says, "I do feel that . . .", when Patricia says, "One of the things that I know is true about students that age," or "I think a lot of kinds this age are just not capable of capturing grammar," they indirectly suggest a source for this knowledge, whether an outside source or their own experience. These voices are in their discourse. When Hank says that "a lot of assessment is in the eye of the beholder," he borrows the speech of the poet who originally was speaking of notions of beauty. Doing so, he seems to give new meaning to the notion of assessment in school. When Bette declares that she is not "one of the teachers" who thrive on their students' failures, those teachers' voices push at her notion of herself. As Bakhtin might say, all these voices (and untold others) are present for these teachers as they talk to me. That their stances seem at times contradictory can be accounted for, I suggest, by their dealing with this range of voices or forces, all present in their classroom lives.

Assessment is impartial/assessment is constructed and partial

This last contradiction is closely coupled with the first two. The conflicting concepts of assessment's being impartial and of its being constructed, and in that sense partial, implicates the burden that is on the teacher to engage in a judging process that can be seen to be value laden while it nonetheless enjoys a widespread reputation of hitting the nail right on the head. In Example 14 below, Bette expresses this conceptual pull well:

14. When I think of assessments, I kind of think of, which I'm not sure if it is *the right way to think about it*, but I kind of think of the grade they'll leave my class with versus what their abilities are. Or what kind of writer they are and sometimes I feel that probably, to make a wild guess, maybe 75% of them, their grade accurately reflects their effort and abilities. And then probably about a quarter of them say their grade, which is my assessment, does not . . . seem to add up to *what their true abilities are*. It may have to do with that *they made a poor effort*; it may have to do with *I didn't get to know the student well enough*. . . .

I suggest that Bette engages in complex interactions within herself, based on her interactions with different voices, to represent the process of assessing students' writing. There is what she calls "the right way to think about it," and thereby she represents some absolute truth in the world, either which she has not yet discovered, or which she surmises that I, her interviewer, know something about. In either case, she appeals to this voice of authority – this unknown authority – as she tries to define her assessor role. Then there is the student's perspective on his own capability – the grade does not match what the student knows about himself. And here is the student's voice, inferred. And then there is the frequent mismatch between effort and performance so that performance only reflects something like attitude or inclination and not capability, an equation that raises the question of what, exactly, we are assessing when we assess. Conflicting voices are at work here, difficult to name. Finally, Bette makes explicit a feeling that I think reflects a range of human relationships, which is that the better you know someone, the better you *know* them. This bit of practical wisdom raises the question of what it is that any assessment, classroom based or state mandated, can actually ever promise to reveal. It also represents a kind of decentering force for Bette in that the conventional voice of the world of assessment is upended by common sense.

Next, in examples 15–20, Hank expresses contradiction around the idea of impartiality:

15. When I start assessing the kids, I do it blindly. I work strictly on a spreadsheet and it's blind, so I don't know who they are. (Hank)

This is the voice of conventional assessment, impartial and objective.

16. But it's pretty hard not to say, oh yeah, she had a good idea.... (Hank).

Human beings leak onto the spreadsheet; impartiality is a slippery concept, and at least two voices or forces collide here.

17. ... so you try to get that human element out of it, but it's difficult, so I try to be as impartial as I can. I think, assessment, it can be so subjective that you have to almost get away from this personality thing.... (Hank)

Assessment almost begs Hank to be subjective, yet some belief in the possibility of being impartial keeps him fighting against the subjectivity. Put a different way, and using Hank's words, he knows that there is little getting around the test-taker's "personality," a force to contend with, yet he also believes that he must try to do just that. His shifts between second-person perspective to first ("you" to "I" and back again) might be said to represent a range of experiences, a range of voices impinging on him as he tries to justify his thrust toward objectivity.

18. Well, here's the deal. I think ego is really tied to teacher ego; it's hard to separate from what might be a better way of assessing. (Hank)

Here is his belief that there is something that "nails down" student performance – but he has not yet found it. Like Bette in Example 14, Hank appeals to the authority "out there," the better way of assessing, while inferring that teachers in general have strong (stubborn?) egos. In wrestling with assessment, then, he represents at least two different voices or forces.

19. If I felt like I had written a great test, and they did well, then I would think, all is well, right? But that may not necessarily be the accurate picture. (Hank)

20. The STAR test results were very dismal for our school . . . and when I saw the scores I was pretty shocked. I said, "I thought they were ready for this. We practiced this and I saw that they [the students] had the skills to do this." (Hank)

In Example 19, Hank surfaces another contradiction, one between "meaningfulness" and what he would call "accuracy" in the absolute sense. In Example 20, uttered in the same breath, the "accurate" test did not in the final analysis seem to reflect what Hank knew to be true about the students' capabilities. Again, the unknown authority, one voice or force, contends with stubborn ego, another, and we see as Bakhtin helps us to the nature of thought and verbal expression.

DISCUSSION

The teachers I talked to each inhabit many worlds – the world of the classroom, which takes shape and identity contingent upon their changing relationships with students and implicit others who inhabit it; the world of test takers and testing, which changes contingently in like ways; the world, in the case of my interviews, of a research context steps away from both classroom and testing and that itself influences these teachers in the moment of the interview. And, of course, countless other worlds, countless other "affiliations" – to use Brandt's (1992) word – through which they understand, make sensible, and create their current perspectives on literacy for their students.

One of the reasons that contradictory perspectives on literacy emerge rests on the contradictory environments in which teachers live and work. Their thoughts and discourse represent these environments.

As indicated at the beginning of this chapter, I want to try to not see as problematic the apparent fact that one can hold such contradictory perspectives on students' literacy, but try to see as problematic that the community of scholars who study literacy, including students' literacy engagement and achievement, have not noticeably taken theoretical contradiction into consideration as part and parcel of teacher thinking, and therefore, of literacy teaching and learning. I do not mean that scholars have not addressed such issues as literacy assessment's being constructed or not or of its being impartial or not; or of literacy itself being variously defined (sometimes in terms of test results). I do mean to say that contradiction itself has not been incorporated into the conceptual frameworks we put forth about literacy dynamics in the context of school.

To incorporate contradiction is, in fact, to take Bakhtin quite seriously. Interestingly, Bakhtin focuses much of his work on the ways that authors filter these kinds of mismatched perspectives or contradictions through the contentious voices of their novels' characters. His point, however, is that these characters merge in the author him- or herself, which is to say that the author, unlike her characters, inhabits the real world where contentious voices compete within a single body. Perhaps that condition is our greatest consistency.

This is not to say that because we may inevitably live with and through contradictions, we cannot as educators do our best to try to create the best possible systems for literacy teaching or testing that we can imagine. However, "contradiction-free" may ultimately be unattainable because it is a concept divorced of the voices of human experience. Expecting teachers to act as if they can reconcile contradiction may be tantamount to expecting them to erase the contexts in which they live and work.

References

Bakhtin, M. M. (1934–35/1981). *Dialogic imagination.* (Trans. M. Holquist). Austin: University of Texas Press.

Brandt, D. (1992). The Cognitive as the social: An ethnomethodological approach to writing process research. *Written Communication, 9*(3), 315–55.

Brandt, D. (2001). *Literacy in American lives.* New York: Cambridge University Press.

Cazden, C. (1988). *Classroom discourse: The language of teaching and learning.* Portsmouth, NH: Heinemann.

Delandshire, G., & Petrosky, A. (1998). Assessment of complex performances: Limitations of key measurement assumptions. *Educational Researcher, 27*(2), 14–24.

Dyson, A. H. (1993). *Social worlds of children learning to write in an urban primary school.* New York: Teachers College Press.

Flower, L. (1994). *The construction of negotiated meaning: A social cognitive theory of writing.* Carbondale: Southern Illinois University Press.

Gopnik, A. (2000). *Paris to the moon.* New York: Random House.

Holquist, M., ed. (1981). *Dialogic imagination.* (Glossary pp. 423–34). Austin: University of Texas Press.

Lakoff, G., & Johnson, M. (1980). *Metaphors we live by.* Chicago: University of Chicago Press.

Morson, G. S. (1986). Dialogue, monologue, and the social: A reply to Ken Hierchkop. In G. S. Morson (Ed.), *Bakhtin: Essays and dialogues on his work.* Chicago: University of Chicago Press.

Reddy, M. (1978). The conduit metaphor: A case of frame conflict in our language about language. In A. Ortony (Ed.), *Metaphor and thought* (2nd ed., pp. 164–201). Cambridge, UK: Cambridge University Press.

Rogoff, B. (1990). *Apprenticeship in thinking: Cognitive development in social context.* Oxford, UK: Oxford University Press.

Sacks, S. (Ed.). (1978). *On metaphor.* Chicago: The University of Chicago Press.

Sfard, A. (1998). On two metaphors for learning and the dangers of choosing just one. *Educational Researcher, 27*(2), 4–13.

Shepard, L. (2000). The role of assessment in a learning culture. *Educational Researcher, 29*(7), 4–14.

Sizer, T. (1985). *Horace's compromise: The dilemma of the American high school.* Boston: Houghton Mifflin.

Sperling, M. (1994). Moments remembered, moments displayed: Narratization, metaphor, and the experience of teaching. *English Education, 26*(3), 142–56.

Sperling, M. (1995). Uncovering the role of role in writing and learning to write: One day in an inner-city classroom. *Written Communication, 12*(1), 93–133.

11

A Bakhtinian Perspective on Learning to Read and Write Late in Life

Judy Kalman

> Before we didn't go to school . . . nobody called us, nobody pushed us, nobody said study, it's necessary.
>
> – Carmen, age 64

Work in the area of adult literacy education in peripheral nations has been dominated by the search for the right method, the implementation of school-like programs adapted for adults, or the explanation of adult educational services' failures to provide quality learning opportunities to underschooled adults (Rivera, 1994; Schmelkes & Kalman, 1996). Little effort has been made to understand what becoming literate or further developing literacy knowledge and know-how entails for a person once they are beyond school age. Some researchers have pointed out that the reading and writing itself is often secondary to other interests, such as opportunities to socialize with others, the need to make a living, or care for one's children (Garcia-Huidoro, 1994; Rockhill, 1993; Stromquist, 1997). Recent international studies (Organization for Economic Cooperation and Development, 1995; Infante, 2000) look at literacy in terms of individual mastery, emphasizing what Wagner (2001) calls the cognitive abilities of reading, writing, and calculating. They study knowledge about literacy with large standardized test materials, similar to school-type evaluations, placing adults' performances within predetermined literacy levels. Even on those test items having to do with so called "real-life" situations, such as writing a check, filling out a form or reading a newspaper, they approach evaluating literacy in terms of skills and abilities similar to evaluation tools of schooling. They develop scales for observing certain benchmarks in what is considered to be "functionality," the appropriate use of literacy in given situations, noting certain levels of achievement but ignoring what it takes to get there, or what is involved in using written language for different purposes. Despite the efforts of these studies to develop portraits of different uses of reading and writing, their approach is decontextualized in the sense that they present generic tasks that could never reproduce the real sociocultural demands that written language use makes of readers and writers. (Barton & Hall, 1999) In general, it is safe to say that adult literacy use and acquisition processes have not been adequately researched, despite the large worldwide population of unschooled and underschooled adults.

In Mexico, approximately one-half of the adult population has not completed a basic education.[1] In absolute terms, there are 19 million adults with less than 6 years of schooling (including 7 million who are considered illiterate) and approximately 16 million who finished primary school but did not go on to complete the obligatory 9 years. This population is the potential student body for adult education programs. Yet, as in other Latin American countries, the adult education opportunities offered by the Secretary of Public Education (SEP) are sorely underattended, the availability of schooling far outweighs the demands made on local agencies by adults. This contradiction implies, among other things, that what the SEP has to offer does not, for a series of reasons, meet learners expectations. Some of the reasons may be that the courses are irrelevant, that it takes too long to progress through the coursework to obtain a primary or secondary certificate, that the services are irregular or that, for some reason, the educational programs simply do not meet adult's needs, spark their interest, or attend to their learning processes.

This chapter reflects on what kinds of learning takes place when becoming literate late in life. On the one hand, there is the obvious challenge of understanding how the writing system works: reading and writing implies being able to interpret texts written by others and produce written language comprehensible to readers who are often unknown. In this chapter, I argue that learning to read and write late in life also involves a gradual and continuous repositioning of the learners' self vis-à-vis written culture. The chapter centers on a case study of one woman's learning to read and write, and how her learning process includes developing a sense of her self as a reader and writer. Carmen is a native of Mixquic, a township on the edge of Mexico City. She has lived there her entire life, as has her family for several generations. She rarely goes out of the town; Mixquic is therefore her main setting for knowledge about literacy and its use (Kalman, 2001). Because she did not go to school as a child and does not work outside of her family context, knowledge and know-how learned in work and school situations are only accessible to her in other types of situations, such as when her grandchildren bring schoolwork to finish at home (Valdés, 1995).

Bakhtin's views about language use offer a suggestive conceptual frame for thinking about her literacy learning. He theorized that language use, including reading and writing, is at once a social, contextual, and historical phenomenon. Inasmuch, he argued, language, is dialogic in nature,

---

[1] The Secretaría de Educación Pública defines an adult as a person 15 years or older.

multiple in meaning, and situationally grounded. Although he did not directly address the issue of language learning, his ideas about meaning and how it is transformed provides a fertile ground for thinking about the construction of literacy knowledge.

The chapter begins with a section centered on a discussion of some of Bakhtin's concepts useful for thinking about literacy development. It is followed by a presentation of the research project and its participants, and then a description of Carmen's knowledge and uses of reading and writing, developed through her daily experiences with written language. Next is an analytical description of her participation in a literacy class, pointing out some key moments in her learning process, and in conclusion, a series of final reflections of how this research might contribute to literacy education programs aimed at unschooled and underschooled youth and adult learners.

USING BAKHTINIAN NOTIONS ABOUT LANGUAGE FOR THINKING ABOUT LITERACY DEVELOPMENT

In contemporary society, literacy is expected to be accomplished in childhood. Before children reach adolescence, if they move continuously through the education system, they will have had at least 7 years of formal schooling. Although literacy learning is by no means confined to the classroom, school is the institution officially in charge of preparing new readers and writers. By the time young people are 12 years old, they are already expected to be fairly fluent readers and writers, and experienced in several genres and written language uses. Although they are not mature readers and writers as of yet, they are believed to be on the road to becoming one, assuming that they stay in school. To think about adult literacy education for unschooled and underschooled young people and adults requires asking questions about what does it mean to become literate later in life and what it means to have minimal access to written language in a society highly dependent on the written word. For this chapter, written language is considered first and foremost language, and Bakhtin's views about language apply to the written channel and an oral one. He underlined the social and interactive nature of verbal communication portraying language as "a living, socio-ideological concrete thing" and "a heteroglot opinion" placing it for each speaker (or "individual consciousness") "on the borderline between oneself and another" (Bakhtin, 1981, p. 293).

The vitality of language lies precisely in its use. For Bakhtin, what makes language mean is its insertion in specific situations where speakers try to understand others and try to make themselves be understood. Meaning emerges in the intersection of multiple voices and contextual conditions: some of the meanings come from public discourses, some from previous conversations, and some from different social voices. The words we speak are never truly new, for they have been spoken before and are weighed with multiple meanings. In this process, speakers (and listeners, readers, and writers) position themselves, and words are splattered with intentions and contextual nuances. Yet, at the moment of their utterance in a particular context, they are newly hued with the specificity of the communicative moment.

Given that language materializes in its use, Bakhtin described it as dialogic, or containing more than one voice. He considered to be dialogized on at least two planes: first, in concrete face-to-face verbal exchanges and, second, in more abstract sense of continuous cultural response. In "Marxism and the Philosophy of Language" signed by Voloshinov[2] (1973), it is noted that

Orientation of the word toward the addressee has an extremely high significance. In point of fact, word is a two sided act. It is determined equally by whose word it is and for whom it is meant. As word it is precisely the product of the reciprocal relationship between speaker and listener, addresser and addressee. Each and every word expresses the "one" in relation to the "other." I give myself verbal shape from another's point of view, ultimately from the point of view of the community to which I belong. A word is a bridge thrown between myself and another. (p. 86)

On this level, dialogue has to do with the mutual shaping of meanings between speakers sharing a specific communicative context. What is said to the listener is shaped by the participants' biographies, their past encounters and conversations, and their purpose for interacting. It is also a way of positioning oneself in a community of speakers or, in this case, of readers and writers. Adults who read and write poorly (or do not read and write at all), and who live in a literate society, are positioned in the world differently than those who read and write fluently. Each time they encounter written language and participate in a literacy event, they do it from a specific social space both because of their literacy practices and because of what is said and believed about their literacy practices (or their lack of them). In this sense being literate, reading and writing independently, resorting to literacy mediators to confront societal and personal literacy need are dialogically construed possibilities and marked participations in that they are social identifiers.

Literacy is also dialogic in the second, more abstract sense. Again, in Voloshinov (1973), we read that

Dialogue can be understood in a broader sense, meaning not only direct face to face, vocalized verbal communication between persons but also verbal communication of any type whatsoever. A book, i.e., a verbal performance in print, is also an element of verbal communication. It is something discussable in actual, real life dialogue, but aside from that it is calculated for active perception, involving attentive reading and inner reponsiveness and for organized printed reaction in the various forms devised but the particular sphere of verbal communication in question (book reviews, critical surveys, defining influence on subsequent works and so on.) (p. 95)

---

[2] There is a historical discrepancy as to whether Voloshinov was one of Bakhtin's pen names or if, in fact, it was a different person. In any event, this book is considered a part of Bakhtin's thought (Morris, 1994).

Writing is dialogic because it evokes a response. In the academic and intellectual spheres, one book leads to another: a paper is written, and a rebuttal is published; a novel comes out, and reviews appear in the newspaper and literary magazines. In other social spaces, this is also true: legal procedures require documentation to be written, financial services require forms to be completed, and schooling requires endless paperwork as well. Each of these provokes its own answers, each of these have consequences for their bearers in the social world. How one presents documents, forms, and paperwork is a type of participating that is both socially marked and evaluated. As I have written elsewhere (Kalman, 1999), people believe that in order to present documentation in government offices or other official agencies they must be typed, anything handwritten is *"feo y malhecho"* (ugly and poorly done), and that the physical appearance of a document has important implications for the outcome of any legal procedures. Adults dealing with official situations, institutions, or commercial establishments who read and write poorly are identified as "illiterate," a stigma synonymous with unintelligent, untrustworthy, and even, uncouth. This is what Bakhtin refers to when he notes that the word is a "socio-ideological concrete thing." In our society, not knowing how to read and write is part of an identity related to marginality and otherness. Part of being considered illiterate, then, is the ideological meaning that accompanies the fact that one does not read and write well, and part of becoming literate includes reconstructing meaning in regards to one's literate self.

The reasons that adults did not go to school or were forced to leave school before developing their knowledge and know-how about reading and writing are many: during times of economic crisis, families cannot afford to keep their children in school (Garcia-Huidoro, 1994; Rivera, 1994). They are needed at home to tend to younger siblings, to take over household responsibilities, or to work. Reading and writing and formal education are seen as secondary, even a luxury, when economic need is great. Furthermore, in households where resources are scarce, schooling is rarely reserved for daughters. In Mexico, the acceptance of educating girls and young women is a fairly recent accomplishment. Women were given the right to vote in the early 1950s, and only since the 1970s have they begun to occupy public office, visible government positions, and professional spaces.

Literacy and illiteracy are also ideologically charged in the sense that socially great expectations are attached to knowing how to use written language, and inversely, serious consequences are related to not being able to read and write. Literacy is believed to secure democratic processes, prosperity, economic development, and competitiveness, as well as personal satisfaction. In 2001, Vicente Fox, elected to the presidency of Mexico,[3]

---

[3] Fox, elected in July of 2000 is the first president of Mexico elected from a party other than the Partido Revolucionario Institucional(PRI), which held the presidency and all other major political offices and posts for 70 years.

presented to the nation his *Plan Nacional de Desarrollo,* the customary policy statement and plan of action made public every 6 years by each in-coming president. In it, he made special emphasis on the need to nurture and develop democracy, noting that the struggle for democracy in Mexico has been severely hindered by several factors, such as "authoritarian attitudes," "paternalism," the omnipresence of the state," "low education levels of the majority of the population," "a general lack of prestige of politics," and the "low levels of reading of newspapers and magazines."[4] In his discourse, he gives the inability to read certain types of publications the same status as authoritarianism, paternalism, and a general mistrust of the political process in his definition of the historical obstacles to democracy. The example shows how saturated literacy (and education) is with ideological meaning in official thinking.

Who is expected to read and write, who can and cannot read and write, what is thought about different ways of reading and writing, what should be read (or written), and what reading and writing is supposed to guarantee socially, politically, economically, and culturally are part of an "official" version of literacy, what Bakhtin (1981) refers to as the authoritative discourse. Unlike dialogic language, the authoritative word is monologic, distant from context, unanswerable, and embodies different sources of authority (tradition, generally accepted truths, official lines). It is an imposition, in the sense that it

Demands that we acknowledge it, that we make it our own; it binds us quite independent of any power it might have to persuade us internally; we encounter it with its authority already fused into it. The authoritative word is located in a distanced zone, organically connected with a past that is felt to be hierarchically higher.... It is therefore not a question of choosing it from among other possible discourses that are its equal. (p. 342)

For adults like Carmen, then, learning to read and write involves not only learning about the writing system or the diverse uses of written language, it means repositioning herself in regards to written language, what she believes about literacy, and what others believe about her in relationship to literacy. Specifically this involves questioning the authoritative discourse concerning literacy, both current lines and versions she has heard over her lifetime.

---

[4] The full quote reads: "El perfil de la cultura política predominante no corresponde al que requiere la vigencia y subsistencia de un sistema político democrático. Dentro de los factores que, a lo largo de décadas, han dado lugar a esta situación se encuentran las insuficiencias de nuestra democracia, las actitudes autoritarias, el paternalismo, la omnipresencia del Estado, el clientelismo, los bajos niveles educativos con que ha contado la población, la ausencia de una contribución sistemática a la formación ciudadana por parte del sistema educativo nacional, la escasez de prácticas ciudadanas, la insuficiente identificación de la población con los partidos políticos, el desprestigio de la política, los bajos niveles de lectura de diarios y revistas, así como la insuficiente promoción de la cultura democrática en la radio y la televisión" (Presidencia de la Republica, 2001, p. 135).

Being a woman in her sixties from an area that is living a rural-to-urban transition, most people assume that she would not be able to read or write. She grew up in a place where written language and materials were scarce, where there was no library, no post office, no telegraph services, and no formal education offered locally beyond the third grade (Kalman, 2004). Learning for her involves distancing herself from the authoritative discourse of literacy and her past experiences with reading and writing. Although Bakhtin (1981) does not discuss learning directly, he does note that "when thought begins to work in an independent, experimenting and discriminating way, what first occurs is a separation between internally persuasive discourse and authoritarian enforced discourse" (p. 345).

Becoming literate late in life involves questioning what is held to be true about literacy and, through participating in new ways in reading and writing events, constructing new meanings for literacy, transforming it from a distant communicative practice performed by others to a collection of practices that may be resorted to in order to fulfill reading and writing needs. Bakhtinian theory suggests that the tensions between the authoritative word (what is said to be) and the internally persuasive discourse (what is experienced to be) results in transformations of meaning or learning. People learning to read and write after living many years with little access to written culture must develop a new significance for literacy, reading and writing need to be inserted in specific situations where they see themselves as capable of accomplishing literacy. It involves resignifying their positions vis-à-vis literacy, in renewing their internally persuasive discourse, separate from the authoritative discourse and creating their "own word." Bakhtin (1981) notes that the creativeness of an independent internally persuasive discourse lies precisely "in the fact that such a word awakens an independent words, that it organizes masses of our words within" (p. 343), words that come from our reflections on the events, actors, and relationships in our everyday lives. It entails finding a new position in the social world. Resignifying literacy, giving it a new meaning implies a reevaluation of one's self as a reader and writer, an integral part of learning to read and write.

THE PLACE, THE PROJECT, AND THE PARTICIPANTS[5]

Community life in Mixquic is a hybrid of its traditional agricultural economy dating to before the conquest, its deep ties to the Catholic Church, the persistence of *nahuatl* culture and more recent urban ways and institutions.

[5] This project ran from 1997 to 2000; Rocío Vargas, Guadalupe Noriega and Guadalupe Díaz Tepepa helped do the field work and data preparation. Macrina Gomez tidied up this manuscript. My appreciation goes to all of them. The first 2 years were supported by the National Academy of Education/Spencer Foundation postdoctoral fellowship grant. My thanks to them for their generosity.

Mixquic's agricultural production is *chinampera*, the Aztec technique of planting in water, through creating floating islets of landfill for cultivation. All women in the study group either owned *chinampas*, or had family members that did, and were involved in production activities that varied depending on the planting cycle. Besides planted crops, there is a strong use of local herbs and medicinal plants that the women gather from their yards, the local pathways through the fields, and around town. Subsistence farming and small-scale commercial crops are still one of the most important local economic activities. Since the 1960s, some townspeople, mostly men, have been employed in either in industrial or service sector jobs or participated in the widespread informal economy of Mexico City. Women, for the most part, are engaged in the traditional agricultural activities, housework, and child-rearing activities. They rarely travel outside of Mixquic, and when they do, it is usually no further than the surrounding towns of Chalco, Tetleco, Tuylehualco, or Tlahuac, the furthest being a 30-minute bus ride away. Cash income is scarce: families live on microeconomies and must make ends meet sometimes for as little as $5 US a day (cf. Benería & Roldán, 1987).

The total current population of Mixquic is 11,400 people, 8 percent is considered illiterate and 36 percent of the population 15 years or older has less than 6 years of schooling. Mixquic's urban infrastructure does not as of yet satisfy the needs of the whole community: 70 percent of the population has running water and sewer connections, 60 percent has either cobblestone or paved streets, and 30 percent of the housing is considered irregular in construction, land ownership, sanitation, electricity, and/or communication services.

As I have described in detail elsewhere (Kalman, 2001, 2004), in 1997, I began a study of unschooled and underschooled women's literacy practices in Mixquic. My entrance into the community was through a literacy circle attended by women, where I offered to support the instructor and hoped that I would meet some of the participants who would help me learn about the uses of literacy in town and how they used literacy in their everyday lives.[6] The classes were part of a program run by the *Instituto Nacional de Educación para los Adultos* (INEA), and as all their educational services,

---

[6] Over the 2 years that I visited Mixquic, classes and interviews were audiorecorded, written products were collected, and a small camera was kept in the class for the participants to use as they pleased. All this material has been transcribed, using the methodological suggestions of Hymes (1986), Gumperz (1984, 1986, 1990), and Coates (1995). Analytical categories are built from the data to reflect how the participants use reading and writing, as well as what they think about what they do. Toward the end of the project, I also conducted a small-scale literacy survey, aided by two women in the group. A total of 234 survey interviews were held, but several of them were discarded for technical reasons. The final corpus of 179 surveys were selected, spanning fifty-nine households, and four generations; approximately 80% of the informants were women. Questions were concerned with reading habits, uses of written language on a daily basis, availability of texts, different contexts for reading and writing, and so on.

depended on a volunteer instructor. Many of the tutors are well meaning, but the commitment to working in difficult conditions, and the lack of training, pay, and support from INEA often lead to the volunteer giving up only after a short amount of time. This was the case for the women's group in Mixquic: the volunteer instructor left the group only several weeks after beginning to work with them. The women in the group wanted me to be their instructor – a responsibility I was unable to fully assume – so I proposed a different solution – that they learn to work independently. I offered to help them work together so the group would not disband. In the class, a few women could read and write to some degree, and one of them had a sixth-grade certificate. I agreed to support them through learning activities and help them organize their efforts to pass the certification exams offered by INEA. In practical terms, this meant that I worked with them on Mondays, and before I left I helped them plan their activities for Wednesdays and Fridays.[7]

Although the discussion of literacy learning and use centers on Carmen because she participates in a study group, it is important to mention some of the women attending the learning sessions. Most of them used reading and writing only occasionally throughout the day: they were born and grew up in a place where the first newspaper stand appeared in the early 1960s, the local post office opened its doors in the early 1980s and there is still no bookstore. Public school existed, but little girls either did not attend, or attended only for a couple of years at most. Few letters were written or received, notices and local news were oral or through television or radio, and learning was done in the confines of the home and in the context of practice. This is not to say, however, that the women have no notion of literacy or do not use reading and writing at all. Over the years, they have picked up many literacy practices and developed numerous communicative strategies to resolve those situations demanding written language use at home, at school, in government agencies and offices, at church, and in other domains (Kalman, 2001, 2004).

The women are now interested in learning to read and write or improving their reading and writing, and have signed up for a local literacy class. As girls, they were not encouraged to go to school: formal education was a financial burden that most families could not endure, and if they were to

---

[7] The number of women participating in this autonomous group varied: at its lowest point there were three, at its high point there were as many as twelve. As in other experiences in adult education, their attendance and commitment varied as the other activities and responsibilities of their lives allowed them to participate. Their ages varied from late teens to 79 years, but the core group of women that participated on a regular and continuous basis were between 42 and 79 years old. They had varying degrees of schooling, but in general terms, fell into two groups: those who did not attend school at all or who had finished just 1 year of schooling, and those who studied up to 3 years. There was one exception, Gudelia, who had a primary certificate.

TABLE 11.1. *Study Group of Women*

Name	Approximate age at start of project (yr)	Formal schooling
Gudelia	42	sixth grade
Carmen	64	first grade
Delfina	79	first grade
Isabel	50	third grade
Joaquina	44	third grade

make the effort to send a child to school, it was almost always a son. A girl's education occurred within the home, preparing her to carry out domestic duties, child care, and some traditional agricultural work. With the exception of one of them, as girls they either did not attend school or attended only briefly. Gudelia (age 44), has a sixth-grade certificate, which for her generation was considered to be a complete basic education. Although the number of women who participated in this study varied, the core group of women are listed in Table 11.1.

Their current reasons for learning to read and write, or improve their reading and writing, vary. Individually, they now have time, whereas entrenched in the responsibilities of housework and child rearing, they were previously unable to develop their own interests. Furthermore, they believe that they are entitled to an education and have a right to learn (even if it is at this stage of their lives). As Stromquist (1997) points out, attending a literacy circle also provides an important opportunity for many women to socialize with other women. Joaquina, a woman in her forties, explained how important her reading sessions became for her (Kalman, 2004; Table 11.2).

These legitimate personal motivations are tied to strong social and cultural forces at play in Joaquina's decision to attend a literacy circle. On a national level, women who for more than half of the twentieth century were confined to domestic domains are now more involved in public life in their community and beyond. More women are publicly visible, holding elected offices and high government positions, working in various sectors of the economy, prominent in the arts and the media and, in general, participating in all aspects of national life. Girls are now enrolled and sent to school on a regular basis and, in 1998, 46.3 percent of university students were female.[8] In the early 1940s a 1–6 grade school was built in town to replace the 1–3 grade school improvised in adobe rooms in an orchard. Although the women in this study still spend their days within the boundaries of their town, they are aware of these changes and witness them in the lives of their

---

[8] Source: *Secretaría de Educación Pública* (1999, p. 77).

TABLE 11.2. *Example 1*

Spanish	English
Un poco me he despejado de todos mis problemas porque pobremente en su casa de usted, las tardes eran de llorar. En las mañanas era de llorar. Y ahora no, por que me apuro, porque se dónde ir, se que hacer.... Ahora me siento bien pues me siento bien, me siento tranquila y digo pues mis hijos puedo decir que fueron mis hijos cuando los tuve en brazos. Ahora ya se casaron, ahora ya que formaron su hogar cada quien, que me dejen a mi. Yo también puedo.	I feel somewhat relieved from my problems now, because before the afternoons at my poor house were for crying. The mornings were for crying. But not now, I hurry, because I know where to go, I know what to do.... Now I feel better, I feel better, more at ease and I say to my self my children were mine when I carried them in my arms. But now they are married, they have their own families, and now they should let me be. I too am able.

own daughters and granddaughters. Both of these factors, the increased availability of schooling and the redefinition of women's roles, along with a heightened sense of wanting to read and write, contribute to their current interest in literacy.

As noted elsewhere (Kalman, 2001), from a first glance, there is not much evidence of literacy in their homes. They do not have an ample supply of the material artifacts that make writing possible (pencils, paper, pens, erasers, pencil sharpeners, and so on); there are no tools such as computers or typewriters visible and, with the exception of the free national textbooks and other school related texts, there are few other books or printed materials to be seen. However, first impressions can be deceiving. They participate in and are responsible for doing at least some of the everyday paperwork related to running their households: paying bills, caring for their family's health, keeping records and saving important papers, and following official procedures. Each of these activities generates a series of written materials that the women must put away and retrieve as needed. Their ability to do this effectively implies sufficient familiarity with printed documents such as bills, certificates, and receipts, at least to the extent that that they can identify them. Most of these different materials have a specific format, logos, symbols, and colors that make them distinguishable from the rest. Official birth, marriage, and death certificates, for example, are printed on legal-size paper and have a reiterated and recognizable format that includes the national emblem, a paragraph at the top of the chapter information organized in the form of a two-column chart, and a list of signatures. Receipts for electricity bills are small 2-inch by 2-inch documents with information about electricity consumption and the light and power company's emblem. There are other types of documents that the women may not have personally, but that they recognize and are knowledgeable of. One such document is the military identification card, or *cartilla*, that all men 18 or older must have. The women know that this is an important identification document for their husbands and sons, and also know the consequences if their family members do not have one. The one "book" that all the women mentioned either reading or having listened to being read is the Bible. They also collect *estampas religiosas*, stories about saints and miracles printed on sheets of papers no bigger than a wallet calendar, particularly those that narrate the life of the local patron saint or the saint of a neighboring community (Kalman, 2001, 2004).

CARMEN'S PREVIOUS KNOWLEDGE

Bakhtin posited that humans cannot help but "pay attention to life" (Holquist, 1990, p. 152), that "being" is synonymous with activity: "seeing, thinking, or practical doing" (Bakhtin, 1993, p. 57). In as much as activity is inevitable, literacy is present for those who do not read and write, and they position themselves in relation to written culture, even if they cannot produce or understand written language. It is in this sense that Street (1993) notes that, unless a person lives in the most isolated geographical conditions, it is difficult to find an adult who does not know something about literacy, even if it is the idea that they are distanced from it.

As in many parts of the world, in Mexico the expansion of the school system has played an important role in the dissemination of written language. Since 1959, the Mexican Secretary of Public Education distributes free textbooks to all students attending primary school. Not only is formal education responsible for teaching reading and writing to young people, but also through schooling, reading and writing practices become available to other family members through schoolbooks, other printed materials, written invitations to school events, notices, report cards, homework assignments, etc., entering the home. Although Carmen did not go to school as a young girl, she is still familiar with what has been referred to as school literacy, the term used to describe those reading and writing practices associated with formal education (Barton & Hamilton, 1998; Street, 1993). She believed that copying, taking dictation, impeccable spelling, reading assigned material and answering "comprehension questions," manipulating and recuperating content from text, and so on were essential to learning to read and write, and that without these types of exercises learning could not really take place.

Although these practices are generated in school, they are by no means restricted to the classroom: homework is often supervised by parents (generally mothers), grandmothers, and siblings, bringing school literacy into the family space. Carmen did not complete the first grade, so it is safe to assume that she built her knowledge about reading and writing in other

TABLE 11.3. *Example 2*

Spanish	English
Quiero anotar todo para después dárselos a estudiar [leer] a mis nietos a mis hijos, porque así no más a lo mejor lo pierdo y ya no, no lo hago, platicarles [la historia] y así teniéndolo por lo menos tengo un recuerdo de esta plática.	I want to write the whole thing down and give it to my grandchildren to study [read] later, because if I don't, and I lose it then I don't do it, tell them, and at least this way I have a souvenir from when I told them [the story].

social spaces. During the first sessions with the study group, I lent the women a collection of children's books to take home to read with their children or grandchildren. A few days later, when we were commenting on what it was like to read to a child, Carmen took out her notebook and showed me the page where she had copied the entire story by hand. Her personal reproduction of the text followed the precise instructions given to children in the first grade in Mexico: between every word she had place a hyphen, the local strategy used to teach word separation. (Kalman, 2004) When I asked her why she had decided to copy the text, she replied as shown in Table 11.3

Somewhere along the line, Carmen learned how to do school copies and what some of the uses of copying are. She reproduced the text by hand so she could reread it with her grandchildren or so her children could read it. Copying the story gave her a memento of her experience; reading or retelling it did not have the same meaning to her. Having a copy meant that she could read it over and over again.

In many situations, it is assumed that not everybody will know how to read and write independently. Carmen's experience at a public medical clinic attests to this. Usually when she went to her appointments, somebody else filled out the forms for her. But one day, she arrived at class and told us triumphantly that she had fooled the receptionist because she took the forms and filled them out herself, without assistance, writing in her name and address. Her idea that she was "fooling" somebody is truly revealing: because it was assumed that she could not write, and she in fact had never filled out her own form before, she had violated a social premise, ever so slightly shifting her position vis-à-vis literacy.

Within the local history, the use of literacy for official purposes has not always been straightforward or legitimate. As reported in elsewhere (Kalman, 2004), the women in the study group shared stories about how wealthy land owners used written documents to swindle local farmers out of their land. Given the high illiteracy/low schooling rate among the *campesinos*, the lack of local title offices to protect land ownership, often the elaboration

TABLE 11.4. *Example 3*

Spanish	English
Se escondía el ingrato señor y se quedaba con todo. No había quien los parara. Todos éramos pobres, se hicieron delegados. Por la ignorancia no nos sabíamos defender.	That vile man would hideout, and keep everything. Nobody could stop them. We were all so poor, and got themselves elected to congress. Because of our ignorance, we could not defend ourselves.

of deeds came into private hands.[9] According to their stories, several unsavory local characters lent money to small-scale farmers and drew up bogus documents that stipulated that if payment in full was not made by a specific date and time, the land owners would automatically receive ownership of the *campesinos'* holdings (Table 11. 4).

Carmen and some of the other women belonged to a sewing cooperative. As head of the shop, Gudelia applied for training courses for the women working there offered through the city government. This involved a great deal of paperwork and Gudelia was asked about the seamstresses ability to read and write as a requirement for receiving job training. Most of the women interviewed in the survey considered domestic work to be their main activity, even those few who held an outside job. Less than half of them reported reading and writing on a regular basis during the day, and those who did noted that their main literacy activities had to do with helping children with their homework. Only in a few very specific cases (a police woman, a nurse, and a couple of women that looked after family stores) did women mention that they read and wrote on the job.

Apparently, as part of the development policies of the 1940s, local authorities built small damns in towns nearby Mixquic, seriously affecting their water supply and agricultural productivity. The women in the study group mentioned this event, noting that many men in the community had to migrate to other parts of the city to look for work (Kalman, 2004; Table 11.5).

It turns out that the rerouting of water not only had an impact on the local economy, but also on the townspeoples' communicative practices. The factory and service jobs were in parts of Mexico City that were sometimes as long as 3 hours away or more, making commuting impossible. Letter writing became an important means of communication. For some of the men to keep in touch with their families, they had to learn to write, some of them just did the best they could, and others used the services of public scribes.

---

[9] According to official statistics in 1950, 35% of the population was considered illiterate; currently, 27% has less than 6 years of schooling.

TABLE 11.5. *Dialogue 1*

Spanish	English
Carmen: Pusieron presas en Tetelco y Tezompa.	Carmen: They built damns in Tetelco and Tezompa.
Delfina: Por el agua, pusieron presas para que no pasara el agua.	Delfina: Because the water, they built damns so the water wouldn't go through.
Carmen: Sí, porque como se terminó el agua ya no tenían en qué trabajar y se tuvieron que ir a trabajar fuera... como ya tenían que estar más tiempo fueras pues tenían que mandar cartas para informarse como estaban, por ejemplo mi cuñado se fue por Tacuba; otros se fueron por Clavería.	Carmen: Yes, because we ran out of water they didn't have work and they had to look for work out of town, and they had to be away for a long time they had to send letters to let everyone know how they were, for example, my brother-in-law went to Tacuba and others went to Clavería.

For several years, Carmen received letters from her daughter, Gudelia, who migrated to Los Angeles to work. Gone for 4 years, unable to return home for a visit, she wrote to her mother and children frequently. In a few of her letters, she narrated her adventures, but mostly she used her letters to continue to participate in family life and in her children's upbringing. For Carmen, these letters have great sentimental value and she keeps them still carefully put away in a plastic bag. Almost every letter is carefully folded in its original envelope. When a letter arrived at Carmen's home, another family member read them to her, often several times.

The above examples illustrate some of what Carmen knows about literacy from her experiences with the way written language is used in the social world. They show she is familiar with some aspects of school literacy, knows about different uses (and abuses) of written language, and recognizes its communicative capacity. Moreover, these examples show how literacy is a marginal activity in her life in terms of personally producing or reading text, yet still is present in the social milieu and important in her life: her daughter and other family members communicated with her through letters when their search for work took them away from Mixquic, written language was a routine part of obtaining public services, and written language can be used to support asymmetrical power relationships. In some of these cases, Carmen had to deal with written text directly; in others, knowledge about certain uses and privileges related to written language was woven into her experience as being poor and female.

TRANSFORMING POSITIONS THROUGH PARTICIPATING IN LITERACY EVENTS

As previously noted, choosing to learn to read and write, or to improve reading and writing, implies resignifying authoritative notions about literacy and finding "one's own word" and stance in regard to reading and writing. For Bakhtin (1981), position is "a particular belief system, with a particular view on the world and its events, with particular value judgments" (p. 312). Becoming literate involves transforming the position of the self in relation to the text and to other readers and writers, questioning some of the established meanings of literacy, and participating in literacy events where the expectations about one's reading and writing allow for the learner to be accepted as a reading and writing subject. For the women in Mixquic, this implies dialogically questioning issues such as women's rights to education, their place in the workplace/home, and their roles as mothers and grandmothers, and responding by constructing new meanings transformed by their own intentions (Bakhtin, 1981). This dialogue occurs both in face-to-face interactions and within inner speech, between speakers and between authoritative discourse and inner persuasive discourse. Often triggered by a learning activity, the women would discuss their views on what it meant to be a good wife or a loving grandmother, or they would reveal their thoughts on how they saw literacy fit into their lives as women, as opposed to when they were younger.

The analysis that follows centers on Carmen as she engaged in literacy activities with others in her group (Gudelia, Estela, Joaquina, Chabela, and Delfina). All are natives of Mixquic and share varying kinship ties (Gudelia is Carmen's daughter, several of them are *comadres*). In the previous section, examples of Carmen's uses and thoughts about literacy were already described: how she saved letters, how she explained that the building of damns affected local communication, how she copied a text, and how she filled out a form without assistance. I center my discussion here on how Carmen positions and repositions herself in the context of her literacy circle, constructing new ways to participate in the learning activities through, with, and around written language.[10]

Carmen went to school for less than a year. She laughed heartily and reminisced that she always preferred to play than pay attention, but she and the other women in the group confided that as girls they were made to feel afraid of going to school. Carmen explained to all of us present why she did not learn to read as a child (Table 11.6).

As good humored as Carmen was about not going to school as a little girl, this comment also shows how her exclusion was related to issues of sexuality,

---

[10] For a longer, more detailed description of many of the examples presented in this section, see Kalman (2004).

TABLE 11.6. *Example 4*

Spanish	English
Antes no íbamos casi a la escuela....sí me invitaba a la escuela, una amiga me invitaba a la escuela [pero] me metieron miedo, dicen vas a venir a la escuela, van revueltos hombres y mujeres y unos son encajosos, las besan [y las abrazan]....nadie nos empujaba, nadie nos llamaba, nadie nos decía estudien, hace falta.	Before we didn't go to school....I was invited to go, a friend invited me but they made me afraid, they said you'll go to school, there's boys and girls mixed up together, and they take advantage, they kiss [and hug] the girls...nobody pushed us, nobody called us, nobody said study, it's necessary.

TABLE 11.7. *Example 5*

Spanish	English
Era una persona muy inteligente, muy valiente, con mucho ánimo, mucha fe, empezó a estudiar a pesar de todo lo que ha sufrido. Pues a ver si la imitamos.	She was very intelligent, very brave, enthusiastic, with faith, she started to study despite everything she had been through. Well. Let's see if we do the same.

gender, and expectations for girls. She claimed that she did not go to school because she did not pay attention as a child, but her lack of schooling is also due to her parents' reluctance to send her based on their concerns about their daughter being in contact with boys who they feared would try to take advantage of her. Carmen noted that girls were not encouraged to go to school and that nobody thought that a formal education was even necessary for them (Kalman, 2004).

In early 1999, one of the main activities of the study group was reading together. At that point the women were sharing *Benita*, the autobiography of Benita Galeana, a social activist in the 1940s. The women in the group admired the protagonist because they identified with her struggle. Like them, Benita was very poor, endured great strife in order to keep and raise her child, and learned to read and write as an adult. Carmen commented about Benita (Table 11.7).

Carmen's response to the reading reveals traces of her inner dialogue about women. She called her "intelligent, brave, enthusiastic" and venerated her persistence and faith. She noted that "she started to study even after all she had been through," not unlike Carmen and her classmates, and dialogically different from what other versions of unschooled women stated as possible or true. Benita not only learned to read and write, she wrote a book, and this was cause for great respect and regard among Carmen and the other women. Through her deference for Benita, Carmen also expressed her thoughts on what many women have to confront and places a high value on a woman's decision to learn to read and write, even in the face of conflict and struggle, particularly when the authoritative version of literacy predominant in Carmen's life left little room for women's education.

When there was still a volunteer instructor organizing the learning activities, the women worked individually in workbooks or in their notebooks doing *planas*, repetitive copy work from a model. As the volunteer's attendance began to slip, Carmen asked me to correct her homework, something I did rather reluctantly. One afternoon in April 1998, Carmen presented me with several *planas*, and she asked me to grade them. As I looked over her exercises, I suggested that she read them out loud. As she read phrases such as *el sol amarillo* (the yellow sun) and *las nubes de algodón* (the cotton clouds), she pronounced each word hesitantly, stopping in spots, sounding out syllables in others, but was able to decipher them. After reading *el perro ladra* (the dog barks), she predicted the next line as saying *el perro corre* (the dog runs), but corrected herself to read *el carro corre* (the car runs). At about that point, I noticed that there was a pamphlet from one of the national political parties on the table, so I picked it up and asked her if she would read the headline. When confronted with this unknown text, the first move Carmen made was to position herself as a nonreader, by telling me that she could recognize the letters but she could not always put them into words quickly (*"es que luego las conozco pero no las puedo juntar rápido"*). In doing so, she distanced herself from the activity at hand and from me as I played the role of "the literate other." But I held out the headline in big blue letters STOP THE OPPRESSION IN CHIAPAS [*Basta de opresión en Chiapas; basta* literally means enough] and coaxed her to try as shown in the following dialogue (Table 11.8).

Several differences and similarities between reading the school-type phrases and reading the newspaper headline should be noted. In the first case, the short deconextualized phrases were not always complete sentences, some were subject–verb constructions and others were noun phrases. Because Carmen had copied them over and over until she filled up a page in her notebook with each one, she was very familiar with them, whereas with the headline she was not. In the case of reading the homework assignment, she presented me with the texts, asked to be "corrected," and was not surprised by my suggestion to read them out loud. I was placed in the position of being the "teacher," and she expected to be evaluated. However, in the case of reading the headline, I defined the activity: I chose the material and I suggested (and encouraged her) to read it out; given my teacher place, she believed that she was obliged to do so. Her response to my prompts were also different: when confronted with the request to read her homework, she

TABLE 11.8. *Dialogue 2*

Spanish	English
Carmen: Basta de . . . aquí dice basta y de . . .	Carmen: Stop . . . here it says "stop," stop the
Kalman: Claro. Basta de . . . que es lo que basta?	Kalman: Right. Stop . . . stop what?
Carmen: A Chi-a . . .	Carmen: In Chi-a . . .
Kalman: A ver, un lugar en el país que conoce donde hay muchos líos que empiece con Chi-á	Kalman: Let's see . . .a place in the country that you know where there has been a lot of trouble that starts with Chi-a
Carmen: Chiapas.	Carmen: Chiapas.
Kalman: Chiapas. A ver. (Señala periódico). "Aquí que dice"	Kalman: Chiapas. Let's see (pointing to newspaper). What does this say?
Carmen: Sí entonces dirá Chiapas.	Carmen: Yes. This says Chiapas.
Kalman: Léamelo todo	Kalman: Read me all of it.
Carmen: Bas-ta de o-pre-si-ón en Chiapas.	Carmen: Sto-op the o-pre-sion in Chiapas.

engaged immediately with the task at hand, but when dealing with reading the newspaper, she first defined the kind of reader she was (knows letters but cannot put them together) before beginning. When reading the homework phrases, Carmen pronounced and anticipated meanings (the dog runs, the car runs) based on her knowledge of what they might say and what she remembered them saying; in reading the headline, my prompts to her were about what the text might say using knowledge about a major current event to help her anticipate its meaning.

In terms of how she actually read the different texts, how she read the unknown material was quite similar to how she read the rehearsed one. In both cases she sounded parts out, stopped, and restarted. When given a clue to context about where the oppression might be, she was able to put the parts of the headline together. In the first case, she positioned herself as an apprentice, ready and willing to be corrected; she readily participated, but with the expectation of being evaluated. In the second case, she distanced herself from the activity, emphasizing what she did not know how to do. She agreed to participate, but only after warning me that she might not be able to read it.

During the same class, the group engaged in a collective writing activity, composing together a class set of rules for borrowing books. Throughout the activity, Carmen sat placidly, sometimes participating in the discussion, but mostly on the sidelines. As the group composed the text, everybody wrote it down in their notebook. Carmen only commented: "I don't know how to write that," an evaluation of her own abilities, as well as a move to occupy a distant position from the activity.

Over the next months, Carmen engaged in several activities such as group reading, collective and individual writing, INEA workbook lessons, map reading, measurements, and registering information. At the beginning of September, the group began a long-term project that involved creating a calendar with descriptions of locally grown herbs and vegetables, with recipes for each one. Carmen participated actively in the discussions. As one of the elder members of the group, she was given the role of expert. Other women turned to her to ask her for information about different plants. When it came to writing or reading texts that were still in the works, she continued to express distance to those activities by pronouncing disclaimers about her abilities. She often prefaced her interaction with the other readers and writers in the room with statements, such as "I am the one who is the farthest behind," "I don't know how to write," "I'm in kinder," or "Better you, you know more" ("*soy la más atrasada*," "*no sé escribir*," "*soy del kinder*," "*mejor usted, que sabe más*").

This assessment of her reading and writing self continued throughout my time with her. However, gradually a new stance began to emerge: when she worked with Estela and Gudelia on writing a description of *epazote*, they named her the group scribe and she accepted. With their help and coaching, she wrote a brief text (Table 11.9).

Only a few months prior, Carmen had sat motionless while the rest of the women wrote together. Now she was the center of her writing group. With the help of the other two women, Carmen repositioned herself within the event and turned oral language into writing. She asked for help as she needed it and confronted this challenge from a new social place. Table 11.10 shows is a transcription of her first draft.

Carmen's writing illustrates some of the aspects of written language she is learning to control. Most of the writing is conventional and legible, albeit incomplete in terms of sentence structure and punctuation. The first word, *Epazote*, is the title of her piece. What follows is a description of the plant. Some of the spelling is unconventional (*volitas* instead of *bolitas*), but at the same time, she shows knowledge of different graphic representations for the same phoneme. Although some of the capital letters are omitted or misplaced, she begins the text after *Epazote* with a capital letter and the third line with one as if starting a new sentence. She uses a letter j to represent both /x/y/y/: she writes *oja, tajo,* and *semija* when the correct spelling would be *hoja, tallo,* and *semilla* (see Fig. 11.1). In general, Carmen is able to put her classmates' oral descriptions down on paper, albeit difficult to decipher or read independently.

TABLE 11.9. *Dialogue 3*

Spanish	English
Carmen: "Y cuál otra vamos a poner" (4 segundos).	Carmen: Now what are we going to write? (4 seconds)
Estela: Es...	Estela: Es...
Carmen: El epazote.(...)	Carmen: Epazote.(...)
Gudelia: Sí. A ver, usted empiece. Epazote.	Gudelia: OK, let's see. You start. Epazote.
Carmen: Para qué te hubiera dicho.	Carmen: What did I tell you for.
Estela: Ora ponle... "a color(//) de color" (inaudible).	Estela: Now, write, what color, what color?
Gudelia: Bueno, ((está bien)). Usted tiene lo de los...	Gudelia: Good, that's ok. You have that...
Estela: Epazote. (3 segs.).	Estela: Epazote.
Gudelia: E-pa-zo-te. Con zeta.	Gudelia: E-pa-zo-te. With a "Z."
Carmen: "Cuál"	Carmen: Which one?
Gudelia: Como tres pero al revés.	Gudelia: Like a three but backward.
Carmen: Ah. "Así" Está muy junto (se ríe), se ve muy mal.(...)	Carmen: Ah. Like this? Its kind of close together (she laughs). It doesn't look good.
Gudelia: E-pa-zo-te.	Gudelia: Epazote.
Carmen: Ya está.	Carmen: It's done.
Gudelia: A ver. Epazote, ajá.	Gudelia: Let's see. Aja.
Carmen: Epazote. Sirve "no"	Carmen: Epazote. That will do, "no."
Gudelia: Ajá. "Cómo es el epazote" A ver.	Gudelia: Aja. What is epazote like, let's see.
Carmen: Ya se lo dije ¿verdad? (...)	Carmen: I already told you, right?(...)
Gudelia: Es verde.... Es verde... redonda.	Gudelia: It's green, round.
Estela: Redonda?	Estela: Round?
Gudelia: Es verde. Y su tallo es redondo.(...)	Gudelia: Its green, the stem is round.(...)
Carmen: "Es qué"	Carmen: It's what?
Gudelia: Redondo...y tiene semilla en forma de bolita.	Gudelia: Round...and it has little ball shaped seeds.
Estela: (dictando) Tiene... semillas...	Estela: (dictating) It..has... seeds..
Carmen: Bolitas, bolitas que me hago, a ver qué hago. ¿Qué otro?	Carmen: little ball...I get a bit confused...what else?
Gudelia: Sus hojas son, su hoja es alargada.(...)	Gudelia: Their leaves are, its leaf is longish.(...)
Carmen: Su hoja larga, nada alargada.	Carmen: Its leaf is long, not longish.

TABLE 11.10. *Example 6*

Transcription	Conventionalized Spanish	Approximate Translation to English
Epazote Su oja es berde tajo tajo redondo in tnesemiya en somonevo lilas su hoja se laga	Epazote Su hoja es verde Tallo tallo redondo tiene Semillas en como en bolitas su hoja es larga	Epazote Its leaf is green Stalk stalk is round it has Seeds like in little balls Its leaf is long

More important than the actual pen strokes, however, are her efforts to get these words down. She positioned herself as an active participant, first suggesting the topic and then accepting the responsibility her classmates gave to her. She worked with them, asking for help as she needed it, attempted to write letters and words that she had not written before, wrote straight from spoken words without a written model to copy, and generally took several important risks in order to fulfill the position of scribe in this event. She seemed to enjoy what she was doing and, even within the tension of accepting so many new challenges at once, was able to laugh and engage with the others. For Carmen, this was a new stance.

Over the next several weeks, she continued participating in reading and writing activities centered on describing the use of locally grown herbs and vegetables. Sometime in November, in the heat of a discussion about how to prepare *verdolagas*, a local sour grass used for cooking, Carmen and Delfina had a disagreement about what to include in the recipe that they were writing together. At one point, Carmen turned to me, and said off the record, "You better let me write this," implying that her long-time friend did not know what she was talking about when it came to *verdolagas*. However, when writing, Carmen required a great deal of assistance, which Delfina gave her. The result was a text that they produced together. As we were going over a checklist of what recipes were or were not yet written, Carmen proudly announced to everyone: "Delfina and I wrote that already," referring to the *verdolaga* recipe. In doing so, Carmen appraised her literacy abilities differently than she had before. In this situation, she publicly defined herself and Delfina as capable of producing text.

Toward the end of the project, Carmen began to extend her activities outside her home. One of her sons had a small store and sometimes she minded it for him. She told me that she waited on customers, took their orders, found the merchandise they asked for, and calculated what they owed. With pride she noted (Table 11.11).

Working in the store offers Carmen new opportunities in more ways than one: it allows her to help her son and engage in a variety of literacy events

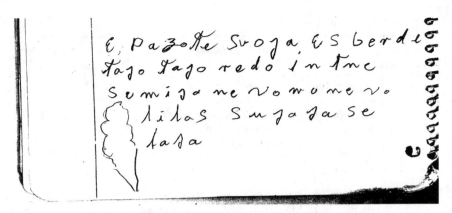

FIGURE 11.1. Example of Carmen's writing.

on a more continuous basis. It is a new responsibility, an opportunity to interact with people, a situation where knowing how to read and write comes in handy. Carmen has given her position to literacy another new turn, she does not think of herself as unable to learn, instead here she has taken the stance of learning, being open to what the store can teach her. This new position is a new place in her world, in the contexts where reading and writing are achieved.

Literacy is a way of being in the world, and involves interacting with others. The construction of a literate stance, a notion of one's self as a reader and writer is an integral part of being literate. For Carmen, and other women like her, the issue of becoming literate or enhancing their use of literacy cannot be understood only in terms of gaining better control over the writing system, learning to read more fluently, or becoming familiar with written genres. An important part of her learning has to do with reevaluating herself as a reader and writer, and redefining her position in regard to written language and the possibility of learning how to use it. Until now, she had construed a notion of herself as distant from literacy, too far behind to be able to learn (*la más atrasada*), but she is now reassessing this stance, using new experiences with written language to question what she once held to be true about literacy and developing her "own word" about what she can or cannot do. In the process, she constructs new knowledge and gains know-how about reading and writing and rethinks her – and other women's – place in the world. Her experiences are embedded in social interaction with others: with her classmates, at the store, around town. Bakhtin described this by noting that "[O]ne's own discourse is gradually and slowly wrought out of others' words that have been acknowledged and assimilated . . . in everyday rounds of our consciousness, the internally persuasive word is half ours and half someone else's" (Bakhtin, 1981, p. 345).

TABLE 11.11. *Example 7*

Spanish	English
Les doy lo que me piden, la tiendita me está enseñando.	I give them what they ask for, the store is teaching me.

LITERACY LEARNING AS REEVALUATED MEANING

For many of the people living in Mixquic, especially for women and girls, it is only recently that literacy is a cultural option for them. In this chapter, learning to read and write late in life is located in the tensions between the authoritative discourse about literacy for women and the inner struggles to question and redefine those beliefs, between the positioned self and written culture, and between socially defined limits and personal experiences. Carmen's quest is at once an effort to examine the restrictions placed on her for the simple reason that she is female and poor, and a process of learning the intricacies of using, producing, and understanding written language. It involves dialogically confronting her recent and past experiences, her previous and emerging positions vis-à-vis written language, and official and authoritative lines about literacy with her own word. This is as much a part of her pursuit for literacy as learning about the inner workings of the writing system, social uses of literacy, text genres, or other aspects that lead to the control of written language. Each process implies positioning herself dialogically to literacy and responding with "her own word." Evidently this is not an all-or-nothing process: it is a gradual reconstruction of meanings through continuous participation in literacy activities.

Bakhtin's ideas about language provide theoretical tools for thinking about the complexity of the learning at hand. By inserting language – written or oral – in the dialogic realm, he encourages us to look for the different and often contradictory components that make up knowledge about literacy/illiteracy. It quickly becomes obvious that this is not just an issue of knowing or not knowing how to read or write. For educated people who read and write well, continuously, and constantly, literacy is part of their identity, just as illiteracy (or low literacy) is part of the identity of the person who does not. He also provides a toolkit for thinking about how change comes about, how one steps back from truths constructed from experience and dominant discourse and reconsiders their validity. According to his theory, this happens when inner persuasive discourse is freed from authoritative discourse to create an independent word, a reorganization of what was once held to be an indisputable truth.

Becoming literate at any stage of life is a specific cultural experience in which inner discourse and exterior voices dialogically meet. When this occurs early in life, potentially it gives time for a gradual accumulation of experiences with reading and writing, and the construction of a literate self, achieved through participating reiteratively in literacy events and interacting with other readers and writers. Contemporary western societies are organized for this to occur, schooling begins by 5 or 6 years of age and throughout basic education literacy plays an important part of the curriculum in several different subject areas. However, when literacy is approached later in life, the institutional support for learning to read and write is weak at best, nonexistent in most situations. Because adults are supposed to know how to read and write, the same kind of heated debates around learning that exist for children do not take place around adult education. Until recently, it was assumed that what was good for children was good for adults, leading most educational programs to mimic child-oriented curriculum (Schmelkes & Kalman, 1996). Unfortunately, programs have mostly paid attention to the a-e-i-o-u's of reading and writing and ignored the significance that literacy learning has for unschooled and underschooled adults.

A Bakhtinian perspective on becoming literate late in life compels us to ask questions about what kinds of learning take place, besides the obvious acquisition of written language. In essence, it is a question of changing identities and, as such, we need to give some thought to what it is we are asking people to do. For Carmen, an important part of learning entailed finding new meanings for literacy, a revaluation of herself in regard to reading and writing. Voloshinov (1973) notes that

No utterance can be put together without value judgment. Every utterance is above all an evaluative orientation. Therefore, each element in a living utterance not only has a meaning but a value ... it is evaluation, after all, which determines that a particular referential meaning may enter the purview of speakers – both the immediate purview and the broader social purview of the particular social group. Furthermore, with respect to changes of meaning, it is precisely evaluation that plays the creative role. A change in meaning is essentially always a reevaluation. (p. 105)

When Carmen announced that she was the "furthest behind" or "in kindergarten," she was also pointing out that other people, particularly her classmates, were ahead of her and knew more about reading and writing than she did. When she noted before the group that she and Delfina had written a recipe together, she was also saying that they were writers, active participants in the calendar project, able to produce written language. In making these statements, she shifts her stance and takes a new "evaluative orientation" for her place in the learning circle and in the world beyond. Each reevaluation implies constructing new meanings for literacy.

From Carmen's process, it is clear that multiple learning takes place when becoming literate late in life. Given the complexity of the process, programs that offer quick fix approaches to literacy for adults are doomed to fail. Learning to read and write at any age is a matter of language development, and in the adult years it includes subtle changes of identity, a reorientation toward other readers and writers, and constructing new meanings and value of written culture. In short, it means redefining one's place in the social world after living a lifetime without access to reading and writing practices.

Worldwide there are 880 million illiterate youth and adults, and some 113 million children who are still out of school. According to the United Nations, "they are the poorest of the poor and most of them are female" (UNESCO, 2001, p. 1). At the 2001 executive board meeting of UNESCO, delegates from around the world renewed their commitment to literacy for all. If the their pledge is sincere, and their intention is to some way alter the asymmetrical distribution of literacy, their efforts will be enhanced by understanding the complexity of literacy practices and the contexts in which they take place. Bakhtin offers important theoretical tools for understanding what it means to become literate late in life and how access to literacy is constructed from the tensions between beliefs and experience, authoritative discourse, and an independent inner voice. To think about ways to promote literacy learning among adults, understanding the complexity of shifting one's position in the social world from distant to written language to a position within written culture is a good place to start.

References

Bakhtin, M. (1981). *The dialogic imagination.* Austin: University of Texas Press.

Bakhtin, M. (1993). *Toward a philosophy of the act.* Austin: University of Texas Press.

Barton, D., & Hall, N. (1999). *Letter writing as social practice.* Amsterdam: John Benjamins Publishing Company.

Barton, D., &. Hamilton., M. (1998). *Local literacies* (1st ed.). London: Routledge.

Benería, L., & Roldán, M. (1987). *The crossroads of class and gender. Industrial homework, subcontracting and household dynamics in Mexico City.* Chicago: The University of Chicago Press.

Coates, J. (1995). *Women talk.* Oxford, UK: Basil Blackwell.

Garcia-Huidoro, J. (1994). Los cambios en las concepciones actuales de la educación de adultos. (Current conceptual changes in adult education). In Unesco-Unicef (Ed.), *La educación de adultos en América Latina ante el próximo siglo.* (Adult education in Latin America into the next century) (pp. 15–50). Santiago de Chile: Unesco-Unicef.

Gumperz, J. (1984). Introduction: Language and the communication of social identity. In J. Gumperz (Ed.), *Language and social identity* (pp. 1–21). Cambridge, UK: Cambrige University Press.

Gumperz, J. (Ed.). (1986). *Directions in sociolinguistics. The ethnography of communication.* New York: Basil Blackwell.

Gumperz, J. (1990). Transcribing conversational exchanges. In J. E. M. Lampert (Ed.), *Transcribing and coding methods for language research.* Hillsdale, NJ: Erlbaum.

Holquist, M. (1990). *Dialogism. Bakhtin and his world.* New York: Routledge.

Hymes, D. (1986). *Foundations in sociolinguistics. An ethnographic approach* (2nd ed.). Philadelphia: University of Philadelphia Press.

Infante, I. (2000). *Alfabetización funcional en 7 países de América Latina.* (Functional literacy in seven latin American countries). Santiago de Chile: Unesco-Orealc.

Kalman, J. (1999). *Writing on the Plaza. The mediated literacy practice of scribes and their clients in Mexico City* (1st ed.). Cresskill, NJ: Hampton Press.

Kalman, J. (2001). Everyday paperwork: Literacy practices in the daily life of un-schooled and underschooled women in a semiurban community of Mexico City. *Linguistics and Education, 12*(4), 1–25.

Kalman, J. (2004). *Saber lo que es la letra. Vías de acceso a la cultura escrita para un Grupo de Mujeres de Mixquic, México*. (To know what writing is: Ways of access to written culture for a group of women in Mixquic, Mexico.) UNESCO Institute of Education International Literacy Research Award 2002. Hamburg: UNESCO Institute of Education.

Morris, P. (1994). *The Bakhtin reader. Selected writings of Bahktin, Medvedev, Voloshinov*. London: Edward Arnold.

Organization for Economic Cooperation and Development (OECD). (1995). *Literacy, economy and society*. Paris: Organization for Economic Cooperation and Development and Statistics Canada.

Presidencia de la Republica (2001). *Plan Nacional de Desarrollo*. Mexico City: Gobierno Federal de los Estados Unidos Mexicanos, p. 169.

Rivera, J. (1994). Educación de adultos en areas urbano-marginales. (Adult education in marginalized urban areas). In UNESCO-UNICEF (Ed.), *La educación de adultos en América Latina ante el próximo siglo* (Adult education in Latin America into the next century) (pp. 51–75). Santiago de Chile: UNESCO-UNICEF.

Rockhill, K. (1993). Gender, language, and the politics of literacy. In B. Street (Ed.), *Cross cultural approaches to literacy* (pp. 156–74). Cambridge, UK: Cambridge University Press.

Schmelkes, S., & Kalman, J. (1996). *Educación de adultos: Estado del arte. Hacia una estrategia alfabetizadora para México*. (Adult education: State of the art. Towards a literacy strategy for Mexico). (1st ed.). México, DF: Instituto Nacional Para la Educación de Adultos.

Secretaría de Educación Pública. (1999). *Perfil de la educación en México*. México City: Secretaría de Educación Pública.

Street, B. (Ed.). (1993). *Cross cultural approaches to literacy* (1st ed.). Cambridge, UK: Cambridge University Press.

Stromquist, N. (1997). *Literacy for citizenship. Gender and grassroots dynamics in Brazil*. Albany: State University of New York Press.

UNESCO. (2001). *Draft proposal and plan for a United Nations literacy decade*. Paris: UNESCO.

Valdés, M. (1995). Inequalities in capabilities in men and women in Mexico. In M. N. J. Glover (Ed.), *Women, culture and development. A study of human capabilities* (pp. 426–32). Oxford: Oxford University Press.

Voloshinov, V. N. (1973). *Marxism and the philosophy of language*. Cambridge, MA: Harvard University Press.

Wagner, D. (2001). *Adult assessment. A historical and analytical review*. Draft background paper prepared for experts meeting on Literacy Assessment Practices in selected developing countries. Paris, June 18–19 2001. International Literacy Institute, University of Pennsylvania and UNESCO.

12

New Times and New Literacies

Themes for a Changing World

James Paul Gee

THE OLD CAPITALISM

Before I talk about new literacies for new times, let me start with old literacies for old times. First, by old times I mean the old capitalism (industrial
capitalism, Fordism). The old capitalism (Drucker, 1999; Kanigel, 1997) is a
social formation that has been transformed by our current high-tech, global
new capitalism (see Castells, 1996; Gee, Hull, & Lankshear, 1996; Greider,
1997; Reich, 1992; Smith,1995). The old capitalism did not disappear, it
still exists as a foregrounded formation in the "developing world" and as a
backgrounded formation in the "developed world" (Drucker, 1999; Greider,
1997).

The old capitalism was born in warfare between workers and bosses over
how work would be done and how fast it should be carried out (Kanigel,
1997). In the end, the workers lost the battle. Thanks to "Taylorism," work
came to be carried out at a pace and in terms of procedures determined
by a "science" of efficiency, not by workers themselves. The craft knowledge of the workers was removed from the workers' heads and bodies and
placed into the science of work, the rules of the workplace, and the dictates
of managers and bosses. A top-down system was created in terms of which
knowledge and control existed at the top (the bosses) and not at the bottom
(the workers). Middle managers conveyed and mediated knowledge, information, and control between the top and the bottom. This became, too,
pretty much how knowledge was viewed in schools: knowledge was a system
of expertise, owned by specialists, and imposed top-down on students.

OLD LITERACIES

Now to "old literacies." Sociocultural studies of literacy (Barton, 1994; Gee,
1996; Street, 1995) have argued that there are as many different "literacies"
as there are socioculturally distinctive practices into which written language

is incorporated. However, one family of literacy practices served, in the old capitalism, as the most significant gate to economic success and sociopolitical power. These were practices that incorporated "academic language." Academic language does not exist just in schools, it exists, as well, out in the world of disciplinary, professional, bureaucratic, official, and public sphere practices and institutions (Schleppegrel & Cecilia Colombi, 2002).

However significant it is, academic language is but one style of language (actually it is composed of a family of related styles). Academic language is acquired in school, although it is facilitated at home by families with a good deal of mainstream educational and cultural capital. It comes to form, for some learners (provided they give it allegiance and identify with it), a specific type of "consciousness" or "worldview," what the Scollons once called "modern consciousness" (Scollon & Scollon, 1981). Modern consciousness is a viewpoint that holds (consciously or unconsciously) that "higher intelligence" is epitomized by explicitness (i.e., low reliance on context), analytic skills, logical (deductive) thought, abstract definitions and generalizations, and sustained attention to, or communication on, a single topic (see also Goody, 1977; Goody & Watt, 1963; Olson, 1977; Ong, 1982).

It is sometimes said, by people influenced by Bakhtin, that academic language, and its attendant form of consciousness, is "monologic." This is not quite right. In fact, like all forms of language, academic language is fully designed to communicate with an "assumed other." The "assumed other" for academic language, however, is a person who backgrounds his or her distinctive individual, social, ethnic, economic, and cultural properties, and, in that sense, fictionalizes him- or herself (Scollon & Scollon, 1981). This backgrounding is done so the person can take on the persona of a rational, generalizing, deductive, "generic," "disinterested," asocial and acultural pursuer of fact and truth. This is to say, such a person seeks to take on the very persona that is also the "voice" or "author" of academic language (by "voice" or "author" here I mean the "presumed author," that is, the persona one must adopt when speaking or writing academic language). In this sense, academic language both creates an "other" and then insists that that the "other" be pretty much like the "author."

When one comes to the acquisition of any form of academic language, there are both significant *losses* and *gains* (Halliday & Martin, 1993; Martin, 1990). To see this, consider the two sentences below. The first (1) is in the social language of the "lifeworld," and the second (2) is in an academic social language. By the "lifeworld," I mean that domain where we speak and act as "ordinary," "everyday," "nonspecialist" people (Habermas, 1984). Of course, different social and culturally groups have different lifeworlds and different lifeworld social languages, although such lifeworld languages do share a good many features that cause linguists to refer to them as "vernacular language."

1. Hornworms sure vary a lot in how well they grow.
2. Hornworm growth exhibits a significant amount of variation.

Subjects of sentences name what a sentence is about (its "topic") and (when they are initial in the sentence) the perspective from which we are viewing the claims we want to make (the sentence's "theme"). The lifeworld sentence above (1) is about hornworms (cute little green worms) and launches off from the perspective of the hornworm. The presence of "sure" helps to cause the subject here ("hornworms") also to be taken as naming a thing with which we are empathizing. The specialist sentence (2) is not about hornworms, but about a trait or feature of hornworms (in particular, one that can be quantified) and launches off from this perspective. The hornworm disappears.

The lifeworld sentence involves dynamic processes (changes) named by verbs ("vary," "grow"). People tend to care a good deal about changes and transformations, especially in things with which they emphasize. The specialist sentence turns these dynamic processes into abstract things ("variation," "growth") through a linguistic device known as "nominalization" (Halliday & Martin, 1993). The dynamic changes disappear. We can also mention that the lifeworld sentence has a contentful verb ("vary"), whereas the specialist one has a verb of appearance ("exhibit"), a class of verbs that is similar to copulas and are not as deeply or richly contentful as verbs like "vary." Such verbs are basically just ways to relate things to each other (in this case, abstract things, to boot).

The lifeworld sentence has a quantity term ("how well") that is not just about amount or degree, but is also "telically evaluative," if I may be allowed to coin a term. "How well" is about both a quantity and evaluates this amount in terms of an end-point or "telos" germane to the hornworm, that is, in terms of a point of good or proper or full growth toward which hornworms are "meant" to move. Some hornworms reach the telos and others fall short. The specialist sentence replaces this "telically evaluative" term with a more precise measurement term that is "Discourse evaluative" (see Gee 1996 for the notion of "Discourse" with a capital "D"). "Significant amount" is about an amount that is evaluated in terms of the goals, procedures (even telos, if you like) of a Discourse (here a type of biology), not a hornworm. It is a particular area of biology that determines what amounts to significant variation and what does not. All our hornworms could be stunted or untypical of well-grown hornworms ("well grown" from a lifeworld, nonspecialist perspective) and still display a significant amount of variation in their sizes.

This last difference is related to another one: the lifeworld sentence contains an appreciative marker ("sure"), whereas the specialist sentence leaves out such markers. The appreciative marker communicates the attitude, interest, and even values of the speaker/writer. Attitude, interest, and values, in this sense, are left out of the specialist sentence.

So, when one has to leave the lifeworld to acquire and then use the specialist language above, these are some of the things that are lost: concrete things like hornworms and empathy for them, changes and transformations as dynamic ongoing processes, and telos and appreciation. What is gained are abstract things and relations among them, traits and quantification and categorization of traits, and evaluation from within a specialized domain. The crucial question, then, is this: *Why would **anyone** – most especially a child in school – accept this loss?*

My view is that people will accept this loss only if they see the gain *as a gain*. So a crucial question in science education, for example, ought to be: *What would make someone see acquiring a scientific social language as a gain?* Social languages are tied to socially situated identities and activities (i.e., people use them to do things while acting as certain kinds of people with characteristic viewpoints, values, and ways of acting, talking, and believing). People can only see a new social language as a gain if they recognize and understand the sorts of socially situated identities and activities that recruit the social language; if they value them or, at least, understand why they are valued; and if they believe they (will) have real access to them or, at least, (will) have access to meaningful versions of them.

Thus, at the outset, acquisition is heavily tied to identity issues. It is tied to the learner's willingness and trust to leave (for a time and place) the lifeworld and participate in another identity, one that, for everyone, represents a certain loss. For some people, as we all know, it represents a more significant loss in terms of a disassociation from, and even opposition to, their lifeworlds, because their lifeworlds are not rooted in the sort of middle-class lifeworlds that have historically built up some sense of shared interests and values with some academic specialist domains (Finn, 1999; Gee, 1996). For such people, the issue is not just a lack of familiarity with the new identity (which is initially an issue for all learners). The issue is, as well, a feeling of opposition or hostility between the new identity they are being asked to assume and other identities they are already comfortable with. Of course, in some cases, this sense of hostility is historically accurate, at least, because some academic domains (e.g., psychology) have historically denigrated certain sorts of people (e.g., people of color, women, and poor people, see Fausto-Sterling, 1985; Gould, 1981).

Using the terms "old literacies" and "old times" can be misleading. Neither has disappeared. Academic language, and its attendant modern consciousness, once believed to be central to what counted as a "schooled" and "intelligent" person (see Berger, Berger, & Kellner, 1973, and Scollon & Scollon, 1981, on the connections between academic language and "modern consciousness"), is now at best *necessary but not sufficient*. By the way, my argument here is not that acquiring facility with academic language ever guaranteed success in society, or necessarily mitigated the effects of racism, for example, but only that people often equated facility with academic language with "intelligence," modernity, and "being educated" (Goody & Watt, 1966; Olson, 1977, 1994; Ong, 1982). Failing to acquire academic language may still bar poor and minority children from power in society, but acquiring academic language (and showing affiliation with school and school-based practices and values) is now, at least, joined by other important centers of action.

To get at where some of these other centers of action are, we will need to turn to new literacies and new times. The new capitalism is all about multiple identities, and enacting and recognizing socially situated identities. Just as we educators are beginning to get a handle on the issues connected to poor and minority children acquiring the languages and identities connected to schooling, the new capitalist world is changing the nature of identities – and their connection to literacies and knowledge – at play in the world.

THE NEW CAPITALISM

What had allowed a relatively peaceful "stand off" between workers and managers in the old capitalism was the great success of the old capitalism in producing commodities (Rifkin, 2000; Thurow, 1999). Commodities are standardized products that become inexpensive enough to be widely available. Changes in science and technology eventually allowed modern conditions of work and the mass production of commodities to be carried out successfully in a great variety of countries, even in some so-called "developing countries." The result was (and is) a global overproduction of commodities and hypercompetition for consumers and markets across the globe (Greider, 1997). The production of commodities (which, of course, continues and will continue across the world) becomes a backgrounded part of the new economy, one that, in general, cannot reap great profits (unless one is first into a market with a new commodity).

There is also another result: many workers cease to be "middle class" (Beck, 2000). The new industrial worker, and the many other sorts of non-middle-class workers to which the new capitalism gives rise, especially temporary and service workers, can no longer afford to live in the sorts of communities, or to live with the degree of stability and security, that made workers in the old capitalism feel securely middle class (Rifkin, 1995). This despite the fact that, in the new capitalism, workers are often asked to think and act more proactively in the business's interest: there is a movement to place the sorts of knowledge and control normally reserved for middle managers back into worker's heads and bodies (from whence Taylor had taken them) (Drucker, 1999). In turn, this has imperiled many middle managers, whose knowledge and supervisory tasks can readily be taken over by front-line workers.

Much work in the new capitalism involves teams and collaboration, based on the idea that in a fast-changing environment, where knowledge goes out of date rapidly and technological innovation is common, a team can behave smarter than any individual in it by pooling and distributing knowledge. Furthermore, in the new capitalism, work is more and more *project based* (Gee et al., 1996; Smith, 1995). A team comes together to carry out a project and when the project changes or is over, the team reassembles and many of its members move on to other projects in the same business or other ones. Security in the new capitalism is rooted not in jobs and wages, but in what I will call one's "*portfolio.*" By one's portfolio, I mean the skills, achievements, and previous experiences that a person owns, and that he or she can arrange and rearrange to sell him- or herself for new opportunities in changed times.

Identities

So, if commodities are not central to the new capitalism, what is? The answer, I believe, is *design* (Kress et al., 2001; Kress & Van Leeuwen, 2001; New London Group, 1996). There are three types of design that reap large rewards in the new capitalism: the ability to design new *identities, affinity groups*, and *networks*. These three types are all deeply interrelated (Gee, 2000–1). In turn, people who are adept at taking on new identities, interacting within affinity groups, and are well connected in networks will flourish.

Let's start with designed *identities*. One type of design typical in the new capitalism (Rifkin, 2000) is the ability to design products, services, or experiences so they create or take advantage of a specific identity connected to specific sorts of consumers (and one and the same individual might constitute several different types of consumer). In turn, businesses seek through the design of such identities to contract an ongoing *relationship* with the consumer in terms of which he or she can be sold ever newer variations on products and services or from which information can be leveraged for sale to other businesses. The product or service itself is not the important element here. After all, many products (as commodities) are getting cheaper and cheaper to make (as the cost of materials – and most especially computer chips – gets lower and lower), and many services don't involve any material things at all (Thurow, 1999). What is important is the identity and relationship associated with the product or service.

Let me give just one example, typical of a myriad of others. Consider the website "palm.com," the site of the Palm™ company, which sells handheld computer organizers. A series of rotating pictures at the top of the site clearly signals the sort of identity the company wants the consumer to assume (e.g., "Find yourself on the road to independence," associated with a picture of the open road, or "Find yourself on the road to freedom," associated with a picture of downhill skiing, or "Follow Wall Street from your street," associated with a picture of the Wall Street sign). Furthermore, the site contains a link to the "The Palm Community," where consumers can swap stories, chat with other Palm users, contribute to a discussion board, give advice to other users, get information on related products and links, download free software, and sign up for a free e-mail newsletter. The Palm company is contracting an ongoing relationship with their consumers, placing them in relationship to (networking them with) each other, and creating an affinity group (see next section).

Affinity Groups and Communities of Practice

Let me now turn to designing *affinity groups*. Affinity groups are increasingly important today, both in business and politics (Beck, 1999; Beck, Giddens, & Lash, 1994; Gee, 2003; Rifkin, 2000). Greens, Saturn owners, members of an elite guarded-gate community, users of Amazon.com, skate boarders, poetry rave fans, or Pokemon fanatics constitute affinity groups that share practices, patterns of consumption, and ongoing relationships to specific businesses and organizations. An affinity group (in the sense I intend here) is a group wherein people form affiliations with each other, often at a distance (that is, not necessarily face to face, though face-to-face interactions can also be involved), primarily through shared practices or a common endeavor (which entails shared practices), and only secondarily through shared culture, gender, ethnicity, or face-to-face relationships (see Rose, 1997, for an important discussion of the relationships between affinity groups as a contemporary form of organization, activism, and social class).

One important type of affinity group today, in schools and workplaces, is "communities of practice" (Wenger, 1998, or what are sometimes called "communities of learners" in schools, Brown, 1994; see also Wenger, McDermott, & Snyder, 2002). Whether in a workplace or school, knowledge functions in a distinctive way in a community of practice. In a community of practice, knowledge is both *intensive* (each person in the practice has special knowledge) and *extensive* (each person in the practice shares some knowledge and functions with others). In a community of practice, knowledge is also *distributed* across people, tools, and technologies, not held in any one person or thing, and *dispersed*, that is people in the practice, using modern information and communication technologies, can draw on knowledge in sites outside the community of practice itself. Finally, much knowledge in a community of practice is *tacit*, that is, built up by daily practice and stored in the routines and procedures the group has evolved. Such knowledge is not easily verbally explicated. New members acquire the knowledge stored in a community of practice by guided participation in the practice, not primarily through direct instruction outside the practice.

Networks

Finally, let me turn to designing *networks*. Another crucial aspect of design in the new capitalism is *networking* people and organizations (Kelly, 1998).

Networking involves designing communicational links between people and organizations. It also crucially involves creating links between people and various sorts of tools and technologies. These tools and technologies not only help create the communicational links that constitute networks, but they are also themselves nodes in the network in which knowledge is stored and across which it is distributed (together with people's minds).

In fast changing times and markets, the more nodes to which one is connected, the more information one receives and the faster one can adapt and change. Networks harness the power of *unfamiliarity*. If people or organizations are networked only with people or organizations like themselves, then everyone in the network pretty much knows what everyone else knows and there is nothing very new to be learned. In slow-changing times, this is fine – maybe even good – because a common core of knowledge can be ever refined. However, if people or organizations are networked with diverse others, then they are going to learn and keep learning new things, things not already in their own repertoire of knowledge and skills. In a fast-changing world, the power of network links to unfamiliar people and organizations is crucial.

Networks that leverage the power of unfamiliarity often have to be large and diffuse, and many of the links are relatively weak links, unlike the strong bonds that people tend to have with those with whom they are familiar and with whom they share a good deal. We come, more and more, to live in a world of many weak links, rather than a few strong ones. This is aided and abetted by the increased *mobility* of many people in the new capitalism, people who move, either physically or virtually, from place to place, creating multiple diffuse weak links to other people and organizations (Bauman, 1998). In fact, in the new capitalist world, mobility is a form and source of power. The mobile classes often leave it to the locals (people who cannot get out or who have few links beyond their area) to clean up (or live with) the messes they have left behind.

Millennials

There is a generation of children today who have lived their entire lives in the new capitalism. These children are part of a new baby boom, a generation that has been called by many names (e.g., Generation Y, Generation XX, Echo Boom, Generation Next, the Bridger Generation, Generation 2K, Millennials) (Howe & Strauss, 2000; O'Reilly, 2000). At the earliest, these children were born in 1982 (and this only for the United States, where the trends that gave rise to Millennials happened earlier than elsewhere – elsewhere in the world they are not yet in their teens, see Howe & Strauss, 2000, Chapter 13).

One interesting way to begin to get at the different sensibilities of many (although, of course, not all) Millennials in comparison to Baby Boomers (people like myself who were initially socialized within the old capitalism and lived through the upheavals of the 1960s and the chaotic dawning of the new capitalism) is to look at the television programs that are helping to socialize the Millennials. Many Baby Boomers cannot stand shows like *Barney & Friends* and *Blue's Clues*, but they rather like *Sesame Street*. Young Millennials like *Sesame Street*, especially the Muppets, but they also like *Barney* and *Blue's Clues*, often more than *Sesame Street*.

Let me take a moment to contrast *Sesame Street* (first aired in 1969) with *Barney & Friends*(first aired in 1991) and *Blue's Clues* (which within months of first airing in 1996 was trouncing *Sesame Street* in the ratings; see Gladwell, 2000, Chapter 3). The themes that emerge from this analysis, by and large, replicate themes that emerge from a contrast between the Baby Boom generation and the Millennial generation, a topic to which I will turn briefly in a moment. Below, I reprint material from the shows' websites about their respective philosophies. I have underlined words that I believe are particularly important for the following discussion:

SESAME STREET

http://www.sesameworkshop.org/faq/answers/0,6113,0,00.html
...designed to use the medium of television to reach and teach preschoolers, and give them skills *that* would provide a successful transition from home to school. The show gave children a head start and provided them with enough confidence to begin learning the alphabet, numbers, and pro-social skills. . . . Everything about the series was a departure from previous children's television programming– from its format to its focus on disadvantaged inner city children, to the way it combined education and entertainment.

BARNEY & FRIENDS

http://www.pbs.org/barney/html/Philosophy.html
The programs are designed to enhance the development of the whole child – the cognitive, social, emotional, and physical domains. . . . A strong emphasis is put on *prosocial skills* such as making friends, sharing, cooperating, and using good manners.

BLUE'S CLUES

http://www.nickjr.com/grownups/home/shows/blue/blues_play_to_learn.jhtml
Play-to-learn is the essence of *Blue's Clues*. *Blue's Clues* was created to celebrate the life of a preschooler – who they are, what they know, and how they experience and learn from everything that they do. . . . Every episode is developed to fulfill the mission of the show: to empower, challenge, and build the self-esteem of preschoolers all the while making them laugh.

Sesame Street is devoted to the transition from home to school, especially in respect to "disadvantaged inner city children." Note that "prosocial skills" for *Sesame Street* are part of a list of school-based things like literacy (the alphabet) and numeracy (numbers). "Prosocial" here appears to mean "knowing how to behave in school." *Sesame Street* is, in many respects, a quite overt form of early schooling, a kind of Head Start program all its own.

Sesame Street combines real people and Muppets in an urban-looking three-dimensional space. It is replete with an often wryly humorous subtext directed at adults (e.g., Monsterpiece Theater), and uses a good deal of metaphorical language and language play that only adults can understand. *Sesame Street* displays, foregrounds, and celebrates social and cultural differences. In fact, the celebration of difference is one of its major themes.

Barney & Friends is not primarily about making the transition from home to school, although it embeds in its shows things like counting or learning shapes. It is primarily about the "whole child" and "prosocial skills" in the sense of cooperation and community, not in the sense of knowing how to behave in school per se. It contains a good deal of play, song, dance, and other sorts of movement of the body, less school-type language than *Sesame Street*. Like *Sesame Street*, it combines real people and fantasy figures, but in a suburban, or even rural, context, not an urban one.

Barney & Friends has little or no subtext directed at adults and engages in little or no metaphorical language of the sort only an adult could understand. Although *Barney & Friends* displays children of different ethnic groups, it does not foreground social or cultural differences. Rather, one of its major themes is commonality and what makes children the same.

Blue's Clues (in which children solve a puzzle using three clues in each episode) takes *Barney & Friends* one step further. It is overtly about "playing to learn," much like *Barney*, which often seems to be about "singing and dancing around to learn," and, thus, in a sense, overtly juxtaposes itself over against or contrasts itself with school (which is not to say it is antischool). It celebrates the life of a preschooler and what preschoolers are and know as they are now, not as they will become in the future. It is about "empowerment," where "empowerment" means feeling smart and being willing to take on intellectual challenges.

Blue's Clues combines one real person (originally "Steve," now gone from the show) with fantasy. Like *Barney*, it is filmed in a setting that looks suburban or even rural, but the setting is two dimensional. It looks like a child's magazine or book in bright primary colors, not like the real world (e.g., the dog "Blue" looks like a cut-out of a child's drawing of a blue dog).

Blue's Clues entirely eschews adult directed subtext and metaphorical language. Characters are named quite literally (e.g., "Blue," a dog that is blue; "Shovel," a shovel; "Pail," a pail). The host often directly faces the camera and interacts with the show's child viewers, giving them ample time to answer his queries and comments. Although *Blue's Clues* occasionally shows culturally diverse children (it rarely shows any humans besides the host), it has next to nothing to do with difference, diversity, or commonality. It is primarily focused on the socially situated cognitive growth of children in interaction with an adult and his cognitive "mediating devices," characters like

Blue, Shovel, Pail, and Slippery Soap, as well as tools like a notebook in which to keep a record of the clues, all of which help the child solve the problems (see the interview with Alice Wilder, director of research for *Blue's Clues*, who makes it clear that the show has been influenced by recent theories of situated cognition, at http://www.nickjr.com/grownups/home/shows/blue/inside/alice_wilder_interview.jhtml).

Sesame Street is designed to entice the parent to watch with the child, assuming the parent (perhaps a poor disadvantaged urban mother) might not. *Sesame Street* assumes (certain) kids need a head start for school, a head start they may not get in their homes (perhaps poor disadvantaged urban homes). *Barney* and *Blue's Clues* do nothing to entice the parent to watch, but their websites make it clear that they absolutely assume a parent is watching with the child, and in an interactive way. Unlike *Sesame Street*, *Barney* and *Blue's Clues* assume parents are so devoted to their children's interests and development (in the case of *Blue's Clues*, most especially their intellectual development) that they do not need a subtext to keep them attending with their child. *Barney* and *Blue's Clues* do not assume that children need a head start for school. Rather, they assume children will develop through play, and that they have homes that will enhance their smartness and add value to their play.

Sesame Street assumes that what children really need they will or ought to get in school or through schooling. It does not compete with school, rather it prepares children for school. *Barney & Friends* takes place alongside school and is a space that enhances school and schooling. When *Barney* shows a classroom, it always seems so inert, the displays and activities left over from the school day only really come alive when Barney and the children enact them into communal song and dance after school. *Blue's Clues* is in a space (Steve's two-dimensional home) completely away from school and, in a sense, it is in competition with school. In many respects, it is better than school. Steve's home, like many of the homes of the children watching *Blue's Clues*, seems to assume that it has a truer sense of who children are and what they know and need than does school.

Sesame Street, on the one hand, and *Barney & Friends* and *Blue's Clues*, on the other hand, orient quite differently toward literacy. Sesame Street overtly stresses and showcases language, literacy, and school skills. *Barney & Friends* does not stress these things, but, rather, stresses the body, play, the whole child, sharing, and commonality. *Blue's Clues* also does not stress language, literacy, or schooling but, rather, stresses thinking, problem solving, and empowerment. In *Barney & Friends* and *Blue's Clues*, children become literate and smart by being and celebrating themselves. In *Sesame Street*, they become literate and smart by learning school-based skills.

Blue's Clues is, in my view, the ultimate Millennial show for small children. Its practices and values are fully aligned with rhetoric about new capitalist workplaces (Drucker, 1999; Gee et al., 1996). New capitalist workplaces (according to this rhetoric) require empowered employees who can think for themselves and who think of themselves as smart and creative people. They require employees who are good at problem solving and who can use various tools and technologies to solve problems. In turn, *Barney & Friends* celebrates things like working together (think of work teams and quality circles), and commonality and community (think of corporate cultures and communities of practice), so commonly stressed in the literature on new capitalist workplaces.

Barney & Friends and *Blue's Clues* are also well aligned with the current practices and views of homes attuned to the new capitalism. Such homes see school as only one site – and, perhaps, not the most important one – for enriching and accelerating their children (Gee, 2000; Gee, Allen, & Clinton, 2001; Gee & Crawford, 1998). Such homes offer their children a plethora of out-of-school tools, technologies, experiences, activities, and sites for the formation of intellectual and social skills that will equip them for elite higher education and success in the new capitalist world. In line with current neoliberal philosophy, homes that cannot leverage such advantages for their children in the free marketplace are entitled only to the basic skills that "accountable" public schools have to offer "off market."

Boomers vs. Millennials

Having talked about some of the shows shaping Millennial children, let me now turn to what popular sources have had to say about the contrasts between Baby Boomers (when they were younger) and Millennials (18 at the oldest, but with the heart of their generation younger). I cannot go into details here, but suffice it to say that the "big picture" is something like what I sketch below (Howe & Strauss, 2000; O'Reilly, 2000; http://millennialsrising.com/survey.shtml). Keep in mind that I am telling a story that applies to well-off children more than to others, although it does also apply to many others thanks in part to the way the Internet and modern media allow trends to spread (and standardize) quickly across diverse groups. In fact, the children who express the Millennial trends I discuss below serve as something of an "attractor" for others in their generation (which does not mean that one effect of this is not resistance).

So here's the story: Many Millennials regret the societal fragmentation and extreme individualism to which the Boomers' earlier assault (in the 1960s and 1970s) on social and governmental institutions gave rise. However, Millennials live in a new capitalist world in which the gap between the poor and the rich has increased. This growing gap has been caused by the very logic of the new capitalism, a logic of increasing returns or a "winner take all" system (Frank & Cook, 1995). By and large, many Millennials appear to find this logic acceptable, natural, and inevitable (Gee, 2000; Gee et al., 2001; Rifkin, 2000).

In the new capitalism, the increase of technological and scientific innovations, the rise of immigration, increases in global trade, and the ability of businesses to get workers at the lowest price across the globe have widened the market-determined difference between high and low wages (Greider, 1997; Thurow, 1999). Over the Millennial childhood, Millennials have seen workers with high educational credentials gain more and more income, while they have seen poor people and immigrants fill unskilled labor positions and the massive supply of service jobs.

All this has created something of a paradox for the Millennials. Millennials want to stress commonality, community, conformity, responsibility, and civic duties, yet they also want to accept as natural large disparities between the rich and the poor, even to the point of accepting as natural the existence, power, and status of an overclass. Of course, this paradox exists in large part because Millennials have seen Baby Boomers in their Yuppie guise (attained when many of them gave up their 1960s rebellion for success in the Reagan neoliberal frontier) come to accept and even celebrate this overclass themselves (Howe & Strauss, 2000).

The acceptance and importance of this overclass is, perhaps, one reason many parents today seek to control their children's time and attention so tightly (Millennials show a significant decline in the amount of time they spend in unstructured activity compared with Gen-Xers as children, see Howe & Strauss, 2000). Such parents believe they must heavily invest in and control their children if they are to end up successful in the hour-glass social structure that constitutes the new capitalism (lots of rich and poor at the top and bottom, and fewer and more vulnerable people in the middle).

It is interesting that polls show the even well-off Millennials like school less with each passing year, but accept it as necessary for their future (Howe & Strauss, 2000; Public Agenda, 1997). Many Millennials see success in school as necessary for the future precisely because they (and their parents) are aware of the role that educational credentials, especially from elite institutions, play in the new capitalist world. At the same time, they are well aware that many of the core credentials, skills, experiences, and identities necessary for success in that world are not gained in school, but rather outside school at home, in activities, camps, travel, and on the Internet.

In terms of how Millennials answer surveys, diversity appears to function quite differently for them than it did for the Baby Boomers (Howe & Strauss, 2000, Chapter 10) The Baby Boomers lived in a world in which the Great Divide was between black and white and race was the key social issue. In the world in which Millennials live, diversity does not mean black or white, it means a great many shades of white, brown, and black: Chinese, Vietnamese, Koreans, Japanese, Malaysians, Asian Americans, Mexicans, Mexican Americans, Indians, Guatemalans, El Salvadorians, Colombians, Peruvians, etc., through a very long list, indeed (and each of these groups comes in many types, income levels, and colors). This is not to claim that race is not objectively crucial in the world still, only that, at least according to surveys, Millennials answer in ways that seem to show that they pay less attention to race (in terms of black and white) than do (or did) Baby Boomers and more attention to a wider array of types of diversity.

In the Millennials' world, segregation is increasing, both in communities and schools (and on television, where blacks and whites now watch quite different shows). But, for the Millennials, segregation is defined more by income than race (Howe & Strauss, 2000). Boomer and Gen-X parents appear to have less and less interest in raising their children in multicultural settings, in part because, although they tend to accept cultural diversity as a value and still care about civil rights, they do not want their children mixing with poor children of any sort.

Gender works differently for Millennials as well (Gilbert & Gilbert, 1998; Howe & Strauss, 2000, Chapter 10). In schools, girls, in nearly every area, are showing more progress than boys. In fact, some colleges are beginning to see fewer applications from boys, less good ones, and more boys dropping out. Even in areas like math and science where boys are still ahead of girls, the girls are fast catching up. Girls appear to be the cultural leading edge of the Millennials, with many Millennial boys caught between following the lead of the girls or retaining the behaviors of Gen-Xers.

Shape-Shifting Portfolio People

The new capitalist literature calls for what I have elsewhere referred to as "shape-shifting portfolio people" (Gee, 1999, 2000). Shape-shifting portfolio people are people who see themselves in entrepreneurial terms. That is, they see themselves as free agents in charge of their own selves as if those selves were projects or businesses. They believe they must manage their own risky trajectories through building a variety of skills, experiences, and achievements in terms of which they can define themselves as successful now and worthy of more success later. Their set of skills, experiences, and achievements, at any one time, constitutes their portfolio. However, they must also stand ready and able to rearrange these skills, experiences, and achievements creatively (that is, to shape-shift into different identities) in order to define themselves anew (as competent and worthy) for changed circumstances. If I am now an "X," and the economy no longer needs "Xs," or "Xs" are no longer the right thing to be in society, but now "Ys" are called for, then I have to be able to shape-shift quickly into a Y.

In earlier work, I have argued that well-off teens today see home, community, school, and society in just such terms (Gee, 1999, 2000; Gee, Allen et al., 2001). They seek to pick up a variety of experiences (e.g., the "right" sort of summer camps, travel, and special activities), skills (not just school-based skills, but a wide variety of interactional, aesthetic, and technological skills), and achievements (honors, awards, projects) in terms of which they can define themselves as worthy of admission to elite educational institutions and worthy of professional success later in life. They think and act, from quite early in life, in terms of their "resume." Note that school (or at least the classroom at school) is not the only, perhaps not even the central, site for filling up one's resume.

Shape-shifting did not start with the Millennials. In fact, as the old capitalism gradually turned into the new, and neoliberalism became hegemonic in much of the Western world, there were calls for such people (e.g., Boyett & Conn, 1992; Drucker, 1989, 1999; Handy, 1989; Peters, 1987), much of these stemming from the success of Japan in the 1980s. Of course, at the time this often meant adults were being asked to think of themselves in new ways. However, the Millennials are a generation in which there are wide-scale expectations, at least among many middle- and upper middle-class families, that children will think of themselves and build themselves in this way from the earliest ages. The old capitalism left a good deal of space for someone to enter the middle class without being a shape-shifting portfolio person (think of all the secure union jobs that paid middle-class wages). The new capitalism leaves much less space in this regard.

Class means something different in the new capitalism than it did in the old. In the old capitalism, there was a broad and massive "middle class" defined by one's ability to consume standardized commodities. In the new capitalism, class is defined by the nature of one's portfolio, the sorts of experiences, skills, and achievements one has accrued (which one shares, by and large, with the "right" sort of people) and one's ability to manage these in a shape-shifting way. One's portfolio surely correlates with one's parents' income (although by no means perfectly), but what matters is the portfolio and the way in which it is viewed and managed. If you have no portfolio or do not view yourself in portfolio terms, then you are at risk in the new capitalism.

Diverse Millennials

To many, it may seem as if my talk of Millennials only applies to well-off young people, perhaps even only well-off white young people. However, lots of young people today who are not well-off or white display Millennial viewpoints and aspirations. Let me briefly discuss but one example. Wan Shun Eva Lam in her excellent article "L2 Literacy and the Design of the Self" (2000) discusses a case that is not at all untypical in a Millennial generation, 35 percent of whom are nonwhite or Latino (Howe & Strauss, 2000).

Lam's focal student, whom she calls "Almon," emigrated at the age of 12 from Hong Kong to the United States. After 5 years in the United States, Almon was frustrated by his skills in English. School only offered him English as a Second Language, bilingual, or remedial courses, courses which stigmatized him as a "low-achieving student" (Lam, 2000, p. 466). Almon believed it was going to be hard for him to develop his "career" (p. 467) in the United States because of his English skills. However, eventually, Almon got involved with the Internet, created his own personal home page on a Japanese pop singer, and "compiled a long list of names of on-line chat mates in several countries around the world, and was starting to write regularly to a few e-mail 'pen pals'" (p. 467). Almon's Internet writing eventually improved his writing in school significantly.

After his experiences with and on the Internet, here is how Almon talked about himself and his future:

> . . . I'm not as fearful, or afraid of the future, that I won't have a future. . . . I didn't feel I belonged to this world. . . . But now I feel there's nothing to be afraid of. It really depends on how you go about it. It's not like the world always has power over you. It was [names of a few chat mates and e-mail pen pals] who helped me to change and encouraged me. If I hadn't known them, perhaps I wouldn't have changed so much. . . . Yeah, maybe the *Internet* has changed me. (Lam, 2000, p. 468)

Almon had chosen to settle his home page in the "Tokyo" section of *Geo-Cities* (an international server) where a global community of Asians gathers around Japanese pop culture. Almon's online chatmates were located in a variety of places, such as Canada, Hong Kong, Japan, Malaysia, and the United States.

Almon's story is one variety of a typical Millennial story. He thinks in terms of his career and future, and evaluates his current skills and experiences in that light. He gains his most important skills, experiences, and identities, including even school-based skills, outside school (indeed, school stigmatizes and deskills him). Although I have not discussed the matter above, Lam (2000) makes it clear that Almon's penpal relationships are mainly with girls, and that his remarks take on some of the values and perspectives that these girls enact on the Internet. Finally, he forms his new identities as part and parcel of an affinity group.

Lam (2000) argues that the genre of electronic dialogue, as a form of communication that relies heavily on writing, "constitutes a highly visible medium for the scripting of social roles" (p. 474). She points out that many of Almon's postings to his female interlocutors "sound both very personal and very much like role play" (p. 475). Almon not only gains new skills and develops new identities on the Internet, but he also learns to shape-shift, to enact different social roles by designing representations of meaning and self through language and other symbols systems (e.g., music, graphics, emoticons) (New London Group, 1996).

There is no doubt that Almon, regardless of his economically based social class, is building a portfolio and learning to think of himself in entrepreneurial terms (in the creation of his own website and in his sense of free agency and control over his own destiny) and in shape-shifting terms. Connected in a affinity-group way, as he is, to a young Asian Diaspora, many of whom are, rich or poor, core Millennials, Almon is not at the margins (expect in the eyes of the school), but at the center of the new capitalist world.

A Note on Learning in the New Capitalist World

One important theme the world in which Millennials are growing up is, I believe, this: thanks to modern technology, young people today are often exposed outside school to processes of learning that are deeper and richer than the forms of learning to which they are exposed in schools. I do not have space here to develop this theme in any full way. Let me give but one example of what I mean.

In recent work (see Gee, 2003), I have been investigating the principles of learning that are built into video and computer games (I discuss video and computer games more in the last section of this chapter). Video and computer games are today a major cultural practice of young people – the video and computer game industry now outsells the movie industry (Poole, 2000). Video and computer games are a prototypical high-tech product of the new capitalism and the businesses that make them, in a highly competitive market, cannot have lots of people fail when they try to learn to play them (just as the makers of *Blue's Clues* have to get their research about what children want and can do right or go out of business).

Taking modern first- and third-person shooter games as an example (e.g., "Half-Life," "Metal Gear Solid," "Deus Ex," "System Shock 2"), here are just a few (there are many more) of the learning principles that the player is (however tacitly) exposed to in learning to play these games. Learning is based on situated practice; there are lowered consequences for failure and taking risks (you've saved the game and can start over); learning is a form of extended engagement of self as an extension of an identity to which the player is committed; the learner can customize the game to suit his or her style of learning; the learning domain (e.g., a training module connected to the game or the first episodes of the game) is a simplified subdomain of the real domain/game; problems are ordered so the first ones to be solved in the game lead to fruitful generalizations about how to solve more complex problems later; explicit information/instruction is given "on demand" "just in time" in the game world; learning is interactive (probing, assessing, and reprobing the world); there are multiple routes to solving a problem; there are intrinsic rewards (within the game) keyed to any player's level of expertise; the game operates at the outer edge of one's "regime of competence" (always doable with the resources you have at that point, never too easy); "basic skills" are not separated from higher-order skills, both are picked up bottom-up by playing the game or several different games of a given type or genre of game; the meaning of texts and symbols is situated in what one does and, thus, never purely verbal or textual;

meaning/knowledge is built up through various modalities (e.g., images, texts, symbols, interactions, abstract design, sound); meaning/knowledge is distributed between the player's mind, the objects and environments in the game world, and other players (who help); knowledge is dispersed as player's go online to get help and discuss strategy; players become members of affinity groups dedicated to a particular game or type of game; and the game constitutes a complex designed system, and the player orients his or her learning to issues of design and the understanding of complex systems.

I could go on, but the point I hope is clear: imagine young people who have been immersed in this sort of learning coming to school to acquire academic language top-down in a setting remote from practice or affinity groups. Such young people experience much better viewpoints on learning in their "trivial" (from a Baby Boomer's perspective) cultural pursuits than they do in the schools Baby Boomers largely control. I should mention, too, that while school-based Baby Boomers give lip service to multicultural diversity and understanding, they rarely extend this understanding to the generational, peer-based, and popular cultures of the young people in school.

At the same time, it is clear that some of the learning principles I have just sketched are often integral to good science instruction (DiSessa, 2000), when such instruction seeks conceptual understanding and not just rote memory of facts. Such learning principles are also supported by a good deal of modern work in cognitive science concerned with how humans learn best (Kirshner & Whitson, 1997). They are also supported in much contemporary work on literacy learning that stresses critical and conceptual learning (Freedman et al., 1999; Rose, 1999). However, they are just the sorts of principles that are drive out of schools by our current mania for testing and accountability.

Schools and Schooling in the New Capitalism

The notion of *experience* has become crucial in the new capitalist world. Shape-shifting portfolio people leverage distinctive experiences to form their portfolios and to underwrite their claims to distinction. New capitalist businesses often see themselves as primarily selling experiences (and relationships) customized to different consumer identities (Rifkin, 2000). Current cognitive science of the sort based on situated cognition (often with a connectionist bent) argues that people primarily reason, not by logical computations and on the basis of abstract generalizations, but by manipulating records of their actual experiences (Barsalou, 1999; Glenberg, 1997; Gee, 1992 – and, remember, *Blue's Clues* is explicitly based on such work in cognitive science). You are what you have experienced, and in the new capitalist world, distinctive experiences are for sale.

In general, outside of certain narrow spheres (e.g., science), the new capitalism has no great use for the persona of a rational, generalizing, deductive, "generic," "disinterested," asocial and acultural pursuer of fact and truth, the persona so central to the old capitalism and modern consciousness (Bauman, 1992). Rather, it values distinctive identities and skills rooted in distinctive and various (but often classbound) experiences. At the same time, the new capitalism has no great use for – perhaps even a fear of– diversity centered in ethnic, cultural, and gender differences when these are not defined in terms of market niches. The diversity the new capitalism revels in is the sort of diversity defined by affinity groups and networks centered in practices that markets create, transform, and sustain. In the new capitalism, these are affinity groups and networks defined by socially and economically distinctive types of knowledge, information, skills, experiences, and lifestyles.

The great barrier today for many poor and minority children (those who come to school without the home-based head start for formal schooling that more affluent children often have), as I see it, is that mastery of academic language and affiliation with school-based values is necessary for success in the new capitalist world, but now only a small part of the whole picture. At the same, the recent standards, testing, and accountability regime has committed to schools to supplying all children, most especially poor children, with no more (and no less) than "the basics." This, of course, fits perfectly with the neoliberal philosophy that underlies the new capitalism.

According to neoliberal philosophy, everything should be on a (free) market and people ought to get what (and only what) they can pay for (Hayek, 1996; Sowell, 1996; von Mises, 1997). If, for humane reasons, there has to be, within a given area, something "off market" (i.e., free or subsidized), then it must be "basic"; otherwise, it will encourage people away from the market and disrupt the market.

This, of course, allows children to begin to fill up their portfolios only if they can draw on family, community, or Internet resources, resources from various sorts of private sites and institutions, and school resources at the margins of the neoliberal central curriculum (in privileged public schools or private schools – private schools experienced a major increase in enrollment in the 1990s – and in special activities and programs at school). In turn, it leaves children without such resources to fill the huge number of service jobs created by the new capitalism and its distinctive workings of class defined in terms of the consumption of status and lifestyle. In the end, we get the Tale of Two Millennial Cities (Howe & Strauss, 2000), a tale not of race, nor of class in traditional terms, but of "kinds of people" – those with and without portfolios, those with small and big portfolios, shape-shifters and non-shape-shifters.

It has not been my intention here to make recommendations for the future. Nonetheless, it seems to me that, for those who care about disadvantaged children, there are two possible courses of action (not necessarily mutually exclusive). One is to give up on public schools, accept their neoliberal function of delivering "the basics" accountably, and work to provide portfolio-forming activities and experiences, as well as political-critical capacities, for disadvantaged children outside school and at school at the margins of the neoliberal curriculum. The other is to fight the neoliberal agenda and make schools sites for creativity, deep thinking, and the formation of whole people, sites in which all children can gain portfolios suitable for success, but success defined in multiple ways, and gain the ability to critique and transform social formations in the service of creating better worlds for all.

BAKHTINIAN THOUGHTS

Bakhtin (1986) captures powerfully how spoken and written words always have two "sources." One source is the whole set of utterances, texts, and institutions that have always already given those words meanings in culture and history. The other source is the individual person speaking or writing here and now, projecting onto the words his or her own "slant," and thereby adding to the cultural and historical possibilities of those words. The same is true, not just of words, but of any other signs or symbols, whether they be images, artifacts, graphs, or what have you.

I have nothing novel to add to Bakhtin scholarship. What I want to do here, rather, is meditate for just a moment on how one contemporary semiotic domain – namely, video and computer games – might illuminate some of the ways in which the dynamic between these two sources of meaning works out, especially in our "new times." Video and computer games are now as influential in the popular culture of young people as are (or were) movies and books (Poole, 2000). It is interesting to note that Bakhtin gained many of insights about language at work in the world from a close study of narration and dialogue in novels. Perhaps, we can also gain some insights from video and computer games.

I focus my discussion on a game named *Arcanum: Of Steamworks and Magick Obscura*. This is a game that takes place in a (virtual) world where once upon a time magic ("magick") ruled, but where technology has now arrived and magic and machines coexist in an uneasy balance. A variety of different groups – Humans, Elves, Gnomes, Dwarves, Orcs, and Ogres, as well as Half-Elves, Half-Orcs, and Half-Ogres (each of which have one Human parent)– cohabit this world, each orientating to the conflicts between magic and technology in different ways.

Before you start playing *Arcanum*, you must construct your character. Each group and gender has different natural characteristics. For example, each group and gender has their own unique degrees of strength, constitution, dexterity, beauty, intelligence, willpower, perception, and charisma (there are no real inequalities here, just differences – a character from any group you choose can fare well or poorly in the world of Arcanum). Each trait will affect how your character (i.e., you) carries out dialogue and action in the world of Arcanum and how other characters in the world respond.

When the game starts you also get five "points" that you can choose to distribute, in any way you want, to your character, thereby changing his or her "natural" state (e.g., a female Half-Elf has a natural strength of 7, but you could use one or more or your five points to make her stronger; the same goes for her other traits). As the game progresses and you gain more worldly experience through various actions in the game, you gain yet more points to distribute, thereby allowing your character to develop in certain ways and not others. These initial and subsequent points can be distributed to your character's primary traits such as strength and dexterity, but they can also be used to build up a wide variety of other skills, such as ability with a bow and arrow, skill with picking locks, or persuasive skills. They can be used to build up ability to cast a wide variety of magic spells or, instead, ability to build a wide variety of technological apparatus, as well. You can choose to have a character primarily oriented to magic or technology or some mixture of the two. By the time you finish *Arcanum*, moving through many quests and interactions, your character is very different from the characters other players would have built, and the game you have played is very different than what it would have been had you built your character differently, initially and throughout the game.

A game like *Arcanum* involves playing with identities in an interesting way. Three different types of identity are at stake. First, there is a *virtual* identity: one's identity as a virtual character in the virtual world of Arcanum. When I played the game, I constructed my character to be a female Half Elf named "Bead." In the virtual world of Arcanum, given the sort of creature Bead is (a female Half-Elf) and how I have developed her in the game at any one point, there are things she can do and things she cannot do. For example, at a certain point in the game, Bead wanted to persuade a town meeting to fund the building of a monument in order to please the mayor of the town. To do this, she needed to be both intelligent and persuasive. Half-Elves are, by nature, pretty intelligent and I had built up Bead to be persuasive during the game (i.e., by giving her points in this area as she gained more experience). Thus, she was able to pull off the task at the town meeting. Thus, these traits (her intelligence and persuasive skills) and her accomplishment at the town meeting – for which she received ample praise – are part of my virtual identity as Bead. In the virtual world of Arcanum, I was the Half-Elf Bead.

A second identity that is at stake in playing a game like *Arcanum* is a *real-world identity*: namely, my own identity as "James Paul Gee," a nonvirtual person playing a computer game. Of course, in the real world I have a good many different nonvirtual identities. I am a professor, a linguist, an Anglo-American, a middle-age Baby Boomer male, a parent, an avid reader, a middle-class person initially raised outside the middle class, a former devout Catholic, a lover of movies, and so on and so forth, through a great many other identities. Any one or more of my real world identities can be engaged, at one point or another, as I am playing *Arcanum*. For example, which of my real-world identities were at play – positively or negatively – when I got such joy at having Bead pick rich people's pockets? When I chose to be a female Half-Elf in the first place?

A third identity that is at stake in playing a game like *Arcanum* is what I will call a *projective identity*, playing on two senses of the word "project," meaning both "to *project* one's values and desires onto the virtual character" (Bead, in this case) and "seeing the virtual character as one's own *project* in the making, a creature whom I imbue with a certain trajectory through time based on my aspirations for what I want that character to be and become." This is the hardest identity to describe, but the most important one for understanding the power of games like *Arcanum*.

A game like *Arcanum* allows me, the player, certain degrees of freedom (choices) in forming my virtual character and developing her throughout the game. In my projective identity, I worry about what sort of "person" I want her to be and what type of history I want her to have had by the time I am done. I want this person and history to reflect my values – although I have to think reflectively and critically about these because I have never had to project a Half-Elf onto the world before. At the same time, this person and history I am building also reflect what I have learned from playing the game and being Bead in the land of Arcanum. A good role-playing game makes me think new thoughts about what I value and what I do not value.

Let me give an example of what I mean: At one point, I had Bead sell a ring a dying old man had given her. I regretted this: it was not, on reflection, the sort of thing I wanted the person I desired Bead to be and become to do (and note, too, that what I want her to be and become is not a clone of myself – in my "real" life I do not pick pockets). It was not an event I wanted her to have in her history – in her trajectory through her virtual life – at the end of the day. So, I started the game again. This projected person – the kind of person I want Bead to be, the kind of history I want her to have, the kind of person and history I am trying to build in and through her – is what I mean by a projective identity. There is a certain Bakhtian-like tension here between what *others* have designed (the people who designed the game and world of *Arcanum*) and what *I myself* make of that design through projecting my real world values and aspirations onto its degrees of freedom. The design exists before I have played, but it is inert until I vitalize with new possibilities.

This tripart play of identities involving a virtual identity, real world identities, and a projective identity is quite powerful. It transcends identification with characters in novels or movies, for instance, because it is both *active* (the player actively does things) and *reflexive*, in the sense that once the player has made some choices about the virtual character, the virtual character is now developed in a way that sets certain parameters about what the player can now further do. The virtual character redounds back on the player and affects his or her further actions.

As a player, I was proud of Bead, at the end of the game, in a way in which I have never been proud of a character in a novel or movie, however much I had identified with them. For a character in a novel or movie, I can identify with the pride they must or should feel, given what they have done or how far they have come. But my pride in Bead is tinged with pride (or, it could have been regret had things turned out differently), at various levels, in and with myself. But this pride is not (just) selfish. In a sense, it is also selfless because it is pride at things that have transcended – taken me outside – my real world self (selves), if I am playing the game reflectively.

Of course, from the standpoint of critical theory, one could readily criticize role-playing games like *Arcanum* for essentializing traits like "intelligence" and "strength," or for distributing them differently to different sorts of creatures. It is, of course, not surprising that computer games indulge in the vices of the cultures they inhabit, although they also offer opportunities to reflect on these matters in a novel form. Be that as it may, I will leave cultural critique of computer games to others and to myself for another time.

What I want to concentrate on here is the way in which the tripart play of and with identities I discussed above can illuminate how identity works elsewhere in the contemporary world. In a good science classroom (good by my standards, at least), children are invited to take on the virtual identity of being a scientist of a certain type in words, deeds, and interactions (after all, they are not "really" scientists and are not going to become scientists any time soon – and, indeed, there are aspects of "real" science and "real" scientists we may not want children imitating). This identity is determined by the values, norms and design work of the teacher as he or she sets of what constitutes in this classroom being-doing a scientist.

This virtual identity impinges on and bridges to the real world identities of different children in the classroom in different ways. Indeed, if children cannot or will not make bridges between some of their real world identities and the virtual identity at stake in the classroom (here, a particular type of scientist)–or if teachers or others destroy or do not help build such bridges – then, once again, learning is imperiled. Children who, for instance, sees themselves as members of families that are adept at technical learning, may have an advantage because they can build a powerful bridge between one of their real world identities ("people like us learn technical stuff – it's no big deal") and the virtual identity at stake in the science classroom ("scientists in the sort of semiotic domain being created in this classroom do not fear or put off technical learning").

However, active and critical learners can do more than simply carry out the role of playing a virtual scientist in a classroom. They can also form a projective identity. If learners are to do this, they must come to project their own values and desires onto the virtual identity of "being a scientist of a certain sort" in this classroom. They must come to see this virtual identity as their own project in the making, an identity they take on that entails a certain trajectory through time defined by their own values, desires, choices, and goals, as these are rooted in the interface of their real world identities and the virtual identity.

The learners, when they take on a projective identity, want the scientist they are "playing" to be a certain sort of person and to have had a certain sort of history in the learning trajectory of this classroom. They have aspirations for this scientist, just as I had aspirations for Bead when I played *Arcanum.* Perhaps, they want *their* scientist to have had a history of having been persistent, resilient in the face of failure, collaborative, risk taking, skeptical, and creative. They want *their* scientist to become *this* sort of person.

If learners in classrooms carry learning so far as to take on a projective identity, something magic happens – a magic that cannot, in fact, take place in playing a computer game. The learner comes to know that he or she has the *capacity*, at some level, to take on the virtual identity as a real world identity. However much I might want to do, I myself, in the real world, have no capacity to become the sort of female Half-Elf I wanted and built Bead to be. But a learner in a good science classroom comes to feel what it is like to have the capacity to be the sort of scientist (and person) they have wanted and built their "character" in the classroom to be. This becomes one of their real world identities.

Learners do not, of course, have to realize this capacity in actuality and become a scientist. They do not even have to believe they could become particularly good scientists – after all, in the projective identity you also learn about your own limitations. It is often enough that they have sensed new powers in themselves. They will, possibly for a lifetime, be able to empathize with, affiliate with, learn more about, and even critique science as a valued, but vulnerable, human enterprise.

Thus, what *others* have designed (a virtual world in a game or classroom) becomes part of myself, my real world identity – my own uniqueness – when and if I engage in the virtual identity as a project of my own, and not just a role to be played by the rules of the game/classroom (for a win or a grade). My projective identity stands at the border of the social (the virtual world created by others) and myself (my real world identities, which themselves are the products of my own past projective work). The social and the individual are inextricably linked.

Of course, such projective identities are often worked out much more creatively in playing computer games than in studying in classrooms, especially classrooms that stress skill and drill, the passive storage of information, and standards that the learner has had no part in forming. In such class-rooms, there are no degrees of freedom for the projective identity to take wing. As young people face the contemporary demand to be shaping-shifting portfolio people, the sort of play with identity that is characteristic of contemporary forms like video and computer games will be practiced by some more than others, more in some schools than others, and sometimes more outside school than in it. Indeed, access to these technologies themselves will be greater for some than for others (and, thus far, they are recruited little or not at all by schools). What if projective identities turn out to be a central form of learning for our "new times"? What if they turn out to be a key site at which the Bakhtian tension between the social/cultural/historical and the individual works itself out in the modern world? I can offer the questions. I have no firm answers.

References

Bakhtin, M. (1986). *Speech genres and other late essays.* Austin: University of Texas Press.
Barsalou, L. W. (1999). Language comprehension: Archival memory or preparation for situated action. *Discourse Processes, 28,* 61–80.
Barton, D. (1994). *Literacy: An introduction to the ecology of written language.* Oxford, UK: Blackwell.
Bauman, Z. (1992). *Intimations of postmodernity.* London: Routledge.
Bauman, Z. (1998). *Globalization: The human consequences.* Cambridge, UK: Polity Press.
Beck, U. (1999). *World risk society.* Oxford, UK: Blackwell.
Beck, U. (2000). *The brave new world of work.* Cambridge, UK: Polity Press.
Beck, U., Giddens, A., & Lash, S. (1994). *Reflexive modernization: Politics, traditions and aesthetics in the modern social order.* Stanford, CA: Stanford University Press.
Berger, P., Berger, B., & Kellner, H. (1973). *The homeless mind: Modernization and consciousness.* New York: Random House.
Boyett, J. H., & Conn, H. P. (1992). *Workplace 2000: The revolution reshaping American business.* New York: Plume/Penguin.
Brown, A. L. (1994). The advancement of learning. *Educational Researcher, 23,* 4–12.
Castells, M. (1996). *The information age: Economy, society, and culture, Volume 1: The rise of the network society.* Oxford, UK: Blackwell.
DiSessa, A. A. (2000). *Changing minds: Computers, learning, and literacy.* Cambridge, MA: MIT Press.
Drucker, P. F. (1989). *The new realities: In government and politics, in economics and business, in society and world view.* New York: Harper Collins.
Drucker, P. F. (1999). *Management challenges for the 21st century.* New York: Harper.
D'Souza, D. (2001). *Virtue of prosperity: Finding values in an age of techno-affluence.* New York: Touchstone Books.
Fausto-Sterling, A. (1985). *Myths of gender: Biological theories about women and men.* New York: Basic Books.
Finn, P. J. (1999). *Literacy with an attitude: Educating working-class children in their own self-interest.* Albany: State University of New York Press.

Frank, R. H., & Cook, P. J. (1995). *The winner-take-all society: How more and more Americans compete for ever fewer and bigger prizes, encouraging economic waste, income inequality, and an impoverished cultural life.* New York: The Free Press.

Freedman, S. W., Simons, E. R., Kalnin, J. S., Casareno, A., & the M-Class Teams (1999). *Inside city schools: Investigating literacy in multicultural classrooms.* New York: Teachers College Press.

Gee, J. P. (1992). *The social mind: Language, ideology, and social practice.* New York: Bergin & Garvey.

Gee, J. P. (1996). *Social linguistics and literacies: Ideology in discourses* (2nd ed.). London: Taylor & Francis.

Gee, J. P. (1999). New people in new worlds: Networks, the new capitalism and schools. In B. Cope & M. Kalantzis (Eds.), *Multiliteracies: Literacy learning and the design of social futures* (pp. 43–68). London: Routledge, 1999.

Gee, J. P. (2000). Teenagers in new times: A new literacy studies perspective. *Journal of Adolescent & Adult Literacy, 43*(5), 412–20.

Gee, J. P. (2000–1). Identity as an analytic lens for research in education. *Review of Research in Education, 25,* 99–125.

Gee, J. P. (2003). *What video games have to teach us about learning and literacy.* New York: Palgrave/Macmillan.

Gee, J. P., Allen, A-R., & Clinton, K. (2001). Language, class, and identity: Teenagers fashioning themselves through language, *Linguistics and Education, 12,* 175–94.

Gee, J. P., & Crawford, V. (1998). Two kinds of teenagers: Language, identity, and social class. In D. Alverman, K. Hinchman, D. Moore, S. Phelps, & D. Waff (Eds.), *Reconceptualizing the literacies in adolescents' lives* (pp. 225–45). Hillsdale, NJ: Erlbaum.

Gee, J. P., Hull, G., & Lankshear, C. (1996). *The new work order: Behind the language of the new capitalism.* Boulder, CO: Westview Press.

Gilbert, R., & Gilbert, P. (1998). *Masculinity goes to school.* London: Routledge.

Gladwell, M. (2000). *The tipping point: How little things can make a big difference.* Boston: Little, Brown and Company.

Glenberg, A. M. (1997). What is memory for. *Behavioral and Brain Sciences, 20,* 1–55.

Goody, J. (1977). *The domestication of the savage mind.* Cambridge, UK: Cambridge University Press.

Goody, J., & Watt, I. P. (1963). The consequences of literacy. *Comparative Studies in History and Society, 5,* 304–45.

Gould, S. J. (1981). *The mismeasure of man.* New York: Norton.

Greider, W. (1997). *One world, ready or not: The manic logic of global capitalism.* New York: Simon & Schuster.

Habermas, J. (1984). *Theory of communicative action* (Vol. 1). (Trans. T. McCarthy). London: Heinemann.

Handy, C. (1989). *The age of unreason.* London: Business Books.

Halliday, M. A. K., & Martin, J. R. (1993). *Writing science: Literacy and discursive power.* Pittsburgh: University of Pittsburgh Press.

Hayek, F. A. (1996). *Individualism and economic order* (reissue ed.). Chicago: The University of Chicago Press.

Howe, N., & Strauss, W. (2000). *Millennials rising: The next great generation.* New York: Vintage Books.

Kanigel, R. (1997). *The one best way: Frederick Winslow Taylor and the enigma of efficiency.* New York: Penguin.

Kelly, K. (1998). *New rules for the new economy: Ten radical strategies for a connected world.* New York: Viking.

Kirshner, D., & Whitson, J. A. (Eds.). (1997). *Situated cognition: Social, semiotic, and psychological perspectives.* Norwood, NJ: Erlbaum.

Kress G., Jewitt, C., Ogborn, J., & Tsatsarelis, C. (2001). *Multimodal teaching and learning: The rhetorics of the science classroom.* London: Contunuum.

Kress, G., & Van Leeuwen, T. (2001). *Multimodal discourse: The modes and media of contemporary communication.* London: Arnold.

Lam, W. S. E. (2000). L2 literacy and the design of the self: A case study of a teenager writing on the Internet. *TESOL Quarterly, 34*(3), 457–82.

Martin, J. R. (1990). Literacy in science: Learning to handle text as technology. In F. Christe (Ed.), *Literacy for a changing world* (pp. 79–117). Melbourne: Australian Council for Educational Research.

New London Group. (1996). A pedagogy of multiliteracies: Designing social futures. *Harvard Educational Review, 66,* 60–92. Reprinted in B. Cope & M. Kalantzis (Eds.), *Multiliteracies: Literacy learning and the design of social futures* (pp. 9–37). London: Routledge, 1999.

Olson, D. R. (1977). From utterance to text: The bias of language in speech and writing. *Harvard Education Review, 47,* 257–81.

Olson, D. R. (1994). *The world on paper: The conceptual and cognitive implications of writing and reading.* Cambridge, UK: Cambridge University Press.

Ong, W. S. J. (1982). *Orality and literacy: The technologizing of the word.* London: Methuen.

O'Reilly, B. (2000, July 24). Meet the future – It's your kids. *Fortune,* 144–68.

Peters, T. (1987). *Thriving on chaos: A handbook for management revolution.* New York: Harper & Row.

Poole, S. (2000). *Trigger happy: Videogames and the entertainment revolution.* New York: Aracade Publishing.

Public Agenda. (1997). *Getting by: What American teenagers really think about their schools.* New York: Public Agenda.

Reich, R. B. (1992). *The work of nations.* New York: Vintage Books.

Rifkin, J. (1995). *The end of work: The decline of the global labor market and the dawn of the post-market era.* New York: Jeremy P. Tarcher.

Rifkin, J. (2000). *The age of access: The new culture of hypercapitalism where all of life is a paid-for experience.* New York: Jeremy Tarcher/Putnam.

Rose, F. (1997). Toward a class-cultural theory of social movements: Reinterpreting new social movements. *Sociological Forum, 12*(3), 461–93.

Rose, M. (1999). *Possible lives: The promise of public education in America.* New York: Penguin.

Schleppegrel, M., & Cecilia Colombi, M. (Eds.). (2002). *Developing advanced literacy in first and second languages: Meaning with power.* Mahwah, NJ: Erlbaum.

Scollon, R., & Scollon, S. B. K. (1981). *Narrative, literacy, and face in interethnic communication.* Norwood, NJ: Ablex.

Smith, H. (1995). *Rethinking America: A new game plan from American innovators: Schools, business, people, work.* New York: Random House.

Sowell, T. (1996). *The vision of the anointed: Self-congratulation as a basis for social policy.* New York: Basic Books.

Street, B. (1995). *Social literacies: Critical approaches to literacy in development, ethnography and education.* London: Longman.

Thurow, L. C. (1999). *Building wealth: The new rules for individuals, companies, and nations in a knowledge-based economy.* New York: Harper Collins.

von Mises, L. (1997). *Human action: A treatise on economics* (4th rev. ed). San Francisco: Fox & Wilkes.

Wenger, E. (1998). *Communities of practice: Learning, meaning, and identity.* Cambridge, UK: Cambridge University Press.

Wenger, E., McDermott, R., & Snyder, W. M. (2002). *Cultivating communities of practice.* Cambridge, MA: Harvard Business School Press.

Voices in Dialogue

Hybridity as Literacy, Literacy as Hybridity: Dialogic Responses to a Heteroglossic World

Alice A. Miano

> What is hybridization? A mixture of two social languages within the limits of a single utterance, an encounter, within the arena of an utterance, between two different linguistic consciousnesses, separated from one another by an epoch, by social differentiation, or by some other factor.
>
> – M. M. Bakhtin, (1981, p. 358)

Compiling this commentary seemed a unique assignment. True, students are often expected to contrast or critique various ideas, arguments, or literary forms in published works. However, for this commentary, we were asked to relate or otherwise make sense, not of texts seemingly congealed in print,[1] but of exchanges created through an ostensibly more tentative, transitory medium, e-mail. Texts produced for publication are generally expected to be developed, edited, and manicured with great care, but an e-mail may be dashed off with little time devoted to spelling or punctuation, let alone to ideas. Yet, despite such perceptions about print vs. electronic media, the ideas in the e-mails that served as sources for this commentary, e-mails from Gee, Kalman, Mahiri, and Sperling, were both thoughtful and thought provoking. At the same time, the process of reading early versions of the authors' contributions to this volume, posing questions to the authors, and then receiving feedback from them via e-mail highlighted for me both the hybrid and dialogic natures (Bakhtin, 1981), not only of e-mail, but also of the writing process itself (see also Brettschneider, this volume). In fact, as I wrote this piece, it occurred to me that it could be viewed as a consolidation of at least two already synthesized forms. On the one hand, it is an essay in the making whose sources for ideas include the texts produced by these authors, books, my own scribblings in notebooks, and oral

---

[1] I say "seemingly" because I consider the supposed permanence of print and of ideas expressed therein (Goody & Watt, 1968; Olson, 1977; Ong, 1982) to be one of the greatest illusions of modern times.

feedback from professors and classmates. On the other hand, it is a compilation of previously disconnected electronic texts, excerpts from various e-mails, now brought together here. This example, I believe, points to a larger phenomenon in which different forms in their emerging hybridity can potentially multiply into various and increasingly hybrid forms.

However, we must keep in mind that this phenomenon of hybridization, the joining of previously separate, stratified forms, may reach a point of invisibility, so that what we contend are hybrid forms today may tomorrow seem "standard" and "unitary" (Bakhtin, 1981, 1986). To provide one example, Bakhtin (1981, 1986) describes the novel as a hybrid yet self-contained, single utterance. From his description, in its early machinations, the novel may have been considered scandalously hybrid, but in everyday conceptions of the novel today, readers tend to focus on the unitary nature of the genre. Conversely, forms now recognized as hybrid may have become visibly so only in light of sudden or unusual circumstances that foreground previously backgrounded conditions (M. Sperling, personal communication, August 15, 2002). In the United States, for instance, civil liberties that we once took for granted are now being differentiated and challenged in the aftermath of September 11. In short, what once seemed hybrid forms (in language or society) may later be viewed as standard, unitary forms, and what once seemed standard and unitary may later be "unpacked" to reveal an underlying hybrid nature.[2] In both cases, the many explorations and elaborations on the theme of hybridity (or hybridization) by Bakhtin (1981, 1986) bring us to a deeper understanding of the multiple combinations and permutations of hybridity in language forms and the impact of this hybridity on linguistic identities. Bakhtin's explorations and elaborations on the theme of hybridity also bring us to a deeper understanding of the societies that produce these language forms and linguistic identities, and likewise are produced by them.

Literacy, in fact, is a case in point. By some it is viewed as a narrowly defined, unitary activity that relates to the production and reception of print only (Goody & Watt, 1968; Olson, 1977; Ong, 1982). Others, however, especially since the clarion call of Street (1984) to view it from an ideological perspective, deconstructed the notion of literacy attempting to reveal its many facets (Gee, 1996; New London Group, 1996; Reyes & Halcón, 2001). Gutiérrez, Baquedano-López, and Alvarez (2001), for instance, examined the hybrid nature of literacy. They argue that transformation, including literacy learning, is stimulated by hybridity in settings that encourage

---

[2] For ease of discussion, I have made the distinction between the viewing of forms as hybrid or unitary as if time were the only factor that might alter such a view. There are, of course, a myriad of social and cultural factors that might alter this perspective. Hybridity, as it were, is in the eye of the beholder.

hybrid language uses. Similarly, the New London Group (1996) speaks of "multiliteracies," a term that "signals multiple communication channels, hybrid text forms, new social relations, and the increasing salience of linguistic and cultural diversity" (Schultz & Hull, 2002, p. 26). The readings in this section, I believe, highlight these insights and point us toward a notion of hybridity in ever-expanding and multiplying forms, perhaps especially with respect to literacy, both conceptualized and actualized. Extrapolating somewhat on Bakhtin's notion, we may further adduce that spiraling hybridization is a predictable dialogic response in a heteroglossic world. As Gee states, "the older forms usually don't disappear. They get into a new set of relationships with each other and with the newer forms" (J. Gee, personal communication, March 6, 2002). The teachers in Mahiri (this volume), "Carmen" in Kalman (this volume), and "Almon" in Gee (this volume, following Lam, 2000) demonstrate some of the outgrowths of this spiraling hybridity, as "slipping into more literate places (among more literate people) opens opportunities for access to literacy" (J. Kalman, personal communication, March 7, 2002). All gain a measure of confidence with their newfound literacies. At the same time, however, Carmen, Mahiri's teachers, and the teachers in Sperling (this volume) also demonstrate that any process of hybridization may not be seamless or uncontested but instead may be challenged by the "centripetal forces" that seek to maintain a "unitary language" (Bakhtin, 1981).

The teachers in the course taught by Mahiri, for instance, present a clear picture of a setting in which hybrid language and social forms flourish, but do not go uncontested. The teachers are learning to become more comfortable with hybridity, both in terms of negotiating multiple literacies (including various technologies) and in terms of socially navigating among diverse cultures. These abilities, I would argue, are multiliteracies based on hybridity that will be increasingly essential, especially for teachers, as we delve further into these "new times." Further, technology-based literacies are not to be discounted.[3] As Mahiri notes, students can use electronic media in order to

create various textual products that . . . carry some of the same learning possibilities as creating written texts – i.e., the texts need to be composed, they need to have a thematic focus, they need to cohere. (J. Mahiri, personal communication, March 17, 2002)

In fact, Mahiri is currently pursuing research on "the notion of transferability between compositional (and cognitive) skills between different textual mediums like electronic texts and traditional written texts."

---

[3] Ong (1982), for instance, disregarded technology-based literacies as "secondary orality" or "post-literate orality," dichotomizing print and oral language and subordinating the latter.

Indeed, perhaps the richness of such technological media emanate from their intrinsically dialogical nature. As Mahiri explains,

technology is inherently dialogical. I think Bakhtin would agree with this. The nature of the dialogues will necessarily vary across mediums, but the essential premise of the dialogic is not limited to or by a particular medium. In this regard, it would be good to bring in the theories of Christina Haas from her book "Writing Technology" where she makes the critical point that all writing (and I would say all communications) systems require some level of technology. So, it's not just electronic systems that are renderings of technology. (J. Mahiri, personal communication, March 17, 2002)

In regard to embracing this hybridity, Mahiri notes a further benefit of electronic communication in the class that he taught:

I think there were ways that the electronic communications allowed students to deal with certain difficult issues easier than if we did not have access to this form of communication. It helped us open up dialogue on these issues and create some level of comfort with dealing with these issues, but we still needed to eventually face each other in class and in person to get the depth of discussion necessary. So, the technology created some additional possibilities, but it also had clear limitations too. I think the way we were able to communicate with each other electronically did help to deepen ties between class members. I tried to show a bit of this in the way the students responded to each other around an issue of race that one of the students raised. (Goody & Watt, 1968; Olson, 1977)

Hybrid forms of communication, then, likewise set the stage for a sharing of diverse ideas (Gutiérrez et al., 2001) and a deepening of the human bond between those who share in this diversity. Mahiri's classroom provides opportunities for transformation through the use of hybrid forms of expression, which likewise help foment assertions of hybrid forms of identity.

As Sperling (this volume) writes, however, the contradictions that emanate from the airing of such hybrid forms, ideas, or identities are frequently seen as undesirable. As such, transformation, as it occurs among Mahiri's group, for instance, is less likely to take place among the teachers of whom Sperling writes. Although Sperling's teachers likewise find themselves working in a variety of "contradictory environments" from which "contradictory perspectives" emerge (Sperling, this volume), their working environment, unlike Mahiri's classroom, does not generally provide an outlet in which to air and confront contradiction. Thus, even though

we all (human beings) shift all the time, . . . either to "fit in" to the social and cultural context that we find ourselves in or to try to shape context to fit our own identities of the moment. (M. Sperling, personal communication, August 15, 2002)

such processes may go unexplored in many classrooms, work environments, home environments, and societies at large. Instead, as Sperling further notes, we don't notice many contradictions largely because they are so much a part of our lives that they are invisible to us – we learn somehow to accommodate to them and to normalize them. For example, so-called "double standards" for gender or race are often based on theoretic contradictions about the nature of human beings, yet they can easily be normalized and therefore [made] invisible. (M. Sperling, personal communication, August 15, 2002)

Again, then, as Gutiérrez et al. (2001) suggest, and as the chapters of Mahiri and of Sperling likewise indicate, schools and education programs are at their best when they cultivate contexts that expose and confront the contradictions that arise from hybridity. In the same vein, denying the existence of hybridization or failing to cultivate an awareness of or ability to notice hybridization, an ability that I have argued is itself a literacy, leaves individuals, systems, and societies less prepared to face the challenges of the twenty-first century, that is, less prepared to face each other.[4]

Where Mahiri's and Sperling's chapters provide perspectives on the cultural worlds of teachers, Gee and Kalman, through "Almon" and "Carmen," give us glimpses of individual struggles vis-à-vis literacy. As with the two sets of teachers, Almon and Carmen likewise present contrasting cases with respect to hybridity and the clashes or contradictions it may engender. Almon is incorporating new electronic literacies into his life and gaining additional literacies as well, reading and writing in English. Carmen, however, is struggling with cultural and literate identities (Ferdman, 1990, 1991) in a community, at least in Carmen's eyes, not yet accustomed to the seemingly hybrid identity of someone who is poor but can also read and write. The mere act of writing her name on a form in the doctor's office places her "internally persuasive discourse" (Bakhtin, 1981) at odds with the "authoritative discourse" (Bakhtin, 1981) of the town, Mixquic, and the society in which she lives. As Kalman notes,

for the women of Mixquic to become literate and incorporate use of reading and writing into their language life, they have to believe that they can. That is an ideological condition, and it directly contradicts what they believe about themselves, what they have experienced, and what they think literacy is. Their ideas are not of spontaneous generation; they are socially constructed and part of authoritative versions of what reading and writing is, who gets to do it, who does not. So "fooling" someone, which is Carmen's word, is like pulling a fast one: not only on the others who witness her literacy use (and thus see her as someone who can fill out her own form and therefore is not illiterate), but herself as well. She is still working on the idea that she can be a reader or writer. Her internally persuasive discourse is at odds

---

4 Bakhtin (1981, 1986), of course, reminds us that the "unitary" and "centripetal forces" that act within language and society will continuously work against the "centrifugal forces" from which hybridization emerges. However, the objects of these terms, as Sperling and Gee have pointed out (see above, and footnotes 2 and 3), are relative to their social and cultural contexts.

with what she has known, the authoritative (or hegemonic, to use Gramsci's term) version of literacy. (J. Kalman, personal communication, March 7, 2002)

As Kalman further explains,

to talk about becoming literate, we must situate our comments in specific lives, times, and places. For the women of Mixquic, we have to take into account what it means for them to face such a multilayered challenge: it challenges what they believe, what they have lived and therefore what they know. As the world has changed around them, some of these beliefs have become shaken and opened up the possibility of believing and experiencing otherwise. (J. Kalman, personal communication, March 7, 2002)

Despite the discourse of seemingly static identities we use to classify each other, then, these identities can be challenged, as Carmen demonstrates, despite the complexity of the endeavor. We must keep in mind, however, as Kalman does and as Bakhtin reminds us, that the challenge is not merely an external one in which an individual clashes with society. In addition, a microcosm of such a clash also churns within the individual. Carmen, when we meet her, finds herself at such a stage. She has not yet fully accepted the notion of a poor woman who can read and write, but she currently challenges it.

Almon, however, once labeled a "low-achieving student" in school (Gee, this volume), has used electronic technologies to transcend the "identity challenge," if you will. Through the creation of a website and frequent chats with online "key pals," Almon has learned the art of tailoring the expression of his identity toward others in an entrepreneurial fashion, an activity that itself seems a hybrid form of Bakhtin's (1981) concept of addressivity. Gee elaborates on this link:

Shape-shifting is certainly related to Bakhtin's notion of addressivity, though the person is addressing not just others, but a whole conception of the world and selfhood in that world. That is, one sees the world as a fast changing, highly risky space that requires the ability to see oneself as a set of resources for – almost a kit for – changing and transforming shapes to fit into ever new circumstances. . . . Shape-shifting is not talking just about adaptation, but how one sees oneself. A shape-shifting portfolio person sees him or herself as an ever re-arrangeable set of skills and experiences that can be shaped anew for each occasion, job, and career move in order to take on a new identity. . . . In the new capitalism – in some spheres and especially for elites – stability is death. Some have gone so far (e.g., Emily Martin) as to suggest that "new times" so value (again in certain spheres and for certain people) flexibility that we will revalue how we think of such labile people as those held to have "ADHD" and "manic depression." Perhaps we will see these as "advantages" and not (just?) diseases. (J. Gee, personal communication, March 6, 2002)

As with Mahiri's teachers, then, Almon's use of new technologies has fomented growth and transformation in terms of his identity and his ability to transcend the limiting identities that, in this case, school officials once placed on him. For, as Gee notes, identity, like language itself and the world that engenders it,

is most certainly heteroglossic.... [O]ne's virtual, real-world, and projective identities constantly interact and can change and transform each other. (J. Gee, personal
communication, March 6, 2002)

In the cases of Almon and Mahiri's teachers, then, the heteroglossia of new technologies seems to have provided both a springboard and a cushion for the voicing of hybrid identities, which act both to embolden expression and likewise to soften the clash of conflicting identities. Sperling, in fact, reflects on the uneasiness of such a clash:

Taking on hybrid roles, if you will, reflects living with complexity and ambiguity,
and no one particularly relishes dealing with the nuances and shades of gray that
complexity and ambiguity necessitate. Thus the challenge. The pay-off...is a deeper
understanding of what it means to be exquisitely human.(M. Sperling, personal
communication, November 11, 2002)

It may be, then, that in these "new times," at least for some, it will be machines and new technologies, with their hybrid, dialogic natures, that help us to more fully realize the expression of our humanity. Mere access to technology, however, be it the computer of Almon or the pen and paper of Carmen, is not enough. Rather, as Gee (this volume) following Wenger (1998) asserts, the sense of a "community of practice," in which knowledge is shared and practices carried out among community members, appears to be the context in which our heteroglossic tendencies can emerge and interact, providing a safe haven in which hybridities can flourish and we can learn to see contradictions, as Sperling suggests, as not so contradictory, but instead transformative, after all.

References

Bakhtin, M. M. (1981). *The dialogic imagination.* Austin: University of Texas Press.
Bakhtin, M. M. (1986). *Speech genres and other late essays.* Austin: University of Texas Press.
Ferdman, B. (1990). Literacy and cultural identity. *Harvard Educational Review, 60*(2):181–204.
Ferdman, B. (1991). Becoming literate in a multiethnic society. In E. Jennings & A. Purves (Eds.), *Literate systems and individual lives: Perspectives on literacy and schooling.* Albany: State University of New York Press.
Gee, J. P. (1996). *Social linguistics and literacies: Ideology in discourse* (2nd ed.). London: Routledge Falmer.
Goody, J., & Watt, I. (1968). The consequences of literacy. In J. Goody (Ed.), *Literacy in traditional societies* (pp. 27–68). Cambridge, UK: Cambridge University Press.
Gutiérrez, K., Baquedano-López, P., & Alvarez, H. H. (2001). Literacy as hybridity: Moving beyond bilingualism in urban classrooms. In M. L. Reyes & J. J. Halcón

(Eds.), *The best for our children: Critical perspectives on literacy for Latino students.* New York: Teachers College Press.

Lam, W. S. E. (2000). L2 Literacy and the design of the self: A case study of a teenager writing on the Internet. *TESOL Quarterly, 34*(3):457–82.

New London Group. (1996). A pedagogy of multiliteracies: Designing social futures. *Harvard Educational Review, 66,* 60–92. Reprinted in B. Cope & M. Kalantzis (Eds.), Multiliteracies: Literacy learning and the design of social futures (pp. 9–37). London: Routledge, 1999.

Olson, D. R. (1977). From utterance to text: The bias of language in speech and writing. *Harvard Education Review, 47:* 257–81.

Ong, W. J. (1982). *Orality and literacy: The technologizing of the word.* New York: Routledge.

Reyes, M. L., & Halcón, J. J. (2001). Introduction. In M. L. Reyes & J. J. Halcón (Eds.), *The best for our children: Critical perspectives on literacy for Latino students.* New York: Teachers College Press.

Schultz, K., & Hull, G. (2002). Locating literacy theory in out-of-school contexts. In G. Hull & K. Schultz (Eds.), *School's out: Bridging out-of-school literacies with classroom practice.* New York: Teachers College Press.

Street, B. (1984). *Literacy in theory and practice.* Cambridge, UK: Cambridge University Press.

Wenger, E. (1998). *Communities of practice: Learning, meaning, and identity.* Cambridge, UK: Cambridge University Press.

PART IV

A CLOSING THOUGHT ON BAKHTINIAN
PERSPECTIVES

13

The Process of Ideological Becoming

Gary Saul Morson

Sarah Freedman and Arnetha Ball describe learning as a dialogic process. It is not merely a transmission of knowledge, but an activity in which whole selves are formed and acquire new capacities for development. We live in a world of enormous cultural diversity, and the various languages and points of view – ideologies in Bakhtin's sense – of students have become a fact that cannot be ignored. Teachers need to enter into a dialogue with those points of view and to help students do the same. For difference may best be understood not as an obstacle but as an opportunity.

The range of "authoritative" and "innerly persuasive discourses" in our classrooms appears to be growing along with our cultural diversity. Freedman and Ball observe: "This rich and complex 'contact zone' inside the classroom yields plentiful opportunity for students to decide what will be internally persuasive for them, and consequently for them to develop their ideologies. This diversity presents both challenges and opportunities as teachers seek to guide their students on this developmental journey" (pp. 8–9, this volume). The journey they have in mind does not so much lead to a particular goal as establish an ever-enriching process of learning.

Freedman and Ball's approach grows out of Bakhtin's key concepts, especially one that has been largely neglected in research on him: "ideological becoming" (see Chapter 1, this volume). The implications of the essays in this volume therefore extend well beyond educational theory and practice to the humanities and social sciences generally. How does a thinking person– and we are all thinking people – develop? What happens when ideas, embodied in specific people with particular voices, come into dialogic contact? What factors guide the creation of a point of view on the world? The specific problematic of pedagogy serves as a lens to make the broader implications of such questions clearer.

AUTHORITY AND TESTING

How does a person develop a point of view on the world, a set of attitudes for interpreting and evaluating it? How systematic is that point of view? Is our fundamental take on the world a philosophy with implicit doctrines or is it more like a set of inclinations and a way of probing? Perhaps it is not one, but a collection of ways of probing, a panoply of skills and habits, which a person tries out one after another the way in which one may, in performing a physical task, reach for one tool after another? What does our point of view have to do with our sense of ourselves, whether as individuals or as members of groups? What role does formal education play in acquiring and shaping it? What happens when contrary evidence confronts us or when the radical uncertainty of the world impinges on us? Whatever that "point of view" is, how does it change over time?

In any given culture or subculture, there tends to be what Bakhtin would call an "authoritative" perspective. However, the role of that perspective is not necessarily authoritarian. Despite Bakhtin's experience as a Soviet citizen, where the right perspective on just about all publicly identified perspectives was held to be already known and certain, he was well aware that outside that circle of presumed certainty life was still governed by opinion. It is not just that rival ideologies – Christian, liberal, and many others – were still present; beyond that, each individual's experiences led to half-formed but strongly held beliefs that enjoyed no formal expression. Totalitarianism was surely an aspiration of the Soviet and other such regimes, but it could never realize its ideal of uniformity – "the new Soviet man" who was all of a piece – for some of the same reasons it could not make a centrally planned economy work. There is always too much contingent, unexpected, particular, local, and idiosyncratic, with a historical or personal background that does not fit.

Bakhtin may be viewed as the great philosopher of all that does not fit. He saw the world as irreducibly messy, unsystematizable, and contingent, and he regarded it as all the better for that. For life to have meaning, it must possess what he called "surprisingness." If individual people are to act morally, they cannot displace their responsibility onto some systematic ideology, whether Marxist, Christian, or any other. What I do now is not reducible to any ethical, political, or metaphysical system; and I – each "I" – must take responsibility for his or her acts at this moment. As Bakhtin liked to say, there is "no alibi."

Authoritative words in their fully expressed form purport to offer an alibi. They say, like Dostoevsky's Grand Inquisitor: we speak the truth and you need not question, only obey, for your conscience to be at rest. Yet, every authoritative word is spoken or heard in a milieu of difference. It may try to insulate itself from dialogue with reverential tones, a special script, and all the other signs of the authority fused to it, but at the margins dialogue waits with a challenge: you may be right, but you have to *convince* me. Once the authoritative word responds to that challenge, it ceases to be *fully* authoritative. To be sure, it may still command considerable deference by virtue of its past, its moral aura, and its omnipresence. But it has ceased to be free from dialogue and its authority has changed from unquestioned to dialogically tested. Every educator crosses this line when he or she gives reasons for a truth.

My daughter once had a math teacher who, when asked why a certain procedure was used to solve an equation, would reply, "because some old, dead guy said so." Of course, no answer could be further from the spirit of mathematics, where logic counts for everything and authority for nothing. Nobody proves the Pythagorean theorem by saying Pythagoras said so. Compare this reply with actually showing the logic of a procedure so the student understands the "why." In that case, one immediately admits that there must be a good reason for proceeding in a certain way, and that it needs to be shown. The procedure does not end up as less sure because of this questioning; quite the contrary. Rather, questioning is seen as intrinsic to mathematics itself, which enjoys its authority precisely because it has survived such questioning.

Even in fields that do not admit of mathematical proof, an authoritative word does not necessarily lose all authority when questioning enters into it. We can give no mathematically sure reason why democracy is preferable to dictatorship or market economies are generally more productive than command economies. But we can give reasons, which admit the possibilities of challenges we had not foreseen and may have to think about. Education and all inquiry are fundamentally different when the need for reasons is acknowledged and when questioning becomes part of the process of learning. Truth becomes dialogically tested and forever testable.

In short, authoritative words may or may not be authoritarian. In the Soviet Union, authoritarian words were the norm and questioning was seen as suspect. One no more questioned Marxism-Leninism than one questioned the law of gravity (a common comparison, suggesting that each was equally sure). What the Party said was right because it was the outcome of sure historical laws guaranteeing the correctness of its rulings. Education reflected this spirit. Bakhtin's embrace of dialogue, then, challenged not so much the economic or historical theories the regime propounded, but its very concept of truth and the language of truth it embraced. Dialogue by its very nature invites questioning, thrives on it, demands it.

It follows from Bakhtin's argument that nonauthoritarian authoritative words are not necessarily weaker than authoritarian ones. After all, one may believe something all the more because one has questioned it, provided that defenders have been willing to answer and have been more or less cogent in their defense. They need not answer all objections perfectly – we are often convinced with qualifications, with a "just in case," with "loopholes."

However, they must demonstrate that the authority is based on generally sound reasons. Morever, for many, enormous persuasive power lies in the very fact that the authoritative belief is so widely held. Everyone speaks it, even if with ironizing quotation marks.

An authoritative word of this nonauthoritarian kind functions not as a voice speaking the Truth, but as a voice speaking *the one point of view that must be attended to*. It may be contested, rejected, or modified, the way in which church dogmas are modified over time by believers, but it cannot be ignored. Think of Huck Finn (discussed by Mark Dressman, this volume). Even when he cannot bring himself to turn in Jim as a runaway slave, he accepts the authority of the social voice telling him that such an action would be right. He does not question that voice, just realizes he will not follow it and will do "wrong." Much of the moral complexity of this book lies in Huck's self-questioning, as he does what we believe to be right but what he thinks of as wrong; and if we read this book sensitively, we may ask ourselves how much of our own behavior is Huckish in this respect. Perhaps our failure to live up to our ideals bespeaks our intuition without overt expression that there is something wrong with those ideals. What Huck demonstrates is that there may be a wisdom, even a belief system, in behavior itself: we always know more than we know, and our moral sensitivity may be different from, and wiser than, our professed beliefs.

OUR OWN AUTHORITATIVE WORDS

The basic power of an authoritative voice comes from its status as the one that everyone hears. Everyone has heard that democracy is good and apartheid is bad, that the environment needs preserving, that church must not be merged with state; and people who spend their lives in an academic environment may add many more to the list. In our academic subculture, we are, almost all of us, persuaded of the rightness of greater economic equality, of plans for inclusion and affirmative action, of abortion rights, of peace, of greater efforts to reach out to all the people in the world in all their amazing diversity. These are our authoritative voices, and these, too, we may accept either because they are simply not to be questioned or because we have sought out intelligent opponents who have questioned them and have thought about, if not ultimately accepted, their answers. Again, educators know the moment when a student from a background different from ours questions one of our beliefs and we experience the temptation to reply like that math teacher. Thinking of ourselves as oppositional, we often forget that we, too, have our own authoritative discourse and must work to remember that, in a world of difference, authority may not extend to those unlike us.

The testable authoritative voice: we hear it always, and though some may disagree with it, they cannot ignore it. Its nonauthoritarian power is based above all on its ubiquity. In a society that is relatively open to diverse values, that minimal, but still significant, function of an authoritative voice is the most important one. It demands not adherence but attention. And such a voice is likely to survive far longer than an authoritarian voice whose rejection is necessarily its destruction. We have all these accounts of Soviet dissidents – say, Solzhenitsyn – who tell their story as a "narrative of rethinking" (to use Christian Knoeller's phrase): they once believed in Communist ideology, but events caused them to raise some questions that by their nature could not be publicly voiced, and that silence itself proved most telling. You can hear silence if it follows a pistol shot. If silence does not succeed in ending private questioning, the word that silence defends is decisively weakened. The story of Soviet dissidents is typically one in which, at some point, questioning moved from a private, furtive activity accompanied by guilt to the opposite extreme, a clear rejection in which the authoritative voice lost all hold altogether. Vulnerability accompanies too much power.

But in more open societies, and in healthier kinds of individual development, an authoritative voice of the whole society, or of a particular community (like our own academic community), still sounds, still speaks to us in our minds. In fact, we commonly see that people who have questioned and rejected an authoritative voice find that it survives within them as a possible alternative, like the minority opinion in a court decision. When they are older, they discover that experience has vindicated some part of what they had summarily rejected. Perhaps the authoritative voice had more to it than we thought when young? Now that we are teachers, perhaps we see some of the reasons for practices we objected to? Can we, then, combine in a new practice both the practices of our teachers and the new insights we have had? When we do, a flexible authoritative word emerges, one that has become to a great extent an innerly persuasive one. By a lengthy process, the word has, with many changes, become our own, and our own word has in the process acquired the intonations of authority.

In much the same way, we react to the advice of our parents. At some point it may seem dated, no more than what an earlier generation unfortunately thought, or we may greet it with the sign of regret that our parents have forgotten what they experienced when our age. However, the dialogue goes on. At a later point, we may say, you know, there was wisdom in what our parents said, only why did they express it so badly? If only I had known! We may even come to the point where we express some modified form of parental wisdom in a convincing voice. We *translate* it into our own idiolect, confident that we will not make the mistakes of our parents when we talk to our children. Then our children listen, and find our own idiolect, to which we have devoted such painful ideological and verbal work, hopelessly dated, and the process may start again.

It is always a difficult moment when we realize that our own voice is now the authority, especially because we have made it different, persuasive in its own terms, not like our parents' voice. When we reflect on how our children see us, we may even realize that our parents' authoritative words may not have been the product of blind acceptance, but the result of a process much like our own. They may have done the same thing we did – question, reject, adapt, arrive at a new version – and that rigid voice of authority we heard from them was partly in our own ears. Can we somehow convey to our students our own words so they do not sound so rigid? We all think we can. But so did our parents (and other authorities).

DIALOGUE, LAUGHTER, SURPRISE

Bakhtin viewed the whole process of "ideological" (in the sense of ideas and values, however unsystematic) development as an endless dialogue. As teachers, we find it difficult to avoid a voice of authority, however much we may think of ours as the rebel's voice, because our rebelliousness against society at large speaks in the authoritative voice of our subculture. We speak the language and thoughts of academic educators, even when we imagine we are speaking in no jargon at all, and that jargon, inaudible to us, sounds with all the overtones of authority to our students. We are so prone to think of ourselves as fighting oppression that it takes some work to realize that we ourselves may be felt as oppressive and overbearing, and that our own voice may provoke the same reactions that we feel when we hear an authoritative voice with which we disagree.

So it is often helpful to think back on the great authoritative oppressors and reconstruct *their* self-image: helpful, but often painful. I remember, many years ago, when, as a recent student rebel and activist, I taught a course on "The Theme of the Rebel" and discovered, to my considerable chagrin, that many of the great rebels of history were the very same people as the great oppressors. There is a famous exchange between Erasmus and Luther, who hoped to bring the great Dutch humanist over to the Reformation, but Erasmus kept asking Luther how he could be so *certain* of so many doctrinal points. We must accept a few things to be Christians at all, Erasmus wrote, but surely beyond that there must be room for us highly fallible beings to disagree. Luther would have none of such tentativeness. He knew, he was sure. The Protestant rebels were, for a while, far more intolerant than their orthodox opponents. Often enough, the oppressors are the ones who present themselves and really think of themselves as liberators. Certainty that one knows the root cause of evil: isn't that itself often the root cause?

We know from Tsar Ivan the Terrible's letters denouncing Prince Kurbsky, a general who escaped to Poland, that Ivan saw himself as someone who had been oppressed by noblemen as a child and pictured himself as the great rebel against traditional authority when he killed masses of people or destroyed whole towns. There is something in the nature of maximal rebellion against authority that produces ever greater intolerance, unless one is very careful. For the skills of fighting or refuting an oppressive power are not those of openness, self-skepticism, or real dialogue. In preparing for my course, I remember my dismay at reading Hitler's *Mein Kampf* and discovering that his self-consciousness was precisely that of the rebel speaking in the name of oppressed Germans, and that much of his amazing appeal – otherwise so inexplicable – was to the German sense that they were rebelling victims. In our time, the Serbian Communist and nationalist leader Slobodan Milosevic exploited much the same appeal. Bakhtin surely knew that Communist totalitarianism, the Gulag, and the unprecedented censorship were constructed by rebels who had come to power. His favorite writer, Dostoevsky, used to emphasize that the worst oppression comes from those who, with the rebellious psychology of "the insulted and humiliated," have seized power – unless they have somehow cultivated the value of dialogue, as Lenin surely had not, but which Eva, in the essay by Knoeller about teaching *The Autobiography of Malcolm X*, surely had.

Rebels often make the worst tyrants because their word, the voice they hear in their consciousness, has borrowed something crucial from the authoritative word it opposed, and perhaps exaggerated it: the aura of righteous authority. If one's ideological becoming is understood as a struggle in which one has at last achieved the truth, one is likely to want to impose that truth with maximal authority; and rebels of the next generation may proceed in much the same way, in an ongoing spiral of intolerance. By contrast, if one's rebellion against an authoritative word is truly dialogic, that is unlikely to happen, or to be subject to more of a self-check if it does. Then one questions one's own certainties and invites skepticism, lest one become what one has opposed. One may even step back and laugh at oneself.

Laughter at oneself invites the perspective of the other. Laughter is implicitly pluralist. Instead of looking at one's opponents as the unconditionally wrong, one imagines how one sounds to them. Regarding earlier authorities, one thinks: that voice of authority, it is not my voice, but perhaps it has something to say, however wrongly put. It comes from a specific experience, which I must understand. I will correct it, but to do that I must measure it, test it, against my own experience. Dialogue is a process of real testing, and one of the characteristics of a genuine test is that the result is not guaranteed. It may turn out that sometimes the voice of earlier authority turns out to be right on some point. Well, we will incorporate that much into our own "innerly persuasive voice." Once one has done this, once one has allowed one's own evolving convictions to be tested by experience and by other convictions, then one may allow the dialogue to continue.

When someone disagrees with us, what do we do? Bakhtin liked to say that in rhetoric (in the narrow sense) there are the unconditionally innocent and unconditionally guilty, which means that the point of an exchange is to destroy the other's point of view and convert him or her, or at least any audience, to ours. However, in dialogue, the destruction of the opponent destroys the very dialogic sphere in which the word lives. One wants not to destroy but to learn from an opponent, to enrich one's own perspective by the exchange. We see the value of realizing how our partial perspective – and all perspectives are partial, in both senses of the word – may appear from the perspective of another, and that may be unsettling. We also see the value of reexamining our own point of view when it becomes clear how strange it may look to another. Part of what a multicultural environment can provide is a constant occasion for seeing, not just that others are different, but also that we are different. In much the same way, one realizes that it is not just those other people who speak with an accent (see Freedman and Ball, this volume).

Others differ from us, moreover, in *unpredictable* ways – ways that our own culture has not even given us terms for. For other cultures are not just the inverse of our own, and if we assume that they are simply carrying our own oppositional attitudes, we are not hearing them. We hear them when we recognize that their concerns, values, and discourse may not fit into our own map, even as the negative pole: we hear them when they begin to *surprise* us.

AUTHENTICITY AND DISAGREEMENT

In *Anna Karenina*, Konstantin Levin, finds himself at a dinner party held by Sviazhsky, a proper liberal with all the currently progressive values held by the educated classes. Levin rapidly becomes frustrated and irritable, because he is trying to work out a problem, but everything Sviazhsky says is utterly predictable and therefore useless. Levin's problem was a common one: why is it that all his attempts, and those of other landowners, to increase productivity and improve the condition of the peasants by borrowing English machines and copying English agricultural practices, either fail to increase yield or actually cause it to decline? Why does what works in England fail in Russia? The failure is evident even to Sviazhsky, whose German accountant has pointed out that his yield on new capital is actually negative, but Sviazhsky still keeps repeating the same formulas and continues to cite "the authority of . . . acknowledged scientific truth or of a currently fashionable book," as Bakhtin puts it.[1] In fact, Sviazhsky does not really think seriously about any topic. If you have heard his views on foreign policy and the peasants, you know his beliefs on education and all other public questions. Like editorials in *The New York Times*, his views are all precisely those that sophisticated people are supposed to believe. To put the point more accurately, holding such beliefs is itself the mark of sophistication.

---

[1] M. M. Bakhtin, *The dialogic imagination: Four essays*, ed. Michael Holquist trans. Caryl Emerson and Michael Holquist (Austin: University of Texas Press, 1981), 342–3. Further references are to DI.

In such a situation, holding the right views is as necessary as wearing the right hat, as Tolstoy says of another character. Defending the wrong views, or even mentioning evidence questioning the right views, becomes a social *faux pas*. Levin wants to talk about the specifics of agriculture, based on his experience with farming. But Sviazhsky answers with the specifics of progressive ideology, based on the experience of social conversation.

From a dialogic perspective, Sviazhsky's predictability is disheartening because there is no otherness from which to learn. Thus, Levin gravitates to someone else, a person with whom he does not agree, but who has arrived at his views by actually reflecting in unpredictable ways on his own experience. This person, who is referred to simply as "the reactionary landowner," utters sentiments that are plainly out of keeping with progressive opinion. He even justifies serfdom (which had been abolished in Russia a decade and a half before).

Sviazhsky reacts with amusement at the landowner's outmoded beliefs. Winking at Levin, Sviazhsky "looked with smiling eyes, and even made a faint gesture of irony to him."[2] In today's discourse, the gesture might be translated as "Get a load of him!" This reaction bothers Levin because, however much he may disagree with the reactionary landowner's conclusions, he recognizes that the landowner has reflected seriously on his own experience, not just learned what he is supposed to believe, as Sviazhsky has:

The landowner unmistakably spoke his own individual thought – a thing that rarely happens – and a thought to which he had been brought not by a desire of finding some exercise for an idle brain, but a thought which had grown up out of the conditions of his life, which he had brooded over in the solitude of his village, and had considered in its every aspect. (AK, 350)

The landowner has responded to specific "conditions of his life," whereas Sviazhsky has accepted a prefabricated progressive ideology. Levin has nothing to learn from the latter because he already knows it and has tried it, but the landowner's opinions allow him to reflect on the specific conditions that have generated them. Perhaps those conditions may show what his own efforts have overlooked. The point (which Tolstoy never tired of making) is that there is a difference between having opinions authorized as sympathetic to the peasants and actually helping them, which may require rejecting some of those opinions when they have been shown not to work. The dialogue suggests a question: are we interested in being reformers, speaking like reformers, and enjoying the good feelings that come with professing proper views, or in actually conducting effective reforms? Anyone really interested in helping others will at some point face this choice. Levin is always arriving at some gathering with views that are totally unexpected. He is surprising;

---

[2] Leo Tolstoy, *Anna Karenina*, the Garnett translation revised by Leonard J. Kent and Nina Berberova (New York: Random House, 1965), 350. Further references are to AK.

and in dialogue he wants to hear the surprising, which may provide a clue to a problem.

What Levin sees in the landowner is the mark of authenticity: thought generated by specific lived conditions. Once Levin has understood those conditions, he can reflect on them and enrich his own thoughts. In Bakhtin's terminology, the landowner's voice becomes part of his inner speech. From now on, he can imagine what the landowner *might* say to some new idea of his and can test that idea against those imagined objections. This is one way we really learn from people different from ourselves: we incorporate their voices *as living presences* within us.

TRANSLATION

In much the same way, when academics teach literature in a dialogic spirit, what they should be after is enriching students with the living voices of others. The voice of the author – of Mark Twain or Tolstoy or Malcolm X – should be felt so palpably that the student can freely *improvise* with it. Let some new situation arise and then try to hear what Twain might have said: when one can do that, one really possesses an author. Or, to switch metaphors, one adds a new way of seeing the world and so has gone from monocular to binocular vision.

In the case of novelists, one can go one step further and incorporate the voice of a compelling character into one's inner speech as well. There is much to be gained when Huck, as well as Twain, speaks within us about things Huck never knew about. As so many of the essays in this volume point out, such appropriation can only happen when students learn actively, participating in the debate, sounding out the voices of characters. Huck lives! As someone who teaches novels all the time, I found especially impressive the experiments undertaken by the contributors to the present volume to make characters' real presences within the lives and thinking of students. When one can, as Bakhtin liked to say, "draw dotted lines" – imagine what a character would say in new circumstances – one has engaged in an activity that allows one to attend with more acumen to voices in real life.

Contrary to what is so often said, it is important for students to read works about people radically different from themselves as long as the voices of those different people can live within them. It is not necessary to teach *The Catcher in the Rye* to get teenagers to love reading. On the contrary, sheer difference can be fascinating, as the phenomenal appeal of Harry Potter to American children who never saw an English school, much less a wizard, attests. I think it is a mistake to assign too much reading about people just like the students. The best way to get students to improve their reading is to inspire them to *want* to read something by engaging their imagination, and we are all fascinated with difference and with imagining ourselves in an alien but fascinating world. Who has not seen a faltering young reader making his or her way through *Harry Potter and the Sorcerer's Stone*?

Students can learn to hear voices of people very different from themselves and imagine themselves in their situation. Of course, if the situation is very different, the teacher may need to help the student *translate* the work by finding analogous situations in their own lives. What one must avoid is what is too often done, teaching *Anna Karenina* or *Huck Finn* as "documents" of other times: if only divorce laws then had been as progressive as they are now, how Anna's fate would be different. Such a smug reading places a distance between us and the characters. We look down on them, but do not learn from them. Instead, we must let the characters speak to us, imagine what they would say about our lives, and then engage in a real dialogue with no guarantee that our views will have the upper hand.

Ask students to imagine how similar moral problems could arise in our changed circumstances. In the case of Levin's conversation with Sviazhsky, for instance, it would not be hard to imagine a social problem that some address like Sviazhsky, with canned progressive answers, whereas others, like Levin, try to probe more deeply after seeing why those answers, although well intentioned, overlook too much. Why, after laughing at Sviazhsky, we may even realize that sometimes we ourselves speak like him. When students learn to engage in this way with a novel, it and its characters come to live within them. Men and women of the past and of very different cultures populate their minds, and the ideas of other times or places figure in their thinking not as dead facts or propositions but as living voices with which they may converse.

Learning to hear difference, to enter into it, becomes excellent practice for doing so in real life. All great novelists have known as much, which is why they make such effort to create a variety of voices and perspectives and to render it possible to identify with characters utterly unlike the author or readers. The point of teaching how a narrator is not necessarily to be identified with the author – how the narrator may be, as the jargon goes, "unreliable" – should be to show how learning means attending to others, including those from cultural and intellectual backgrounds foreign to us (see Freedman and Ball, this volume). We are all narrators, after all, and we hear narrations all the time. In life as in novels, a narrator does not have to be reliable or authoritative in order to be worth hearing and learning from. We can often learn a great deal by just infusing ourselves with a narrator's take on, or even *mis*take about, a situation. However, to do so we must enter into the narrator's perspective and imagine what it would be like to feel and see and speak in the narrator's manner.

LANGUAGES AND LEARNING

In Russia, the educated and the peasants were separated by an enormous cultural gap, much greater than that existing between social classes elsewhere in Europe. Due to Russia's rapid Westernization under Peter the

Great, which affected only the aristocrats, Russia soon had two cultural nations, observing entirely different customs and seeing the world in very different ways. Whenever an aristocrat or educated person confronts a peasant in a classic Russian novel, this difference becomes central, and so many of these scenes become comedies or tragedies of misunderstanding. In the early nineteenth century, aristocrats were raised speaking French as a first language (as any reader of *War and Peace* will recall), and so the two nations literally spoke different languages. For a while, the very act of writing in Russian was already a statement.

Thus, the problems we have come to regard as multicultural were present in Russia to an exaggerated degree even among people of the same religion and ethnic stock. Yet, Russia, although an extreme case, is not unique: we can recover a time when speaking Anglo-Saxon rather than French was a culturally charged act in England and speaking Czech, rather than German, was a bold thing for an educated Czech to do. Think of the role of an imperial language like English in India or French in much of Africa today, or even of the dominant local language over many smaller rivals in a multiethnic African or Asian country. Even when that kind of language difference does not obtain, great differences in "languages" (in Bakhtin's sense of modes of speaking and thinking) may remain – differences that carry with them important differences in worldview. As the essays in this volume attest, language and dialect difference is important not just linguistically, but also ideologically (see Freedman and Ball, this volume). Levin differs from Sviazhsky because he regards such differences as something to learn from and not just as the mark of superstition or backwardness that needs to be educated away. He knows that the peasants have something to teach him, and he learns to improve agriculture when he begins actually listening to them and trying to improve conditions by starting from their perspective.

SCHOOLS AND SCREAMING FITS

We see the difference between Sviazhsky's and Levin's approach when the conversation turns to schools. Sviazhsky wants to ignore the multicultural question entirely. He is motivated by a progressivist and universalist ideology, according to which peasants are the same as aristocrats, but at a lower level. He wants, benevolently, to teach them as much as they can learn about the knowledge that the educated classes possess, but he cannot imagine that, even in farming, which the peasants do every day of their lives, they have anything to teach him. Sviazhsky's explanation for why agricultural reforms fail is that Russian peasants are less educated than European ones, and so one needs to school the peasants and make them into appropriate objects of reform.

The idea that what the peasants needed was schools was a truism of the time, a view one would not even think to question, which is just what tempted Tolstoy to question it. Tolstoy had himself set up schools for peasants and, as Levin knew that received opinion about agriculture was wanting, Tolstoy knew the same about education. Tolstoy was, as people liked to say, a "*nyetovshchik*" (one who says "*nyet*," or no, to received opinion). Levin clearly is voicing the author's skepticism when expressing his own.

Levin asks, just *how* are we to educate the peasants? What he has in mind is the specifics of education – exactly what will be taught, and how? Is the same education that one would give an aristocrat what the peasants need and want? If so, why do peasants refuse to send their children to the schools that do exist? Perhaps we need first to determine what *they* think they need and then, with our superior knowledge of what is available, find a way to satisfy *those* needs better than they could do themselves? In our terms, that would mean a dialogic approach to the curriculum, one that respects different cultures, values, and ways of life. It would be, to adopt Carol Lee's concept, a "hybrid language approach."

Such questions have never crossed Sviazhsky's mind. When Levin asks, "But how are we to educate the people?", Sviazhsky replies with a canned answer, "To educate the people three things are needed: schools, schools, and schools" (AK, 356). We recognize in this witticism the voice of authoritative opinion, constantly repeated, the pedagogic equivalent to our own saw that makes real estate valuable is location, location, and location. Levin cannot get him to appreciate that not just schools but the right kind of schools really matter. Again, dialogue with Sviazhsky is impossible and Levin recognizes that he is encountering one of the superstitions of the educated.

For the educated have opinions they accept entirely without question even when experience refutes them, no less than peasants do. We call superstition the untenable beliefs of others. Levin tries to make this point by telling a story:

The day before yesterday I met a peasant woman in the evening with a little baby, and asked her where she was going. She said she was going to the village sorceress; her boy had screaming fits, so she was taking him to be doctored. I asked, 'Why, how does the wise woman cure screaming fits?' 'She puts the child on the hen roost and repeats some charm . . . ' (AK, 357)

Missing the point of the story, Sviazhsky interrupts to reply: " 'Well, you're saying it yourself! What's needed to prevent her from taking her child to the hen roost to cure it of screaming fits is just. . . . 'Sviazhsky said, smiling good-humoredly" (AK, 357). The good-humored smile represents the confident sense that all proper opinion is behind him; it is what insulates him from dialogue. We have all encountered that smile when asking a real question, answered automatically with the smirk of those who are in the know. As teachers, perhaps the most important thing we can do is to avoid accompanying an answer with such a smile or smirk.

If we are inclined to respond to Levin's story as Sviazhsky does, by saying that the peasant woman's superstition is just why she needs our schools, Levin's answer to this interruption pertains to us as well:

"Oh, no!" said Levin with annoyance, "that method of doctoring I mean merely as a simile for doctoring the people with schools. The people are poor and ignorant – that we see as surely as the peasant woman sees the baby is ill because it screams. But in what way this trouble of poverty and ignorance is to be cured by schools is as incomprehensible as how the hen roost affects the screaming. What has to be cured is what makes him poor." (AK, 357)

Sviazhsky isn't thinking, isn't interested in thinking: he cares about sub-scribing to the right opinion. He responds by citing a (then progressive) authority: "Well, in that, at least, you're in agreement with Spencer, whom you dislike so much" (AK, 357). Substitute Foucault for Spencer and you have the equivalent answer today.

One can tell from such an answer what Sviazhsky schools would be like: they would teach the currently fashionable dogma the way the Church teaches the catechism. The peasants would be passive, if resistant, recipients of such knowledge. They could learn, but they could not answer. They would carry around with them another authoritative word, which would be remote from their own experience and anything but innerly persuasive.

NOTHING CONCLUSIVE

A belief in truly dialogic ideological becoming would lead to schools that were quite different. In such schools, the mind would be populated with a complexity of voices and perspectives it had not known, and the student would learn to think with those voices, to test ideas and experiences against them, and to shape convictions that are innerly persuasive in response. This very *process* would be central. Students would sense that whatever word they believed to be innerly persuasive was only tentatively so: the process of dialogue continues. We must *keep the conversation going*, and formal education only initiates the process.

The innerly persuasive discourse would not be final, but would be, like experience itself, ever incomplete and growing. As Bakhtin observes of the innerly persuasive word:

Its creativity and productiveness consist precisely in the fact that such a word awakens new and independent words, that it organizes masses of our words from within, and does not remain in an isolated and static condition. It is not so much interpreted by us as it is further, that is, freely, developed, applied to new material, new conditions; it enters into interanimating relationships with new contexts. . . . The semantic structure of an innerly persuasive discourse is *not finite*, it is *open*; in each of the new contexts that dialogize it, this discourse is able to reveal ever newer *ways to mean*. (DI, 345–6)

We not only learn, we also learn to learn, and we learn to learn best when we engage in a dialogue with others and ourselves. We appropriate the world of difference, and ourselves develop new potentials. Those potentials allow us to appropriate yet more voices. Becoming becomes endless becoming.

We talk, we listen, and we achieve an open-ended wisdom. Difference becomes an opportunity (see Freedman and Ball, this volume). Our world manifests the spirit that Bakhtin attributed to Dostoevsky: "nothing conclusive has yet taken place in the world, the ultimate word of the world and about the world has not yet been spoken, the world is open and free, everything is in the future and will always be in the future."[3] Such a world becomes our world within, its dialogue lives within us, and we develop the potentials of our ever-learning selves.

Let me draw some inconclusive conclusions, which may provoke dialogue. Section I of this volume, "Ideologies in Dialogue: Theoretical Considerations" and Bakhtin's thought in general suggest that we learn best when we are actually learning to learn. We engage in dialogue with ourselves and others, and the most important thing is the value of the open-ended process itself.

Section II, "Voiced, Double Voiced, and Multivoiced Discourses in Our Schools" suggests that a belief in truly dialogic ideological becoming would lead to schools that were quite different. In such schools, the mind would be populated with a complexity of voices and perspectives it had not known, and the student would learn to think with those voices, to test ideas and experiences against them, and to shape convictions that are innerly persuasive in response. Teachers would not be trying to get students to hold the right opinions but to sense the world from perspectives they would not have encountered or dismissed out of hand. Students would develop the habit of getting inside the perspectives of other groups and other people. Literature in particular is especially good at fostering such dialogic habits.

Section III, "Heteroglossia in a Changing World" may invite us to learn that dialogue involves really listening to others, hearing them not as our perspective would categorize what they say, but as they themselves would categorize what they say, and only then to bring our own perspective to bear. We talk, we listen, and we achieve an open-ended wisdom.

The chapters in this volume seem to suggest that we view learning as a perpetual *process*. That was perhaps Bakhtin's favorite idea: that to appreciate life, or dialogue, we must see value not only in achieving this or that result, but also in recognizing that honest and open striving in a world of uncertainty and difference is itself the most important thing.

What we must do is keep the conversation going.

---

[3] Mikhail Bakhtin, *Problems of Dostoevsky's poetics*, ed. and trans. Caryl Emerson (Minneapolis: University of Minnesota Press, 1984), 166.

Author Index

Abazovic, D., 9, 19, 21
Abelson, R. P., 136
Ackerman, J., 62
Ajdukovic, D., 9, 10, 20, 30
Allen, A. R., 290, 291, 292
Allen, J. G., 112, 160
Althusser, L., 80
Altwerger, B., 76
Alvarez, H. H., 308, 310, 311
Alvermann, D. E., 198
Applebee, A., 79, 175
Appleman, D., 34
Arac, J., 42
Atwell, N., 112
Au, K., 79
Auerbach, E. R., 80

Bakhtin, M. M., 6, 8, 45, 55, 57, 66, 68, 81, 87–89, 102, 107, 108, 113–114, 123, 124, 129, 131, 133, 172–175, 177, 178, 199–312
Balderrama, M., 79
Ball, A. F., 4, 9, 11, 13, 16, 78, 131, 137, 197
Baquedano-Lopez, P., 79, 131, 308, 310, 311
Barkin, F., 76
Barron, D., 70
Barsalou, L. W., 296
Barthes, R., 58
Bartholomae, D., 175, 176
Bartolome, L., 79, 86, 89
Barton, D., 263, 279
Baugh, J., 70
Bauman, Z., 286, 297
Bazerman, C., 61–63, 72
Beck, U., 283, 285

Beneria, L., 259
Bentley, A. F., 38
Bereiter, C., 129
Berger, B., 282
Berger, P., 282
Berkenkotter, C., 62
Bernstein, B., 80
Bero
    Blotner and Bero, in progress, 10
Biber, D., 78, 80
Bigenho, F., 198
Bird, T., 198
Biro
    Ajdukovic, Corkalo, Biro, et al., 10
Bissex, G. L., 172
Blachowicz, C., 112
Blake, R., 137
Bloome, D., 125
Blotner
    Blotner and Bero, in progress, 10
Bolinger, D., 70
Bordieu, P., 80, 113
Bowles, S., 80
Boyett, J. H., 293
Brandt, D., 235, 250
Brannon, L., 79
Brettschneider, A., 307
Britton, J., 79
Brown, A. L., 285
Buchanan, J., 172
Butler, J. E., 87

Cain, C., 172, 174, 175, 193, 197, 199
Calkins, L., 112
Canagarajah, S., 80

333

Subject Index

Other Books in the Series (*continued from p. iii*)

Cognition and Tool Use: The Blacksmith at Work
Charles M. Keller and Janet Dixon Keller

Computation and Human Experience
Philip E. Agre

Situated Cognition: On Human Knowledge and Computer Representation
William J. Clancey

Communities of Practice: Learning, Meaning, and Identity
Etienne Wenger

Learning in Likely Places: Varieties of Apprenticeship in Japan
John Singleton

Talking Mathematics in School: Studies of Teaching and Learning
Magdalene Lampert and Merrie L. Blunk

Perspectives on Activity Theory
Yrjö Engeström, Reijo Miettinen, and Raija-Leena Punamäki

Dialogic Inquiry: Towards a Sociocultural Practice and Theory of Education
Gordon Wells

Vygotskian Perspectives on Literacy Research: Constructing Meaning Through Collaborative Inquiry
Carol D. Lee and Peter Smagorinsky

Technology in Action
Christian Heath and Paul Luff

Changing Classes: School Reform and the New Economy
Martin Packer

Building Virtual Communities: Learning and Change in Cyberspace
K. Ann Renninger and Wesley Shumar

Adult Learning and Technology in Working-Class Life
Peter Sawchuk

Vygotsky's Educational Theory in Cultural Context
Alex Kozulin, Boris Gindis, Vladimir S. Ageyev, and Suzanne M. Miller